The Handbook of Historically Black Colleges & Universities

The Third Edition

www.collegeresources.com

Jireh & Associates, Inc.
Wilmington, DE 19899-1374

The Handbook of Historically Black Colleges & Universities

The Third Edition

Comprehensive Profiles of Black Colleges and Universities

Compiled by Toni Hodge Kennard

Published by:
Jireh & Associates, Inc.
P.O. Box 1374
Wilmington, DE 19899-1374

Maria Y. Moore, Coordinating Editor
Quisa B. Wright, Associate Editor

Printed in the United States

Third Edition

The Handbooks are available at special discounts when purchased in bulk quantities for school districts, businesses, associations, institutions or school sales promotions. Please call our Special Sales Department in Delaware at (302/325-4221.

Text design by Maria Y. Moore

Jacket design by Nina Harris

Cover Photography by Don Henderson

ISBN: 0-9632669-3-4 $35.50
Library of Congress ISSN: 1521-9771

City of Wilmington
Delaware

September 1998

Dear Reader:

It gives me great pleasure to welcome you to the third edition of the *Historically Black Colleges and Universities Handbook*.

The *Historically Black Colleges and Universities Handbook* is a useful reference tool for students, school counselors and administrators, and historians alike. Within these pages is a wealth of information on Historically Black Colleges and Universities such as major courses of study, enrollment statistics, historical information, campus services, admissions and financial aid information, and much more.

As the first Black mayor of the City of Wilmington, Delaware and a graduate of historically Black Morehouse College in Atlanta, Georgia, it is important to me that all people learn about the contributions that Historically Black Colleges and Universities have made during the course of United States history. By purchasing this *Handbook*, you, too, are making a commitment to supporting and learning more about these fine institutions.

Thank you to Ms. Toni Hodge Kennard and the publishers of the *Historically Black Colleges and Universities Handbook* for their dedication to informing others about the good things our institutions of higher learning have to offer.

Sincerely,

James H. Sills, Jr.
Mayor

ACKNOWLEDGMENTS

It goes without saying that this edition would not be a reality if it were not for the God whom I serve. (In faith I type these words as funding for the production of this third edition remains undetermined.) Failure is always a possibility, if one sees failure as the end. I, however, see it as an opportunity for a new approach, an opportunity to trust God AGAIN.

Special acknowledgment to one of the original Seattle YMCA Teen Black Achievers for whom the first 1992 edition of this Handbook was published; Mr. Dana Norwood, 1998 Tuskegee University graduate in Aeronautical Engineering. I am so proud of your accomplishment and am blessed that I could be a part of your growth and development. May God's hand continue to hold you.

A special thanks to Nina Harris for her graphic artistry and consultation. And with deep appreciation and gratitude, many thanks to my "Financial Guru", Margo Reign, for her guidance and direction throughout the critical planning stages of this project.

DEDICATION

This Third Edition is dedicated to my sisters of the faith: Etta Baldwin, Brenda Littleton, Pat Robinsonel Powell, and Brenda Daniels who sent me prayers, cards and letters of encouragement when I needed it the most. And to a very special young lady who comes through for me every time I really need her, my Coordinating Editor and daughter, Maria Moore.

Most of all to my mother, Marie Hodge, who when things looked really dim for the production of this edition, encouraged me not to give up. The words, "Hang in there kiddieo!" were her constant refrain. Thank you!

A SPECIAL NOTE:

To Quisa: Keep your head up little lady and seek the Lord in all you do and nothing shall be impossible for you.

**TONI
HODGE
KENNARD**

Ms. Kennard is an educational consultant with Jireh & Associates, Inc. She authored the First Edition of the Handbook of Historically Black Colleges in 1992, the Second Edition in 1995 and now the Third Edition in 1999.

Ms. Kennard is a devoted Christian, a wife and the mother of two daughters, Maria Yvonne and Quisa Brianne. She was born in Jackson, MS and is an alumnae of Jackson State University, Seattle Central Community College, and Western Washington University in Washington state and holds two Associate degrees and a BA in Business Administration.

Ms. Kennard conducts *College Resources for the 21st Century*, a consortium of college preparatory workshops held at high schools, middle schools, churches, and youth-related organizations. The workshops target first-generation college students and their parents and address the financial aid process, early college preparation, college information resources, recommended high school courses, the admissions application process and useful websites for the college seeker.

ABOUT THE AUTHOR

She also conducts Study Skills Seminars covering such topics as: Test-Taking Tips, How to Study, How to Take Notes, Improving Your Memory, and Time Management.

Since 1993, she has served as the Advisory Committee Chairwoman for the National YMCA Black Achievers Program, a career exploration project for youth.

Ms. Kennard is also a highly sought after storyteller; describing her presentation style as *"Personified Poetry: Storytelling with a Twist."*

She takes a poem or a monologue; gives it a character profile, a name, adds a twist to bring life to that character, then... it's **Show Time!**

Her character portfolio includes a family of four females: Mama, Chic, Slim and Sadie. They deliver poems, songs and monologues suited for organizational luncheons, banquets, conferences, reunions, classroom demonstrations, school assemblies or special church entertainment. Her presentations bring a new dimension to cultural entertainment.

To find out how your school, PTA, college fair event, church, or youth-related organization can utilize Ms. Kennard's services, call, write or email her.

Jireh & Associates, Inc.
P.O. Box 1374
Wilmington, DE 19899-1374
Phone: (302) 325-4221

E-Mail: jai-inc@erols.com

DON HENDERSON
Photographic Craftsman
Certified Professional Photographer

Henderson is a portrait artist specializing in capturing memorable moments through custom environmental photography. Don's passion for his art has allowed him to photograph some of the most influential people of our time. His ability to record history through the lens, and his unique style of marrying the individual to the environment is captivating.

For twenty years, Henderson has been in search of the *perfect* image and his quest for photographic excellence is in direct proportion to his many accomplishments within the photography industry.

Operating a full-service photography business in Delaware has been a dream realized for Henderson and his charismatic personality and public relations skills has established him as one of the best *"people"* photographers in the Delaware Valley Area.

THE COVER ARTIST

When your goal is to be the absolute best, at all times, in every aspect of your craft, the educational process is daily. This attitude has attracted Al Gilbert, Canadian Master Photographer, who has for six years served as a mentor for personal growth, business principles and photographic techniques. Other professional influences include such talents as Andre Torre, Master Photographer and Gerald Hilton.

Don has been sanctioned by the Professional Photographers of America International to instruct professional photographers in "preparing for certification". Additionally, Henderson's photographic writings have been published internationally; he has developed a comprehensive business program, an Advanced Lighting Program, and is currently producing an easy-to-understand photography course for children.

In 1966, Henderson founded the Tri-State Minority Alliance of Professional Photographers and it still exists today. The primary function of this organization is to educate minority professional photographers in business principles and photographic techniques.

In February 1998, Henderson accepted an appointment as a Regional Director for the Professional Photographers Minority Network, a national organization.

FOREWORD
by HENRY PONDER

NAFEO President
National Association for Equal Opportunity in Higher Education

This new edition of the Handbook of Historically Black Colleges & Universities is published in the hope and conviction that it will be more useful than its predecessors for precisely, the over 20,000 persons that Toni Hodge Kennard had in mind when she presented the original Handbook. I can certainly imagine that she expected that the book would be very welcome to those that needed "comprehensive information" about the one-hundred sixteen historically black colleges and universities, and, that it would be "pertinent to any prospective student to assist them in making advised decisions about their college selection." That is, for potential students of all sorts for whom the appropriate college to attend had not yet flashed into mind.

The success of the Handbook as a practical aid to students, I am sure, has been immense in the publication of the first and second editions. It is my hope that thousands of person have, and will put Kennard's hard work to its widest, proper, use as a tool for identifying those attributes and characteristics of an historically black college or university that best suits their individual needs. Hundreds, too, have used Kennard's work as a browsing book, a book that stimulates thought and exploration because it uniquely collects the most important information about black colleges, and provides that information in an easy-to-follow format.

The publishing of this edition comes at a time when the development of higher education in the United States has meant the opening up of colleges and universities to an ever-increasingly large and more diverse group of persons. The black college was a "selfish creation," in that it was created for the clear purpose of maintaining segregation. Out of the euphoria that welled up in the hearts and minds of many Americans as the barriers of segregation fell, a belief arose that black colleges might no longer be needed. "After all, what were these school but alternatives to the white colleges that were beginning to open their doors?" But black colleges were never mere alternatives to white colleges and can never be replaced by them.

The record shows that black colleges are safe harbors for African American youth -- places for them to grow straight and tall, protected for a few crucial years from the stark realities of American society. At a black college, an African American student's race is at the same time irrelevant and central. It is irrelevant in that the student is simply that: a student, not an African American student. He is the norm, not the exception. It is central, in that blackness is the essence of the black college. It is in the black experience that black colleges are grounded. It is to the understanding and solution of African Americans' problems that the best black colleges and this Handbook are dedicated.

Kennard's hope that her book would "materially assist" students in their search for the answer to the correct college of their choice is further realized with the revision of this Handbook. It takes faith, hard work and dedication along with some managerial skills to make progress in any area. As many students, counselors, parents and others look to utilize this invaluable resource, I hope that each understands that one's attitude is far more important that aptitude in making progress in any situation. The editor and publisher believe that the new edition of *The Handbook of Historically Black Colleges and Universities* constitutes the best approach yet made to helping those that are indeed searching for information about these schools. Use it wisely.

A Student's Message

PREPARING FOR COLLEGE
by
Kimberly Baldwin
1998 George Mason University Graduate

College is a big step in one's life. It is a place to help improve and create new skills; develop socially, personally and of course, educationally.

For some, it may be their first time leaving their safety nest -home, and becoming a more mature and independent individual which can be frightening, to say the least. For others, it may seem like just an extended vacation.

But whichever perspective, college is a different world --filled with new experiences and challenges. So what should you do when you are away from home and there is nobody telling you what to do or when to go to class? First, of all be thankful that God has made provisions for you to go to school be it technical school, community college or university. It is a blessing!

Second, you should sit down and spend some time with yourself to figure out what you would like to do in the future (besides making money). Where do you see yourself in the next five to ten years? This should be the time where you separate yourself from the expectations of other people and begin developing your own expectations.

Thirdly, there are a lot of temptations that will arise while in college, but keep these words in mind --"Be smart!" Think about your future, family and more importantly, you, before subjecting yourself to something that you may regret later. A couple of questions that I asked myself whenever I needed to make a critical decision were: "Are these people going to help me get an "A" in my classes?, Do they care about my future?; Will they or this help pay my bills? If the answer is "No", then I don't need them or need to do this." Surround yourself people who are genuine; people that demonstrate a positive and healthy lifestyle.

Now ladies, when you are dating a guy, you will want to choose a gentleman with the 5 C's: Christ, Car, Cash, Character and Class.

Fourthly, don't get discouraged. When you set your mind on your goals and what it is you want to do, don't let people or grades get the best of you. There will probably be a lot of things to be discouraged about but remember, "You are more than a conqueror..." God has made you fully equipped with the "AA" --Armor and Authority. So use it! No weapon formed against you shall prosper! My approach was to take all discouragement and disappointments and present them as new challenges to run over (my sprinter's view!). Don't let anyone lower your self-esteem by disrespecting you and that means respecting yourself first.

Lastly and more importantly, Pray--Pray--Pray. I know it may seem hard to grow spiritually during your college years, but the one thing that can be devastating, detrimental to your health even, is not keeping your connection with God. (That of course, presumes that you have one in the beginning.) If you do not have a connection with Him, the wisest thing to do is to get one BEFORE you go to college. Be forewarned and thus forearmed!

College can be a fun, rewarding and successful time of your life, but pray and be smart. Don't let your first year be your last.

September 1998

Letters from Tuskegee University

November 13, 1992

Dear Ms. Toni,

Hi, how ya doin'? I am doing o.k. --just trying to survive the college experience. It is a lot harder than I thought. I know everyone was telling me it would be hard but this is ridiculous. I'm going to make it though because I'm a 5-Star Achiever (smile).

There are a lot of things going on here that no one could have told me except another Tuskegee student. Being at a historically Black college, I didn't expect to see so many white teachers and even some students. There are also many East Indian teachers here. I'm really starting to miss home. I didn't think I would this much.

I can't quite remember, but isn't it about time for Black Achievers to start again? I am really glad I got involved in that program. Hopefully, when I get back for my summer break, I can help with Black Achievers like it helped me. I would like to tutor. If there are any trips planned for colleges, I'd like to go because it's one thing to hear about college from someone who has been out for some years but to hear from someone you know who is still in college is even better.

How is Maria and Quisa? Tell them I said, Hi! I'll try to write again before Winter break. Thanks for all your help and support.

Love,
Dana Norwood
YMCA Black Achiever

July 9, 1996

Dear Ms. Toni,

Hi! How are you doing? I'm back in Seattle for the Summer. I was so happy to get back home. Unfortunately, I wasn't able to get an internship this Summer. My original plan was to go to summer school but that fell through because there weren't many classes that I needed to take being offered. So at the last minute, I decided to come home. But I do have some very good prospects including several people who want me at Boeing. So God willing, that's where I will be next Summer.

I'm just taking it easy and getting some leisure reading done. I'm in the middle of _Soul on Ice_, by Eldridge Cleaver and I'll probably read _Makes Me Wanna Holler_ by Nathan McCall after that. Speaking of books, I really liked your 2nd Edition. The day I got it I barely got to look at it. All my friends kept wanting to see it and look up stuff. We had it out for about 2 hours before I could put it away! Thanks again for the copy...

I don't know if I told you or not but I will have officially double majored in Aerospace Engineering and Physics starting this Fall. I have seventy-one more credits to graduate. If I take 18 hours a semester, I'll graduate in the Spring of 1998. I have narrowed my specialty fields down to two: Aircraft Structures including Vibrations and Fatigue Analysis or Aircraft Propulsion. Do you have E-mail?

Well, got to go. Hope to hear from you soon. Tell your family hello.

Love,
Dana Norwood
Graduated June 1998

HOW TO USE THIS BOOK

There are 110 historically Black colleges and universities (HBCUs) in the United States and the Virgin Islands and this book contains most of them. Source of this data comes from completed surveys sent to each school. It is our desire to provide the most comprehensive information about these schools for prospective students, librarians, counselors, parents/guardians and human resource personnel to assist them in making advised decisions or locating information. For added convenience and access, each page is perforated. Additionally, fax numbers, web addresses and admissions officers names have been included (if provided by the school). Among the profiles, you will find a NEW section of **Admissions Applications** provided by some of the schools. You are welcome to photocopy or pull out these applications. However, **please note:** The admissions applications included in this Handbook should only be used for the college or university indicated on it. In most cases, additional forms which could not be included due to space restrictions, will be necessary for complete application to the school.

This book is also intended to heighten the public's awareness of HBCUs, their development, and their contributions to this nation. The last section in the book includes a listing of the schools by state, and a listing of the schools by religious affiliation.

Every effort has been made to make this handbook as complete and accurate as possible. However, there may be errors both typographical and in content. Therefore, this handbook should not be used as the ultimate source of HBCU information and each student is encouraged to contact the institutions directly to verify or clarify information.

SCHOOL INFO
The year the college was established, location and any affiliations are indicated here. The types of degrees offered; the academic calendar system the college follows; the accrediting organization; the faculty size; freshman campus enrollment; president or chancellor's name, address, telephone and fax numbers are included here.

WHAT DO I NEED? (ADMISSIONS)
This section describes the criteria used by the college in its selection and/or admissions process. The important criteria is often indicated and if special considerations or requirements are applicable they too will be noted. Fall term application deadlines and costs are also indicated. This information is not all-inclusive however, and additional considerations may apply depending on the program of study.

Jireh & Associates, Inc.
HBCU Third Edition

UNIQUE PROGRAMS
Special programs that the college offers are listed here. These programs may lead to a degree, provide an opportunity for advanced or foreign study i.e., honors program, double major, independent study, cross-registration etc.

GRADUATION/ACADEMIC REQUIREMENTS
Required general education courses for all or most students are listed here; the number of hours required for an associate or bachelor's degree; number of in-residence hours; and number of hours in major may be indicated.

STUDENT SERVICES
Services that enhance a student's academic skills or provide social assistance i.e., tutoring, on-campus daycare, personal counselors, health services, or remedial instruction are listed in this section. Again, these are not all-inclusive and the student should contact the college directly if they are inquiring about a particular service not listed.

WHAT'S MY MAJOR?
These are the major areas of study offered by the college under the associate or bachelor program. Some colleges may have more entries than we had space under this category and in those instances, we will refer the student to the college catalog.

Historical & Special Interest Info: This area may include in addition to historical information, special features of the college campus, its services, its special or unique programs, awards, affiliations, and UNCF membership.

CONTACT INFORMATION
Admissions Officer's name, address, telephone, web address and fax numbers are outlined in this section.

$$$ DOLLARS & SENSE $$$
This information is based on full-time (12 hrs) enrollment in the academic year. Some colleges were in the process of revising their costs when we requested this information and therefore may not be the exact amounts. As indicated on the profile, the out-of-state fee is not included in the total cost figure.

FINANCIAL AID
Significant telephone and FAX numbers, deadline dates for application, notification and replies are indicated here including financial aid form requirements; types of available scholarships and aid. Must contact this department directly for applications for financial aid.

SPORTS
This section includes the varsity sports and athletic programs offered at the school.

ALPHABETICAL LISTING OF SCHOOLS

Profiles in this book are listed alphabetically.
An index of schools by state is included in the back of the book.

SCHOOL	CITY	STATE	ADMISSIONS OFFICER	PHONE #	FAX₁	Page
ALABAMA A & M UNIVERSITY	HUNTSVILLE,	AL	James Heyward	(205) 851-5000	(205) 857-5249	1
ALABAMA STATE UNIVERSITY	MONTGOMERY,	AL	Billy Brooks	(334) 229-4100	(334) 834-6861	2
ALBANY STATE UNIVERSITY	ALBANY,	GA	Patricia Price	(912) 430-4646	(912) 430-3936	3
ALCORN STATE UNIVERSITY	LORMAN,	MS	Emanuel Banks	(601) 877-6147	(601) 877-6347	4
ALLEN UNIVERSITY	COLUMBIA,	SC	Christopher Baughn	(803) 376-5735	(803) 376-5733	5
ARKANSAS BAPTIST COLLEGE	LITTLE ROCK,	AR	Annie Hightower	(501) 374-7856	(501) 372-0321	6
ATLANTA METROPOLITAN COLLEGE	ATLANTA,	GA	Clifton Rawles	(404) 756-4004	(404) 756-4407	7
BARBER-SCOTIA COLLEGE	CONCORD,	NC	Al Coffield	(704) 789-2902	(704) 789-2935	8
BENEDICT COLLEGE	COLUMBIA,	SC	Gary Knight	(803) 256-4220	(803) 253-5167	9
BENNETT COLLEGE	GREENSBORO,	NC	Linda Torrence	(800) 413-5323	(910) 378-0513	10
BETHUNE-COOKMAN COLLEGE	DAYTONA BEACH,	FL	Richard F. Pride	(800) 448-0228	(904) 257-5338	11
BISHOP STATE COMMUNITY COLLEGE	MOBILE,	AL	Ms. Delayne Banks	(334) 690-6412	(334) 431-5403	12
BLUEFIELD STATE COLLEGE	BLUEFIELD,	WV	John Caldwell	(304) 327-4065	(304) 325-7747	13
BOWIE STATE UNIVERSITY	BOWIE,	MD	Carlene Wilson	(301) 464-6563	(301) 464-7521	14
CENTRAL STATE UNIVERSITY	WILBERFORCE,	OH	Carl Penn	(800) 388-2781	(937) 376-6648	15
CHEYNEY UNIVERSITY	CHEYNEY,	PA	Ms. Sharon L. Cannon	(610) 399-2046	(800) 243-9639	16
CHICAGO STATE UNIVERSITY	CHICAGO,	IL	Addie R. Epps, Director	(773) 995-2513	(773) 995-3820	17
CLAFLIN COLLEGE	ORANGEBURG,	SC	Michael Zeigler	(803) 535-5346	(803) 531-2860	18
CLARK ATLANTA UNIVERSITY	ATLANTA,	GA	Peggy Wade, Interim	(404) 880-8017	(404) 880-6174	19
CLINTON JUNIOR COLLEGE	ROCK HILL,	SC	Cheryl J. McCullough Dir.	(803) 327-7402	(803) 327-3261	20
COAHOMA COMMUNITY COLLEGE	CLARKSDALE,	MS	Rita Hanfor	(800) 844-1222	(601) 627-9451	21
COMPTON COMMUNITY COLLEGE	COMPTON,	CA	Ms. Carita Scott	(310) 900-1600	(310) 639-8260	22
CONCORDIA COLLEGE	SELMA,	AL	Ms. Gwendolyn Moore	(334) 874-7143	(334) 874-5755	23
COPPIN STATE COLLEGE	BALTIMORE,	MD	Allen Mosley	(410) 383-5990	(410) 523-7238	24
CUYAHOGA COMM. COLLEGE	CLEVELAND,	OH	Dr. Sammie Tyree Cox	(216) 987-4000	(216) 987-4130	25
DELAWARE STATE UNIVERSITY	DOVER,	DE	Jethro C. Williams	(800) 464-4357	(302) 739-2856	26
DENMARK TECHNICAL COLLEGE	DENMARK,	SC	Ms. Michelle McDowell	(803) 793-5176	(803) 793-5942	27
DILLARD UNIVERSITY	NEW ORLEANS,	LA	Darrin Q. Rankin	(504) 283-8822	(504) 286-4895	28
DREW UNIV. OF MEDICINE & SCIENCE	LOS ANGELES,	CA	Cesar Hernandez	(213) 563-4950	(213) 569-0597	29
EDWARD WATERS COLLEGE	JACKSONVILLE,	FL	Richard F. Pride Jr	(904) 366-2715	(904) 366-2528	30
ELIZABETH CITY STATE UNIV.	ELIZABETH CITY,	NC	Jeff King	(252) 335-3305	(919) 335-3537	31
F.H. LAGUARDIA COMM COLLEGE	LONG ISLAND,	NY	Lavora Desvigne, Acting	(718) 482-7200	(718) 482-5112	32
FAYETTEVILLE STATE UNIV.	FAYETTEVILLE,	NC	Charles Darlington	(910) 486-1371	(910) 437-2512	33
FISK UNIVERSITY	NASHVILLE,	TN	Anthony Jones	(800) 443-3475	(615) 329-8774	34
FLORIDA A&M UNIVERSITY	TALLAHASSEE,	FL	Barbara Cox	(850) 599-3796	(850) 561-2428	35
FLORIDA MEMORIAL COLLEGE	MIAMI,	FL	Peggy Martin	(800) 822-1362	(305) 626-3106	36
FORT VALLEY ST. UNIVERSITY	FORT VALLEY,	GA	Dr. Mildred Hill	(912) 825-6307	(912) 825-6155	37

ALPHABETICAL LISTING OF SCHOOLS

Profiles in this book are listed alphabetically.
An index of schools by state is included in the back of the book.

SCHOOL	CITY	STATE	ADMISSIONS OFFICER	PHONE #	FAX:	Page
GRAMBLING STATE UNIVERSITY	GRAMBLING,	LA	Nora Bingaman	(318) 274-3138	(318) 274-3292	38
HAMPTON UNIVERSITY	HAMPTON,	VA	Leonard Jones	(800) 624-3328	(757) 727-5095	39
HARRIS-STOWE STATE COLLEGE	ST. LOUIS,	MO	Valerie Beeson	(314) 340-3300	(314) 340-3322	40
HINDS COMMUNITY COLLEGE - Utica	UTICA,	MS	Elistene Turner	(601) 885-6062	(601) 885-6026	41
HOWARD UNIVERSITY	WASHINGTON,	DC	Ms. Richetta Johnson	(800) 822-6363	(202) 806-4465	42
HUSTON-TILLOTSON COLLEGE	AUSTIN,	TX	Thomas Clifton VanDyke	(512) 505-3026	(512) 505-3190	43
JACKSON STATE UNIVERSITY	JACKSON,	MS	Dr. Gene Blakley	(601) 968-2100	(601) 973-3445	44
JARVIS CHRISTIAN COLLEGE	HAWKINS,	TX	Linda Rutherford	(903) 769-5733	(903) 769-4842	45
JOHNSON C. SMITH UNIV.	CHARLOTTE,	NC	Jean Frye	(704) 378-1011	(704) 378-1242	46
KENNEDY-KING COLLEGE	CHICAGO,	IL	Welton T. Murphy	(773) 602-5000	(773) 602-5247	47
KENTUCKY STATE UNIVERSITY	FRANKFORT,	KY	Laronistine Dyson	(502) 227-6813	(502) 227-5950	48
KNOXVILLE COLLEGE	KNOXVILLE,	TN	J. Harver GIllespie	(423) 524-6525	(423) 524-6686	49
LANE COLLEGE	JACKSON,	TN	Evelyn Brown	(901) 426-7532	(901) 426-7594	50
LANGSTON UNIVERSITY	LANGSTON,	OK	Willy Anderson	(888) 370-1897	(405) 466-2966	51
LAWSON STATE COMM. COLLEGE	BIRMINGHAM,	AL	Ms. Myra Davis, Registrar	(205) 925-2515	(205)929-6316	52
LEMOYNE-OWEN COLLEGE	MEMPHIS,	TN	Jean Saulsberry	(901) 774-9090	(901) 942-6272	53
LEWIS COLLEGE OF BUSINESS	DETROIT,	MI	Frank L. Gillespie, IV,	(313) 862-6300	(313) 862-1027	54
LINCOLN UNIVERSITY	JEFFERSON,	MO	Jimmy Arrington	(573) 681-5599	(573) 681-5889	55
LINCOLN UNIVERSITY	LINCOLN	PA	Dr. Robert Laney, Jr.	(610) 932-8300	(610) 932-1209	56
LIVINGSTONE COLLEGE	SALISBURY,	NC	Ms. Diedre Stewart	(704) 638-5502	(704) 638-5426	57
MARY HOLMES COLLEGE	WEST POINT,	MS	Brenda Carter	(601) 494-6820	(601) 494-6625	58
MEHARRY MEDICAL COLLEGE	NASHVILLE,	TN	Sharon Hurt	(615) 327-6223	(615) 327-6228	59
MILES COLLEGE	BIRMINGHAM,	AL	Ms. Brenda Grant-Smith	(800) 445-0708	(205) 929-1668	60
MISSISSIPPI VALLEY STATE UNIV.	ITTA BENA,	MS	Maxine Rush	(601) 254-3347	(601) 254-7900	61
MOREHOUSE COLLEGE	ATLANTA,	GA	Andre Patillo	(404) 681-2800	(404) 524-5635	62
MOREHOUSE SCHOOL OF MEDICINE	ATLANTA,	GA	Dr. Angela Franklin	(404) 752-1650	(404) 752-1512	63
MORGAN STATE UNIVERSITY	BALTIMORE,	MD	Clelsia Miller	(800) 332-6674	(410) 319-3684	64
MORRIS BROWN COLLEGE	ATLANTA,	GA	Rev. Debora S. Grant	(404) 220-0152	(404) 659-4315	65
MORRIS COLLEGE	SUMTER,	SC	Queen W. Spann	(803) 775-9371	(803) 773-3687	66
N. CAROLINA A&T STATE UNIV.	GREENSBORO,	NC	John Smith	(910) 334-7946	(910) 334-7478	67
N. CAROLINA CENTRAL UNIV.	DURHAM,	NC	Ms. Nancy Rowland	(919) 560-6100	((919) 560-5462	68
NORFOLK STATE UNIVERSITY	NORFOLK,	VA	Dr. Frank Cool	(757) 683-8396	(757) 683-2078	69
OAKWOOD COLLEGE	HUNTSVILLE,	AL	Ms. Tanya Bowman, Assoc.	(800) 824-5312	(205) 726-7154	70
PAINE COLLEGE	AUGUSTA,	GA	Ellen King	(800) 476-7703	(706) 821-8293	71
PAUL QUINN COLLEGE	DALLAS,	TX	Ralph Spencer	(214) 302-3520	(214) 302-3613	72
PHILANDER SMITH COLLEGE	LITTLE ROCK,	AR	Ms. Beverly Richardson	(501) 375-9845	(501) 370-5225	73
PRAIRIE VIEW A&M COLLEGE	PRAIRIE VIEW,	TX	Deborah Dungey	(409) 857-2618	(409) 857-2699	74

ALPHABETICAL LISTING OF SCHOOLS

Profiles in this book are listed alphabetically.
An index of schools by state is included in the back of the book.

SCHOOL	CITY	STATE	ADMISSIONS OFFICER	PHONE #	FAX₁	Page
ROXBURY COMMUNITY COLLEGE	ROXBURY CROSSING,	MA	Dr. Rudolph Jones	(617) 541-5310	(617) 427-5316	75
RUST COLLEGE	HOLLY SPRINGS,	MS	JoAnn Scott	(601) 252-8000	(601) 252-6107	76
SAINT AUGUSTINE'S COLLEGE	RALEIGH,	NC	Keith Powell	(919) 516-4012	(919) 516-5801	77
SAINT PAUL'S COLLEGE	LAWRENCEVILLE,	VA	Mary Ransom	(804) 848-3984	(804) 848-0403	78
SAVANNAH STATE COLLEGE	SAVANNAH,	GA	Dr. Roy A. Jackson	(912) 356-2181	(912) 356-2256	79
SELMA UNIVERSITY	SELMA,	AL	Estella Davis-Baynes, Ira	(334) 872-2533	(334) 872-7746	80
SHAW UNIVERSITY	RALEIGH,	NC	Keith Smith	(800) 214-6683	(919) 546-8271	81
SHORTER COLLEGE	NORTH LITTLE	AR	Ms. Delores Voliber	(501) 374-6305	(501) 374-9333	82
SOJOURNER-DOUGLASS COLLEGE	BALTIMORE,	MD	Diana Samuels	(410) 276-0306	(410) 675-1810	83
SOUTH CAROLINA STATE UNIVERSITY	N.E. ORANGEBURG,	SC	Dorothy Brown	(800) 260-5956	(803) 536-8990	84
SOUTHERN UNIV. at BATON ROUGE	BATON ROUGE,	LA	Wayne Brumfield	(504) 771-2430	(504) 771-2500	85
SOUTHERN UNIV. AT SHREVEPORT	SHREVEPORT,	LA	Ms. Artie Reed	(800) 458-1472	(318) 674-3313	86
SOUTHERN UNIV. NEW ORLEANS	NEW ORLEANS,	LA	Dr. Laura Hardester	(504) 286-5314	(504) 286-5320	87
SOUTHWESTERN CHRISTIAN COLLEGE	TERRELL,	TX	Thomas Fitzgerald	(972) 524-3341	(972) 563-7133	88
SPELMAN COLLEGE	ATLANTA,	GA	Victoria Valle	(404) 681-3643	(404) 215-7788	89
STILLMAN COLLEGE	TUSCALOOSA,	AL	Mason Bonner	(205) 349-4240	(205) 366-8996	90
TALLADEGA COLLEGE	TALLADEGA,	AL	Dr. Edward L. Hall	(800) 633-2440	(205) 362-2268	91
TENNESSEE STATE UNIVERSITY	NASHVILLE,	TN	Dean John Cade	(615) 963-5131	(615) 963-5108	92
TEXAS COLLEGE	TYLER,	TX	Dr. T Meek Dean of	(903) 593-8311	(903) 593-0588	93
TEXAS SOUTHERN UNVERSITY	HOUSTON,	TX	Joyce Waddell	(713) 313-7011	(713) 313-7471	94
TOUGALOO COLLEGE	TOUGALOO,	MS	Carolyn Evans	(601) 977-7770	(601) 977-6185	95
TRENHOLM STATE TECH. COLLEGE	MONTGOMERY,	AL	Ms. Carolyn Silverman	(334) 832-9000	(334) 832-9777	96
TUSKEGEE UNIVERSITY	TUSKEGEE,	AL	Elva Bradley	(334) 727-8500	(334) 724-4402	97
UNIV. OF ARKANSAS PINE BLUFF	PINE BLUFF,	AR	Ms. Kwurly Floyd	(501) 543-8000	(501) 543-8014	98
UNIV. OF MARYLAND E. S.	PRINCESS ANNE,	MD	Dr. Rochell Peoples	(410) 651-6410	(410) 651-7922	99
UNIV. OF THE VIRGIN ISLANDS	ST.THOMAS,	US	Judith Edwin	(809) 776-9200	(809) 693-1155	100
UNIVERSITY OF D. C.	WASHINGTON,	DC	Michael O'Leary	(202) 274-5000	(202) 994-0325	101
VIRGINIA STATE UNIVERSITY	PETERSBURG,	VA	Lisa Winn	(804) 524-5906	(804) 524-5055	102
VIRGINIA UNION UNIVERSITY	RICHMOND,	VA	Gil Powell	(804) 257-5600	(804) 524-5055	103
VOORHEES COLLEGE	DENMARK,	SC	Cedric W. Baker	(803) 793-3351	(803) 793-3068	104
WEST VIRGINIA STATE COLLEGE	INSTITUTE,	WV	Robin Green, Assoc. Dir.	(304) 766-3221	(304) 766-5182	105
WILBERFORCE UNIVERSITY	WILBERFORCE,	OH	Kenneth Christmon	(973) 376-2911	(937) 376-4751	106
WILEY COLLEGE	MARSHALL,	TX	Frederick Pryor	(903) 927-3300	(903) 938-8100	107
WINSTON-SALEM STATE UNIV.	WINSTON-SALEM,	NC	Dr.Alvin Schexnider	(910) 750-2000	(910) 750-2079	108
XAVIER UNIVERSITY OF LOUISANA	NEW ORLEANS,	LA	Winston Brown	(504) 486-7411	(504) 482-1508	109

COLLEGE PROFILES

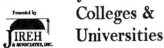

Historically Black Colleges & Universities

ALABAMA A & M UNIVERSITY

HUNTSVILLE, AL

Web Site:
www.aamu.edu

SCHOOL INFO

Established in 1875, 4-year public land grant coed university, suburban campus located in Huntsville, Alabama, 95 miles north of Birmingham.

ACCREDITATON:
Southern Association of Colleges & Schools

CAMPUS ENROLLMENT:
Undergraduate: 3,524 men & women full-time. **Transfer Students:** 134. **Part-Time:** 328.
Graduate: 1,411 men & women. **Freshman Ethnic Enrollment:** Native Am/Alskn-395; Af Am-1100; Asian/Pac Is-17; Cauc-834; Hisp-18; Other-38

WHAT DO I NEED?

The minimum required SAT combined score is 650 and the minimum ACT composite is 18. SAT/ACT (ACT preferred); and score report should be received by July 1. Application fee $10.

UNIQUE PROGRAMS

The following programs are available: accelerated program, double majors, dual enrollment with high school students, adult degree program, honors programs, cooperative education, internships, liberal arts, engineering liberal arts and health science combination, cross-registration with other institutions.

ACADEMIC REQUIREMENTS

Minimum GPA for freshmen is 2.0 and majors must be declared by end of second year.

Core curriculum: Art, economics, English, biological/physical sciences, health, history, humanities, mathematics, music, philosophy, physical education or military science, psychology (general) or sociology. Associate: 67-79 hrs. Bachelor's: 127-142 hrs.

STUDENT SERVICES

Campus student services include: career and personal counseling, employment services for undergraduates, freshman orientation, health services, learning center, placement services, special counselor, tutoring, special advisor for adult students, veterans counselor, services for disabled, campus security, services for speech disorders and learning disabilities, remedial instruction . ROTC: Army.

ADDRESS:

ALABAMA A & M UNIVERSITY
P.O. BOX 1357
HUNTSVILLE,   AL   35762
Principal Official: John T. Gibson

TYPES OF DEGREES AWARDED:
AS, BA, BS, M.Ed, MS, MBA, PhD, Ed.S., BSTS

ACADEMIC CALENDAR:
Semester. Summer sessions.

CONTACT INFORMATION

Admissions Officer: James Heyward
Phone: (205) 851-5000   **Fax:** (205) 857-5249
Web Site: www.aamu.edu

DOLLARS AND SENSE

TUITION & FEES:	$2,312.00
ROOM & BOARD:	$3,993.00
BOOKS & SUPPLIES:	$600.00
OTHER EXPENSES:	$950.00
OUT OF STATE TUITION:	$4,322.00
*ANNUAL TOTAL:	$7,855.00

(*Annual Total does not include out-of-state tuition .)

FINANCIAL AID

Financial Aid Phone: (205) 851-5400
Financial Aid Fax: (205) 851-5755
Closing date July 15; applicants notified on a rolling basis beginning around May 1; must reply within 2 weeks. FAFSA accepted. Pell grants, loans, jobs available. Academic, music/drama, athletic, leadership, band scholarships available.

SPORTS

Varsity Sports: Basketball, cross-country, track and field, tennis, volleyball, football, soccer NCAA.

WHAT MAJOR?

Associate: Civil engineering technology, electrical/engineering technology, mechanical engineering technology, printing production technology.

Bachelor's: Accounting, agribusiness, agribusiness education and non-teaching, agribusiness management, agricultural economics, animal sciences, art education, apparel, biology, business administration, chemistry, civil engineering, civil engineering technology, commerical and advertising art, computer science, crop science, early childhood education, economics, education, electrical engineering, elementary education, English, environmental science, food science, finance, French, history, home economics education, horticulture, hospitality food systems management, industrial arts education, industrial technology, marketing, mathematics, medical technology, mechanical engineering, merchandising and design, middle school education, music education, office systems management, physical education, physics, political science, pre-nursing, pre-veterinary medicine, printing production & management, psychology, secondary education, special education, sociology, soil science, speech pathology, technical studies, telecommunications, trade & industrial education, urban planning.

Graduate Programs: The Masters, specialist, and doctoral degrees are offered under the School of Graduate Studies. Masters degrees are offered in 32 of the undergraduate majors. The Ph.D. is offered in Plant and Soil Science, Applied Physics, and Food Science.

Historical & Special Interest:

Alabama Agricultural and Mechanical University was founded in 1875 as a co-educational institution within the city limits of Huntsville. The university offers fully accredited academic programs, including five undergraduate areas of concentration: School of Agriculture and Environmental Science; Arts and Sciences; Business, Education and Engineering and Technology. The institution serves more than 5,300 students. The University yields a well-rounded population of multi-racial students. Under a strong $5 million research program, NASA contracted with the University's Physics Department to test the possibilities of growing crystals in space aboard Space Lab 3 in 1985.

Master Key: *A man is twice miserable when he fears his misery before it comes.*

HBCU Third Edition
© Jireh & Associates, Inc.
Wilmington, DE

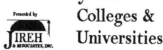
ALABAMA STATE UNIVERSITY

MONTGOMERY, AL

Web Site:
http://www.alasu.edu/

SCHOOL INFO

Established in 1867. 4-year public university, coed on urban campus in state capital, Montgomery; 91 miles from Birmingham.

ADDRESS:

ALABAMA STATE UNIVERSITY
P.O. BOX 271
MONTGOMERY,   AL   36101-0271
Principal Official: Dr. William H. Harris

ACCREDITATON:
S. Assoc.of Colleges & Schools; Assoc. of Collegiate Bus. Schools & Pgms; Nat'l Council for Accred. of Teacher Ed.

CAMPUS ENROLLMENT:
Undergraduate: 1,842 men & 2,372 women full-time. 564 part-time. **Transfer Studemts:** 191. **Graduate:** 217 men & 559 women. **Freshman Ethnic Enrollment:** Native Am/Alskn-1; Af Am-4,954; Asian/Pac Is-8; Cauc-543; Hisp-13; Other-35

WHAT DO I NEED?

Diploma from accredited high school with 2.0 GPA or GED and can demonstrate contribution to university educational program. Minimum ACT score of 20 or equivalent SAT score for applicants with diplomas from unaccredited high schools. No application fee. No closing date, June 1 priority date.

UNIQUE PROGRAMS

The following programs are available: transfer program: 2-year; cooperative education, education specialist degree, honors program, internships, teacher preparation, visiting/exchange student program, weekend college, cross-registration; liberal arts/career combination in engineering.

ACADEMIC REQUIREMENTS

Majors must be declared by end of first year.

Core curriculum: computer science, English, history, geography, humanities, mathematics, philosophy/religion, biological/physical sciences, social sciences. Associate: 63 hrs (hrs in major: 24); Bachelor's: 129 hrs (hrs in major:59).

STUDENT SERVICES

Campus student services include: learning center, remedial instruction, special counselor, tutoring.
ROTC: Air Force

TYPES OF DEGREES AWARDED:
AA, AS, BA, BS, BSW, BME, MA, MS, MED,

ACADEMIC CALENDAR:
Semester.

CONTACT INFORMATION

Admissions Officer: Billy Brooks
Phone: (334) 229-4100   **Fax:** (334) 834-6861
Web Site: http://www.alasu.edu/

DOLLARS AND SENSE

TUITION & FEES:	$2,090.00
ROOM & BOARD:	$3,560.00
BOOKS & SUPPLIES:	$800.00
OTHER EXPENSES:	$2,110.00
OUT OF STATE TUITION:	$1,500.00
*ANNUAL TOTAL:	$8,560.00

(*Annual Total does not include out-of-state tuition .)

FINANCIAL AID

Financial Aid Phone: (334) 229-4712
Financial Aid Fax: (334) 229-4924

No closing date; priority given to applications received by April 1. Students must apply through the FAFSA. Scholarships: Academic, Music/Drama, Athletic, Teacher Ed, Presidential, Honor's Dean's & Minority. Pymt Plans: Promissory Notes & Academic Mgmt. Svcs.

SPORTS

Varsity Sports: Baseball, basketbal, cross-country, tennis, football), golf, track and field, softball, volleyball. NCAA

WHAT MAJOR?

Associate: Pre-Elementary Education, Child Development, Business Management and Administration, Office Administration.

Bachelor: Accounting, art, art education, banking and finance, biology, business administration, business management, business economics, chemistry, communications (Journalism/Mass), community services, computer sciences, computer information systems, criminal justice studies, elementary education, English, French, graphic arts, health information management, health education, history, laboratory technology, marine biology, marketing and purchasing, mathematics, music, music education, music performance, office administration, parks and recreation management, physical education, physics, political science and government, pre-elementary education, psychology, public relations, radio/television, secondary education, social work, Spanish, special education (MR), speech, theatre arts.

Master: Agency counseling, biology, elementary educaion, educational administration, guidance counseling, health education, history, library educational media, mathematics, music education, music performance, physical education, pre-elementary education, physical education, reading education, secondary education, special education (MR, LD).

Historical & Special Interest:
Originally the Lincoln Normal School, a private institution, Alabama State University began in Marion, AL in 1867, 10 years after the "Emancipation Proclamation" and eight years after 4 million slaves were freed penniless. It became the first state supported, historically Black institution and was for many years the only school of its kind in the southern states. On 113.5 acres in Montgomery, Alabama, ASU has more than 5,500 students in seven major units: University College, the College of Arts and Sciences, the College of Business Adminisration, the College of Education, the School of Music, the School of Graduate Studies and Continuing Education, and the Division of Aerospace Studies. E.D. Nixon papers from the civil rights movement and the Black history collection are housed at ASU.

Master Key: *The man on his feet carries off the share of the man sitting down. African Proverb*

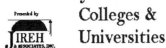
ALBANY STATE UNIVERSITY

ALBANY, GA

Web Site:
www.alsnet.peachnet.edu

SCHOOL INFO

Established in 1903. 4-year public liberal arts, coed college on urban campus in small city 176 miles south of Atlanta.

ACCREDITATON:
Southern Association of Colleges & Schools

CAMPUS ENROLLMENT:
Undergraduate: Full-time women and men: 2782. **Graduate:** Full-time: 331 women and men. **Freshman Ethnic Enrollment:** NA-0; Af Am-1,244; Asian/Pac Is-4; Cauc-29; Hisp-0; Other-0

WHAT DO I NEED?

School achievement record, test scores, essay and interview considered important. SAT or ACT. College-preparatory program. Foreign language must have 2 units in same language. Scores by September 1. No fee. Closing date September 1. Deferred and early admission program available. Notification on a rolling basis; replies within one week. Interview required for provisional students.

UNIQUE PROGRAMS

The following programs are available: cooperative education, cross registration, double major, dual enrollment of high school students, education specialist degree, honors program, internships, teacher prepartion, weekend college, liberal arts/career combination in engineering, health sciences.

ACADEMIC REQUIREMENTS

Minimum GPA for freshmen 2.0 and major must be declared by end of second year.

Core curriculum: Arts/fine arts, English, History, Mathematics, science and social science. Bachelors: 186 hrs.

STUDENT SERVICES

Campus student services include: aptitude testing, career and personal counseling, freshman orientation, health services, learning center, placement service for graduates, minority student advisor, remedial instruction, special counselor, services for handicapped, tutoring, veterans counselor, . ROTC: Army.

WHAT MAJOR?

ADDRESS:

ALBANY STATE UNIVERSITY
504 COLLEGE DRIVE
ALBANY,   GA   31705
Principal Official: Dr. Portia Holmes Shields

TYPES OF DEGREES AWARDED:
AA, BA, BS, MS, MBA

ACADEMIC CALENDAR:
Quarter. Summer sessions limited.

CONTACT INFORMATION

Admissions Officer: Patricia Price
Phone: (912) 430-4646   **Fax:** (912) 430-3936
Web Site: www.alsnet.peachnet.edu

DOLLARS AND SENSE

TUITION & FEES:	$2,124.00
ROOM & BOARD:	$3,225.00
BOOKS & SUPPLIES:	$750.00
OTHER EXPENSES:	$1,680.00
OUT OF STATE TUITION:	$4,461.00
*ANNUAL TOTAL:	$7,779.00

(*Annual Total does not include out-of-state tuition .)

FINANCIAL AID

Financial Aid Phone:
Financial Aid Fax:

No closing date; priority given to applications received by June1. FAFSA accepted. Notifications on a rolling basis beginning July 1; must reply within 2 weeks. Academic, state/district residency, leadership scholarships available.

SPORTS

Varsity Sports: Baseball, basketball, cross-country, football, tennis, track and field, volleyball. NCAA.

Bachelor's: Accounting, allied health, biology, business management, chemistry, computer sciences, criminal justice studies, French, health education, history, junior high education, mathematics education,middle grades education, music, music education, nursing, physical education, political science and government, preelementary education, psychology, science education, secondary education, secretarial and related programs, social science education, social work, sociology, Spanish, special education, speech/communication/theater education.

Graduate Degree Programs:
Business Administration, Criminal Justice, Education, Nursing, Public Administration, and Educational Administration and Supervision.

Historical & Special Interest:
The university was founded by Dr. Joseph Winthrop Holley in 1903 as a Bible and Manual Training Institute and became a state assisted school in 1917. Today, Albany State University is a regional institution serving a 24-county area and the population of Southwest Georgia with programs that anticipate and respond to community and individual needs. Albany State University is the senior unit of the University System of Georgia.

The University is student-driven and has taken on a statewide mission with the 1989 opening of the Center for the Study of the Black Male with satellite programs at three sister institutions. A "Total-Quality Approach" guarantees a broad-based curriculum and builds in student goals which focus on breadth of knowledge as well as the kind of knowledge gained. Academic achievement must translate to competency in the workplace and commitment to the community. Student-teacher ratio is 20 to one, and currently ASU has one computer available for every 13 students at computer clusters located conveniently throughout the campus. Its strategic plan includes literacy training programs, partnerships with four local high schools and computer literacy levels among all personnel as well as students. Currently for every 12 students, there is one terminal with plans to reduce the number to seven to one.

Master Key: *A bank is a place where they lend you an umbrella in fair weather and ask for it back when it begins to rain. Robert Frost*

HBCU Third Edition
© Jireh & Associates, Inc.
Wilmington, DE

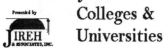
ALCORN STATE UNIVERSITY

LORMAN, MS

Web Site:
www.alcorn.lorman.edu

SCHOOL INFO

Established in 1871. 4-year public coed university on rural campus in small town; 40 miles from Natchez, 80 miles from Jackson.

ACCREDITATON:
Southern Association of Colleges & Schools

CAMPUS ENROLLMENT:
Undergraduate: 2741 men & women. **Graduate:** 185 men and women. **Transfer students:** 72.

WHAT DO I NEED?

Academic record, test scores considered important. College preparatory. SAT or ACT (ACT preferred); scores by July 21. No fee; no closing date and priority to applications received by July 21; notifications on a rolling basis. Music applicants must audition; interview required for nursing applicants. Deferred and early admission program available.

UNIQUE PROGRAMS

The following programs are available: accelerated program, cooperative education, double major, honors program, independent study, internships, teacher preparation.

ACADEMIC REQUIREMENTS

Freshmen must maintain a minimum 2.0 and majors must be declared by end on second year.

Core curriculum: Arts, English, history, humanities, mathematics, biological/physical sciences, social sciences. Associate: 70 hrs (34 in major). Bachelor's: 128 (44 in major).

STUDENT SERVICES

Campus student services include: academic center, preadmission summer program, remedial instruction, special counselors, special services for disadvantaged students, tutoring. ROTC: Army.

ADDRESS:

ALCORN STATE UNIVERSITY
BOX 300
LORMAN,   MS   39096
Principal Official: Dr. Clinton Bristow, Jr.

TYPES OF DEGREES AWARDED:
A, BA, BS, MS.

ACADEMIC CALENDAR:
Semester. Summer sessions limited.

CONTACT INFORMATION

Admissions Officer: Emanuel Banks
Phone: (601) 877-6147   **Fax:** (601) 877-6347
Web Site: www.alcorn.lorman.edu

DOLLARS AND SENSE

TUITION & FEES:	$2,895.00
ROOM & BOARD:	$2,612.00
BOOKS & SUPPLIES:	$300.00
OTHER EXPENSES:	$728.00
OUT OF STATE TUITION:	$5,586.00
*ANNUAL TOTAL:	$6,535.00

(*Annual Total does not include out-of-state tuition .)

FINANCIAL AID

Financial Aid Phone: (601) 877-6190
Financial Aid Fax: (601) 877-6110
No application closing date; priority given to applications received by April 14, notifications on a rolling basis beginning about July 1; must reply within 30 days. FAFSA accepted. Academic, music/drama, athletic, alumni affiliation, minority scholarships available.

SPORTS

Varsity Sports: Baseball, basketball, cross-country, football, golf, gymnastics, tennis, track and field, wrestling. NAIA, NCAA.

WHAT MAJOR?

Associate: Drafting and preengineering.

Bachelors: Accounting, agricultural economics, agricultural education, agricultural sciences, agronomy, animal sciences, applied mathematics, biology, business administration, business education, business management, chemistry, computer sciences, criminal justice studies, drafting and design technology, economics, education of the emotionally handicapped, electronic technology, elementary education, English, English education, food sciences and human nutrition, health education, health sciences, history, home economics, home economics education, industrial arts education, industrial technology, institutional management, institutional home/management/supporting programs, journalism, mathematics, mathematics education, music, music education, nursing, nutritional education, nutritional sciences, physical education, political science and government, predentistry, prelaw, premedicine, prepharmacy, preveterinary, psychology, recreation and community services technologies, science education, secondary education, secretarial and related programs, social science education, social studies education, social work, soil sciences, special education, technical education, textiles and clothing, trade and industrial education.

Historical & Special Interest:

The University offers instruction in the following seven divisions: Agriculture and Applied Science, Arts and Sciences, Business and Economics, Education and Psychology, Graduate Studies, and Nursing. Alcorn boasts an extensive research program, a program of cooperative extension and an agricultural and forestry experiment station.
Alcorn is one of the state's two land-grant universities. Of the 151 faculty members, approximately 50% of them hold doctoral degrees.

Master Key: *A clever man commits no minor blunders. Goethe*

HBCU Third Edition
© Jireh & Associates, Inc.
Wilmington, DE

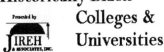
ALLEN UNIVERSITY
COLUMBIA, SC

Web Site:
Not provided.

SCHOOL INFO

Established in 1870. 4-year private liberal arts, coed college. Affiliation with African Methodist Episcopal Church on urban campus in small city.

ADDRESS:

ALLEN UNIVERSITY
1530 HARDEN STREET
COLUMBIA,   SC   29204
Principal Official: Dr. Davis T. Shannon Sr., President

TYPES OF DEGREES AWARDED:
BA, BS.

ACADEMIC CALENDAR:
Semester. Summer sessions limited.

CONTACT INFORMATION

Admissions Officer: Christopher Baughn
Phone: (803) 376-5735   **Fax:** (803) 376-5733
Web Site: Not provided.

ACCREDITATON:
Southern Association of Colleges & Schools

CAMPUS ENROLLMENT:
Undergraduate: 560 men and women. **Transfer Students- 40.**

DOLLARS AND SENSE

TUITION & FEES:	$4,750.00
ROOM & BOARD:	$4,210.00
BOOKS & SUPPLIES:	$300.00
OTHER EXPENSES:	$0.00
OUT OF STATE TUITION:	$0.00
*ANNUAL TOTAL:	$9,260.00

(*Annual Total does not include out-of-state tuition .)

WHAT DO I NEED?

Open admissions. Application fee $10 may be waived based on need. Personal interview required.

UNIQUE PROGRAMS

The following programs are available: Transfer program: 2-year; cooperative education, education specialist degree, honors program, internships.

FINANCIAL AID

Financial Aid Phone:
Financial Aid Fax:
FAFSA accepted. 100% of freshmen receive some form of aid.

ACADEMIC REQUIREMENTS

Freshmen must earn a minimum 2.0 in order to remain in good standing. Majors must be declared by the end of the 2nd year.

Core curriculum: Fine arts, computer science, English, foreign languages, history, humanities,mathematics, philosophy / religion, biological/physical science and social science.

STUDENT SERVICES

Campus student services include: academic center, tutoring, career and personal counseling, placement services.

SPORTS

Men & Women Basketball Team, track and field competion.

WHAT MAJOR?

Associate: Business and office, business data processing and related programs, business data programming, computer, science technologies, secretarial and related programs.

Bachelor's: American studies, biology, business administration, elementary education, English, history, mathematics, political science and government, secretarial and related programs, sociology.

Historical & Special Interest:

Founded in 1870 under the auspices of the African Methodist Episcopal Church, Allen University is the oldest historically black college in South Carolina. Five buildings on the Allen University campus have been awarded the "Historic District Status" by the United States Department of Interior. Allen recognizes the need for a challenging curriculum and personalized instruction in its six academic departments: Humanities, Mathematics and Sciences, Social Science, Business and Economics, English, Foreign Languages and Education, Teacher Education, and Physical Education.

Allen has produced 10 college presidents from its doors, contributing significantly to our society admist an educational revolution for Black America.

Master Key: *A critic is a legless man who teaches running. Anonymous*

HBCU Third Edition
© Jireh & Associates, Inc.
Wilmington, DE

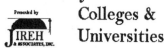
ARKANSAS BAPTIST COLLEGE

LITTLE ROCK, AR

Web Site:
Not provided.

SCHOOL INFO

Established in 1884. 4-year private liberal arts college, coed, affiliated with American Baptist Churches in the USA on urban campus in small city; in downtown area.

ACCREDITATON:
North Central Association of Colleges & Schools

CAMPUS ENROLLMENT:
*Undergraduate: Full-time and part-time: 167 women and 139 men.

ADDRESS:

ARKANSAS BAPTIST COLLEGE
1600 BISHOP STREET
LITTLE ROCK,   AR   72202
Principal Official: Dr. W. Thomas Keaton

TYPES OF DEGREES AWARDED:
AA, BA, BS.

ACADEMIC CALENDAR:
Semester. Summer sessions.

CONTACT INFORMATION

Admissions Officer: Annie Hightower
Phone: (501) 374-7856   **Fax:** (501) 372-0321
Web Site: Not provided.

WHAT DO I NEED?

Academic record, recommendations, special talents, interviews and alumni relations considered important. Provisional applicants may be admitted however; a 2.0 GPA must be attained by end of 1st semester. Application fee $10 may be waived based on need; notifications on a rolling basis beginning around June 30. No application deadline. Fall term application closing date is 2 wks prior to registration.

UNIQUE PROGRAMS

The following programs are available: Dual major, independent study and transfer program.

ACADEMIC REQUIREMENTS

Minimum GPA of 1.5 for freshmen, all other classifications must maintain GPA of 2.0 and a major must be declared by end of first year.

Core curriculum: English, history, mathematics, philosophy, physical sciences, social sciences. Associate: 62 hrs. Bachelor's: 124 hrs. Hours required in residence: 15 and 30 respectively.

DOLLARS AND SENSE

TUITION & FEES:	$2,200.00
ROOM & BOARD:	$3,600.00
BOOKS & SUPPLIES:	$500.00
OTHER EXPENSES:	$100.00
OUT OF STATE TUITION:	
*ANNUAL TOTAL:	$6,400.00

(*Annual Total does not include out-of-state tuition .)

FINANCIAL AID

Financial Aid Phone: (501)374-7856
Financial Aid Fax: (501) 375-9257

Application closing date May 1. Notifications around August 15; must reply by August 20. FAFSA accepted.

STUDENT SERVICES

Campus student services include: aptitude testing, campus day care, developmental studies program in English, reading and mathematics; employment services, freshman orientation, health services, career, personal and veterans counseling, placement services, tutoring.

SPORTS

Varsity Sports: Basketball, softball, and volleyball.

WHAT MAJOR?

Associate: Adult continuing education, business administration, business and office, computer science, Christian education, secretarial science.

Bachelor's: Accounting, business administration, computer science, elementary education, religion/Christian education, secondary education, social science.

Historical & Special Interest:

Arkansas Baptist College offers a liberal arts oriented academic program leading to terminal degrees in Natural and Physical Science, Social Science, Education, and Business Administration. It provides the following service programs to the local community and the state:

1) A Kiddie Kollege for preschoolers; and

2) Non-credit career extension program through the Arkansas Baptist Convention.

Master Key: *A diplomat is a man who always remembers a woman's birthday but never remembers her age.*
Robert Frost

HBCU Third Edition
© Jireh & Associates, Inc.
Wilmington, DE

ATLANTA METROPOLITAN
ATLANTA, GA

Web Site:
Not provided.

SCHOOL INFO

Established in 1974. 2-year public junior coed college on urban campus in very large city; 2 miles from downtown.

ACCREDITATON:
Southern Association of Colleges & Schools

CAMPUS ENROLLMENT:
Undergraduate: 1700. **Transfer students:** 430. **Freshman ethnic enrollment:** Native American-2, African American-695, Asian-3, Caucasian-11, Hispanic-3.

WHAT DO I NEED?

Test scores and high school GPA important. SAT/ACT. Scores by May 1. College-preparatory program. Application fee $10. Closing date September 1. Notification on a rolling basis; beginning March 1. Deferred and early admission program available.

UNIQUE PROGRAMS

The following programs are available: cooperative education, dual enrollment of high school students, internships, weekend college, cross-registration, 2-year transfer program.

ACADEMIC REQUIREMENTS

Minimum GPA for freshmen 1.8 and major must be declared on application.

Core curriculum: English, history, mathematics, biological/physical sciences, social sciences. Associate: 97 hours (30 in major).

STUDENT SERVICES

Campus student services include: aptitude testing, career and personal counseling, employment service for undergraduates, health services, learning center, placement service for graduates, remedial instruction, special counselor, services for handicapped, tutoring, veterans counselor.

ADDRESS:

ATLANTA METROPOLITAN COLLEGE
1630 STEWART AVENUE S.W.
ATLANTA,   GA   30310
Principal Official: Dr. Harold Wade

TYPES OF DEGREES AWARDED:
AA, AS, AAS.

ACADEMIC CALENDAR:
Quarter. Summer sessions extensive.

CONTACT INFORMATION

Admissions Officer: Clifton Rawles
Phone: (404) 756-4004   **Fax:** (404) 756-4407
Web Site: Not provided.

DOLLARS AND SENSE

TUITION & FEES:	$1,300.00
ROOM & BOARD:	$0.00
BOOKS & SUPPLIES:	$400.00
OTHER EXPENSES:	$100.00
OUT OF STATE TUITION:	$2,420.00
*ANNUAL TOTAL:	$1,800.00

(*Annual Total does not include out-of-state tuition.)

FINANCIAL AID

Financial Aid Phone: (404) 756-4002
Financial Aid Fax: (404) 756-4834

No closing date; priority given to applications received by August 20. Notifications on a rolling basis beginning July 1; must reply within 2 weeks. FAFSA accepted. All aid based on need. 25% freshmen received some form of financial aid.

SPORTS

Varsity Sports: Basketball, softball, tennis, track and field.

WHAT MAJOR?

Associate: Accounting, agriculture engineering, agricultural sciences, air conditioning/heating/refrigeration mechanics, aircraft mechanics, anthropology, automotive mechanics, automotive technology, biological and physical sciences, business management, business and office, business data processing and related programs, business data programming, business education, carpentry, chemistry, computer sciences, construction, criminology, dental laboratory technology, diesel engine mechanics, drafting, economics, education, electrical and electronics equipment repair, electrical installation, elementary education, engineering-related technologies, English, fine arts, foreign languages (multiple emphasis), forestry and related sciences, geography, geology, graphic and printing production, history, home economics, humanities, information sciences and systems, journalism, law enforcement and corrections technologies, liberal/general studies, marketing and distribution, masonry/tile setting, mathematics, medical illustrating, medical laboratory technologies, medical records administration, medical records technology, mental health/human services, music, nursing, occupational therapy, office supervision and management, physical therapy, political science and government, preelementary education, protective services, psychology, public affairs, radiograph medical technology, recreation and community services technologies, science technologies, secretarial and related programs, social work, sociology, speech/debate forensics, teacher aide, urban studies.

Historical & Special Interest:

Atlanta Metropolitan College is a coed, non-residential institution offering programs leading to associate degrees in Arts and Science and Applied Science. The campus sits on a wooded 83-acre tract of land and a lake.

The College offers a variety of programs through the Division of Extension and Public Service including non-degree courses, workshops, seminars, lectures and conferences. An extensive program of Developmental Studies assists students who require further development of basic skills in English, Mathematics and Reading.

Master Key: *A people that values its priviledges above its principles soon loses both. Dwight D. Eisenhower*

HBCU Third Edition
© Jireh & Associates, Inc.
Wilmington, DE

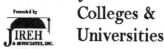
BARBER-SCOTIA COLLEGE

CONCORD, NC

Web Site:
Not provided.

SCHOOL INFO

Established in 1867. Private, coed, 4-year liberal arts college. Presbyterian Church affiliation on urban campus in large town; 20 miles from Charlotte.

ACCREDITATON:
Southern Association of Colleges & Schools

CAMPUS ENROLLMENT:
Undergraduate: 704. Transfer students: 21. Freshman ethnic enrollment: Not Available

WHAT DO I NEED?

Open admission. SAT or ACT (SAT preferred) for placement and counseling only; score report by August 17. $10 application fee which may be waived with need; no closing date notifications on a rolling basis beginning about January 25. Deferred admission program available. Interview recommended.

UNIQUE PROGRAMS

The following programs are available: double major, cross-registration, honors program, independent study, internships, teacher preparation,

ACADEMIC REQUIREMENTS

Freshmen must earn a minimum 2.0 and majors must be declared by end of second year.

Core curriculum: Arts/fine arts, computer science, humanities, English, foreign languages, history, mathematics, biological/physical sciences, philosophy/religion, social sciences. Bachelor's: 125 hrs (45 in major).

STUDENT SERVICES

Campus student services include: academic center, aptitude testing, career and personal counseling, employment service for undergraduates, health services, placement services, reduced course load program, remedial instruction, special counselor, tutoring, services for handicapped. ROTC: Army, Naval.

WHAT MAJOR?

Bachelor's: Accounting, biology, business administration and management, business and management, computer programming, computer mathematics, elementary education, hotel/motel and restaurant management, mathematics, mathematics education, parks and recreation management, physical education, secondary education, sociology.

Historical & Special Interest:

Barber-Scotia College was originally Scotia Seminary, a preparatory school for young Negro Women and remained so for more than a generation. In 1916 significant changes in policy and programs expanded the curricula and changed the name to Scotia Women's College.

In 1930 the College merged with the Barber Memorial College of Anniston, Alabama and in 1932 the name Barber-Scotia College was adopted. The College was then converted to a coed institution in 1954. Barber-Scotia College is a UNCF school.

ADDRESS:

BARBER-SCOTIA COLLEGE
145 CABARRUS AVE. W.
CONCORD,   NC   28025
Principal Official: Dr. Samuel Potts

TYPES OF DEGREES AWARDED:
BA, BS.

ACADEMIC CALENDAR:
Semester.

CONTACT INFORMATION

Admissions Officer: Al Coffield
Phone: (704) 789-2902   **Fax:** (704) 789-2935
Web Site: Not provided.

DOLLARS AND SENSE

TUITION & FEES:	$10,800.00
ROOM & BOARD:	$3,220.00
BOOKS & SUPPLIES:	$736.00
OTHER EXPENSES:	$1,000.00
OUT OF STATE TUITION:	
*ANNUAL TOTAL:	$15,756.00

(*Annual Total does not include out-of-state tuition .)

FINANCIAL AID

Financial Aid Phone: (704) 789-2909
Financial Aid Fax: (704) 789-2624

No application closing date but priority given to applications received by March 1; notifications on a rolling basis beginning about April 15; must reply within 2 weeks. FAFSA accepted. Pell grants, loans, jobs available. Academic, athletic, music/drama, state/district residency, religious affiliation scholarships available.

SPORTS

Varsity Sports: Basketball, softball, tennis, track and field. NAIA.

Master Key: *Acting is not being emotional, but being able to express emotion. Kate Reid*

HBCU Third Edition
© Jireh & Associates, Inc.
Wilmington, DE

8

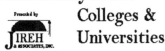
BENEDICT COLLEGE
COLUMBIA, SC

SCHOOL INFO

Established in 1870. 4-year private liberal arts, coed college. Affiliation with American Baptist Churches in the USA on urban campus in downtown Columbia; 120 miles from Charleston.

ACCREDITATON:
Southern Association of Colleges & Schools

CAMPUS ENROLLMENT:
Undergraduate: 941 men & 1054 women. **Part-Time:** 52 men & 87 women. **Freshman ethnic enrollment:** African American - 2133, Caucasian - 5.

WHAT DO I NEED?

Open admissions. SAT or ACT for counseling; scores by August 1. Application fee $25 may be waived based on need. No closing date; notifications on a rolling basis; replies within 4 weeks. Deferred admission program available.

UNIQUE PROGRAMS

The following programs are available: accelerated program, double major, dual enrollment of high school students, external degree, honors program, internships, teacher preparation, weekend college; liberal arts/career combination in engineering.

ACADEMIC REQUIREMENTS

Freshmen must earn a minimum 2.0 and majors must be declared by end of second year.

Core curriculum: arts/fine arts, computer science, English, foreign languages, history, humanities, mathematics, biological/physical sciences, philosophy/religion, social sciences. Bachelor's: 125 hrs (24 in major).

STUDENT SERVICES

Campus student services include: academic center, aptitude testing, career and personal counseling, employment service for undergraduates, health services, language and mathematics labs, placement services, preadmission summer program, reduced course load program, special counselor, tutoring, veterans counselor ROTC: Air Force, Army.

WHAT MAJOR?

Bachelor's: Accounting, art, biology, business administration, chemistry, computer sciences, child & family development, criminal justice, economics, early childhood education, elementary education, English, Environmental Health Science, history, mathematics, media arts, music, physics, political science, religion & philosophy, social work.

Historical & Special Interest:

Benedict College is a private Baptist Convention-related, fully accredited four-year college offering programs leading to the Bachelor of Arts, Bachelor of Science, and Bachelor of Social Work degrees. Benedict College is located in an urban center and situated on a 20-acre campus in downtown Columbia, South Carolina, the capital city. Since 1973 Benedict has had the largest enrollment of South Carolina residents of all 20 private, four-year colleges in the state. Benedict College now ranks third in total enrollment among private colleges in the state.

Still a relatively young institution, Benedict caters to the intellectual, cultural and emotional needs of students endeavoring careers as professionals and/or paraprofessionals in government, industry, commerce, education and church-related occupations.

Benedict College is a UNCF school.

ADDRESS:

BENEDICT COLLEGE
1600 HARDEN STREET
COLUMBIA,　　　　SC　　29204
Principal Official: Dr. David H. Swinton

TYPES OF DEGREES AWARDED:
BA, BS

ACADEMIC CALENDAR:
Semester. Summer sessions limited.

CONTACT INFORMATION

Admissions Officer: Gary Knight
Phone: (803) 256-4220　**Fax:** (803) 253-5167
Web Site: www.icusc.org/benedict

DOLLARS AND SENSE

TUITION & FEES:	$6,820.00
ROOM & BOARD:	$3,620.00
BOOKS & SUPPLIES:	$700.00
OTHER EXPENSES:	$784.00
OUT OF STATE TUITION:	
*ANNUAL TOTAL:	$11,924.00

(*Annual Total does not include out-of-state tuition.)

FINANCIAL AID

Financial Aid Phone:　(803) 253-5105
Financial Aid Fax:　(803) 253-5325

No closing date priority given to applications received by January 1; notifications on a rolling basis beginning about January 1; must reply by June 30 or within 2 weeks. FAFSA accepted. Federal and State Pell grants, loans, jobs based on need. UNCF, SC Aptitude, Academic and athletic scholarships available.

SPORTS

Varsity Sports: Baseball & football, basketball, volleyball, cross-country, golf, softball), track and field. NAIA.

Master Key: *Any fool can criticize, condemn, and complain —and most fools do. Dale Carnegie*

HBCU Third Edition
© Jireh & Associates, Inc.
Wilmington, DE

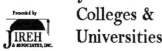
BENNETT COLLEGE
GREENSBORO, NC

Web Site:
www.bennett.edu

SCHOOL INFO

Established in 1873. Private, women-only,4-year liberal arts college. United Methodist Church affiliation on urban campus in small city; 295 miles south of Washington, D.C. and 35 miles north of Atlanta, GA.

ACCREDITATON:
Southern Association of Colleges & Schools

CAMPUS ENROLLMENT:
Undergraduate: 635 women. **Transfer students:** 28 women. **Freshman ethnic enrollment:** African American-189.

WHAT DO I NEED?

Academic record, test scores, essay required and interview recommended for provisional students, and recommendations important. College preparatory program. SAT/ACT (SAT preferred) scores by August 1. Application fee $10 which may be waived for applicants with need; no closing date and notifications on a rolling basis; replies within 4 weeks. Early admission program available.

UNIQUE PROGRAMS

The following programs are available: accelerated program, cooperative education, double major, cross-registration, honors program, independent study, internships, student-designed major, teacher preparation; liberal arts/career combination in engineering.

ACADEMIC REQUIREMENTS

Must earn 1.75 to remain in good standing. Declaration of major by end of 2nd year.

Core curriculum: English, foreign languages, history, humanities, mathematics, biological/physical sciences, philosophy/religion, social sciences. Bachelor's: 124 hrs (60 in major).

STUDENT SERVICES

Campus student services include: academic center, aptitude testing, career and personal counseling, employment service for undergraduates, freshmen orientation, health services, campus daycare, placement services, preadmission summer program, reduced course load, remedial instruction, special counselor, tutoring. ROTC: Air Force, Army.

WHAT MAJOR?

Associate: Secretarial and related programs.

Bachelor's: Accounting, biology, business administration , business management, chemistry, communications, computer sciences, elementary education, English, English education, fashion merchandising, food sciences and human nutrition, health sciences, home economics, home economics education, humanities and social sciences, junior high education, liberal/general studies, mathematics, mathematics education, music education, physical education, political science and government, predentistry, preelementary education, premedicine, psychology, science education, secondary education, social science education, social work, sociology, special education, textiles and clothing.

Historical & Special Interest:

Bennett College was founded as a coed institution in 1873 and re-organized as a four-year, liberal arts women's college in 1926. Bennett offers the Bachelor of Arts and Sciences in Interdisciplinary Studies and Bachelor of Sciences degrees in four academic disciplines: education, humanities, natural sciences, and social sciences.

The Bennett woman has the option to concentrate on one major area, combine two or more majors for a specialized career goal or design her own non-traditional program of study.

Bennett College is a UNCF school.

ADDRESS:

BENNETT COLLEGE
900 E. WASHINGTON ST.
GREENSBORO,   NC   27401
Principal Official: Dr. Gloria R. Scott

TYPES OF DEGREES AWARDED:
AA, BA

ACADEMIC CALENDAR:
Semester.

CONTACT INFORMATION

Admissions Officer: Linda Torrence
Phone: (800) 413-5323   **Fax:** (910) 378-0513
Web Site: www.bennett.edu

DOLLARS AND SENSE

TUITION & FEES:	$12,730.00
ROOM & BOARD:	$2,500.00
BOOKS & SUPPLIES:	$900.00
OTHER EXPENSES:	$1,500.00
OUT OF STATE TUITION:	$12,168.00
*ANNUAL TOTAL:	$17,630.00

(*Annual Total does not include out-of-state tuition .)

FINANCIAL AID

Financial Aid Phone: (336)370-8677
Financial Aid Fax: (336)378-0513

Application closing date April 15; notifications on a rolling basis beginning about April 15; must reply within 15 days. FAFSA accepted. Pell grants, loans, jobs available. Academic, athletic, alumni affiliation, religious affiliation scholarships available.

SPORTS

Varsity Sports: Basketball, tennis, volleyball. Intramural Sports: Basketball, softball, swimming, tennis, volleyball.

Master Key: *When ambition goes out the door, poverty comes in the window.*

HBCU Third Edition
© Jireh & Associates, Inc.
Wilmington, DE

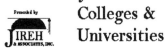
BETHUNE-COOKMAN COLLEGE

DAYTONA BEACH, FL

Web Site:
www.bethune.cookman.edu

SCHOOL INFO

Established in 1904. 4-year private liberal arts college, coed, residential, affiliated with United Methodist Church on urban campus in small city; 60 miles from Orlando.

ACCREDITATON:
Southern Association of Colleges & Schools

CAMPUS ENROLLMENT:
Undergraduate: 2157 Total; 879 men & 1287 women. **Transfer students:** 29 men & 87 women. **Freshman ethnic enrollment:** Asian-3, A.A.- 2168, Caucasian-14, Hispanic-3, Other-22, Int'l-112.

WHAT DO I NEED?
Most important are School achievement record, 2.25 GPA, and student evaluation report. A report of scores on the SAT or ACT is suggested. Non-refundable application fee $25; Closing date for Fall semester July 30 and Nov. 30 for Spring semester; notification on rolling basis. Deferred and early admissions and Advanced Placement program available.

UNIQUE PROGRAMS
The following programs are available: accelerated programs, double major, pre-professional programs; honors program, Continuing Education Program; Army & Air Force ROTC; internships, cooperative education; community service; teacher preparation, dual degree in engineering available.

ACADEMIC REQUIREMENTS
Majors declared on application. Based on entry-level placement test scores, students may be required to take basic skills courses prior to college-level. Minimum GPA of 1.85 for freshmen; and 2.0 for all other classes.

Spend at least one full year of residence in study at the College; compete satisfactorily a major in a field of study with a min. 124 semester hrs with a cum. GPA of not less than "C" or 2.0; pass all the subtests of the College-Level Academic Skills Test; pass a senior exit examination; complete a Senior Seminar and senior research paper.

STUDENT SERVICES
On-campus housing; freshmen and new student orientation; religious services; health services; athletic programs; SGA, Men's and Women's Senate, School publications-performing groups- drama, choir, bands, major area clubs, religious organ., fraternal organ., honor societies, svc. & social organ., aptitude testing; career and person counseling; employment and placement service, financial aid counselor, library and learning resource center, tri-learning center, tutoring and computer laboratories.

WHAT MAJOR?

ADDRESS:

BETHUNE-COOKMAN COLLEGE
640 DR. MARY MCLEOD BETHUNE BLVD.
DAYTONA BEACH, FL 32114-3099
Principal Official: Dr. Oswald P. Bronson, Sr.

TYPES OF DEGREES AWARDED:
BA, BS.

ACADEMIC CALENDAR:
Fall & Spring Semester. 8-week Summer Session.

CONTACT INFORMATION

Admissions Officer: Richard F. Pride
Phone: (800) 448-0228 **Fax:** (904) 257-5338
Web Site: www.bethune.cookman.edu

DOLLARS AND SENSE

TUITION & FEES:	$7,280.00
ROOM & BOARD:	$4,274.00
BOOKS & SUPPLIES:	$600.00
OTHER EXPENSES:	$2,300.00
OUT OF STATE TUITION:	
*ANNUAL TOTAL:	$14,454.00

(*Annual Total does not include out-of-state tuition .)

FINANCIAL AID

Financial Aid Phone: (800) 553-9369
Financial Aid Fax: (904) 255-9284

Financial Aid is awarded according to individual financial need and/or academic potential in the form of loans, grants, scholarships or part-time on-campus employment (used solely for school related expenses). Priority date for FAFSA applications is March 1.

SPORTS
Varsity Sports: Baseball, basketball, cross-country, football, golf, tennis, track and field. Intramural: Basketball, cross-country, Golf, Softball, Tennis, Track & Field, volleyball. Mid-Eastern Athletic Conference of NCAA.

Bachelor's: Accounting, biology, biology education, business administration, business education, chemistry, chemistry education, computer information systems, computer science, criminal justice, gerontology, elementary education, varying exceptionalities, specific learning disabilities, English, English education, mass communications, modern languages, modern languages education, history, hospitality management, international business, mathematics, mathematics education, medical technology, music, music education, nursing, physics, physics education, physical education, political science, pre-engineering, psychology, religion and philosophy, social studies education, sociology. Liberal Studies.

Historical & Special Interest:
Bethune-Cookman College's mission is to serve in the Christian tradition the educational, social, and cultural needs of its student --traditional and non-traditional and to develop in the desire and capacity for continuous intellectual and professional growth, leadership and service to others. The mission further includes commitment to moral and personal values.
The year was 1904 when a very determined young black woman, Mary McLeod Bethune opened the Daytona Educational and Industrial Training School for Negro Girls. It underwent several stages of growth and development through the years. It became a co-ed high school with the merger in 1923 of Cookman Institute for Boys of Jacksonville, founded in 1872 by the Reverend D.S.B. Darnell and the Institute for Girls of Daytona Beach. A year after the merger, the institution became affiliated with the Methodist Church, evolved into a junior college by 1931. The name was later changed to Bethune-Cookman College. In 1941, the Florida State Dept. of Education approved a 4-yera baccalaureate program offering liberal arts and teacher education. Mrs. Bethune retired in 1942 at which time James E. Colston became president until 1946 when Mrs. Bethune resumed the presidency for a year. In 1943, the first group of graduates received the Bachelor of Science Degree in Elementary Education. Richard V. Moore, Sr. became president in 1947. Under his tenure the college was accredited by the Southern Association of Colleges and Schools in 1970, joined the United Negro College Fund and other academic and professional organizations. A rapidly increasing student enrollment led to construction of more student housing and classroom buildings. In addition, nine continuing education centers are in operation for students throughout the state. Bethune-Cookman College is a UNCF school.

Master Key: *A man wrapped up in himself makes a very small bundle. Anonymous*

HBCU Third Edition
© Jireh & Associates, Inc.
Wilmington, DE

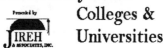
BISHOP STATE COMMUNITY
MOBILE, AL

Web Site:
Not provided.

SCHOOL INFO
Established in 1963. 2-year public community, junior college, coed on urban campus in small city; 1.5 miles from downtown.

ADDRESS:

BISHOP STATE COMMUNITY COLLEGE
351 N.BROAD STREET
MOBILE,　　　　　AL　　36603-6401
Principal Official:　Dr. Yvonne Kennedy

TYPES OF DEGREES AWARDED:
AA, AS, AAS.

ACADEMIC CALENDAR:
Semester . Summer sessions limited.

CONTACT INFORMATION

Admissions Officer:　Ms. Delayne Banks
Phone:　(334) 690-6412　**Fax:** (334) 431-5403
Web Site:　Not provided.

ACCREDITATON:
Southern Association of Colleges & Schools

CAMPUS ENROLLMENT:
Undergraduate: 4194 men & women. **Transfer students:** 133.

WHAT DO I NEED?
Open admission. Application fee $5. No closing date; priority given to applications received by August 15; notifications on a rolling basis beginning around August 15. Test Required: SAT or ACT (ACT preferred). Deferred and early admissions program available.

UNIQUE PROGRAMS
The following programs are available: accelerated program, 2-year transfer program, cooperative education, cross-registration, dual enrollment of high school students, internships, weekend college, honors program.

ACADEMIC REQUIREMENTS
Minimum GPA for freshmen is 1.5 and majors must be declared on enrollment.

Core curriculum: English, history, humanities, mathematics, biological/physical sciences, social sciences. Associate requirement: 96 hours.

DOLLARS AND SENSE

TUITION & FEES:	$1,440.00
ROOM & BOARD:	$0.00
BOOKS & SUPPLIES:	$300.00
OTHER EXPENSES:	$20.00
OUT OF STATE TUITION:	$2,880.00
*ANNUAL TOTAL:	$1,760.00

(*Annual Total does not include out-of-state tuition .)

FINANCIAL AID

Financial Aid Phone:　(334)690-6861
Financial Aid Fax:　(334)438-5403

No closing date; priority given to applications received by June 15; notifications on a rolling basis beginning around July 20. Reply within 1 week. FAFSA accepted. All Pell grants, loans, and jobs based on need. Academic, music/drama, athletic, leadership scholarships available.

STUDENT SERVICES
Campus student services include: career and personal counseling, employment service for undergraduates, health services, learning center, learning center, placement service for graduates, preadmission summer program, reduced course load, remedial instruction, special counselor, tutoring, veterans counselor, services for handicapped.

SPORTS
Varsity Sports: Baseball, basketball. NJCAA.

WHAT MAJOR?
Associate: Accounting, biology, biomedical equipment technology, business administration, business management, business and office, business data programming, chemical technology, chemistry, communications, computer sciences, drafting, economics, education, electrodiagnostic technologies, elementary education, emergency medical technologies, English, fine arts, funeral services/mortuary science, history, interpreter for the deaf, liberal/general studies, library assistant, marketing management, mathematics, medical assistant, medical laboratory, medical laboratory technologies, medical records administration, medical records technology, mental health/human services, music, nursing, predentistry, prelaw, premedicine, prepharmacy, preveterinary, psychology, radiograph medical technology, secondary education, secretarial and related programs, sociology, special education, teacher aide.

Historical & Special Interest:

Bishop State Community College was at one time the Alabama State College Branch, started in Mobile, Alabama in 1927. In 1936, the College began offering a two-year curriculum as a part of the parent institution, Alabama State University. The College became an independent junior college in 1965 and the name was changed to Mobile State Junior College. In honor of its first president, Dr. S.D. Bishop, the name of the institution was changed again by a 1971 legislative act. Bishop marked its 50th year of operation in 1985-86 and is the largest two-year school on the Alabama Gulf Coast after its recent merger with Southwest State Technical College and Carver State Technical College. With a student enrollment of well over 4,000, Bishop State offers a wide variety of courses. One of the more popular programs is the generic and career mobility nursing programs and the physical assistant therapist program. Bishop State's basketball team, the Matadors, plays in the Southern Division of the Alabama College Conference as well as the women's team..

Master Key: *Be aware that a halo has to only fall a few inches to become a noose. Dan McKinnon*

HBCU Third Edition
© Jireh & Associates, Inc.
Wilmington, DE

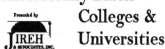
BLUEFIELD STATE COLLEGE
BLUEFIELD, WV

Web Site:
www.bluefield.wvnet.edu

SCHOOL INFO

Established in 1895. 4-year public comprehensive college with a community college component. Campus setting on 45-acre campus in Terrace Hills of SW Virginia; approx. 95 miles from Charleston.

ACCREDITATON:
North Central Association of Colleges & Schools

CAMPUS ENROLLMENT:
Undergraduate: 2,931 men and women total. **Transfer Students:** 351. **Freshman ethnic enrollment :** Native American/Alskn: 2; African American: 42; Asian: 3; Caucasian: 407.

WHAT DO I NEED?
Open admissions to associate degree prgm. except Allied Health. High school diploma or equivalent required. SAT or ACT for admissions and placement. Test scores due by August 23. No application fee. Notifications on a rolling basis. Early admissions program available.

UNIQUE PROGRAMS
Bachelor of Science: Accountancy, Adolescent Education, Applied Science, Architectural Engr. Tech., Bus. Admin., Civil Engr. Tech., Computer Science, Criminal Justice Admin., Early/Middle Ed., Electr. Engr. Tech., Mathematics, Middle/Adolescent Educ., Mining Engr. Tech., Physical Ed. (non-teaching). SEE CATALOG FOR MORE PROGRAMS OF STUDY.

ACADEMIC REQUIREMENTS
Freshmen must earn a minimum 1.8 and majors must be declared on application.

An overall 2.0 GPA is required for all degrees except for accountancy (2.75 in all accounting courses & teacher ed.- 2.50 GPA). Associate: 64 hrs. Bachelor's: 128 hrs (36 hrs. in major). Core curriculum: Computer science, English, humanities, mathematics, sciences, social science.

STUDENT SERVICES
Campus student services include: academic center, aptitude testing, career and personal counseling, employment services for undergraduates, health services, multi-cultural counselor, campus daycare, placement services, remedial instruction, services for handicapped, summer orientation program, tutoring, veterans counselor.

ADDRESS:

BLUEFIELD STATE COLLEGE
219 ROCK STREET
BLUEFIELD,   WV   24701
Principal Official: Dr. Robert E. Moore

TYPES OF DEGREES AWARDED:
AS, AAS, BA, BS, BSET.

ACADEMIC CALENDAR:
Semester. Summer sessions limited.

CONTACT INFORMATION

Admissions Officer: John Caldwell
Phone: (304) 327-4065   **Fax:** (304) 325-7747
Web Site: www.bluefield.wvnet.edu

DOLLARS AND SENSE

TUITION & FEES:	$2,110.00
ROOM & BOARD:	$0.00
BOOKS & SUPPLIES:	$300.00
OTHER EXPENSES:	$10.00
OUT OF STATE TUITION:	$5,126.00
*ANNUAL TOTAL:	$2,420.00

(*Annual Total does not include out-of-state tuition .)

FINANCIAL AID

Financial Aid Phone: (304) 327- 4011
Financial Aid Fax: (304) 325-7747
Notifications on a rolling basis beginning around June15; must reply within 2 weeks. FAFSA accepted. Pell grants, loans, jobs based on need. Academic, athletic, scholarships available.

SPORTS
Varsity Sports: Baseball, basketball, bowling, cross-country, golf, softball. NAIA, NCAA II.

WHAT MAJOR?
Associates: Applied science (Lab science), architectural engineering technology, civil engineering technology, computer science, electrical engr. technology, engineering, general business, general education, law enforcement, mechnical engr. tech., radiologic tech., secretarial science, and technical nursing.

Bachelor's: Accountancy, adolescent education, applied science, architectural engin. tech., business administration, civil engineering technology, computer science, criminal justice administration, early/middle education, electrical engineering tech., engineering, English, general business, benderal education, history, law enforcement, mathematics, mechanical engineering tech., middle/adoles. education, mining engr. technologies, physical education (non-teaching), practical nursing, radiologic tech., regents Bachelor of Arts, secretarial science, social science, technical nursing.

Historical & Special Interest:

Bluefield State College was founded in 1895 as an academy and normal school for African-American students under the name of Bluefield Colored Institute. The name was changed to Bluefield State Teachers College in 1931, and 12 years later, was amended to Bluefield State College, in recognition of the College's expanded mission and curriculum offerings. During the early 1950's, Bluefield State College enrolled approximately 350 full-time students. The college was integrated in 1954, and by the early 1960's, Bluefield became a comprehensive 4-yr institution offering programs in arts and sciences, business, engineering technology, and teacher education. Subsequently, the college implemented a variety of 2-yr and 4-yr career technical programs. Bluefield is the only 4-yr public college in West Virginia that services its students entirely on a commuting basis.

During the 1991-92 academic year, Bluefield served as the host site for the Shott Lecture Series appearance and speech by Dr. Henry Kissinger, and hosted a 14-event Black History month series. The college also assited in arrangements for the appearance in Bluefield of NFL Hall of Fame football coach Tom Landry.

Master Key: *Good luck is a lazy man's estimat of a worker's success.*

HBCU Third Edition
© Jireh & Associates, Inc.
Wilmington, DE

BOWIE STATE UNIVERSITY

BOWIE, MD

Web Site:
www/bowiestate.edu

SCHOOL INFO

Established in 1865. 4-year public coed university on suburban campus in a very large town; 25 miles from Baltimore and 17 miles from Washington, D.C.

ACCREDITATON:
Middle States, MD DoE, Accrd. Teacher Ed.,

CAMPUS ENROLLMENT:

Undergraduate: 834 men /1314 women. **Trans.** 350 men & women. P-T: 967 m&w. **Grad:** 1957 men & women. **Ethnic enrollment:** Native American-20, African American-3838, Asian-119, Caucasian-936, Hispanic-59, Foreign-95.

WHAT DO I NEED?

In-State: Minimum GPA 2.2, and SAT score of 900. GED accepted. Out-of-State: 2.6 GPA with SAT score of 950. Scores due by June 1. Application fee $35 which may be waived based on need. Closing date April 1; applicants notified on a rolling basis; must reply by June 1 or within 7 days if notified after 6/1.

UNIQUE PROGRAMS

The following programs are available: Cooperative education, cross-registration, dual degree in Engineering, concurrent enrollment, inter-institutional enrollment, honors program, National Student Exchange, Model for Excellence (MIE Science and Math).

ACADEMIC REQUIREMENTS

Minimum GPA of 2.0 and majors must be declared by end of second year.

General Education Requirements: English Composition 6 credits, Arts and Humanities 9 credits, history, humanities, mathematics, science 7/8 credits, Math 3 credits, Emerging Issues 3 credits, social sciences 12 credits and Institution Requirements 6 credits. Bachelor's: 120 hours.

STUDENT SERVICES

Campus student services include: academic center, career and personal counseling, employment services for undergraduates, freshman orientation, health svcs., peer counseling for women, placement services, preadmission summer prgm., reduced course load program, remedial instruction, special counselor, tutoring, services for handicapped. ROTC: Army.

ADDRESS:

BOWIE STATE UNIVERSITY
14000 JERICHO PARK ROAD
BOWIE,   MD   20715
Principal Official: Dr. Nathaniel Pollard Jr., President

TYPES OF DEGREES AWARDED:
BA, BS, BSN, MA, MS, Med, MSN.

ACADEMIC CALENDAR:
Semester. Summer 3 sessions, Mini-mester (Jan).

CONTACT INFORMATION

Admissions Officer: Carlene Wilson
Phone: (301) 464-6563   **Fax:** (301) 464-7521
Web Site: www /bowiestate.edu

DOLLARS AND SENSE

TUITION & FEES:	$3,657.00
ROOM & BOARD:	$4,650.00
BOOKS & SUPPLIES:	$900.00
OTHER EXPENSES:	$2,250.00
OUT OF STATE TUITION:	$7,792.00
*ANNUAL TOTAL:	$11,457.00

(*Annual Total does not include out-of-state tuition .)

FINANCIAL AID

Financial Aid Phone: (301) 464-6544
Financial Aid Fax: (301) 464-7814

No Aid applications closing date priority given to those applications received by July 1; applicants notified on a rolling basis beginning on or about June 1; must reply within 2 weeks. FAFSA accepted. Pell grants, SEOG, Perkins, Direct loans, work-study, Ed. Assistance/Guaranteed Access, Senatorial, & Diversity Grants available. Full-ride, Tuition & Fees, Tuition, Thurgood Marshall scholarships available. Paymnt Options: AMS.

SPORTS

Varsity Sports: Baseball, soccer, basketball, football, softball, tennis, track and field, volleyball. NCAA.

WHAT MAJOR?

Bachelor's: Applied mathematics, art education, biology, business administration, communications, computer sciences, criminal justice/law enforcement, dramatic arts, education, elementary education, English, English education, fine arts, history, international studies, journalism, mathematics education, music education, nursing, physical education, political science and government, preelementary education, psychology, public administration, pure mathematics, science education, secretarial management, social science education, social work, sociology, speech and linguistics.

Historical & Special Interest:
Bowie State University is an outgrowth of the first school opened in Baltimore January 9, 1865 by the Baltimore Association for the Moral and Educational Improvement of Colored People, organized in 1864 to engage in its self-appointed mission on a statewide basis. The first normal school classes were held in the African Baptist Church. In 1868, with the aid of a grant from the Freedmen's Bureau, the Baltimore Association purchased from the Society of Friends a building at Courtland and Saratoga Streets for the relocation of its Normal School.

This institution was re-organized solely as a normal school to train Negro teachers in 1893. With occasional financial support from the city of Baltimore in 1870 and the state in 1872, the Baltimore Normal School received a legacy from a fund for the education of freed Negro children in the state of Maryland established by Nelson Wells before his death in 1843. On April 8, 1908 the school requested permanent status and funding as an institution for the education of Negro teachers. The state legislature authorized its Board of Education to assume control of the school. The same law redesignated the institution as Normal School No. 3 and subsequently relocated on a 187-acre tract in Prince George's County. In 1914 it became known as Maryland Normal and Industrial School at Bowie. With state authorization in 1935, a four-year program for the training of elementary teachers was begun and the school was renamed the Maryland State Teachers College at Bowie. In 1951, with approval, the College established a teacher preparation program with a core curriculum for junior high schools and ten years later permission was granted for secondary education programs. In 1963, a liberal arts program was started and the name was changed to Bowie State University.

Master Key: *Stay clear of a man who does not value his own character. He will surely not value yours.*

CENTRAL STATE UNIVERSITY

WILBERFORCE, OH

Web Site:
www.cesvxb.ces.edu

SCHOOL INFO

Established in 1887. 4-year public, coed university campus in rural community; midway between Cincinnati and Columbus.

ACCREDITATON:
North Central Association of Colleges & Schools

CAMPUS ENROLLMENT:
Undergraduate: 3261 men & women. **Transfer students:** 155 men & women. **Freshman ethnic enrollment : Not available.**

WHAT DO I NEED?

Open admissions; out-of-state residents must have GPA 2.0. ACT score for counseling and placement only; scores by September 1. Application fee: $15 may be waived based on need. Closing date August 1; notifications on a rolling basis. Interview recommended. Deferred and early admission programs.

UNIQUE PROGRAMS

The following programs are available: cooperative education, cross-registration, double major, educational specialist degree, honors program, independent study, internships, weekend college; liberal arts/career combination in engineering.

ACADEMIC REQUIREMENTS

Freshmen must earn a minimum 2.0 and majors must be declared by end of second year.

Core curriculum: English, humanities, mathematics, biological/physical sciences, social sciences. Associates : 111 hrs (39 hrs in major). Bachelor's: 189 hrs (70 hrs in major).

STUDENT SERVICES

Campus student services include: academic center, aptitude testing, career counseling, employment service for undergraduates, health services, international counselor, placement services, reduced course load, remedial instruction, special counselor, tutoring, veterans counselor.

ADDRESS:

CENTRAL STATE UNIVERSITY
1400 BRUSH ROW ROAD
WILBERFORCE, OH 45384
Principal Official: Dr. John W. Garland

TYPES OF DEGREES AWARDED:
AAS, BA, BS.

ACADEMIC CALENDAR:
Quarter. Summer sessions limited.

CONTACT INFORMATION

Admissions Officer: Carl Penn
Phone: (800) 388-2781 **Fax:** (937) 376-6648
Web Site: www.cesvxb.ces.edu

DOLLARS AND SENSE

TUITION & FEES:	$8,013.00
ROOM & BOARD:	$0.00
BOOKS & SUPPLIES:	$250.00
OTHER EXPENSES:	$0.00
OUT OF STATE TUITION:	$11,988.00
*ANNUAL TOTAL:	$8,263.00

(*Annual Total does not include out-of-state tuition .)

FINANCIAL AID

Financial Aid Phone: (800)234-2782
Financial Aid Fax: (800)234-2782

Closing date August 1; priority given to applications received by May 15; notifications on a rolling basis beginning about May 15; must reply within 2 weeks. FAFSA accepted. All jobs based on need. Academic, music/drama, art, state/district residency, leadership, religious and alumni affiliation, minority scholarships available.

SPORTS

Varsity Sports: Baseball, basketball, football, tennis, track and field, volleyball. NAIA Division I.

WHAT MAJOR?

Associate: Child development/care/guidance.

Bachelor's: Accounting, allied health, art, advertising graphics, art education, art studio, anthropology, banking and finance, biology, business administration, business management, business economics, chemistry, communications, computer sciences, dance, data processing, dramatic arts, earth sciences, economics, education, education of the culturally disadvantaged, education of the emotionally handicapped, education of the mentally handicapped, electrical/electronics/communications engineering, elementary education, English, English literature, French, geography, geology, health sciences, history, information sciences and systems, international relations, journalism, junior high education, manufacturing technology, marketing management, mathematics, mechnanical engineering, medical laboratory, military science, music, philosophy, physics, political science and government, pre-elementary education, prelaw, pre-dentistry, pre-medicine, physchology, public administration, radio/television technology, remedial education, secondary education, secretarial and related programs, social sciences, social work, sociology, Spanish, special education, specific learning disabilities, speech.

Historical & Special Interest:
Center for Studies of Urban Literacy is one of Central State University's Centers of Excellence with three major components: Research, Development, and Service to meet the literacy needs of Central University predominately urban population. The main campus sits on 60-acres in rural Greene County. Amongst the newly constructed buildings are the Paul Roberson Cultural and Performing Arts Center, a Library/College of Education Building, and the historic landmark, Galloway/Alumni Tower.

Articulations (Intercollegiate Curriculum Partnerships) at Central State engages in the development of a set curriculum partnerships with several community colleges in an effort to assure compatibility between specially designed programs at each of the community colleges. University College (UC) evaluates the academic preparation of all incoming students in order to certify readiness for enrollment in a major curriculum.

Master Key: *Temptations, like misfortunes, are sent to test our moral strength.*

HBCU Third Edition
© Jireh & Associates, Inc.
Wilmington, DE

CHEYNEY UNIVERSITY

CHEYNEY, PA

Web Site:
Not provided.

SCHOOL INFO

Established in 1837. 4-year public liberal arts, coed teacher's college on rural campus in rural community; 20 miles from Philadelphia.

ADDRESS:

CHEYNEY UNIVERSITY
CHEYNEY ROAD
CHEYNEY, PA 19319
Principal Official: Dr. W. Clinton Pettus

ACCREDITATON:
Middle States Association of Colleges & Schools

CAMPUS ENROLLMENT:
Undergraduate: 1100 men & women. **Transfer students:** 75 men & women. **Graduate:** 200 men & women. **Freshman ethnic enrollment:** Native American-<1%, African American-97%, Asian-<1%, Caucasian-1%, Hispanic-1%

WHAT DO I NEED?

High school class rank, GPA, counselor recommendation, test scores, and extracurricular activities. College prep. program. SAT or ACT (SAT preferred); scores by June 30. Application fee $20; no closing date; priority given to applications received by June 30; notifications on a rolling basis beginning about January 1; replies within 4 weeks. Portfolio recommended for art applicants. Deferred and early admission program available.

UNIQUE PROGRAMS

The following programs are available: accelerated program, cooperative education, ACT101 (PA Residents), cross-registration, double major, dual enrollment of high school students, education specialist degree, honors program, independent study, internships, teacher preparation.

ACADEMIC REQUIREMENTS

Freshmen must earn a minimum 2.0 GPA and a minimum of 128 credit hrs. and majors must be declared by end of first year.

Core curriculum: English, humanities, mathematics, biological/physical sciences, social sciences. Bachelor's: 128 hrs (55 in major).

STUDENT SERVICES

Campus student services include: academic assistance center, aptitude testing, career and personal counseling, employment service for undergraduates, freshman orientation, health services, campus daycare, placement services, pre-admission summer program, reduced course load program, remedial instruction, special counselor, tutoring, veterans counselor, limited academic services for handicapped. ROTC: Army.

WHAT MAJOR?

Bachelor's: Biology, business management, chemistry, clothing and textiles management/production/services, communications, computer sciences, criminal justice, dramatic arts, economics, early childhood education, elementary education, English, fine arts, food sciences and human nutrition, French, geography, history, home economics education, hotel/motel and restaurant management, industrial arts education, industrial technology, mathematics, medical laboratory technologies, music, music business management, parks and recreation management, political science and government, preelementary education, psychology, radio/television technology, secondary education, social sciences, social work, sociology, Spanish, special education, textiles and clothing.
Graduate Programs: M.Ed. Elementary Education, Special Education, Educational Administration and Supervision, Elementary or Secondary Administrative Certificate, Elementary or Secondary Principalship; M.S. Adult Continuing Education, General Science, and Special Education Certificate Programs.

Historical & Special Interest:
Cheyney University originated in 1837 making it the oldest institution of higher learning founded for Black students in the United States. In the 1829 will of its founder, a Quaker, Richard Humphreys bequeated $10,000, one tenth of his estate for the education of "the descendants of the African race". At that time, the Quaker trustees, purchased 133-acre farm on Old York Road on Philadelphia's outskirts and established an agricultural school. In 1842, the school assumed a new charter and title, The Institute for Colored Youth. In 1764, at the age of fourteen, he came to Philadelphia to apprentice with a gold and silversmith. During his childhood, Humphreys saw Black men and women working as slaves on his own father's plantation. Much later in life, after he had become a successful craftsman, he watched as the Blacks were continually mistreated. He saw that the accomplished Black tradesman were overlooked when they competed for jobs against other skilled laborers. Richard witnessed disaster for Black artisans. This was when Humphreys began his mission and charged in his will that his thirteen fellow Quakers design "...an institution...to instruct the descendants of the African race in school learning, in the various branches of the Mechanik Arts trades and in agriculture, in order to prepare and fit and qualify them to act as teachers."

TYPES OF DEGREES AWARDED:
BA, BS, BS Ed, M Ed, MS.

ACADEMIC CALENDAR:
Semester. Summer sessions limited.

CONTACT INFORMATION

Admissions Officer: Ms. Sharon L. Cannon
Phone: (610) 399-2046 **Fax:** (800) 243-9639
Web Site: Not provided.

DOLLARS AND SENSE

TUITION & FEES:	$1,961.00
ROOM & BOARD:	$2,185.00
BOOKS & SUPPLIES:	$400.00
OTHER EXPENSES:	$375.00
OUT OF STATE TUITION:	$4,560.00
*ANNUAL TOTAL:	$4,921.00

(*Annual Total does not include out-of-state tuition .)

FINANCIAL AID

Financial Aid Phone: (610) 399-2302
Financial Aid Fax: (610) 399-2411

Closing date August 1; priority given to applications received by May 1; notifications on a rolling basis beginning about September 15; must reply within 2 weeks. FAFSA accepted. Pell grants, loans, jobs based on need. Academic, and merit-based scholarships available. AMS payment plan accepted.

SPORTS

Varsity Sports: Div. II Football, wrestling, basketball, cross-country, tennis, track and field, volleyball. NCAA.

Master Key: *A lie has no legs to stand on, yet it seems to get around quite easily.*

HBCU Third Edition
© Jireh & Associates, Inc.
Wilmington, DE

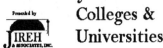
CHICAGO STATE UNIVERSITY

CHICAGO,   **L**

Web Site:
www.csu.edu

SCHOOL INFO

Established in 1867. 4-year public university on urban campus in a very large city; 12 miles south of Chicago Loop.

ACCREDITATON:
N. Cntrl Assoc. of Colleges & Secondary Schools

CAMPUS ENROLLMENT:
Undergraduate: 6892 men & women. **Graduate:** 2570 men & women. **Transfer students:** 626 men & women. **Freshman ethnic enrollment:** Native American-1, African American-610, Caucasian-9, Hispanic-27.

WHAT DO I NEED?

Academic record, test scores, GPA. College Preparatory Program completed, and all considered important. SAT or ACT (ACT preferred). Scores due by July 15. Application fee $20 (effective 9/97). Priority to applications received by July 15; applicants notified on rolling basis. Deferred admission program available.

UNIQUE PROGRAMS

Accelerated program, double major, dual enrollment of high school students, honors pgm, independent study, internships, student-designed major, study abroad, teacher prep., visiting/ exchange student program, 5-year BA-BS degree in some majors; pgms for mature adults (University Without Walls), Individualized Curriculum, Board of Governors.

ACADEMIC REQUIREMENTS

Minimum GPA for freshmen 2.0 and major must be declared on application.

Core curriculum: English, humanities, mathematics, biological/physical sciences, social sciences. Bachelor's: 120 hours (42 in major).

STUDENT SERVICES

Campus student services include: Women's Center, Academic Support Office aptitude testing, campus daycare, career and personal counseling, employment services for undergraduates, Wellness Center, learning center, placement services, remedial instruction, special counselor, special advisor for adult students, Disabled Student Services, tutoring, veterans counselor. ROTC: Air Force, Army.

WHAT MAJOR?

Bachelor's: African American Studies, Accounting, art and design, finance, business education, bilingual/bicultural education, biological and physical sciences, biology, business administration, chemistry, computer science, criminal justice, economics, education of the mentally handicapped, elementary and early childhood education, English, engineering studies, geography, history, health information administration, hospitality management, business management, information systems, mathematics, medical records administration, music, nursing, occupational education, physics, political science, physical education & recreation, elementary education, premedicine, pre-dental, psychology, radio/television, secondary education, sociology/anthropology, Spanish, speech, special education.

Special Programs:
BA & BS Individualized Curriculum
BA& BS University Without Walls
BA Board of Governors

Historical & Special Interest:

Founded in 1867, Chicago State University's alumni, a leader in teacher education, comprise nearly two-thirds of all teachers in the Chicago Public School System. It offers 36 undergraduate majors and 16 graduate-granting programs through the College of Arts and Science, Business, Education, Nursing and Allied Health Professions.

Its library includes some 250,000 volumes of teaching and learning materials. Chicago State University is accredited by the North Central Association of Colleges and Secondary Schools and the National Council for Accreditation of Teacher Education on both undergraduate and graduate level.

ADDRESS:

CHICAGO STATE UNIVERSITY
9501 SOUTH KING DR./Cook Adm 200
CHICAGO,   IL   60628
Principal Official: Dr. Dolores Cross

TYPES OF DEGREES AWARDED:
BA, BS, MA, MS.

ACADEMIC CALENDAR:
Semester. Summer sessions limited.

CONTACT INFORMATION

Admissions Officer: Addie R. Epps, Director
Phone: (773) 995-2513   **Fax:** (773)995-3820
Web Site: www.csu.edu

DOLLARS AND SENSE

TUITION & FEES:	$2,496.00
ROOM & BOARD:	$5,170.00
BOOKS & SUPPLIES:	$825.00
OTHER EXPENSES:	$1,200.00
OUT OF STATE TUITION:	$6,660.00
*ANNUAL TOTAL:	$9,691.00

(*Annual Total does not include out-of-state tuition .)

FINANCIAL AID

Financial Aid Phone: (773) 995-2304
Financial Aid Fax:

No closing date, priority given to applications received by April 15. Notifications on a rolling basis beginning June 1. Reply within 2 weeks. FAFSA accepted. Freshmen with outstanding academic ability and talent are eligible for Scholars Program full-tuition scholarship. Federal Pell grants, loans, and jobs available and based on need. Academic, music/drama, art, athletic, leadership scholarships available. Deferments.

SPORTS

Varsity Sports: Basketball, volleyball, cross-country/track, and tennis, baseball and wrestling. Mid-Continent NCAA I.

Master Key: *Before God we are equally wise and equally foolish. Albert Einstein*

HBCU **Third Edition**
© Jireh & Associates, Inc.
Wilmington, DE

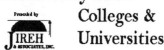

Historically Black Colleges & Universities

CLAFLIN COLLEGE

ORANGEBURG, SC

Web Site:
www.icusc.org/claflin

SCHOOL INFO

Established in 1869. 4-year private liberal arts, coed college. Affiliation with United Methodist Church on 25-acre urban campus in Orangeburg; 40 miles south of Columbia.

ACCREDITATON:
Southern Association of Colleges & Schools

CAMPUS ENROLLMENT:

Undergraduate: 940 men & women. **Transfer students:** 23 men & women. **Freshman ethnic enrollment:** African American-406, Hispanic-3

WHAT DO I NEED?

Academic record, SAT or ACT (SAT preferred), scores by September 1. C ounselor or high school official recommendation, personal background, experience, apparent character traits, educational objectives and health record considered. Application fee $10 may be waived based on need. No closing date; priority to applications received by July 30; notifications on a rolling basis; replies within 6 weeks.

UNIQUE PROGRAMS

The following programs are available: cross-registration, double major, honors program, internships.

ACADEMIC REQUIREMENTS

Freshmen must earn a minimum 1.65 and majors must be declared on application.

Core curriculum: computer science, English, foreign languages, humanities, mathematics, biological/physical sciences. Bachelor's: 124 hrs (38 in major).

STUDENT SERVICES

Campus student services include: academic center, aptitude testing, career and personal counseling,, employment service for undergraduates, health services, placement services, reduced course load program, remedial instruction, special counselor, tutoring, veterans counselor ROTC: Air Force, Army.

WHAT MAJOR?

Bachelor's: Art education, biology, business administration, business and computer science, computer sciences, education, elementary education, engineering and engineering-related technologies, English, English education, fine arts, history, mathematics, mathematics and computers science, mathematics education, music, office supervision and mangement, physical education, secondary education, social sciences, sociology, theological studies.

ADDRESS:

CLAFLIN COLLEGE
400 COLLEGE AVENUE
ORANGEBURG,   SC   29115-4498
Principal Official: Mr. Henry N. Tisdale

TYPES OF DEGREES AWARDED:
BA, BS.

ACADEMIC CALENDAR:
Semester. Summer sessions limited.

CONTACT INFORMATION

Admissions Officer: Michael Zeigler
Phone: (803) 535-5346   **Fax:** (803) 531-2860
Web Site: www.icusc.org/claflin

DOLLARS AND SENSE

TUITION & FEES:	$6,068.00
ROOM & BOARD:	$3,314.00
BOOKS & SUPPLIES:	$1,200.00
OTHER EXPENSES:	$180.00
OUT OF STATE TUITION:	
*ANNUAL TOTAL:	$10,762.00

(*Annual Total does not include out-of-state tuition .)

FINANCIAL AID

Financial Aid Phone: (803)535-5344
Financial Aid Fax: (803) 531-2860

Closing date June 1; notifications on a rolling basis beginning about June 1; must reply within 2 weeks. FAFSA accepted. Pell grants, loans, jobs based on need. Academic and athletic scholarships available.

SPORTS

Varsity Sports: Basketball, cross-country, softball, track and field, volleyball. NAIA.

Historical & Special Interest:

In 1869, two United Methodist Church laymen from Massachusetts--William and Lee Claflin began with only a teacher training center and a technical training center with which to realize their dream and vision. Today, Claflin features many new centers including a fine arts center, physical education center, science center. The mission however, is still the same; to prepare students for a better life not just for making a living. Claflin College is a UNCF school.

Master Key: *Blessed are they who can laugh at themselves, for they shall never cease to be amused. Anonymous*

HBCU Third Edition
© Jireh & Associates, Inc.
Wilmington, DE

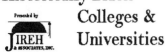

Historically Black Colleges & Universities

CLARK ATLANTA UNIVERSITY

ATLANTA, GA

Web Site:
www.cau.edu/cau

SCHOOL INFO
Established in 1869. 4-year private liberal arts, coed college with United Methodist Church affiliation on urban campus in very large city; 2 miles from downtown.

ACCREDITATON:
Southern Association of Colleges & Schools

CAMPUS ENROLLMENT:
Undergraduate: 3364 men & women . **Graduate:** 1229 men & women. **Transfer students:** 276 men & women. **Freshman ethnic enrollment:** African American-753, Asian-5, Caucasian-1, Other-38

WHAT DO I NEED?
Test scores and high school GPA important. SAT/ACT (SAT preferred). SAT preferred. College-preparatory program. Scores by August 1. Fall term application fee $20 may be waived based on need. High school transcripts, 2 recommendations required. Closing date March 1 and applicants notified on or about March 1. Replies within 30 days of acceptance. Early admission program available.

UNIQUE PROGRAMS
The following programs are available: accelerated program, cooperative education, double major, dual enrollment of high school students, honors program, independent study, internships, study abroad, cross-registration, combined bachelor's/graduate program in business administration, teacher preparation.

ACADEMIC REQUIREMENTS
Minimum GPA for freshmen 1.76 and major must be declared by end of second year.

Core curriculum: computer science, English, foreign languages, history, humanities, mathematics, biological/physical sciences, philosophy/religion, and social sciences. Bachelor's: 122 hours (36 in major).

STUDENT SERVICES
Campus student services include: aptitude testing, career and personal counseling, employment service for undergraduates, health services, learning center, placement services, reduced course load program, remedial instruction, special counselor, tutoring, veterans counselor. ROTC: Air Force, Army, Navy.

ADDRESS:

CLARK ATLANTA UNIVERSITY
J. P. BRAWLEY DR. AT FAIR ST, S.W.
ATLANTA,   GA   30314
Principal Official: Dr. Thomas W. Cole, Jr.

TYPES OF DEGREES AWARDED:
BA, BS, M, D

ACADEMIC CALENDAR:
Semester.

CONTACT INFORMATION

Admissions Officer: Peggy Wade, Interim
Phone: (404) 880-8017   **Fax:** (404) 880-6174
Web Site: www.cau.edu/cau

DOLLARS AND SENSE

TUITION & FEES:	$9,980.00
ROOM & BOARD:	$3,500.00
BOOKS & SUPPLIES:	$630.00
OTHER EXPENSES:	$840.00
OUT OF STATE TUITION:	
*ANNUAL TOTAL:	$14,950.00

(*Annual Total does not include out-of-state tuition .)

FINANCIAL AID

Financial Aid Phone:
Financial Aid Fax:

Closing date May 15; priority given to applications received by April 15. Notifications on a rolling basis beginning May 15; must reply within 2 weeks. FAFSA accepted. Pell grants, loans, jobs available. Academic, music/drama, athletic, scholarships available.

SPORTS
Varsity Sports: basketball, football, track and field. Intramural Sports: cross-country, tennis.

WHAT MAJOR?
Bachelor's: Accounting, advertising, African women's studies, art education, banking and finance, business administration, business economics, business education, chemical engineering, chemistry, child development/care/guidance, civil engineering, communications, computer sciences, criminology, dramatic arts, economics, education, English, English education, fashion design, food sciences and human nutrition, foreign languages (multiple emphasis), foreign languages education, French, German, health education, history, journalism, junior high education, marketing management, mass media arts, mathematical and computer sciences, mathematics, mathematics education, mechanical engineering, medical records technology, medical illustrating, medical laboratory technologies, medical records technology, music, music education, nutritional sciences, office supervision and management, pharmaceutical chemistry, philosphy, physical education, physical therapy, physics, political science and government, psychology, public relations, radio/television technology, religion, science education, secondary education, secretarial and related programs, social science education, social sciences, social work, sociology, Spanish, speech/debate/forensics.

Historical & Special Interest:
Clark Atlanta University is the result of a 1988 incorporation of Atlanta University and Clark College. Atlanta University was founded in 1865 as a teachers college with a commitment to high standards of excellence and in 1929 it became an exclusive graduate and professional institution. Later, Atlanta developed schools of Education, Social Work, Library Science, Business Administration, and several Schools of Arts and Sciences.

Clark College was founded in 1869 with Methodist affiliation established to serve African Americans with a commitment to high standards of intellectual achievement. In 1888, Clark College developed the independent Gammon Theological Seminary and has sinced evolved from a teacher and minister concentration to a diversity of college disciplines in the social and natural sciences and the arts and humanities.
Both schools share the commitment to close cooperation within other sister institutions in the Atlanta University Center and to serving the educational nees of students of diverse racial, national and socioeconomic backgrounds.
Clark-Atlanta University is a UNCF school.

Master Key: *A teacher affects eternity. They can never tell where their influence stops. Henry B. Adams*

HBCU Third Edition
© Jireh & Associates, Inc.
Wilmington, DE

CLINTON JUNIOR COLLEGE

ROCK HILL,   SC

Web Site:
Not provided.

SCHOOL INFO

Clinton Junion College is located in a small city.

ADDRESS:

CLINTON JUNIOR COLLEGE
1029 CRAWFORD ROAD
ROCK HILL,   SC   29730
Principal Official: Dr. Cynthia M. Russell, President

ACCREDITATON:
Applied for Southern Assoc. Colleges & Schools

CAMPUS ENROLLMENT:
Undergraduate: 69 (full-time); 35 (part-time). **Freshman Ethnic Enrollment:** African American - 100%

WHAT DO I NEED?
Open admissions policy. High School completion or GED accepted. Application closing date July 18.

UNIQUE PROGRAMS
Special counseling for student with learning disabilities. Completion of high school diploma or GED accepted.

ACADEMIC REQUIREMENTS

STUDENT SERVICES

WHAT MAJOR?
Associates Degrees Only: Liberal Arts, Business Administraton, Religion.

TYPES OF DEGREES AWARDED:
A.A.

ACADEMIC CALENDAR:
Semesters.

CONTACT INFORMATION

Admissions Officer: Cheryl J. McCullough Dir.
Phone: (803) 327-7402   **Fax:** (803) 327-3261
Web Site: Not provided.

DOLLARS AND SENSE

TUITION & FEES:	$500.00
ROOM & BOARD:	$1,028.00
BOOKS & SUPPLIES:	$250.00
OTHER EXPENSES:	$350.00
OUT OF STATE TUITION:	$0.00
*ANNUAL TOTAL:	$2,128.00

(*Annual Total does not include out-of-state tuition .)

FINANCIAL AID

Financial Aid Phone:
Financial Aid Fax:
Institutional financial aid, work-study, income-based tuition reduction program. FAFSA accepted. Payment options available.

SPORTS
Varsity sports: Basketball.

Master Key: *Rather fail with honor than succeed by fraud. Sophodes*

HBCU Third Edition
© Jireh & Associates, Inc.
Wilmington, DE

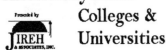
COAHOMA COMMUNITY COLLEGE

CLARKSDALE, MS

Web Site:
Not provided.

SCHOOL INFO

Established in 1949. Public, 2-year community coed college in rural community.

ACCREDITATON:
Southern Association of Colleges & Schools

CAMPUS ENROLLMENT:
Undergraduate: 851 men & women. **Transfer students:** 38 men & women.

ADDRESS:

COAHOMA COMMUNITY COLLEGE
ROUTE 1, BOX 616
CLARKSDALE,   MS   38614
Principal Official: Dr. Vivian Presley

TYPES OF DEGREES AWARDED:
AA, AAS.

ACADEMIC CALENDAR:
Semester.

CONTACT INFORMATION

Admissions Officer: Rita Hanfor
Phone: (800) 844-1222   **Fax:** (601) 627-9451
Web Site: Not provided.

WHAT DO I NEED?

High school graduation or GED certificate not required with open admission to degree programs and vocational programs. Transcript or record of previous educational training required.

UNIQUE PROGRAMS

The following programs are available: Health Careers Opportunity Program, Single-Parent/Displaced Homemaker Program, Upward Bound,

ACADEMIC REQUIREMENTS

Students are required to earn a 2.0 GPA to be in good standing.

Associate: 65 hrs. Students must earn an average of 2 quality points for each semester hour completed; meet their financial obligations at Coahoma; and complete the last 15 semester hours at Coahoma.

DOLLARS AND SENSE

TUITION & FEES:	$3,268.00
ROOM & BOARD:	$0.00
BOOKS & SUPPLIES:	$500.00
OTHER EXPENSES:	$400.00
OUT OF STATE TUITION:	$5,687.00
*ANNUAL TOTAL:	$4,168.00

(*Annual Total does not include out-of-state tuition .)

FINANCIAL AID

Financial Aid Phone: (601) 627-2571
Financial Aid Fax:

FAFSA accepted. Institutional financial aid applications must be received by April 1 to be given top priority. Pell grants, loans, jobs available. Presidential, departmental, music, athletic, minority honors, and memorial award scholarships available.

STUDENT SERVICES

Campus student services include: Career planning/placement/follow-up, counseling and guidance services, extra-class activities, food services, health services, housing services, orientation, religious life, student organizations, student discipline, student government, testing services.

SPORTS

Varsity Sports: Baseball, basketball, track and field.

WHAT MAJOR?

Most of these programs are designed for the student who plans to continue his/her education beyond the two-year college level.

Associate: Accounting, administrative support services, art, biology, chemistry, computer technology/science, criminal justice, economics, early childhood education, elementary education, English & foreign language, general business, general education, health/physical education, mathematics, mathematics education, medical technology, pre-agriculture, pre-dental hygiene, pre-forestry, pre-law, pre-medical, pre-nursing, pre-optometry, pre-pharmacy, pre-physical therapy, pre-veterinary, printing/graphic management, radio/television, science education, social science, social science education, social work, technical business,

Vocational Programs: Auto body and fender repair, automechanics, automotive diesel mechanics, barbering, carpentry, combination welding, construction masonry, cosmetology, farm/tractor and implement mechanics, heat/air conditioning/refrigeration and wiring, industrial electricity, machine shop, print/graphics/reprographics.

Historical & Special Interest:

In 1924, the Coahoma County Agricultural High School was established, making it the first county in Mississippi to provide an agricultural high school for Negroes under the then existing "separate but equal" doctrine of education. The junior college curriculum was added in 1949, and the name of the institution was changed to Coahoma Junior College and Agricultural High School. Approval of the Board of Trustees of Coahoma Junior College and the State Board for Comunity and Junior Collegs, Coahoma Junior College's name was changed to Coahoma Community College effective July 1, 1989.

Master Key: *I do not know what the future holds but I know who holds the future.*

HBCU Third Edition
© Jireh & Associates, Inc.
Wilmington, DE

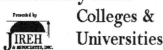
COMPTON COMMUNITY COLLEGE

COMPTON, CA

Web Site:
Not provided.

SCHOOL INFO

Established in 1927. 2-year public community coed college on urban campus in small city; 25 miles from southeast of Los Angeles.

ADDRESS:

COMPTON COMMUNITY COLLEGE
1111 EAST ARTESIA BLVD
COMPTON,   CA   90221
Principal Official: Dr. Ulis Williams

TYPES OF DEGREES AWARDED:
AA, AS.

ACADEMIC CALENDAR:
Semester. Summer sessions limited.

CONTACT INFORMATION

Admissions Officer: Ms. Carita Scott
Phone: (310) 900-1600   **Fax:** (310) 639-8260
Web Site: Not provided.

ACCREDITATON:
Western Association of Colleges & Schools

CAMPUS ENROLLMENT:

Undergraduate: 5294 men & women. **Transfer students:** 562 men & women. **Freshman ethic enrollment:** Native American-3, African American-872, Mexican American-506, Asian-42, Caucasian-81

WHAT DO I NEED?

Open admissions. Applicants under 18 must have graduated from high school or passed the California High School Certificate of Proficiency Test. No application fee; no closing date; applicants notified on a rolling basis. Deferred and early admission program available.

DOLLARS AND SENSE

TUITION & FEES:	$390.00
ROOM & BOARD:	$0.00
BOOKS & SUPPLIES:	$410.00
OTHER EXPENSES:	$10.00
OUT OF STATE TUITION:	$3,060.00
*ANNUAL TOTAL:	$810.00

(*Annual Total does not include out-of-state tuition .)

UNIQUE PROGRAMS

The following programs are available: accelerated program, cooperative education, honors program, cross-registration, 2-year transfer program.

FINANCIAL AID

Financial Aid Phone: (310) 900-1618
Financial Aid Fax: (310) 900-1681

Closing date May 15; applicants notified around August 1. FAFSA accepted. Pell grants, loans, jobs available. Academic, music/drama, art, athletic, state/district residency, leadership, alumni affiliation, religious affiliation, minority scholarships available.

ACADEMIC REQUIREMENTS

Minimum GPA for freshmen 2.0 and majors must be declared by end of first year.

Core curriculum: computer science, English, humanities, mathematics, biological/physical sciences, social sciences. Associate: 64 hours (18 in major).

STUDENT SERVICES

Campus student services include: campus daycare, career and personal counseling, employment service for undergraduates, freshman orientation, learning center, placement services, reduced course load program, remedial instruction, special counselor, services for handicapped, tutoring,veterans counselor.

SPORTS

Varsity Sports: Baseball, basketball, cross-country, football, tennis, track and field.

WHAT MAJOR?

Associate: Accounting, automotive technology, banking and finance, business computer/console/peripheral equipment operation, business data entry equipment operation, business data processing and related programs, business data programming, drafting, engineering and engineering-related technologies, graphic and printing production, graphic arts technology, law enforcement and corrections technologies, liberal/general studies, marketing and distribution, medical assistant, nursing, personal services, photographic technology, practical nursing, precision metal work, protective services, public affairs, radiograph medical technology, real estate, recreation and community services technologies, respiratory therapy technology, science technologies, secretarial and related programs, teacher aide.

Historical & Special Interest:

Located on a beautiful eighty-three acre campus in Compton, California, Compton Community College is one of the oldest public community colleges in the State, established in 1927. Its enrollment, over 5,000, is predominantly– 70 percent, Black and a high percentage of its faculty hold earned doctoral degrees. It is a member of the California Community College System with 107 colleges campuses.

The campus enjoys a modern computerized and video-cable Learning Skills Center, a state-of-the-art Allied Health Building and Early Childhood Development Center, and a library with over 55,000 volumes.

Enjoying the most trips to the Junior Rose Bowl than any other community college in the nation, Compton Community College is the home of the Tartars.

Master Key: *Education is a progressive discovery of our own ignorance. Will Durant*

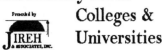
CONCORDIA COLLEGE
SELMA, AL
Web Site:
http://www.cord.edu

SCHOOL INFO
Established in 1922. 2-year private junior, liberal arts college, coed, affiliated with Lutheran Church-Missouri Synod. Suburban campus in large town; 50 miles from Montgomery.

ADDRESS:

CONCORDIA COLLEGE
1804 GREEN STREET
SELMA,   AL   36701
Principal Official: Dr. Julius Jenkins

TYPES OF DEGREES AWARDED:
AA

ACADEMIC CALENDAR:
Semester. Summer sessions limited.

ACCREDITATON:
Southern Association of Colleges & Schools

CONTACT INFORMATION

Admissions Officer: Ms. Gwendolyn Moore
Phone: (334) 874-7143   **Fax:** (334) 874-5755
Web Site: http://www.cord.edu

CAMPUS ENROLLMENT:
Undergraduate: 354 men & women. **Freshman ethnic enrollment: Not available.**

WHAT DO I NEED?
Open admissions. SAT or ACT (ACT preferred) for placement and counseling only; score report by August 15. Application fee $5 may be waived based on need; notifications on a rolling basis beginning around August 15. Deferred admissions progam available.

DOLLARS AND SENSE

TUITION & FEES:	$8,150.00
ROOM & BOARD:	$2,800.00
BOOKS & SUPPLIES:	$400.00
OTHER EXPENSES:	$150.00
OUT OF STATE TUITION:	$0.00
*ANNUAL TOTAL:	$11,500.00

(*Annual Total does not include out-of-state tuition .)

UNIQUE PROGRAMS
The following programs are available: independent study and 2-year transfer program.

FINANCIAL AID

Financial Aid Phone: (334) 874-7143
Financial Aid Fax: (334) 874-3728

No closing date; applicants notified on a rolling basis beginning about June 15; must reply within 2 weeks. FAFSA accepted. Pell grants, jobs available based on need.

ACADEMIC REQUIREMENTS
Minimum GPA for freshmen is 2.0 and majors must be declared by end of second year.

Core curriculum: English, history, humanities, mathematics, philosophy/religion, biological/physical sciences, social sciences. Associate: 64 hours.

STUDENT SERVICES
Campus student services include: career and personal counseling, employment services for undergraduates, freshman orientation, health services, learning center, preadmission summer program, reduced course load program, remedial instruction, special counselor, tutoring, special advisor for adult students, veterans counselor, services for handicapped.

SPORTS
Varsity Sports: Basketball. Intramural Sports: Baseball, softball, table tennis, tennis, volleyball. NJCAA.

WHAT MAJOR?
Associate: Accounting, biology, business administration, business education, computer science, economics, English, general science, health & physical education, history, mathematics, music education, music performance, music theory & composition, office administration, psychology, religion theology, reading education, secretarial science, sociology.

Historical & Special Interest:

Concordia College began in 1922 and was formerly known as Alabama Lutheran Academy and Junior College. This college was the result of the work of a young black woman, Miss Rosa Young, who was concerned about the spiritual and educational welfare of young Black children in this area of Alabama. Concordia, with its 383 students, is the only Black Lutheran College in America. According to its mission, "Concordia seeks friends with vision who understand what a college can do for young people and in turn, what young people with Christian values and quality education can do for the world."

Master Key: *Worry is like a rocking chair, it gives you something to do but gets you nowhere.*

HBCU Third Edition
© Jireh & Associates, Inc.
Wilmington, DE

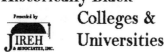

Historically Black Colleges & Universities

COPPIN STATE COLLEGE
BALTIMORE, MD

SCHOOL INFO

Established in 1900. 4-year public liberal arts coed college on urban campus in a very large city; 50 miles from Washington, D.C.

ADDRESS:

COPPIN STATE COLLEGE
2500 WEST NORTH AVENUE
BALTIMORE,   MD   21216
Principal Official: Dr. Calvin W. Burnett

TYPES OF DEGREES AWARDED:
BA, BS, MA, MS.

ACADEMIC CALENDAR:
Semester. Summer sessions.

CONTACT INFORMATION

Admissions Officer: Allen Mosley
Phone: (410) 383-5990   **Fax:** (410) 523-7238
Web Site: http://coeacl.coppin.umd.edu

ACCREDITATON:
Middle States Association of Colleges & Schools

CAMPUS ENROLLMENT:
Undergraduate: 832 men & 2304 women. **Graduate:** 130 men & 377 women. **Freshman ethnic enrollment:** NA-24; AA-3,418; Asian-7; Caucasian-101; Hispanic-21.

WHAT DO I NEED?
Test scores and academic record in college preparatory curriculum, test scores, minimum GPA 2.5, and recommendation from counselor/school. SAT or ACT (SAT preferred); scores by August 1 and required for all nursing school applicants. Application fee $20 which may be waived based on need. Closing date July 15; applicants notified on a rolling basis. Deferred and early admission Program available.

UNIQUE PROGRAMS
The following programs are available: cooperative education, double major, dual enrollment of high school students, honors program, independent study, internships, teacher preparation, weekend college.

DOLLARS AND SENSE

TUITION & FEES:	$6,662.00
ROOM & BOARD:	$5,684.00
BOOKS & SUPPLIES:	$500.00
OTHER EXPENSES:	
OUT OF STATE TUITION:	$14,520.00
*ANNUAL TOTAL:	$12,846.00

(*Annual Total does not include out-of-state tuition.)

ACADEMIC REQUIREMENTS

Minimum GPA of 2.0 and majors must be declared by end of second year.

Core curriculum: fine arts, English, meida arts, history, mathematics, management science, philosophy, biological/physical sciences, social sciences. Bachelor's: 120 hours (43 in major)

FINANCIAL AID

Financial Aid Phone: (410) 383-5830
Financial Aid Fax: (410) 728-2979
Aid applications closing date May 1; applicants notified on or about June 1; must reply within 2 weeks. FAFSA accepted. Pell grants, loans, jobs are available. Athletic, state/district residency, and freshman honors scholarships available. Deferred Payment Plan available.

STUDENT SERVICES
Campus student services include: academic resource center, aptitude testing, career and personal counseling, career development, student activities, advising, health services, placement services, remedial instruction, tutoring, many services for the learning disabled and handicapped, veterans counselor. ROTC: Army.

SPORTS

Varsity Sports: Basketball, baseball, bowling, cross-country, tennis, track and field, volleyball, softball. NCAA.

WHAT MAJOR?

Bachelor's: Biology, business administration, chemistry, computer sciences, counseling psychology, criminal justice studies, education of the emotionally & mentally, multiple, and physically handicapped, elementary education, English, English literature, history, law enforcement and corrections, mathematics, nursing, philosophy, predentistry, prepharmacy, prephysical therapy, psychology, secondary education, social sciences, social work, sociology, special education, specific learning disabilities.

Graduate Programs:
Criminal Justice, Rehabilitation Counseling, Special Education, Adult and General Education, Master of Arts in Teaching, Psychology.

Historical & Special Interest:

Coppin State College, established in 1900 is the only public senior college in the University of Maryland System and its unique mission is to focus on the needs and aspirations of the urban inner city population. Coppin provides the traditional yet diverse liberal arts programs and through majors in Computer Science, Nursing, Management Science, Criminal Justice, Early Childhood and Elementary Education, Special Education, and Physical Education for the Handicapped. Affiliation with the new University of Maryland System will allow Coppin to expand its existing programs with the University beyond the current Dentistry, Engineering, Pharmacy, and Social Work.

Coppin has garnered the description as the area's "Community School" because of its cooperative programs with area businesses and the city schools and production of graduates who have taken their position in front-line and middle administrative positions within Baltimore and Maryland as a whole.

Master Key: *Everybody wants to go to heaven but nobody wants to die.   Joe Louis*

HBCU Third Edition
© Jireh & Associates, Inc.
Wilmington, DE

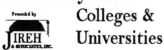
CUYAHOGA COMM. COLLEGE
CLEVELAND, OH

Web Site:
www.tir-c.cc.oh.us

SCHOOL INFO
Established in 1963. 2-year public, community college campus in large urban city in downtown corridor.

ACCREDITATON:
North Central Association of Colleges & Schools.

CAMPUS ENROLLMENT:
Undergraduate: 6864 men & women. **Freshman ethnic enrollment : Not available.**

WHAT DO I NEED?
Open admissions process. Special admission requirements for programs in health technology

UNIQUE PROGRAMS
The following programs are available: cooperative education, honors program.

ACADEMIC REQUIREMENTS
A minimum 1.0 GPA must earned by freshmen and majors must be declared on application.

Core curriculum: English, humanities, mathematics, and social sciences.Core curriculum: English, humanities, mathematics, social science.Associate degre: 93 hours (45 in major).

STUDENT SERVICES
Campus student services include: academic center, aptitude testing, counseling.

ADDRESS:

CUYAHOGA COMM. COLLEGE
2900 COMM. COLLEGE AVE.
CLEVELAND, OH 44115-2878
Principal Official: DR. JERRY SUE OWENS

TYPES OF DEGREES AWARDED:

ACADEMIC CALENDAR:
Quarter. Summer sessions limited.

CONTACT INFORMATION

Admissions Officer: Dr. Sammie Tyree Cox
Phone: (216) 987-4000 **Fax:** (216) 987-4130
Web Site: www.tir-c.cc.oh.us

DOLLARS AND SENSE

TUITION & FEES:	$1,485.00
ROOM & BOARD:	$0.00
BOOKS & SUPPLIES:	$675.00
OTHER EXPENSES:	$525.00
OUT OF STATE TUITION:	$2,475.00
*ANNUAL TOTAL:	$2,685.00

(*Annual Total does not include out-of-state tuition .)

FINANCIAL AID

Financial Aid Phone:
Financial Aid Fax:
All jobs based on need. FAFSA accepted.

SPORTS

WHAT MAJOR?
Associate: Accounting, computer technology, health technology, office and secretarial related programs.

Historical & Special Interest:

Located in downtown Cleveland, Cuyahoga is one of three modern, well-equipped campuses located in the College district. As Ohio's fourth largest institution of higher learning, Cuyahoga boasts services, programs and day, evening, and weekend classes to an annual student population of over 6,000.

With that they offer more than 40 career programs, 36 transfer programs, an elders' campus for senior citizens, a displaced homemaker program, a youth development program, credit by television, and a credit-in-escrow program for high school students.

The largest public high technology training and demonstration facility in Northeastern Ohio is the College's Unified Technologies Center.

Master Key: *The world is composed of givers and takers. The takers eat better, but the givers sleep better.*

HBCU Third Edition
© Jireh & Associates, Inc.
Wilmington, DE

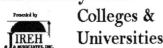
DELAWARE STATE UNIVERSITY

DOVER, DE

Web Site:
www.dsc.edu

SCHOOL INFO

Established in 1891. 4-year public liberal arts coed college on surburban campus in large town.

ADDRESS:

DELAWARE STATE UNIVERSITY
1200 N. DUPONT HIGHWAY
DOVER,   DE   19901
Principal Official: Dr. William B. DeLauder

ACCREDITATON:
Middle States Association of Colleges & Schools

CAMPUS ENROLLMENT:
Undergraduate: 2695 men & women. **Graduate:** 286 men & women. **Transfer students:** 184 men & women. **Freshman ethnic enrollment:** Native American-2, African American-451, Asian-6, Caucasian-106, Hispanic-5, Other-10.

WHAT DO I NEED?
High school GPA, test scores and state residency most important. Test scores only used in conjunction with GPA. Fall applications $10 fee. Closing date July 1, priority given to those received by June 1; notification on rolling basis and replies must be received by May 15. Interview recommended for nursing, and academically weak applicants. ACT or SAT (SAT preferred); score report by August 15.

UNIQUE PROGRAMS
The following programs are available: cooperative education, double major, dual enrollment of high school students, honors program, independent study, internships, teacher preparation, visiting/exchange student program, weekend college, Cooperative Engineering, Freshmen Enhancement Program; liberal arts/career combination in engineering.

ACADEMIC REQUIREMENTS

Minimum GPA for freshmen 1.7 and majors must be declared by end of first year.

Core curriculum: English, humanities, mathematics, biological/physical sciences, social sciences. Bachelor's: 121 hours (30 in major).

STUDENT SERVICES
Campus student services include: aptitude testing, campus daycare, career and personal counseling, freshman orientation, health services, learning center, placement services, reduced course load program, remedial instruction, special counselor, services for handicapped, special advisor for adult students, tutoring,veterans counselor. ROTC: Air Force, Army.

TYPES OF DEGREES AWARDED:
BA, BS, MA, MS, MBA.

ACADEMIC CALENDAR:
Semester. Summer sessions.

CONTACT INFORMATION

Admissions Officer: Jethro C. Williams
Phone: (800) 464 -4357   **Fax:** (302) 739-2856
Web Site: www.dsc.edu

DOLLARS AND SENSE

TUITION & FEES:	$2,996.00
ROOM & BOARD:	$4,884.00
BOOKS & SUPPLIES:	$400.00
OTHER EXPENSES:	$350.00
OUT OF STATE TUITION:	$7,140.00
*ANNUAL TOTAL:	$8,630.00

(*Annual Total does not include out-of-state tuition .)

FINANCIAL AID

Financial Aid Phone:
Financial Aid Fax:
No closing date; priority given to applications received by May 1, notifications on rolling basis beginning around June 1; must reply by within 2 weeks. FAFSA accepted. Available scholarships: Academic, music, drama, athletic, state/district residency, leadership, alumni affiliation, and minority.

SPORTS
Varsity Sports: Baseball, basketball, cross-country, football, tennis, track and field, volleyball, wrestling. NCAA.

WHAT MAJOR?
Bachelor's: Accounting, agricultural business/education/sciences, air traffic control, airline piloting and navigation, art education, biology/education/with botany, business management, chemical engineering/laboratory technology, chemistry/education, child development/care/guidance, civil engineering, communications, community health work, computer technology, criminal justice technology, dramatic arts, driver and safety education, education of exceptional children, electrical/electronics and communications engineering, elementary education, engineering and related technologies, English, English education, environmental health, fine arts, fire protection, fishing and fisheries, food sciences and human nutrition,foreign languages education, French, health education, history, home economics/education, horticultural science, hotel/motel and restaurant management, journalism, junior high education, library technology, marketing and distributive education, marketing management, mathematics, mathematics education, music, music education, nursing, parks & recreation management, physical education, physics, physics education, plant sciences, political science and government, preelementary education, psychology, recreation and community services technologies, renewable natural resources, science education, secretarial and related programs, social studies education, social work, sociology, Spanish, special education, speech communication, theater education, textiles and clothing, trade and industrial education, vegetation management, wildlife management.

Historical & Special Interest:

Delaware State College is located on a 400 acre complex and is one of this nation's publicly supported 1890 land-grant institutions. The College's program is organized into 20 academic departments for undergraduates seeking a B.A., B.S. and the Bachelor of Technology. It also offers Masters degrees in Curriculum and Instruction, Business Administration, Social Work, Special Education, Chemistry, Biology, Physics and Science Education. The Cooperative Engineering Program with the University of Delaware allows students to benefit from the combined resources. A unique Outreach/off-campus Bachelor degree program in Elementary Education, Social Work, and Occupational Teacher Education allows for a more accessible higher education for Sussex County residents.

Master Key: *If you wish to eliminate your enemy, make him your friend.*

DENMARK TECHNICAL COLLEGE

DENMARK, SC

Web Site:
www.dtc401.dentec.sc.us

SCHOOL INFO

Established in 1948. 2-year public technical, coed college. Affiliation with United Methodist Church on urban campus in large town; 40 miles from Columbia.

ACCREDITATON:
Southern Association of Colleges & Schools

CAMPUS ENROLLMENT:
Undergraduate: 597 men & women. **Transfer students:** 19 men & women.   **Freshman ethnic enrollment:** African American-439, Caucasian-21

WHAT DO I NEED?
Open admissions. Selective admission to some programs and interview recommended. Application fee $5 may be waived based on need. No closing date; notifications on a rolling basis beginning about April 1.   Deferred admission program available.

UNIQUE PROGRAMS
The following programs are available: cooperative education, 2-year transfer program, cross-registration, independent study, internships.

ACADEMIC REQUIREMENTS

Freshmen must earn a minimum 1.5 and majors must be declared on application.

Core curriculum: English and mathematics. Associate degree in major 122 hrs.

STUDENT SERVICES
Campus student services include: academic center, aptitude testing, career and personal counseling, employment service for undergraduates, freshman orientation, health services, placement services, reduced course load program, remedial instruction, special counselor, tutoring, veterans counselor, services for handicapped. ROTC: Air Force, Army.

WHAT MAJOR?
Associate: Accounting, air conditioning/heating/refrigeration mechanics, automotive technology, business and office, business data processing and related programs, computer programming, computer technology, criminal justice technologies, electronic technology, engineering and engineering-related technologies, industrial technology, machine tool operation/machine shop, secretarial and related programs.

Historical & Special Interest:

Denmark Technical College was established in 1947 as a an all Black trade school then named Denmark Branch of the South Carolina Trade School and remained so until 21 years later in 1969 when it became a member of the South Carolina technical education system of colleges along with its sixteen member colleges.

Denmark is the only South Carolina technical college which maintains a student resident campus. It is a comprehensive two-year college offering a variety of college transfer programs and averages 700 students per term and employing 121 staff and faculty.

Bus service is provided for students in Allendale, Barnwell, & Bamberg counties.

ADDRESS:

DENMARK TECHNICAL COLLEGE
P.O.BOX 327
DENMARK,   SC   29042-0327
Principal Official: Dr. Joanne Boyd-Scotland

TYPES OF DEGREES AWARDED:
AA, AS.

ACADEMIC CALENDAR:
Quarter. Extensive summer sessions.

CONTACT INFORMATION

Admissions Officer: Ms. Michelle McDowell
Phone: (803) 793-5176   **Fax:** (803) 793-5942
Web Site: www.dtc401.dentec.sc.us

DOLLARS AND SENSE

TUITION & FEES:	$1,080.00
ROOM & BOARD:	$2,842.00
BOOKS & SUPPLIES:	$300.00
OTHER EXPENSES:	$0.00
OUT OF STATE TUITION:	$2,160.00
*ANNUAL TOTAL:	$4,222.00

(*Annual Total does not include out-of-state tuition .)

FINANCIAL AID

Financial Aid Phone: (803)793-5161
Financial Aid Fax: (803)793-5942

Closing date August 15; notifications on a rolling basis beginning about May 15; must reply within 2 weeks. FAFSA accepted. Pell grants, loans, jobs based on need. Academic scholarships available.

SPORTS

Varsity Sports: Baseball, basketball, softball.
Intramural Sports: Basketball.

Master Key: *A delay is not a denial.*

HBCU Third Edition
© Jireh & Associates, Inc.
Wilmington, DE

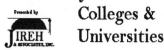

Historically Black Colleges & Universities

DILLARD UNIVERSITY
NEW ORLEANS, LA

SCHOOL INFO
Established in 1869. 4-year private liberal arts coed college, affiliated with United Church of Christ and United Methodist Church on a 46-acre urban campus in New Orleans.

ADDRESS:

DILLARD UNIVERSITY
2601 GENTILLY BLVD.
NEW ORLEANS,   LA   70122
Principal Official: Dr. Samuel DuBois Cook

TYPES OF DEGREES AWARDED:
BA, BS, BSN.

ACADEMIC CALENDAR:
Semester. Summer sessions limited.

CONTACT INFORMATION

Admissions Officer: Darrin Q. Rankin
Phone: (504) 283-8822   **Fax:** (504) 286-4895
Web Site: www.dillard.edu

ACCREDITATON:
Southern Association of Colleges & Schools

CAMPUS ENROLLMENT:
*Undergraduate: 587 men & women. **Transfer students:** 52 men & women. **Freshman ethnic enrollment :** Not available.

WHAT DO I NEED?
Test scores, class rank, participation in extracurricular activities and community svc. considered. College Prep. program. ACT or SAT scores due by April 15. Application fee $10 may be waived with need. Closing date May 15; notifications on rolling basis; priority to applications received by April 15; must reply within 2 weeks. Interview recommended and essay required. Early and deferred admission program available.

UNIQUE PROGRAMS
The following programs are available: double major, dual enrollment of high school students, internships, honors program, Japanese studies, independent study, study abroad, teacher preparation, liberal arts/career combination in engineering.

ACADEMIC REQUIREMENTS
Minimum GPA for freshmen 2.0 by end of first semester and major must be declared by end of first year.

Core curriculum: arts/fine arts, computer science, English, foreign languages, history, humanities, mathematics, philosophy/religion, biological/physical sciences, social sciences. Bachelor's: 130 hours (36 in major).

STUDENT SERVICES
Campus student services include: aptitude testing career counseling, employment services for undergraduates, freshman orientation, health services, learning center, personal counseling, placement services, preadmission summer program, reduced course load program, remedial instruction, special counselor, tutoring. ROTC: Air Force, Army, Naval.

DOLLARS AND SENSE

TUITION & FEES:	$8,480.00
ROOM & BOARD:	$4,550.00
BOOKS & SUPPLIES:	$900.00
OTHER EXPENSES:	$200.00
OUT OF STATE TUITION:	
*ANNUAL TOTAL:	$14,130.00

(*Annual Total does not include out-of-state tuition .)

FINANCIAL AID

Financial Aid Phone: (504) 286-4677
Financial Aid Fax: (504) 283-5456

Application closing date June 1, priority given to applications received by April15. Notifications on a rolling basis beginning June 1. Reply within 2 weeks. FAFSA accepted. Pell grants, loans, and jobs available and based on need. Academic (merit and university) and athletic scholarships available. Payment option plans available.

SPORTS

Varsity Sports: Basketball, Tennis, Cross-country. Intramural Sports: Basketball, football golf, gymnastics, softball, swimming, table tennis, tennis, track and field, volleyball. NAIA.

WHAT MAJOR?
Bachelor's: Applied mathematics, allied health, art education, biology, business administration, business management, business economics, chemistry, communications, computer sciences, criminology, dramatic arts, economics, education, education of the deaf and hearing impaired, education of the emotionally handicapped, education of the gifted and talented, education of the mentally handicapped, elementary education, English, education fine arts, foreign languages education, French, health education, history, junior high education, mathematics, mathematics education, music and music education, nursing, philosophy, physical education, physics, political science and government, predentistry, preelementary education, prelaw, premedicine, prepharmacy, preveterinary, psychology, reading education, science education, social work, sociology, Spanish, special education, specific learning disabilities, urban studies.

Historical & Special Interest:

Located on a 48.2 acre tract in a lovely residential section of New Orleans, Dillard's campus has been called on of the nation's most beautiful. The atmosphere of learning is quietly conveyed by oak-shaded walkways, 19 handsome buildings and green landscaped lawns.
Dilliard dates back to 1869 when the American Missionary Association of the Congregational Church founded Straight University and, on July 8, the Freedman's Aid Society of the Methodist Episcopal Church established Union Normal School. Straight University and Union Normal School were subsequently renamed Straight College and New Orleans University, respectively. Both institutions offered instruction on the elementary level then expanded to secondary, collegiate and professional levels.

On June 6, 1930, New Orleans University and Straight College merged to form Dillard University, which elected to follow the practices of the two parent institutions inmaking no distinction as to race, religion or sex in the admisstion of students or in the selection of faculty. The University was named in honor of James Hardy Dillard, whose distinguished service in the education of Negroes in the South forms an important chapter in the history of American education. Dillard University is a UNCF school.

Master Key: *The problem that infuriates you the most is the problem that God has assigned you to solve. Murdock*

HBCU Third Edition
© Jireh & Associates, Inc.
Wilmington, DE

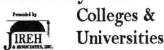
SCHOOL INFO

Established in 1966. 4-year private college of health science. Located in a very large city (Los Angeles).

ACCREDITATON:
Candidate.

CAMPUS ENROLLMENT:
Undergraduate full-time: 102 women and and 33 men.

ADDRESS:

DREW UNIV. OF MEDICINE & SCIENCE
1621 E. 120TH STREET
LOS ANGELES,   CA   90059
Principal Official: Dr. Charles Francis

TYPES OF DEGREES AWARDED:
AS, BS.

ACADEMIC CALENDAR:
Semester.

CONTACT INFORMATION

Admissions Officer: Cesar Hernandez
Phone: (213) 563-4950   **Fax:** (213) 569-0597
Web Site: www.corewu.edu

WHAT DO I NEED?

College preparatory program plus some programs may require: anatomy, botany, chemistry, physics. SAT scores, academic record and recommendations important. Min. SAT-V 510; SAT-M 510. A $20 application fee is required with a January 30th application closing date.

DOLLARS AND SENSE

TUITION & FEES:	$4,200.00
ROOM & BOARD:	
BOOKS & SUPPLIES:	$0.00
OTHER EXPENSES:	$100.00
OUT OF STATE TUITION:	$0.00
*ANNUAL TOTAL:	$4,300.00

(*Annual Total does not include out-of-state tuition .)

UNIQUE PROGRAMS

The College of Allied Health provides a combined bachelor's/graduate program in medicine.

FINANCIAL AID

Financial Aid Phone: (323) 563-4824
Financial Aid Fax: (323)569-0597

Closing date February 28; notifications around June 1. SAAC/CSS, in-state; FAFSA accepted. Pell grants, loans, jobs based on need. Academic, music/drama, art, athletic scholoarships available.

ACADEMIC REQUIREMENTS

Minimum GPA of 2.3 for freshmen and major must be declared on application.

Core curriculum: computer science, English, humanities, mathematics, biological/physical sciences, social sciences. Associate: 79 hours (44 in major); Bachelor's: 158 hours (94 in major).

STUDENT SERVICES

Campus student services include: advanced placement testing, campus daycare, career and personal counseling, freshman orientation, health services, learning center, placement services, tutoring, services for handicapped, veterans counselor.

SPORTS

Information not available.

WHAT MAJOR?

Associate: Medical records administration and technology, radiograph medical technology.

Bachelor's: Physician's Assistant.

Historical & Special Interest:

Opened in 1966, Drew University is one of the newest institutions of medical education in the United States. The school's medical education and research is based on services provided to the community. It provides general medical care at the Martin Luther King, Jr. General Hospital and inpatient psychiatric services at the Augustus Hawkins Mental Health Unit.

Drew University utilizes a unique recruiting mechanism that ensures a constant stream of young people who are prepared to enter health careers, a magnet high school is on campus and it is the home of a headstart program which enrolls over 1,100 children annually.

Master Key: *Learn from the mistakes of others..you can't live long enough to make them all yourself.*

HBCU Third Edition
© Jireh & Associates, Inc.
Wilmington, DE

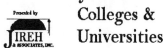
EDWARD WATERS COLLEGE

JACKSONVILLE,   FL

Web Site:
www.ewc.edu

SCHOOL INFO

Established in 1866. 4-year private liberal arts, coed college affiliated with African Methodist Episcopal Church on urban campus in a very large city; 150 miles from Orlando.

ACCREDITATON:
Southern Association of Colleges & Schools

CAMPUS ENROLLMENT:
Undergraduate: 989 men & women. **Transfer students:** 63 men & women.

WHAT DO I NEED?

Open admissions. Application fee $10 may be waived based on need. No closing date; applicants notified on a rolling basis and must reply by registration. Deferred admission program available.

UNIQUE PROGRAMS

The following programs are available: accelerated program, cooperative education, double major, independent study, internships, cross-registration.

ACADEMIC REQUIREMENTS

Minimum GPA for freshmen 2.0.

Information not available.

STUDENT SERVICES

Campus student services include: aptitude testing, career and personal counseling, employment service for undergraduates, health services, learning center, placement services, preadmission summer program, reduced course load, remedial instruction, special counselor, tutoring. ROTC: Army.

ADDRESS:

EDWARD WATERS COLLEGE
1658 KINGS ROAD
JACKSONVILLE,   FL   32209
Principal Official: Dr. Jimmy R. Jenkins Sr.

TYPES OF DEGREES AWARDED:
BA, BS.

ACADEMIC CALENDAR:
Semester. Summer sessions limited.

CONTACT INFORMATION

Admissions Officer: Richard F. Pride Jr
Phone: (904) 366-2715   **Fax:** (904) 366-2528
Web Site: www.ewc.edu

DOLLARS AND SENSE

TUITION & FEES:	$5,340.00
ROOM & BOARD:	$4,150.00
BOOKS & SUPPLIES:	$892.00
OTHER EXPENSES:	$500.00
OUT OF STATE TUITION:	
*ANNUAL TOTAL:	$10,882.00

(*Annual Total does not include out-of-state tuition .)

FINANCIAL AID

Financial Aid Phone: (904)366-2528
Financial Aid Fax:
No closing date for applications; notification on a rolling basis. FAFSA accepted. Jobs based on need.

SPORTS

No athletic programs offered.

WHAT MAJOR?

Bachelor's: Business Administration: accounting, management, organization management, airway science mgmt., computer information systems; Education & Human Services: elementary education, health education, physical education; Teacher Certification: early childhood education, nursery & kindergarten, emotionally handicapped, hearing impaired; Secondary Education: biology, chemistry, English, health education, mathematics, physical education, social science; Arts & Sciences: biology, chemistry, computer science, criminal justice, English, mathematics, psychology, religion and philosophy, sociology, political science, dual degree with Univ. of Miami: chemistry/engineering, mathematics/engineering; Interdisciplinary Studies: public administration, international relationships; Mass Communications: journalism, radio & television.

Historical & Special Interest:

Edward Waters College was founded in 1866 as the Brown Theological Institute and is the oldest historically Black institution of higher education in the state of Florida. The College has an open admission policy and is a four-year accredited, liberal arts, coeducational institution located in the cultural and financial hub of Jacksonville.

The College is commited to implementing programs designed to ensure an educational experience of the highest quality for all students with varying academic strengths, weaknesses and financial need.

Edward Waters College is a UNCF school.

Master Key: *Injustice is only as powerful as your memory of it. Murdock*

HBCU Third Edition
© Jireh & Associates, Inc.
Wilmington, DE

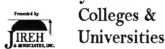
ELIZABETH CITY STATE UNIV.

ELIZABETH CITY, NC

Web Site:
www.ecsu.edu

SCHOOL INFO

Established in 1891. 4-year public liberal arts college on rural campus in large town; 50 miles south of Norfolk, Virginia.

ACCREDITATON:

Southern Association of Colleges & Schools

CAMPUS ENROLLMENT:

Undergraduate: 2019 men & women. **Transfer students:** 148 men & women. **Freshman ethnic enrollment : Not available.**

WHAT DO I NEED?

Test scores important. H.S. diploma or GED equivalent acceptable. Special consideration to residents of 16 neighboring counties. College preparatory program. SAT or ACT ; scores by August 15. Non-refundable application fee: $15; no closing date and notifications on a rolling basis; replies as soon as possible. Deferred admission program available.

UNIQUE PROGRAMS

The following programs are available: cooperative education, double major, honors program, independent study, internships, teacher preparation, weekend college program.

ACADEMIC REQUIREMENTS

Freshmen must earn a minimum 1.45 and majors must be declared by end of second year.

Core curriculum: English, foreign languages, history, mathematics, biological/physical sciences, social sciences. Bachelor's: 126 hrs (36 in major).

STUDENT SERVICES

Campus student services include: academic center, aptitude testing, career and personal counseling, employment service for undergraduates, freshmen orientation, health services, placement services, preadmission summer program, reduced course load program, remedial instruction, special counselor, services for handicapped, tutoring. ROTC: Army.

ADDRESS:

ELIZABETH CITY STATE UNIV.
1704 WEEKSVILLE ROAD
ELIZABETH CITY, NC 27909
Principal Official: Dr. Mickey L. Burnim, Chancellor

TYPES OF DEGREES AWARDED:
BA, BS, BSED.

ACADEMIC CALENDAR:
Semester. Summer sessions.

CONTACT INFORMATION

Admissions Officer: Jeff King
Phone: (252) 335-3305 **Fax:** (919) 335-3537
Web Site: www.ecsu.edu

DOLLARS AND SENSE

TUITION & FEES:	$5,248.00
ROOM & BOARD:	$0.00
BOOKS & SUPPLIES:	$0.00
OTHER EXPENSES:	$370.00
OUT OF STATE TUITION:	$11,542.00
*ANNUAL TOTAL:	$5,618.00

(*Annual Total does not include out-of-state tuition .)

FINANCIAL AID

Financial Aid Phone: (252) 335-3283
Financial Aid Fax: (252) 335-3716

No closing date; priority given to applications received by May 1; notifications on a rolling basis beginning about June 1; must reply within 3 weeks. FAFSA accepted. Pell grants, loans, jobs available. Academic, athletic, music/drama, minority and incentive scholarships available.

SPORTS

Varsity Sports: Baseball, basketball, tennis, football, softball, track and field, volleyball, wrestling. NAIA, NCAA.

WHAT MAJOR?

Bachelor's: Accounting, applied mathematics, art education, biology, business administration, business education, chemistry, computer sciences, criminal justice studies, elementary education, English, English education, geology, history, industrial arts education, industrial technology, junior high education, mathematics, mathematics education, music, music marketing, physical education, physics, political science and government, psychology, science education, social sciences, social studies education, social work, sociology, special education.

Historical & Special Interest:

Elizabeth State University was established by House Bill 383 introduced in the North Carolina General Assembly by Hugh Cale, a Black Representative from Pasquotank County. Initially, the institution was created, by law, as a normal school for the specific purpose of "teaching and training teacher" of the "colored race" to teach in the common schools" of North Carolina and thus named Elizabeth City State Colored Normal School. It began operation on January 4, 1892 with a budget of $900, a two-member faculty, and a student enrollment of 23.

It moved to its present and permanent location on September 9, 1912 and from 1891 and 1928 the curriculum expanded from elementary and secondary school level courses to two-year "normal" courses. The institution was elevated from a two-year normal to a four-year teachers' college in 1937 and the Secondary-School Department was discontinued in 1931. Effective March 30, 1939, by an Act of Legislature, the school's name was changed to Elizabeth City State Teachers' College and a second purpose was given: the training of elementary school principals for rural and city schools.

The first 26 Bachelor of Science degrees in Elementary Education were awarded on May 19, 1939. Curricular offerings were expanded between 1959-1963 from a single Elementary Education major to 12 additional degree-granting programs. Ten departments of instruction came into existence, the Vocational-Technical Program was organized and by a 1963 legislative Act, the school's name was changed to Elizabeth City State College and again in 1969 to Elizabeth City State University.

Master Key: *Trust God's leadership, He knows the way.*

HBCU Third Edition
© Jireh & Associates, Inc.
Wilmington, DE

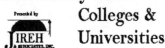
F.H. LAGUARDIA COMM COLLEGE

LONG ISLAND, NY

Web Site:
Not provided.

SCHOOL INFO

Fiorello H. LaGuardia is one of 17 undergraduate colleges of the City University of NY and serves the growing neighborhoods of Western Queens as well as the greater NYC metro area.

ACCREDITATON:
Commission of Higher Education of the Middle States Association of Colleges and Schools.

CAMPUS ENROLLMENT:
LaGuardia's student population represents over 100 nations with many arriving to the United States from their home countries specifically to study at LaGuardia.

WHAT DO I NEED?

All applicants admitted as day students are required to complete the college's cooperative education requirement. There are three application options: Undergraduate Freshman- application fee is $40.00, Undergraduate Transfer- application fee is $50.00, and Non-degree Application for Admission- application fee is $40.00. Applicants must submit a high school diploma and transcript, or their equivalent, a GED and scores.

UNIQUE PROGRAMS

Students receive academic support through tutorial support services and academic and transfer counseling. A variety of non-credit programs in continuing education provide over 20,000 students an opportunity to take courses. Advanced placement, Quick-Start Pgm, Bridges to the Future Program, College Discovery Pgm, College Opportunity to Prepare for Employment (COPE), Honors exchange and study abroad program.

ACADEMIC REQUIREMENTS

The University instituted the Freshman Skills Assessment Program, FSAP: three tests in reading comprehension, mathematics, and writing to assess readiness in the basic learning skills.

Advance Placement and College Level Examination Program.

STUDENT SERVICES

Cooperative education, academic and career counseling program, personal counseling cluster, job placement office, cooperative education, adult and continuing education, transfer and freshman skills assessment program, veteran's program.

ADDRESS:

F.H LAGUARDIA COMM COLLEGE
31-10 Thomson Ave., M-147
LONG ISLAND,   NY   11101
Principal Official: Raymond C. Bowen, President

TYPES OF DEGREES AWARDED:
AA, AAS, AS and Certificate Programs

ACADEMIC CALENDAR:
Semester. Two enhanced / 18-week semesters.

CONTACT INFORMATION

Admissions Officer:
Phone: (718) 482-7200   **Fax:**
Web Site: Not provided.

DOLLARS AND SENSE

TUITION & FEES:	$2,612.00
ROOM & BOARD:	$1,500.00
BOOKS & SUPPLIES:	$500.00
OTHER EXPENSES:	$675.00
OUT OF STATE TUITION:	$1,538.00
*ANNUAL TOTAL:	$5,287.00

(*Annual Total does not include out-of-state tuition .)

FINANCIAL AID

Financial Aid Phone:
Financial Aid Fax:
FAFSA accepted. Federal Pell Grants, FSEOG, Federal Perkins Loan, Federal Work-Study and Federal Direct Loan and Federal Direct Parent Loan Program. Child of Veteran Award, Child of Deceased Police Officer / Firefighter Award, nursing scholarships, Persian Gulf Veteran Tuition Award, Vietnam Veterans Tuition Award.

SPORTS

Basketball, volleyball, soccer.

WHAT MAJOR?

Accounting, commercial foodservice management, commercial photography, computer information systems, dietetic technician, education, education associate: The Bilinqual Child, emergency medical technician / paramedic, fine arts, human services, liberal arts and sciences, managerial studies, mortuary science, nursing, occupational therapy assistant, paralegal studies, physical therapist assistant, school foodservice management, secretarial science, travel and tourism, veterinary technology.

The LaGuardia Performing Arts Center (LPAC), located on themain campus of LaGuardia Community College, is commited to presenting culturally and tehnically diverse programming of the highest quality. With technical features that rival those of many theaters in Manhattan, and a location which makes it easily accessible from Midtown and the largest theater of its kind in Western Queens.

Master Key: *Image reates desire. You will what you imagine.* J.G. Gallimore

FAYETTEVILLE STATE UNIV.

FAYETTEVILLE, NC

Web Site:
www.fsufay.edu

SCHOOL INFO

Established in 1867. 4-year public, coed liberal arts college on urban campus in small city; 60 miles from Raleigh, North Carolina.

ADDRESS:

FAYETTEVILLE STATE UNIV.
1200 MURCHISON ROAD
FAYETTEVILLE, NC 28301
Principal Official: Dr. Willis B. McLoud

TYPES OF DEGREES AWARDED:
AA, BA, BS, MA, MBA.

ACADEMIC CALENDAR:
Semester. Summer sessions.

CONTACT INFORMATION

Admissions Officer: Charles Darlington
Phone: (910) 486-1371 **Fax:** (910) 437-2512
Web Site: www.fsufay.edu

ACCREDITATON:
Southern Association of Colleges & Schools

CAMPUS ENROLLMENT:
Undergraduate: 3124 men & women. **Graduate:** 778 men & women. **Transfer Students:** 460. **Freshman ethnic enrollment :** Not available.

WHAT DO I NEED?

Test scores, school achievement record, and GPA important. College preparatory program. SAT/ACT (SAT preffered); score report by August 31. Application fee: $15. Closing date August 15; priority to applications received by June 1 and notifications on a rolling basis. Interview recommended for academically weak. Must reply within one week. Deferred and early admission program available.

UNIQUE PROGRAMS

The following programs are available: accelerated program, cooperative education, double major, honors program, independent study, internships, teacher preparation, weekend college program.

DOLLARS AND SENSE

TUITION & FEES:	$5,476.00
ROOM & BOARD:	$0.00
BOOKS & SUPPLIES:	$707.00
OTHER EXPENSES:	$160.00
OUT OF STATE TUITION:	$9,079.00
*ANNUAL TOTAL:	$6,343.00

(*Annual Total does not include out-of-state tuition .)

ACADEMIC REQUIREMENTS

Freshmen must earn a minimum 2.0 and majors must be declared by end of second year.

Core curriculum: English, foreign languages, history, humanities, mathematics, biological/physical sciences, social sciences. Bachelor's: 120 hrs.

FINANCIAL AID

Financial Aid Phone: (910)486-1325
Financial Aid Fax: (910) 486-1423

No closing date; priority given to applications received by May 1; notifications on a rolling basis beginning about May 1; must reply within 8 weeks. FAFSA accepted. Pell grants, loans, jobs available. Academic, athletic, music/drama, minority scholarships available.

STUDENT SERVICES

Campus student services include: academic center, aptitude testing, career and personal counseling, employment service for undergraduates, campus daycare, health services, placement services, preadmission summer program, remedial instruction, special counselor, services for handicapped, tutoring,veterans counselor. ROTC: Air Force.

SPORTS

Varsity Sports: Basketball, cross-country, golf, football, tennis, track and field, volleyball . NCAA.

WHAT MAJOR?

Associate: Business and office, liberal/general studies, secretarial and related programs.

Bachelor's: Accounting, biology, business administration, business education, business and office, chemistry, computer and information sciences, criminal justice studies, dramatic arts, economics, elementary education, English, English education, geography, health education, history, marketing and distribution, mathematics, mathematics education, medical laboratory, music education, physical education, political science and government, psychology, public administration, science education, social sciences, sociology, speech/debate/forensics, visual and performing arts.

Historical & Special Interest:

Since 1972, Fayetteville State University has been a constituent institution of the University of North Carolina System however, its was established in 1867 as Howard School making it the second oldest state supported institution in North Carolina and one of the oldest teacher education institutions in the South. The school's name was changed in 1939 to Fayetteville State Teachers College and the school began its first four-year curriculum. The name was again changed to Fayetteville State University. A Liberal Arts program was begun in 1963 which has grown to offering bachelor degrees in 26 disciplines and associate degrees in 25 disciplines. The School now offers master's degrees in Business Administration, Biology, History, and Teaching. A doctoral degree in Educational Leadership is also available.

The campus began with one building and now has 40 buildings which sit on 156 acres of beautiful campus grounds.

Master Key: *One man with courage is a majority. Andrew Jackson*

HBCU Third Edition
© Jireh & Associates, Inc.
Wilmington, DE

Historically Black Colleges & Universities

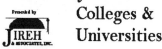

Presented by
JIREH
& ASSOCIATES, INC.

FISK UNIVERSITY
NASHVILLE, TN

Web Site:
www.fisk.edu

SCHOOL INFO

Established in 1867. 4-year private liberal arts, coed college. Affiliation with United Church of Christ on urban campus in large city; 216 miles from Memphis.

ACCREDITATON:

Southern Association of Colleges & Schools

CAMPUS ENROLLMENT:

Undergraduate: 845 men and women. **Graduate:** 29 men & women. **Transfer students:** 0.
Freshman ethnic enrollment: African American-236

WHAT DO I NEED?

High school class rank, academic record, test scores, essay and recommendations . College preparatory program. SAT or ACT; scores by April 1. Application fee $15 may be waived based on need. Closing date June 15; notified on a rolling basis; replies within 30 days. Audition required for music applicants. Deferred and early admission program available.

UNIQUE PROGRAMS

The following programs are available: cooperative education, cross-registration, double major, honors program, independent study, internships, student-designed major, study abroad, teacher preparation; liberal arts/career combination in engineering.

ACADEMIC REQUIREMENTS

Freshmen must earn a minimum 2.0 an majors must be declared by end of second year.

Core curriculum: computer science, English, foreign languages, history, mathematics, philosophy/religion, biological/physical sciences, social sciences. Bachelor's: 120 hrs (30 in major).

STUDENT SERVICES

Campus student services include: academic center, aptitude testing, career and personal counseling, freshman orientation, health services, placement services, special counselor, tutoring, veterans counselor. ROTC: Air Force, Army.

WHAT MAJOR?

Bachelor's: Accounting, art history and appreciation, banking and finance, biology, business administration and management, business and management, business economics, chemistry, computer and information sciences, dramatic arts, economics, elementary education, English, entertainment management, French, history, mathematics, music, music history and appreciation, physics, political science and government, pre-medicine, psychology, public administration, religion and philosophical studies, sociology, Spanish, speech/debate/forensics.

Historical & Special Interest:

Barely six months after the end of the Civil War, and just two years after the Emancipation Proclamation, three men--John Ogden, the Reverend Erastus Milo Cravath, and the Rev. Edward P. Smith--established Fisk School in Nashville, named in honor of General Clinton B. Fisk of the Tennessee Freedmen's Bureau, who provided the new institution with facilities in former Union Army barracks near the present site of Nashville's Union Station. In these facilities Fisk convened its first classes on January 9, 1866. The first students ranged from seven to seventy, but shared common experiences of slavery and poverty--and an extraordinary thirst for learning.

The American Missionary Association--later a part of the United Church of Christ sponsored the work of Fisk's founders and continues its affiliation today. Ogden, Cravath and Smith shared a dream of an educational institution that would be open to all, regardless of race, and that would measure itself by the "highest standards, not of Negro education, but of American education at its best." Their dream was incorporated as Fisk University on August 22, 1867. Fisk's world famous Jubilee Singers originated as a group of traveling students who through their music, set out from Nashville in 1871, taking the entire University treasury with them for travel expenses, praying that they would be able to raise enough money to keep the doors open. Their electrifying performances soon became known throughout the United States and Europe.
The University's Molecular Spectroscopy Research Laboratory is internationally recognized. In 1930, some 63 years later, Fisk became the first African-American institution to gain accreditation by the Southern Association of Colleges Schools. Fisk University is a UNCF school.

ADDRESS:

FISK UNIVERSITY
17TH AVENUE NORTH
NASHVILLE,   TN   37208
Principal Official: Dr. Rutherford H. Adkins, Interim

TYPES OF DEGREES AWARDED:
BA, BFA, BS, MA.

ACADEMIC CALENDAR:
Semester.

CONTACT INFORMATION

Admissions Officer: Anthony Jones
Phone: (800) 443-3475   **Fax:** (615) 329-8774
Web Site: www.fisk.edu

DOLLARS AND SENSE

TUITION & FEES:	$7,078.00
ROOM & BOARD:	$4,350.00
BOOKS & SUPPLIES:	$600.00
OTHER EXPENSES:	$1,050.00
OUT OF STATE TUITION:	
*ANNUAL TOTAL:	$13,078.00

(*Annual Total does not include out-of-state tuition .)

FINANCIAL AID

Financial Aid Phone:
Financial Aid Fax:

No closing date; priority given to applications received by April 15; notifications on a rolling basis beginning about March 15; must reply within 2 weeks. FAFSA accepted. Pell grants, loans, jobs based on need. Academic scholarships available.

SPORTS

Varsity Sports: Baseball, basketball, cross-country, golf, tennis, volleyball, track and field. NCAA.

Master Key: *Everyone has his day and some days are just longer than others.*

HBCU Third Edition
© Jireh & Associates, Inc.
Wilmington, DE

FLORIDA A&M UNIVERSITY

TALLAHASSEE, FL

Web Site:
www.famu.edu

SCHOOL INFO

Established in 1887. 4-year public coed university on urban campus in small city; 169 miles from Jacksonville.

ADDRESS:

FLORIDA A&M UNIVERSITY
ADMINISTRATION OFFICES
TALLAHASSEE, FL 32307
Principal Official: Dr. Frederick S. Humphries

ACCREDITATON:
Southern Association of Colleges & Schools

CAMPUS ENROLLMENT:
Undergraduate: 9666 m&w. **Graduate:** 572 m&w. **Transfer students:** 455 m&w; Part-Time: 1,145. **Ethnic enrollment:** African Amer.-9621, Cauc. -790, Hispanic-128, Amer. Ind.-5; Asian- 101

WHAT DO I NEED?
Academic record and test scores important: SAT or ACT . Scores by July 1. Application fee $20. Closing date May 13th. Notification on a rolling basis. Interviews recommended for health, architecture and pharmacy.

UNIQUE PROGRAMS
The following programs are available: accelerated program, cooperative education, double major, dual enrollment of high school students, honors program, independent study, internships, teacher preparation, weekend college, cross-registration; liberal arts/career combination in engineering, health sciences.

ACADEMIC REQUIREMENTS
Minimum GPA for freshmen 2.0 and major must be declared by end of second year.

Core curriculum: English, foregin languages, history, humanities, mathematics, biological/physical sciences, social sciences. Associate: 60 hours. Bachelor's: 120 hours (30 in major).

STUDENT SERVICES
Campus student services include: aptitude testing, career and personal counseling, employment services, freshman orientation, health services, placement service for grads,learning center, reduced course load program, services for handicapped, special counselor, tutoring, veterans counselor . ROTC: Air Force, Army, Naval.
Learning Disabled: Varied support services: counseling, advocacy, academic advisement, prescriptive plans of study, indiv. & group instruct.

WHAT MAJOR?
Associate: Liberal/general studies.

Bachelor's: Accounting, actuarial sciences, African-American studies, agriculture business, agricultural sciences, animal sciences, architectural technologies, architecture, art education, banking and finance, biology, business management, business education, chemical engineering, chemistry, civil engineering, civil technology, computer sciences, criminal justice studies, dramatic arts, economics, electrical/electronics/communications, engineering, electronic technology, elementary education, English, English education, entomology, fine arts, graphic arts technology, health care administration, history, industrial arts education, industrial engineering, journalism, landscape architecture, mathematics, mathematics education, mechanical engineering, medical records administration, music, music education, music performance, nursing, office supervision and management, ornamental horticulture, pharmacy, philosphy, physical education, political science and government, predentistry, premedicine, psychology, religion, respiratory therapy technology, science education, social studies education,social work, sociology, trade and industrial education, visual and performing arts. Graduate degrees awarded in 32 major fields of study including pharmacy.

Historical & Special Interest:

FAMU was founded in 1887 as a co-educational institution and was designated a land-grant college in 1891. It became a university in 1953 on a 419-acre campus. FAMU's School of Business and Industry includes the National Entrepreneurial Development Center, the first of its kind at an HBCU, with a placement rate of approximately 100 percent. The School of Nursing, established in 1904, was the first baccalaureate nursing program in Florida (and the first at any HBCU) and is fully accredited by the National League of Nursing.
The National Merit Scholarship Corporation released information in October 1991 showing FAMU ranking second nationwide in recruiting National Achievement Scholars. FAMU is a UNCF school.

TYPES OF DEGREES AWARDED:
AA, BA, BS, MA, MS, MBA, PhD.

ACADEMIC CALENDAR:
Semester. Summer , Fall, Spring sessions.

CONTACT INFORMATION

Admissions Officer: Barbara Cox
Phone: (850) 599-3796 **Fax:** (850) 561-2428
Web Site: www.famu.edu

DOLLARS AND SENSE

TUITION & FEES:	$2,459.00
ROOM & BOARD:	$3,580.00
BOOKS & SUPPLIES:	$1,000.00
OTHER EXPENSES:	$680.00
OUT OF STATE TUITION:	$8,750.00
*ANNUAL TOTAL:	$7,719.00

(*Annual Total does not include out-of-state tuition .)

FINANCIAL AID

Financial Aid Phone: (850) 599-3730
Financial Aid Fax: (850) 599-2730

Fall term closing date for aid applications May 12th. FAFSA accepted. Must reply within 2 wks. Pell grants, loans, jobs available. **Scholarships:** President's Scholars Award; Life Gets Better; Disting. Scholars Award; Adopted High School & Distr.; Community College Schol. Other scholarships: Army, Air Force, Navy ROTC; School of Bus. & Industry; College of Pharmacy, Engineering Science & Tech.

SPORTS
Varsity Sports: Baseball, basketball, football, golf, softball, swimming, tennis, track and field, volleyball. NCAA.

Master Key: *Courage is doing what you are afraid to do. There can be no courage unless you are scared.*
Eddie Rickenbacker

HBCU Third Edition
© Jireh & Associates, Inc.
Wilmington, DE

FLORIDA MEMORIAL COLLEGE

MIAMI, FL

Web Site:
www.fmc.edu

SCHOOL INFO

Established in 1879. 4-year private coed college of arts and sciences. Affiliated with American Baptist Churches in the USA, Southern Baptist Convention, Progressive Missionary Convention, Educational Baptist Convention, and Baptist General State Convention on urban campus

ACCREDITATON:
Southern Association of Colleges & Schools

CAMPUS ENROLLMENT:
Undergraduate: 1489 men & women. **Transfer students:** 119 men & women. **Freshman ethnic enrollment:** Not available.

WHAT DO I NEED?

Academic record, test scores, interviews, recommendations, essays and special talent considered. SAT/ACT; Scores by July 1. College-prep. program. Application fee $15 (may be waived). Closing date July 1. Priority given to applications received by April 1. Notification on a rolling basis; must reply by August 1. Interview recommended and essay required. Deferred admission program available.

UNIQUE PROGRAMS

The following programs are available: accelerated program, cooperative education, double major, dual enrollment of high school students, honors program, independent study, internships, teacher prepartion, weekend college, teacher certification, entreprenurial institute in conjunction with 5 area colleges.

ACADEMIC REQUIREMENTS

Minimum GPA for freshmen 2.0 and major must be declared by end of second year.

Core curriculum: computer science, English, foreign languages, history, philosophy/religion, humanities, mathematics, biological/physical sciences, social sciences. Bachelor's: 124 hours (30 in major).

STUDENT SERVICES

Campus student services include: aptitude testing, career and personal counseling, campus ministry, employment service for undergraduates, freshman orientation, health services, learning center, placement services, preadmission summer, reduced course load program, remedial instruction, special counselor, tutoring. ROTC: Air Force, Army.

WHAT MAJOR?

Bachelor's:

Accounting, air traffic control, airway science, art education, aviation computer technology, aviation management, business management, business and management, business economics, chemistry, clinical psychology, community psychology, computer sciences, criminal justice studies, data processing, economics, elementary education, English, English education, mathematics, mathematics education, medical laboratory technologies, music, music education, physical education, physical sciences, recreation and community services technologies, religion, religious education, secondary education, social sciences, sociology, transporation management, urban studies.

Historical & Special Interest:

Florida Memorial College is one of the oldest academic centers in Florida. Founded in 1879 as the Florida Baptist Institute for Negroes in Live Oak, Florida. The American Baptist Home Mission Society gave its full support and the first regular school year began in 1880.

In 1892, the Florida Baptist Academy was established in Jacksonville, Florida which later changed its name to Florida Normal and Industrial Institute. It was there, that two brothers James Weldon Johnson and J. Rosamond Johnson wrote the words and music to what has become the Negro National Anthem: "Lift Every Voice and Sing" in 1900. In 1918, the school moved to St. Augustine where the famous bell was purchased that was once used to call the slaves together for orders. College historian state that this bell was cast at the same foundry as the Liberty Bell which is enshrined in Philadelphia. The bell now rings each day at noon to remind students of their religious heritage.

In 1941, the school in Live Oak and the school in St. Augustine merged changing its limiting offerings from the junior college classification to a four year liberal arts institution. The first graduating class came out in 1945 and in 1950, the name was changed to Florida Normal and Industrial Memorial College and in 1963, the name was changed again to Florida Memorial College. In 1968, it received a new home in Miami, Florida.

ADDRESS:

FLORIDA MEMORIAL COLLEGE
15800 NW 42ND AVENUE
MIAMI,   FL   33054
Principal Official: Dr. Albert E. Smith

TYPES OF DEGREES AWARDED:
BA, BS.

ACADEMIC CALENDAR:
Semester. Summer sessions limited.

CONTACT INFORMATION

Admissions Officer: Peggy Martin
Phone: (800) 822-1362   **Fax:** (305) 626-3106
Web Site: www.fmc.edu

DOLLARS AND SENSE

TUITION & FEES:	$9,586.00
ROOM & BOARD:	$0.00
BOOKS & SUPPLIES:	$0.00
OTHER EXPENSES:	$930.00
OUT OF STATE TUITION:	$6,350.00
*ANNUAL TOTAL:	$10,516.00

(*Annual Total does not include out-of-state tuition .)

FINANCIAL AID

Financial Aid Phone: (800)822-1362
Financial Aid Fax: (305)626-3106

No closing date; priority given to applications received by April 1. FAFSA accepted. Notifications on a rolling basis; must reply within 10 days. Academic, athletic, minority scholarships available.

SPORTS

Varsity Sports: Baseball, basketball, track and field, volleyball. NAIA.

Master Key: *Man punishes the action, but God the intention.*

HBCU Third Edition
© Jireh & Associates, Inc.
Wilmington, DE

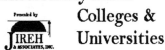
FORT VALLEY ST. UNIVERSITY

FORT VALLEY, GA

Web Site:
oprater@fvs3.fvsc.peachnet.edu

SCHOOL INFO
Established in 1895. 4-year public coed college of arts and sciences on rural campus in small town; 30 miles from Macon.

ACCREDITATON:
Southern Association of Colleges & Schools

CAMPUS ENROLLMENT:
Undergraduate: 2560 men & women. **Graduate:** 464 men & women. **Freshman ethnic enrollment:** African American-93.1%, Caucasian-6.3%, Hispanic & Other-.6%.

WHAT DO I NEED?
High school transcript, SAT test scores important. SAT or ACT. College-preparatory program. Scores by September 5. No application fee. Closing date August 25; and applicants notified on rolling basis beginning on February 1. Reply required within 4 weeks. Early admission program available. Auditions recommended for music education applicants.

UNIQUE PROGRAMS
The following programs are available: cooperative education, double major, dual enrollment of high school students, external degree, honors program, internships, student-designed major, study abroad, teacher preparation program.

ACADEMIC REQUIREMENTS
Minimum GPA for freshmen 2.0. Major must be declared by end of second year.

Core curriculum: Arts/fine arts, English, foreign languages, history, mathematics, biological/physical sciences, philosophy/religion, and social sciences. Associate: 90 hours (20 in major). Bachelor's: 180 hours (30 in major).

STUDENT SERVICES
Campus student services include: career and personal counseling, placement service for graduates, health services, learning center, reduced course load program remedial instruction, special counselors and advisor for adult students, tutoring, veterans counselor. ROTC: Army.

ADDRESS:

FORT VALLEY ST. UNIVERSITY
P.O. BOX 4531 EVSC
FORT VALLEY, GA 31030
Principal Official: Dr. Oscar L. Prater

TYPES OF DEGREES AWARDED:
AA, AS, BA, BS, MA, MS, Ed.S.

ACADEMIC CALENDAR:
Quarter. Summer sessions limited.

CONTACT INFORMATION

Admissions Officer: Dr. Mildred Hill
Phone: (912) 825-6307 **Fax:** (912) 825-6155
Web Site: oprater@fvs3.fvsc.peachnet.edu

DOLLARS AND SENSE

TUITION & FEES:	$2,340.00
ROOM & BOARD:	$3,385.00
BOOKS & SUPPLIES:	$906.00
OTHER EXPENSES:	$500.00
OUT OF STATE TUITION:	$6,273.00
*ANNUAL TOTAL:	$7,131.00

(*Annual Total does not include out-of-state tuition.)

FINANCIAL AID

Financial Aid Phone:
Financial Aid Fax:
Closing date May 1; priority given to applications received by April 15. Notifications on a rolling basis beginning June 1. FAFSA accepted. Pell grants, loans, jobs available. Academic, music/drama, athletic, alumni affiliation, religious affiliation, minority scholarships available.

SPORTS
Varsity Sports: baseball, basketball, cross-country, football, tennis, track and field. NCAA

WHAT MAJOR?
Associate: Engineering and engineering-related technologies, secretarial and related programs.

Bachelor's:

Accounting, agricultural business, and management, agricultural economics, agricultural education, agricultural engineering, agricultural sciences, agronomy, animal sciences, biology, botany, business administration, business and management, business economics, business education, chemistry, commercial design, computer sciences, criminal justice studies, criminology, economics, education,elementary education, English, English education, food sciences and human nutrition, foreign languages education, French, health education, history, home economics, home economics education, horticultural science, individual and family development, journalism, mass communications, mathematics, mathematics education, music education, nutritional sciences, physical education, physics, political science and government, psychology, school psychology, science education, secondary education, secretarial and related programs, social science education, social work, sociology, textiles and clothing, zoology. Graduate degrees awarded in 2 major fields of study.

Historical & Special Interest:

Fort Valley State College was founded in 1895 as the Fort Valley Normal and Industrial School and in 1939, merged with the Forsyth State Teachers and Agricultural College and given the name of Fort Valley State College.

It is a 1890 land-grant college offering over 40 undergraduate majors and five graduate programs and located on 1,375 acres in the scenic Peach County in middle Georgia. The school has a grant funded by the U.S. Agency for International Development which supports project activities in Africa and the Caribbean.

Master Key: *Experience is a good school, but the fees are high. Heinrich Heine*

HBCU Third Edition
© Jireh & Associates, Inc.
Wilmington, DE

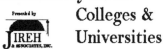
GRAMBLING STATE UNIVERSITY

GRAMBLING,   LA

Web Site:
Not provided.

SCHOOL INFO

Established in 1901. 4-year public coed university on urban campus in a small town; 35 miles from Monroe, 70 miles from Shreveport.

ACCREDITATON:
Southern Association of Colleges & Schools

CAMPUS ENROLLMENT:
*Undergraduate: Full-time: 5665 women and men. **Graduate:** 485 men and women.

WHAT DO I NEED?

Open admissions. A 2.0 GPA required for all out-of-state students. SAT or ACT (ACT preferred) for placement and counseling; scores by July 15.

UNIQUE PROGRAMS

The following programs are available: cooperative education, double major, educations specialist degree, honors program, independent study, weekend college, cross-registration.

ACADEMIC REQUIREMENTS

Minimum GPA for freshmen 2.0 by end of first semester and major must be declared by end of second year.

Core curriculum: English, humanities, mathematics, biological/physical sciences, social sciences. Associate: 67 hours. Bachelor's: 128 hours.

STUDENT SERVICES

Campus student services include: employment services for undergraduates, learning center, personal counseling, placement service for graduates, reduced course load program, remedial instruction, special counselor, veterans counselor, services for handicapped, tutoring. ROTC: Air Force, Army.

ADDRESS:

GRAMBLING STATE UNIVERSITY
P.O. BOX 607, 100 MAIN ST.
GRAMBLING,   LA   71245
Principal Official: Dr. Raymond A. Hicks

TYPES OF DEGREES AWARDED:
AA, AS, BA, BS, MS, D.

ACADEMIC CALENDAR:
Semester. Summer sessions limited.

CONTACT INFORMATION

Admissions Officer: Nora Bingaman
Phone: (318) 274-3138   **Fax:** (318) 274-3292
Web Site: Not provided.

DOLLARS AND SENSE

TUITION & FEES:	$3,088.00
ROOM & BOARD:	$3,954.00
BOOKS & SUPPLIES:	$600.00
OTHER EXPENSES:	$930.00
OUT OF STATE TUITION:	$6,450.00
*ANNUAL TOTAL:	$8,572.00

(*Annual Total does not include out-of-state tuition .)

FINANCIAL AID

Financial Aid Phone: (318) 247-3811
Financial Aid Fax: (318) 274-2398

No closing date, priority given to applications received by March15. Notifications on a rolling basis beginning April 15. Reply within 2 weeks or by May 1. FAFSA accepted. Merit scholarships offered by invitation only on Scholarship Day. Pell grants, loans, and jobs available and based on need. Academic, music/drama, art, athletic, leadership, state/district residency, religious affiliation, minority scholarships available.

SPORTS

Varsity Sports: basketball, basebal, cross-country, football, golf, softball, tennis, track and field.

WHAT MAJOR?

Associate: Accounting, automotive technology, business and office, business data processing and related programs, construction, drafting, electrical technology, law enforcement and corrections technologies, marketing and distribution, secretarial and related programs.
Bachelor's:

Accounting, African-American studies, anthropology, applied mathematics, art education, art history and appreciation, Asian studies, automotive technology, biology, business administration, business management, business education, chemistry, communications, computer sciences, criminal justice studies, cytotechnology, data processing, dramatic arts, economics, electrical technology, elementary education, English, English education, history, home economics education, hotel/motel and restaurant management, industrial arts education, information sciences and systems, institutional/home management/supporting programs, journalism, Latin American studies, law enforcement and corrections, marketing and distributive education, mathematics, mathematics education, medical records technology, music, music history and appreciation, and music education, nursing, occupational therapy, physical education, physical therapy, physics, political science and government, prelaw, psychology, public administration, radio/television technology, rehabilitation counseling/services, respiratory therapy technology, science education, secondary education, secretarial and related programs, social sciences, social work, sociology, Spanish, special education, speech correction, speech pathology/audiology, statistics, urban studies.

Historical & Special Interest:
Grambling State University was established in 1901 and now serves over 6,000 students. It offers preliminary training for medicine, law and dentistry. Its multi-purpose facility also offers opportunities for cooperative education and non-credit continuing education programs for the citizens of Grambling and North Louisiana. With full accreditation by the Southern Association of Colleges and Schools and the National Council for Accreditation of Teacher Education, Grambling has added a unique offering to its curriculum a Graduate School for the Ed.D. in Developmental Education.

Master Key: *Evil knows where evil sleeps. African Proverb*

HBCU Third Edition
© Jireh & Associates, Inc.
Wilmington, DE

Historically Black
Colleges &
Universities

JIREH
& ASSOCIATES, INC.
Presented by

HAMPTON UNIVERSITY
HAMPTON, VA

Web Site:
www.cs/hamptonu.edu

SCHOOL INFO

Established in 1868. 4-year private, liberal arts coed college on urban campus in Hampton by the Chesapeake Bay; 10 miles from Norfolk.

ACCREDITATON:
Southern Association of Colleges & Schools

CAMPUS ENROLLMENT:
Undergraduate: 5582 men and women. **Graduate:** 384 men & women. **Freshman ethnic enrollment:** Not available.

WHAT DO I NEED?

Academic record and test scores. SAT/ACT; scores by June 30. Application fee $10. Closing date February 15; notifications on a rolling basis around March 1; must reply by April 1. Music applicants must audition. Deferred and early admissions program available.

UNIQUE PROGRAMS

The following programs are available: accelerated program, cooperative education, cross-registration, honors program, independent study, internships, study abroad, teacher preparation; combined liberal/arts career program in engineering.

ACADEMIC REQUIREMENTS

Freshmen must earn a minimum 2.0 and majors must be declared by end of first year.

Core curriculum: English, foreign languages, history, humanities, mathematics, biological/physical sciences, social sciences. Bachelor's: 124 hrs (83 in major).

STUDENT SERVICES

Campus student services include: academic center, aptitude testing, career and personal counseling, employment services for undergraduates, freshman orientation, placement services, preadmission summer program, reduced course load program, remedial instruction, special counselor, tutoring, veterans counselor, services for handicapped. ROTC: Army, Naval.

ADDRESS:

HAMPTON UNIVERSITY
QUEEN-TAYLOR ST.
HAMPTON,   VA   23668
Principal Official: Dr. William R. Harvey

TYPES OF DEGREES AWARDED:
BA, BS, MA, MS, MBA.

ACADEMIC CALENDAR:
Semester. Summer sessions limited.

CONTACT INFORMATION

Admissions Officer: Leonard Jones
Phone: (800) 624-3328   **Fax:** (757) 727-5095
Web Site: www.cs/hamptonu.edu

DOLLARS AND SENSE

TUITION & FEES:	$14,518.00
ROOM & BOARD:	$0.00
BOOKS & SUPPLIES:	$600.00
OTHER EXPENSES:	$0.00
OUT OF STATE TUITION:	
*ANNUAL TOTAL:	$15,118.00

(*Annual Total does not include out-of-state tuition .)

FINANCIAL AID

Financial Aid Phone: (800) 624-3341
Financial Aid Fax: (757) 727-5095

Closing date June 1; priority given to applications received by March 31; notifications on a rolling basis beginning around March 1; must reply within 2 weeks. FAFSA accepted. Pell grants, loans, jobs based on need. Academic, athletic, music/drama, state/district residency, minority scholarships available.

SPORTS

Varsity Sports: Basketball, football, golf, rifle , tennis, track and field, volleyball . NCAA.

WHAT MAJOR?

Bachelor's: Accounting, air traffic control, architecture, art history and appreciation, aviation management, banking and finance, biology, business administration and management, banking and finance, biology, business administration and management, business and management, chemical engineering, chemistry, commercial art, communications, computer and information sciences, criminal justice studies, dramatic arts, economics, education, education of the deaf and hearing impaired, education of the emotionally handicapped, education of the mentally handicapped, electrical/electronics and communications engineering, elementary education, English, fashion merchandising, food sciences and human nutrition, gerontology, history, home economics, individual and family development, journalism, junior high education, marine biology, mathematics, music, nursing, physical education, physics, political science and government, preelementary education, prelaw, premedicine, psychology, radio/television, secondary education, secretarial and related programs, social work, sociology, special education, speech correction, speech/pathology/audiology, sports medicine, textiles and clothing.

Historical & Special Interest:

Hampton University was founded by General Samuel Chapman Armstrong in 1868 to train selected young Black men and women to teach and lead their people. Hampton is Virginia's only coeducational, non-denominational, private four-year college. It offers 41 baccalaureate degrees and offers Master degrees in nine areas.

The student-faculty ratio at Hampton is 14 to 1, allowing for a great deal of personalized interaction between student and teacher. The University holds membership in the Council of Graduate Schools, the Council of Independent Colleges in Virginia, and the American Council on Education. Over 25 schools and institutions have come into existence as a result of Hampton and its graduates. Its alumni founded ten institutions among them, Tuskegee University, St. Paul's College and Bowling Green Academy.

Master Key: *To measure the man, measure his heart. Malcolm S. Forbes*

HARRIS-STOWE STATE COLLEGE

ST. LOUIS, MO

Web Site:
www.mwsc.edu/~cwa/harris.html

SCHOOL INFO

Established in 1857. 4-year public coed teachers college on urban campus in a very large city.

ACCREDITATON:
North Central Association of Colleges for Teacher Education.

CAMPUS ENROLLMENT:
Total enrollment: 1700 men and women.

ADDRESS:

HARRIS-STOWE STATE COLLEGE
3026 LACLEDE AVE.
ST. LOUIS,   MO   63103
Principal Official: Dr. Henry Givens, Jr.

TYPES OF DEGREES AWARDED:
BS.

ACADEMIC CALENDAR:
Semester. Summer sessions limited.

CONTACT INFORMATION

Admissions Officer: Valerie Beeson
Phone: (314) 340-3300   **Fax:** (314) 340-3322
Web Site: www.mwsc.edu/~cwa/harris.html

WHAT DO I NEED?

High school GPA, test scores, recommendations, curriculum considered. Interview required.   No fee; no closing date and applicants notified on a rolling basis. CRDA. Deferred admission program available.

UNIQUE PROGRAMS

The following program is available: academic advisement and program planning, academic support center, communications skills laboratory, cross-registration, tutorial service, testing service.

DOLLARS AND SENSE

TUITION & FEES:	$2,502.00
ROOM & BOARD:	$0.00
BOOKS & SUPPLIES:	$500.00
OTHER EXPENSES:	$415.00
OUT OF STATE TUITION:	$5,009.00
*ANNUAL TOTAL:	$3,417.00

(*Annual Total does not include out-of-state tuition .)

ACADEMIC REQUIREMENTS

Freshmen must successfully complete 9 hours or 75% of hours attempted, the lesser of the two. Teacher certification programs available.

Bachelor's: 128 semester hours.

FINANCIAL AID

Financial Aid Phone: (314) 340-3500
Financial Aid Fax: (314) 340-3503

No closing date and notifications on a rolling basis. FAFSA accepted. Pell grants, loans, jobs, memorial, academic, alumni, and honors scholarships, available.

STUDENT SERVICES

Campus student services include: career and personal counseling, employment service for undergraduates, health services, mathematics and communications laboratories, placement services, preadmission summer program, reduced course load program, remedial instruction, tutoring, . ROTC: Air Force.

SPORTS

Varsity Sports: baseball and soccer, basketball, track and volleyball.

WHAT MAJOR?

Associate: Microtechnology Lab.

Bachelor's: Early Childhood, Elementary Education, Middle School/Junior High Education, urban studies planning.

Historical & Special Interest:
Harris-Stowe's earliest predecessor was founded in 1857 by the St. Louis Public Schools as a normal school for whites only and was later named Harris Teachers College in honor of William Torrey Harris Superintendent of Instruction in the St. Louis Public Schools. Harris Teachers College had begun to offer in-service education for St. Louis white teachers as early as 1906.

In 1920, the Harris became a four-year undergraduate institution, authorized to grant a Bachelor of Arts in Education Degree. In 1924, the College received accreditation by the American Association of Colleges for Teacher Education and the National Council for the Accreditation of Teacher Education. Its second predessor institution was Stowe Teachers College which began in 1890 as a normal school for black future teachers of elementary schools in the City of St. Louis. This normal school was also founded by the St. Louis Public School System and was an extension of the Sumner High School. In 1924, the Sumner Normal School became a four-year institution with authority to grant the baccalaureate degree. In 1929, its name was changed to Stowe Teachers College in honor of Harriet Beecher-Stowe, the novelist and abolitionist.

As the first of several steps to integrate the public schools of St. Louis in 1954, the Board of Education merged the two institutions and kept the name Harris Teachers College. Later, in response to the many requests from alumni of Stowe Teachers College and members of the Greater St. Louis Community, the Board of Education agreed to restore to the College's name the word "Stowe," and drop the word, "teachers." In 1979, the General Assembly of the State of Missouri enacted a bill, 703, to add Harris Stowe College to its membership of the State system of public higher education and its name was changed again to add the word "State," and has since then been known as Harris-Stowe State College.

Master Key: *Experience is a hard teacher. She gives the test first and the lessons afterwards. Anonymous*

HBCU Third Edition
© Jireh & Associates, Inc.
Wilmington, DE

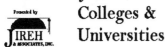
HINDS COMMUNITY COLLEGE -

UTICA, MS

Web Site:
www.hinds.cc.ms.us/index.htm

SCHOOL INFO

Hinds provides convenient education centers in six locations: Two Jackson campuses, Rankin, Raymond, Utica or Vicksburg-Warren County campus.

ACCREDITATON:
Commission on Colleges of the Southern Association of Colleges & Schools to award the AA, AAS & certificates.

CAMPUS ENROLLMENT:
With five campuses, Hinds' enrollment has soared over the 10,000 mark. This represents the largest single institution enrollment at any state community college. Housing is available on the Raymond and Utica campuses only.

WHAT DO I NEED?

Open door policy. High school diploma and transcript or GED transcript required. ACT score minimum 18. Registration fee $25 required at time of registration. Special requirements for admission to certain health related programs.

UNIQUE PROGRAMS

College Credit by Examination, Challenge Exam Program, Advance Placement, Cooperative Education and Job Placement and child care.

ACADEMIC REQUIREMENTS

A student who earns less than a 1.75 GPA during a fall or spring semester will enter on scholastic probation the next semester.

Hinds will guarantee to its academic graduates and other students who have met the requirements (up to 64 cr hr transfer plan) transferability of credits to MS colleges that cooperated in selection guidelines.

STUDENT SERVICES

Counseling services, orientation program, disability support services, deaf and hearing impaired services, veteran affairs, computer-based career information system, learning resource center. Housing is available on the Raymond and Utica campuses only.

ADDRESS:

HINDS COMMUNITY COLLEGE - Utica
Utica Campus
UTICA,   MS   39175
Principal Official: Dr. Clyde Muse

TYPES OF DEGREES AWARDED:

ACADEMIC CALENDAR:
Semester. Summer Sessions available.

CONTACT INFORMATION

Admissions Officer: Elistene Turner
Phone: (601) 885-6062   **Fax:** (601) 885-6026
Web Site: www.hinds.cc.ms.us/index.htm

DOLLARS AND SENSE

TUITION & FEES:	$3,270.00
ROOM & BOARD:	$974.00
BOOKS & SUPPLIES:	$825.00
OTHER EXPENSES:	$150.00
OUT OF STATE TUITION:	$5,686.00
*ANNUAL TOTAL:	$5,219.00

(*Annual Total does not include out-of-state tuition .)

FINANCIAL AID

Financial Aid Phone: (601) 885-7011
Financial Aid Fax: (601) 885-6026

Institutional financial aid and scholarships, federal loans, grants and work-study, income-based tuition reduction program. Payment options available. FAFSA accepted.

SPORTS

Varsity Sports: Baseball, basketball, football, golf, soccer, softball, tennis, track.

WHAT MAJOR?

Accountancy, accounting, agriculture, American studies, anthropology, architecture, art, athletic trainer, biochemistry, biology, biomedical sciences, broadcast journalism, business administration, business educaton, business information systems and quantitative analysis, chemistry, clothing and textiles, coaching and sports administration, commercial aviation, communications, community and regional planning, computer science, criminal justice, dietetics, distributive education, education for the deaf, engineering, engineering technology, English, environmental health, environmental science, exercise science, family and human development, family life studies, fashion merchandising, foods and nutrition, food science technology, foreign languages, forensic science, forestry, history, health info tech., interior design, microbiology, medical technology, music, nursing, nutrition, occupational therapy, office adminstration, religious, paralegal studies, psychology, pre-dentistry, law, medicine, optometry, pharmacy & veterinary science, social sciences, speech, theatre, transportation, urban studies, wildlife & fisheries, zoology.

Historical & Special Interest:

What began in 1917 as a small agricultural high school in the center of Hinds County, is today one of the most progressive post-secondary education institutions in the state. Hinds County Agricultural High School in Raymond was established under the presidency of W. M. Taylor. In its first year, the institution enrolled 117 students who were taught by a faculty of eight. The school was one of several agricultural high school which sprang up in the state during this period and a year later the school became part of the first statewide junior colleges. The first year of junior college work was offered during the 1922-23 school session. Technical programs blossomed during the late 1960s and an associate of applied science degree for two-yr technical students was approved. Dr. Muse became president in 1978 and Hinds enrollment soared over 10,000 mark. This represented the largest single institution enrollment at any state community college. The Pearl-Rankin vocational/technical campus was opened in 1983. In 1984, the Jackson Branch on Sunset joined with the Nursing/Allied Health Center at Chadwick Dr. In 1990, the Vicksburg-Warren County Branch, known as the Academic and Technical Building was added to serve high school students and adult learners. Hinds is now more than ever living up to its name as "The College for All People."

Master Key: *Our aspirations are our possibilities. Robert Browning*

HBCU Third Edition
© Jireh & Associates, Inc.
Wilmington, DE

HOWARD UNIVERSITY
WASHINGTON, DC

Web Site:
www.howard.edu

SCHOOL INFO

Established in 1867. 4-year private college of arts and sciences, business, engineering, health science, music, nursing, pharmacy, teacher's college, coed on urban campus in a very large city located in northwest section of city.

ACCREDITATON:
Middle States Association of Colleges & Schools & others.

CAMPUS ENROLLMENT:
Undergraduate: 2,337 men & 3,827 women FT. 521 PT. **Graduate:** 1,552 men & 2,011 women. **Transfer students:** 166 men & 273 women. **Freshman ethnic enrollment:** Native Am.-1%, African Am.-85%, Asian-2%, Caucasian-2%, Latino-1%, Other-10%.

WHAT DO I NEED?

SAT scores, academic record, and test scores important. SAT/ACT; score report by April 1 for placement and counseling only. Application fee $45; closing date April 1; notification on a rolling basis; reply within 4 wks. Interview recommeded for pharmacy and pharmacological sciences, and fine arts applicants; audition required for music/drama.

UNIQUE PROGRAMS

The following programs are available: cross-registration, double major, dual enrollment of high school students, accelerated degree, ESL, advanced placement, honors program, independent study, internships, student-designed major, study abroad, teacher preparation, visiting & exchange student program; combined bachelor's graduate program Howard Scholars Program.

ACADEMIC REQUIREMENTS

Minimum GPA of 2.0 for freshmen and major must be declared by end of second year.

Core curriculum: English, foreign languages, mathematics, social sciences. Bachelor's: 127 hours.

STUDENT SERVICES

Campus student services include: aptitude testing, campus daycare, career and personal counseling, employment services for undergraduates, freshman orientation, health services, learning center, placement services, reduced course load program, remedial instruction, special counselor, tutoring, services for handicapped, veterans counselor. ROTC: Air Force, Army.

ADDRESS:

HOWARD UNIVERSITY
2400 SIXTH ST. N.W.
WASHINGTON,   DC   20059
Principal Official: Mr. H. Patrick Swygert

TYPES OF DEGREES AWARDED:
BA, BArch, BBA, BM, BME, BS, BFA, M, D, F.

ACADEMIC CALENDAR:
Semester. Summer sessions.

CONTACT INFORMATION

Admissions Officer: Ms. Richetta Johnson
Phone: (800) 822-6363   **Fax:** (202) 806-4465
Web Site: www.howard.edu

DOLLARS AND SENSE

TUITION & FEES:	$9,805.00
ROOM & BOARD:	$5,992.00
BOOKS & SUPPLIES:	$770.00
OTHER EXPENSES:	$500.00
OUT OF STATE TUITION:	
***ANNUAL TOTAL:**	$17,067.00

(*Annual Total does not include out-of-state tuition .)

FINANCIAL AID

Financial Aid Phone: (202) 806-2800
Financial Aid Fax: (202) 806-2818

Closing date April 1; notifications on a rolling basis around May 15; must reply within 4 weeks. FAFSA accepted. Pell grants, loans, work-study and Howard Student Employment Pgm. Academic, music/drama, art, athletic scholoarships available. Payment options available.

SPORTS

Varsity Sports: Baseball , basketball, cross-country, diving, football, gymnastics, soccer, swimming, tennis, track and filed, volleyball, wrestling. NCAA.

WHAT MAJOR?

Bachelor's: Architecture & Environmental Design: Architecture; Area Studies: African studies, Afro-American Studies; Biological Sciences: Biology, microbiology; Business Management: Accounting , finance, hospitality management, insurance education, international business, management, marketing; Communications: Communications Sciences & Disorders, human communication studies, journalism, radio/Television/film; Computer & Information Sciences: Systems and computer sciences, computer systems and analysis; Education: Early Childhood ed., elementary ed., health ed., human development, music ed., physical ed., recreation and leisure, secondary teacher ed.; Engineering: chemical engineering, civil engineering, electrical engineering, mechanical engineering, systems and computer science; Fine & Applied Arts: Acting, Art Management, Art History, Ceramics, composition, dance arts, design, electronic studio, experimental studio, fashion merchandising, instrumental emphasis, interior design, jazz studies, music business, music education, music history, music therapy, musical theatre, orchestral instruments, painting, photography, piano, pre-directing, printmaking sculpture, theatre arts administration, theatre education, voice; Foreign Languages; Health Professions: Clinical laboratory science, dental hygiene, nursing, nutritional sciences, occupational therapy, physical therapy, physician assistant, radiation therapy technology; Mathematics: Math; Military Science: Aerospace Studies, military science (Army); Physical Sciences: Astrophysics, chemistry, physics; Social Sciences: Admin. of Justice, anthropology, economics, history, political science, sociology.
Graduate Degrees Offered:
Master of: Arts, of Arts in Public Admin., of Arts in Teaching, of Arts in Religious Studies, of Business Admin., of Comparative Jurisprudence, of Education, of Engineering (Civil, Elec., Mech.), of Fine Arts, of Music Ed., of Public Admin., of Science, of Science in Nursing, of Computer Science, of Social Work, of Science in Physical Therapy; Doctor of Education, of Ministry and Doctor of Philosophy.

Historical & Special Interest:
Howard University was established as a private, coeducational and multiracial school since its inception in 1867. The University consists of 16 fully accredited schools and colleges and was named after General Oliver Otis Howard, Commissioner of the Freedmen's Bureau. Howard's faculty consists of the largest concentration of Black scholars and Ph.D's of any single college or university.

Master Key: *You will always remember what you teach. Murdock*

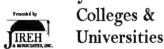
HUSTON-TILLOTSON COLLEGE

AUSTIN, TX

Web Site:
www.htc.edu

SCHOOL INFO

Established in 1876. 4-year private liberal arts coed college with United Church of Christ and United Methodist Church affiliation on urban campus in large city; 78 miles north of San Antonio.

ACCREDITATON:
Southern Association of Colleges & Schools

CAMPUS ENROLLMENT:
*Undergraduate: Full-time: 696 men and women.

ADDRESS:

HUSTON-TILLOTSON COLLEGE
1820 EAST 8TH ST.
AUSTIN,   TX   78702
Principal Official: Dr. Joseph Turner
McMilllian, Jr.

TYPES OF DEGREES AWARDED:
BA, BS.

ACADEMIC CALENDAR:
Semester. Summer sessions limited.

CONTACT INFORMATION

Admissions Officer: Thomas Clifton VanDyke
Phone: (512) 505-3026   **Fax:** (512) 505-3190
Web Site: www.htc.edu

DOLLARS AND SENSE

TUITION & FEES:	$5,550.00
ROOM & BOARD:	$4,416.00
BOOKS & SUPPLIES:	$0.00
OTHER EXPENSES:	$450.00
OUT OF STATE TUITION:	
*ANNUAL TOTAL:	$10,416.00

(*Annual Total does not include out-of-state tuition .)

WHAT DO I NEED?

Academic record, SAT or ACT test scores and interview considered. Minimum in-state ACT composite 14; out-of-state 16. College preparatory program. Application fee $10. No closing date ; priority to applications received by March 1; notifications on a rolling basis. Auditions recommended for music applicants. Deferred admission program available.

UNIQUE PROGRAMS

The following programs are available: cooperative education, double major, honors program, independent study, internships, teacher preparation, weekend college; liberal arts/career combination in engineering, health sciences.

ACADEMIC REQUIREMENTS

Freshmen must earn a minimum 1.5 and majors must be declared by end of second year.

Core curriculum: computer science, English, foreign languages, history, humanities, mathematics, philosophy/religion, biological/physical sciences, social sciences. Bachelor's: 120 hrs (30 in major).

FINANCIAL AID

Financial Aid Phone: (512) 505-3026
Financial Aid Fax: (512)505-3192

Closing date March 1; notifications on a rolling basis beginning around May 15; must reply by June 1. FAFSA accepted. Pell grants, loans, jobs based on need.

STUDENT SERVICES

Campus student services include: academic center, aptitude testing, career and personal counseling, employment service for undergraduates, health services, placement services, remedial instruction, special counselors, veterans counselor, services for handicapped, tutoring. ROTC: Army.

SPORTS

Varsity Sports: Baseball, basketball, tennis, and volleyball. NAIA.

WHAT MAJOR?

Bachelor's: Accounting, banking and finance, biology, business administration and management, business and office, chemistry, communications, computer and information sciences, economics, education, elementary education, engineering, English, history, hotel/motel and restaurant management, marketing management, mathematics, music, nursing, personal management, physical education and recreation, political science and government, predentistry, prelaw, premedicine, prepharmacy, radio/television, secondary education, sociology.

Historical & Special Interest:

Huston-Tillotson College was chartered in 1952 with the merger of two former institutions, Samuel Huston College and Tillotson College. Tillotson was founded in 1875 upon an earlier secondary school sponsored by the American Missionary Association, whose principal founder was a pioneer teacher, Miss Elizabeth Evans. The College was made possible by the Rev. George Jeffrey Tillotson, a retired minister of Wethersfield, Connecticut, who selected the site. The first $5,000 for erection of Allen Hall was given by D.A. Allen of Salem, OH. Allen Hall was designated as "the first building in the State of Texas for the higher education of Negroes, and also the first of its kind west of the Mississippi.

The School was chartered in 1877 as Tillotson Collegiate and Normal Institute and opened to students on January 17, 1881 and in 1894 was renamed Tillotson College. It was organized as a private liberal educational corporation in 1909; reorganized as a junior college in 1925; as a woman's college in 1926; and again as a senior college in 1931, returning to co-educational status. Samuel Huston College was organized by the Rev. George Warren Richardson on February 22, 1876, at Dallas, Texas, and held its first classes in St. Paul Methodist Episcopal Church. The school was adopted by the Methodist Episcopal Church as the educational institution of the West Texas Conference and known as Andrews Normal College, although actually named West Texas Conference School in 1878. It moved to Austin in 1890 and in 1900 began operations as Samuel Huston College. Named after Mr. Samuel Huston, a farmer from Marengo, Iowa, Mr. Huston gave $9,000 for the erection of Lovinggood Hall its first building.

Master Key: *First, do more than you are paid for, before expecting to be paid for more than you do. Murdock*

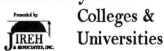
JACKSON STATE UNIVERSITY

JACKSON, MS

Web Site:
www.jsums.edu

SCHOOL INFO

Established in 1877. 4-year public coed university on urban campus in small capital city of Jackson. 190 miles west of New Orleans.

ACCREDITATON:
Southern Association of Colleges & Schools

CAMPUS ENROLLMENT:
Undergraduate: 5456 men & women. **Graduate:** 857 men & women. **Transfer students:** 142 men & women. **Freshman ethnic enrollment:** Native American-3, African American-1571, Asian-8, Caucasian-61, Hispanic-2, Other-13

WHAT DO I NEED?

Academic record, residency and test scores considered important. ACT/ SAT (ACT preferred); scores by August 1. No fee; no closing date and priority given to applications received by August 15; notifications on a rolling basis beginning about January 1. Music applicants must audition. Deferred and early admission program available.

UNIQUE PROGRAMS

The following programs are available: cooperative education, double major, education specialist degree, honors program, independent study, internships, teacher preparation, visiting/exchange student program, weekend college, cross-registration; combined bachelor's graduate program in business administration.

ACADEMIC REQUIREMENTS

Freshmen must maintain a minimum 2.0 and majors must be declared by end of second year.

Core curriculum: English, history, mathematics, biological/physical sciences, social sciences. Bachelor's: 128 (30 in major).

STUDENT SERVICES

Campus student services include: academic center, aptitude testing, campus daycare, career and personal counseling, employment svcs for undergraduates, freshmen orientation, health svcs, placement services, preadmission summer program, reduced course load program, remedial instruction, tutoring, services for handicapped, veterans counselor. ROTC: Army.

ADDRESS:

JACKSON STATE UNIVERSITY
1400 J.R. LYNCH ST.
JACKSON,   MS   39216
Principal Official: Dr. James E. Lyons, Sr.

TYPES OF DEGREES AWARDED:
BA, BS, MA, MS, MBA, EdD, EdS, PhD.

ACADEMIC CALENDAR:
Semester. Summer sessions.

CONTACT INFORMATION

Admissions Officer: Dr. Gene Blakley
Phone: (601) 968-2100   **Fax:** (601) 973-3445
Web Site: www.jsums.edu

DOLLARS AND SENSE

TUITION & FEES:	$6,168.00
ROOM & BOARD:	$0.00
BOOKS & SUPPLIES:	$700.00
OTHER EXPENSES:	$200.00
OUT OF STATE TUITION:	$9,146.00
*ANNUAL TOTAL:	$7,068.00

(*Annual Total does not include out-of-state tuition .)

FINANCIAL AID

Financial Aid Phone: (601)968-2227
Financial Aid Fax: (601)968-2237

No application closing date; priority to applications received by April 14, notifications on a rolling basis beginning about July 1; must reply within 30 days. FAFSA accepted. Pell grants, loans, jobs available. Academic, leadership, music/drama, athletic, alumni affiliation, state/district residency, minority scholarships available.

SPORTS

Varsity Sports: Baseball, basketball, cross-country, football, golf, rifle, tennis, track and field, volleyball. NCAA.

WHAT MAJOR?

Bachelor's: Accounting, atmospheric sciences and meteorology, banking and finance, biology, business administration, business economics, business management, chemistry, city/community/regional planning, communications, computer programming, computer technology, criminal justice studies,data processing, dramatic arts, economics, education, education of the emotionallly handicapped/exceptional children/the deaf & hearing impaired/gifted and talented/mentally handicapped/visually handicapped/physically handicapped, electronic technology, English, English literature, health education, health sciences, history, human and animal pathology, industrial technology, information sciences and systems, journalism, law enforcement and corrections, marine biology, marketing and distribution, mathematics, music, music performance, nursing, office supervision and management, pharmacy, physical education, physics, political science and government, predentistry, preelementary education, prelaw, premedicine, prepharmacy, preveterinary, psychology, public relations, radio/television and technology, remedial education, school psychology, secondary education, secretarial and related programs, social science education, social sciences, social work, sociology, Spanish, special education, speech correction, speech/debate/forensics, urban studies.

Historical & Special Interest:
Jackson State University was founded by the American Baptist Home Mission Society in 1877 in Natchez, Mississippi. Dr. Charles Ayer of New York opened the school on October 23, 1877 with twenty students and it operated as a private church school for 63 years. The school prospered in Natchez until November 1882 when the Society moved it to Jackson, a more central location in the state.

After the American Baptist Home Mission Society withdrew its support from the University in 1934, it became apparent that state support would be needed if the school were to continue. Dr. Jacob L. Redix was elected president in 1940 as the first president under state control. The state assumed support for the specific purpose of training rural and elementary teachers, thus the curriculum was reorganized and subsequently two years of college work were offered. The curriculum was raised by the Board of Trustees in 1942 to a full four-year teacher education program, leading to a B.S. in Education.

Master Key: *Never complain about what you permit. Murdock*

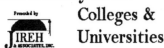
JARVIS CHRISTIAN COLLEGE

HAWKINS, TX

Web Site:
Not provided.

SCHOOL INFO

Established in 1912. 4-year private liberal arts coed college with Christian (Disciples of Christ) affiliation on rural campus in rural community; 100 miles east of Dallas.

ACCREDITATON:
Southern Association of Colleges & Schools

CAMPUS ENROLLMENT:
Undergraduate: Full-time: 261 men and 286 women. Part-time: 5 men and 3 women.

ADDRESS:

JARVIS CHRISTIAN COLLEGE
Highway 80 East
HAWKINS,   TX   75765
Principal Official: Dr. Sebetha Jenkins

TYPES OF DEGREES AWARDED:
BA, BS.

ACADEMIC CALENDAR:
Semester. Summer sessions limited.

CONTACT INFORMATION

Admissions Officer: Linda Rutherford
Phone: (903) 769-5733   **Fax:** (903) 769-4842
Web Site: Not provided.

WHAT DO I NEED?

Academic record, alumni relation, test scores school or community activities, recommendations, religious affiliation or commitment, and interview considered. SAT or ACT (ACT preferred) scores by August 15. Application fee $15. No closing date; notifications on a rolling basis beginning around January 25; must reply by August 15. Interview recommended. Deferred admission program available.

UNIQUE PROGRAMS

The following programs are available: cooperative education, double major, honors program, independent study, study abroad, teacher preparation, combined bachelor's/graduate program in law.

ACADEMIC REQUIREMENTS

Freshmen must earn a minimum 1.5 and majors must be declared by end of second year.

Core curriculum: arts/fine arts, English, history, humanities, mathematics, philosophy/religion, biological/physical sciences, social sciences. Bachelor's: 124 hrs (30 in major).

DOLLARS AND SENSE

TUITION & FEES:	$6,694.00
ROOM & BOARD:	$3,485.00
BOOKS & SUPPLIES:	$500.00
OTHER EXPENSES:	
OUT OF STATE TUITION:	
*ANNUAL TOTAL:	$10,679.00

(*Annual Total does not include out-of-state tuition .)

FINANCIAL AID

Financial Aid Phone: (800) 292-9517
Financial Aid Fax: (903) 769-4842

No closing date; priority given to applications received by June 1; notifications on a rolling basis; must reply within 2 weeks. FAFSA accepted. Music/drama, state/district residency, leadership, religious affiliation scholarships available.

STUDENT SERVICES

Campus student services include: academic center, aptitude testing, career and persoanl counseling, freshman orientation, health services, campus daycare, placement service for graduates, preadmission summer program, reduced course load program, remedial instruction, special counselor, tutoring, services for handicapped.

SPORTS

Varsity Sports: Baseball, basketball, softball, track and field, and volleyball. NAIA.

WHAT MAJOR?

Bachelor's: Biology, business administration, chemistry, communications, education, English, generic special education, history, human performance, interdisciplinary studies in education, mathematics, music, reading, religion, sociology. **Minors:** Accounting, art, biology, business administration, chemistry, computer science, computer management information systems, criminal justice, English, generic special education, history, human performance, management, marketing, mathematics, music, political science, psychology, reading religion, sociology, speech.

Historical & Special Interest:

Jarvis Christian College was founded in 1912 by Major and Mrs. Ida Van Zandt Jarvis, two early philanthropists for whom the school was named. Today Jarvis Christian College is a fully accredited, independent, co-educational, church-related college, with 650 students.

Though it is characterized as a Historically Black College, the student population is diverse, serving Black, white and Hispanic students from across the country. Jarvis Christian College offers sixteen majors/specializations within four academic divisions: Business Administration, Education, Science and Mathematics, and Humanities and Social Science.

Jarvis Christian College is a UNCF school.

Master Key: *Present neglect make future regret.*

HBCU Third Edition
© Jireh & Associates, Inc.
Wilmington, DE

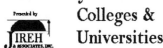
JOHNSON C. SMITH UNIV.

CHARLOTTE, NC

Web Site:
www.jcsu.edu

SCHOOL INFO

Established in 1867. 4-year private (formerly affiliated with Presbyterian Church), coed liberal arts college located in the largest city in the Carolinas on 100 acres.

ACCREDITATON:
Southern Association of Colleges & Schools

CAMPUS ENROLLMENT:
Undergraduate: 584 men & 843 women. **Transfer students:** 34 men & women. **Freshman ethnic enrollment:** Not available

WHAT DO I NEED?

Completion of accredited high school, extra curricular, AP & honors courses and GPA important. College preparatory program. Scores by August 1. ACT or SAT required. Application fee: $20 which may be waived based on need. Closing date June 15 and notifications on a rolling basis. If accepted, a $100 nonref. matriculation fee and $100 nonref. room reservation fee is required to reserve place.

UNIQUE PROGRAMS

The following programs are available: Teaching & Learning center, accelerated program, cooperative education, double major, honors program, internships, international studies, weekend college program, visiting/exchange student program, cross-registration; liberal/arts career combination in engineering.

ACADEMIC REQUIREMENTS

Freshmen must earn at least 122 hours with a minimum 2.0 GPA.

Core curriculum: art/fine arts, English, foreign languages, history, mathematics, biological/physical sciences, philosophy/religion, social sciences. Bachelor's: 122 hrs (30 in major).

STUDENT SERVICES

Campus student services include: academic center, aptitude testing, campus daycare, career and personal counseling, employment service for undergraduates, freshmen orientation, freshman mentoring program, health services, placement services, reduced course load program, special counselor, tutoring. ROTC: Air Force.

WHAT MAJOR?

Bachelor's: Biology, business administration, chemistry, communication arts, computer engineering and computer sciences, elementary education, English, English education, health education, history, applied mathematics, mathematics/physics, mathematics education, music business management, music education, physical education, political sciences, psychology, secondary education, social science education, social sciences, social work, sociology. **Preprofessional programs:** dentistry, law, medicine, pharmacy.

Historical & Special Interest:

Johnson C. Smith University was established in 1867 as a college for Negroes. It is a small coed university situated on 85 acres under private control and affiliated with the Presbyterian Church.

The University has developed Centers of Excellence in International Studies, Liberal Studies, Honors College, Banking and Finance, Education and Mathematics and Sciences --the first of its kind on any historically Black college campus.

Johnson C. Smith University is a UNCF school.

ADDRESS:

JOHNSON C. SMITH UNIV.
100 BEATIES FORD RD.
CHARLOTTE, NC 28216
Principal Official: Dr. Dorothy Cowser Yancy

TYPES OF DEGREES AWARDED:
BA, BS.

ACADEMIC CALENDAR:
Semester . Summer sessions limited.

CONTACT INFORMATION

Admissions Officer: Jean Frye
Phone: (704) 378-1011 **Fax:** (704) 378-1242
Web Site: www.jcsu.edu

DOLLARS AND SENSE

TUITION & FEES:	$6,713.00
ROOM & BOARD:	$3,253.00
BOOKS & SUPPLIES:	$638.00
OTHER EXPENSES:	$938.00
OUT OF STATE TUITION:	
*ANNUAL TOTAL:	$11,542.00

(*Annual Total does not include out-of-state tuition .)

FINANCIAL AID

Financial Aid Phone: (800) 782-7503
Financial Aid Fax:

Closing date May 1; notifications on a rolling basis beginning about May 15; must reply within 2 weeks. FAFSA accepted. Federal Pell grants, loans, jobs available. Academic, athletic, music/drama, minority scholarships available.

SPORTS

Varsity Sports: Basketball, golf, football, softball, tennis, track and field, volleyball. NCAA.

HBCU Third Edition
© Jireh & Associates, Inc.
Wilmington, DE

KENNEDY-KING COLLEGE

CHICAGO, L

Web Site:
Not provided.

SCHOOL INFO

Founded in 1935 as a junior college. It is one of seven schools in the City Colleges of Chicago System.

ACCREDITATON:
North Central Association of Colleges & Schools

CAMPUS ENROLLMENT:
Undergraduate: 2,620 Total. **Transfer Students:** 43 Total.

WHAT DO I NEED?

Open admissions; no application fee; CCC College Placement Examination; Applicants notified on a rolling basis.

UNIQUE PROGRAMS

Honors programs; independent studies; internships and weekend classes.

ACADEMIC REQUIREMENTS

Minimum GPA 2.0 and major must be declared at registration.

Associate Degrees: 60-64 credit hrs. (42 hrs. Gen. Ed for AA & AS; 15 hrs. Gen Ed. AAS).

STUDENT SERVICES

Academic advising, Office of Academic Resources and Services; Career Center, Child Care Center, University Transfer Ctr., College Bookstore, Disabled Student Services, Job Placement, Student Activities, Veterans Affairs, Counseling, Library.

ADDRESS:

KENNEDY-KING COLLEGE
6800 S. WENTWORTH AVE.
CHICAGO,   IL   60621-3798
Principal Official: Dr. Wayne D. Watson

TYPES OF DEGREES AWARDED:
AA, AAS, AS; Advanced and Basic Certificates.

ACADEMIC CALENDAR:
Semester (Fall, Spring & Summer).

CONTACT INFORMATION

Admissions Officer: Welton T. Murphy
Phone: (773) 602-5000   **Fax:** (773) 602-5247
Web Site: Not provided.

DOLLARS AND SENSE

TUITION & FEES:	$1,285.00
ROOM & BOARD:	$0.00
BOOKS & SUPPLIES:	$150.00
OTHER EXPENSES:	$150.00
OUT OF STATE TUITION:	$5,990.20
*ANNUAL TOTAL:	$1,585.00

(*Annual Total does not include out-of-state tuition .)

FINANCIAL AID

Financial Aid Phone: (773) 602-5133
Financial Aid Fax: (773) 602-5247
FAFSA accepted. Pell Grant (BEOG, SEOG), Federal Work Study, Illinois Student Assistance Commission Monetary Award; Veteran's Educational Benefits.

Scholarships Available: City Colleges of Chicago "Harold Washington Scholarship" (Academic), and Athletic scholarships.

SPORTS

Intercollegiate: Men's Basketball. Intramural: Basketball, softball, volleyball, and swimming; NJCAA.

WHAT MAJOR?

Associate Arts: African American Studies, Art, Business Administration, English, History, Humanities, Journalism, Literature, Law, Physical Education, Political Science, Psychology, Social Work, Sociology, Speech & Drama, Teaching.

Associate Science: Biological and Biomedical Sciences, Health Sciences, Pharmacy, Chemistry, Physics, and Mathematics.

Associate Applied Science: Accounting, Computer Information Systems, Merchandising and Marketing, Mid-Management, Office Information Systems, Radio/TV Broadcasting, Theater Technology, Air Conditioning, Automotive Technology, Graphic Communications, Dental Hygiene, Nursing, Child Development/Social Services, Mental Health.

Historical & Special Interest:

Kennedy-King College, formerly known as Woodrow Wilson Junior College, was established in the Fall of 1935 at 6800 South Stewart St. as one of three colleges in the Junior College System of the City of Chicago operated by the Chicago Board of Education. In 1969 the name was officially changed from Woodrow-Wilson Junior College to Kennedy-King College in honor of Robert F. Kennedy and Rev. Dr. Martin Luther King, Jr. Its mission is to provide affordable, high-quality, comprehensive education and training opportunities to Chicago residents.

Master Key: *The best portion of a good man's life —his little nameless, unremembered acts of kindness and of love.*
William Wadsworth

HBCU Third Edition
© Jireh & Associates, Inc.
Wilmington, DE

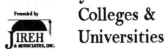

Historically Black Colleges & Universities

KENTUCKY STATE UNIVERSITY

FRANKFORT, KY

Web Site:
www.kysu.edu

SCHOOL INFO

Established in 1886. 4-year public university on urban campus in a large town; 50 miles east of Louisville.

ACCREDITATON:
Southern Association of Colleges & Schools

CAMPUS ENROLLMENT:
Undergraduate: 2465 men & women. Graduate: 75 men & women. Transfer students: 177 men & women. Freshman ethnic enrollment: Not available.

WHAT DO I NEED?

Open admissions to associate degree program. High school GPA and test scores important. ACT only. *Special requirements for out-of-state applicants. College Prep. program; scores by July 15. No application fee; no closing date; notifications on rolling basis. *Special requirements for Whitney College of Leadership studies applicants. Interview recommended for nursing. Early admission program available.

UNIQUE PROGRAMS

The following programs are available: cooperative education, double major, dual enrollment of high school students, internships, study abroad, student-designed major, teacher prep., visiting/exchange program, weekend college; liberal arts/career combination in engineering, health sciences.

ACADEMIC REQUIREMENTS

Minimum GPA for freshmen unreported and major must be declared by end of second year.

Core curriculum: Arts/fine arts, English, foreign languages, history, humanities, mathematics, philosophy/religion, biological/physical sciences, social sciences. Associate: 64 hours. Bachelor's: 128 hours (30 in major).

STUDENT SERVICES

Campus student services include: aptitude testing, campus daycare, career and personal counseling, communication skills center and student support services, employment services, freshman orientation, health services, marriage and family counseling, placement services, preadmission summer program, reduced course load program, remedial instruction, special counselor, special advisor for adult students, services for handicapped, tutoring, veterans counselor. ROTC: Air Force, Army.

WHAT MAJOR?

Associate: Child development and family relations, child development/care/guidance, computer and information sciences, criminal justice studies, drafting, drafting and design technology, electronic technology, food service management, liberal/general studies, nursing, office supervision and management.

Bachelor's: Applied mathematics, art education, biology, business administration, chemistry, child development/care/guidance, clothing and textiles management/production/services, computer sciences, criminal justice studies, elementary education, English, history, liberal/general studies, mathematics, medical technology, microcomputer software, music and music education, music performance, physical education, political science and government, preelementary education, social work, sociology, studio art, textiles and clothing.

Historical & Special Interest:

Kentucky State University is one of two 1890 land-grant institutions in Kentucky chartered in 1886 as the State Normal School for Colored Persons. The second state-supported institution of higher learning in Kentucky established during the centennial year. The new School was unanimously selected to be located in the town of Frankfort and with a donation from the city of $1,500 a site on a scenic bluff overlooking the town was purchased. The school opened on October 11, 1887 with three teachers and 55 students.

The School graduated its first graduating class of five students in the spring of 1890. A high school was organized in 1893. In 1903, the name was changed to Kentucky Normal and Industrial Institute for Colored Persons. The name was changed again in 1926 to Kentucky State Industrial College for Colored Persons. The high school was discontinued and the name was changed again in 1938 to Kentucky State College for Negroes. The term "for Negroes" was dropped in 1952. Whitney M. Young, Jr. College of Leadership Studies, Liberal studies Great Books Program where students study classic works of literature, history, philosophy, mathematics and science.

ADDRESS:

KENTUCKY STATE UNIVERSITY
EAST MAIN STREET
FRANKFORT,   KY   40601
Principal Official: Dr. George Reid

TYPES OF DEGREES AWARDED:
AA, AS,BA, BS, M.

ACADEMIC CALENDAR:
Semester. Summer sessions limited.

CONTACT INFORMATION

Admissions Officer: Laronistine Dyson
Phone: (502) 227-6813   **Fax:** (502) 227-5950
Web Site: www.kysu.edu

DOLLARS AND SENSE

TUITION & FEES:	$2,120.00
ROOM & BOARD:	$3,700.00
BOOKS & SUPPLIES:	$1,080.00
OTHER EXPENSES:	$120.00
OUT OF STATE TUITION:	$6,090.00
*ANNUAL TOTAL:	$7,020.00

(*Annual Total does not include out-of-state tuition .)

FINANCIAL AID

Financial Aid Phone: (502)227-5968
Financial Aid Fax: (502)227-5950

Application closing date April 15, priority given to applications received by March15. FAFSA accepted. Notifications on a rolling basis beginning July 1. Reply within 2 weeks. Pell grants, loans, and jobs available and based on need. FAF required for Grant-in-Aid scholarships. Academic, music/drama, art, athletic, leadership scholarships available.

SPORTS

Varsity Sports: Baseball, basketball, cross-country, football, golf, softball, tennis, track and field, volleyball (W). NCAA.

Master Key: *Find out what you like doing best and get someone to pay you for doing it. Katherine Whitehorn*

HBCU Third Edition
© Jireh & Associates, Inc.
Wilmington, DE

Historically Black Colleges & Universities

Presented by JIREH & ASSOCIATES, INC.

KNOXVILLE COLLEGE
KNOXVILLE, TN
Web Site:
www.falcon.nest.kxcol.edu

SCHOOL INFO
Established in 1875. 4-year private liberal arts, coed college. Affiliation with Presbyterian Church (USA) on 39-acre urban campus in Knoxville.

ADDRESS:

KNOXVILLE COLLEGE
901 COLLEGE STREET
KNOXVILLE,   TN   37921
Principal Official: Dr. Barbara Hatton

TYPES OF DEGREES AWARDED:
AA, BA, BS.

ACADEMIC CALENDAR:
Semester (August - May)

CONTACT INFORMATION

Admissions Officer: J. Harver GIllespie
Phone: (423) 524-6525   **Fax:** (423) 524-6686
Web Site: www.falcon.nest.kxcol.edu

ACCREDITATON:
Southern Association of Colleges & Schools

CAMPUS ENROLLMENT:
Undergraduate: 914 men & women. **Transfer students:** 62 men & women. **Freshman ethnic enrollment: Not available.**

WHAT DO I NEED?
High school GPA 2.0, test scores, recommendations, extra-curricular activities important. College preparatory program. SAT or ACT scores by September 1. Application fee $20 may be waived based on need. No closing date; notifications on a rolling basis beginning around January 2. Audition required for music applicants. Deferred admission program available.

UNIQUE PROGRAMS
Knoxville offers a strong foundation in the liberal arts and a variety of major programs preparing students for careers or for post graduate or professional study in the following areas: Arts & Humanities, Business & Social Sciences, Educational, Natural Sciences & Mathematics. Others include: cooperative education, cross-registration, double major, independent study, internships.

ACADEMIC REQUIREMENTS
Freshmen students expected to maintain a 1.5 GPA and majors must be declared by end of second year.

Successful completion of Senior Comp. Exam; and proficiency in English, reading & basic mathematics. Core curriculum: Arts/fine arts, computer science, English, history, humanities, mathematics, philosophy/religion, sciences physical and social. Bachelor's: 124 hrs (45 in major) Associate's: 65.

DOLLARS AND SENSE

TUITION & FEES:	$5,320.00
ROOM & BOARD:	$0.00
BOOKS & SUPPLIES:	$600.00
OTHER EXPENSES:	$120.00
OUT OF STATE TUITION:	
*ANNUAL TOTAL:	$6,040.00

(*Annual Total does not include out-of-state tuition .)

FINANCIAL AID

Financial Aid Phone: (423) 524-6681
Financial Aid Fax:

No closing date; notifications on a rolling basis. FAFSA accepted. Pell grants (Knoxville College Grant), loans, jobs based on need. Academic, music/drama scholarships available.

STUDENT SERVICES
The college provides developmental educational programs. Campus student services include: career and personal counseling, co-curricular services, employment services for undergraduates, freshman orientation, health services, placement services, remedial instruction, special counselor, tutoring, veterans counselor. ROTC: Air Force, Army.

SPORTS
Varsity Sports: Basketball, baseball, football, tennis, volleyball. NCAA.

WHAT MAJOR?
Associate: Medical assistant, pre-health biology, pre-physical therapy, general program at Morristown Campus; secretarial and office administration.

Bachelor's: Accounting, allied health, biological and physical sciences, biology, botany, business, business economics, chemistry, communications, computer science, economics, education, elementary education, English, English, health administration, history, hotel/motel and restaurant management, humanities and social sciences, junior high education, liberal/general studies, mathematics, medical technology, music, physical education physical sciences, physics, political science, prelaw, psychology, recreation and community services technologies, secondary education, sociology, teacher education, zoology.

Historical & Special Interest:

The main campus of Knoxville College is located in Knoxville, Tennessee, an important industrial, technological, educational and cultural center. The second campus is located in Morristown, Tennessee.

Knoxville College was founded in 1875 as part of the missionary effort of the United Presbyterian Church of North America to promote religious, moral, and educational leadership among the freedmen. Its student body and faculty is multi-racial although predominantly Black.

Knoxville College is a UNCF school

Master Key: *96% of the people hired are hired based on appearance. Murdock*

HBCU Third Edition
© Jireh & Associates, Inc.
Wilmington, DE

LANE COLLEGE
JACKSON, TN

Web Site:
www.lane-college.edu

SCHOOL INFO

Established in 1882. 4-year private liberal arts, coed college. Affiliation with Christian Methodist Episcopal Church on suburban campus in northeast Jackson.

ADDRESS:

LANE COLLEGE
501 LANE AVENUE
JACKSON,   TN   38301
Principal Official: Dr. Wesley C. McClure

TYPES OF DEGREES AWARDED:
BA, BS.

ACADEMIC CALENDAR:
Semester.

CONTACT INFORMATION

Admissions Officer: Evelyn Brown
Phone: (901) 426-7532   **Fax:** (901) 426-7594
Web Site: www.lane-college.edu

ACCREDITATON:
Southern Association of Colleges & Schools

CAMPUS ENROLLMENT:
Undergraduate: 534 men & women. **Transfer students:** 27 men & women. **Freshman ethnic enrollment:** African American-134.

WHAT DO I NEED?

Non-refundable application fee of $25. Academic achievement record, test scores, recommendations, school activities. An applicant must be at least 16 and a graduate of an accredited or approved high school. ACT/SAT (ACT preferred). Test scores by July 15. Applicants not meeting the qualifications will be considered if there is evidence of seriousness and ability to do college-level work.

DOLLARS AND SENSE

TUITION & FEES:	$4,796.00
ROOM & BOARD:	$3,200.00
BOOKS & SUPPLIES:	$400.00
OTHER EXPENSES:	$400.00
OUT OF STATE TUITION:	
*ANNUAL TOTAL:	$8,796.00

(*Annual Total does not include out-of-state tuition .)

UNIQUE PROGRAMS

The following programs are available: and services for students to complete their academic studies and preparations; center for academic skills development; Communication Arts Laboratory; Cooperative program, Educational and Curriculum Computer Laboratory, honors program, internships, special services program helps to increase the retention of students at the college through tutoring, transfer program.

ACADEMIC REQUIREMENTS

Every student is expected to receive a passing grade in at least 14 hours during the first year of enrollment. A minimum of 1.25 GPA. Majors must be declare by end of second year.

Core curriculum: Arts, computer science, English, foreign languages, history, humanities, mathematics, philosophy/religion, biological/physical sciences, social sciences. Bachelor's: 124 hours (35 in major).

FINANCIAL AID

Financial Aid Phone: (901) 426-7537
Financial Aid Fax: (901) 426-7652

A variety of federal, state, and institutional aid is available to students as well as academic scholarships unique to Lane College and the UNCF. FAFSA accepted.

STUDENT SERVICES

Campus student services include: career and personal counseling, community referral services, employment services for undergraduates, freshman orientation, health services, placement services, remedial instruction, special counselor, tutoring, veterans counselor.

SPORTS

Varsity Sports: Basketball, baseball, cross-country, football, tennis, track. NCAA.

WHAT MAJOR?

Bachelor's: Art, accounting, business administration, business general, communication arts, chemistry, computer science, economics, elementary/secondary education, English, engineering, French, geography, health/physical education and recreation, history, mathematics, physics, religion, sociology, Spanish, speech and drama.

Historical & Special Interest:

In 1882, Lane College was founded as the C.M.E. High School by the Colored Methodist Episcopal Church in America. Plans and efforts to establish the school began as early as 1878 but the great epidemic of 1878 handicapped the efforts. Bishop Isaac Lane came to take charge of the Tennessee Conference as presiding bishop. He met with the committee, gave advice, and helped formulate plans for the founding of the school. On January 1, 1880, four acres were purchased for $240.

The school began its first session in November, 1882 with Miss Jennie E. Lane as teacher and January of the next year, Professor J.H. Harper of Jackson, Tennessee, took over the work and carried out the expired term. Under his leadership, the school was chartered under the law of the State of Tennessee and the name was changed to Lane Institute.

In 1887, Reverend T. F. Saunders, a member of the Memphis Conference of the M.E. Church, South, was appointed the first president and made numerous contributions to the institute and to the youth enrolled there. A college department was organized in 1896 and the name of the school was changed from Lane Institute to Lane College. From 1903 to 1907, Reverend J. A. Bray was elected president after which Dr. J.F. Lane, son of the founder, was elected president and served for thirty-seven years. Lane College is a UNCF school.

Master Key: *Gambling: The sure way of getting nothing for something. Wilson Mizner*

HBCU Third Edition
© Jireh & Associates, Inc.
Wilmington, DE

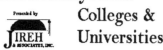
LANGSTON UNIVERSITY
LANGSTON, OK

Web Site:
www.lunet.edu

SCHOOL INFO

Established in 1897. 4-year public liberal arts, coed teacher's college on rural campus in rural community; 18 miles east of Dayton, Ohio.

ADDRESS:

LANGSTON UNIVERSITY
P.O. BOX 907
LANGSTON,   OK   73050
Principal Official: Dr. Ernest L. Holloway

TYPES OF DEGREES AWARDED:
BA, BS, MA.

ACADEMIC CALENDAR:
Semester. Summer sessions limited.

CONTACT INFORMATION

Admissions Officer: Willy Anderson
Phone: (888) 370-1897   **Fax:** (405) 466-2966
Web Site: www.lunet.edu

ACCREDITATON:
North Central Association of Colleges & Schools

CAMPUS ENROLLMENT:
Undergraduate: Full-time: 2765 men and women.

WHAT DO I NEED?

High school GPA (2.8 minimum), and test scores. College preparatory program. Minimum ACT composite: 16. SAT or ACT (ACT preferred); scores by September 9; priority date for scores: March 1. No fee. No closing date; priority given to applications received by March 1; notifications on a rolling basis. Audition recommended for music applicants. Early admissions programs available.

DOLLARS AND SENSE

TUITION & FEES:	$4,910.00
ROOM & BOARD:	$3,000.00
BOOKS & SUPPLIES:	$600.00
OTHER EXPENSES:	$0.00
OUT OF STATE TUITION:	$2,100.00
*ANNUAL TOTAL:	$8,510.00

(*Annual Total does not include out-of-state tuition .)

UNIQUE PROGRAMS

The following programs are available: cooperative education,dual enrollment, honors program, internships, liberal arts/career combination in health sciences.

ACADEMIC REQUIREMENTS

Freshmen must earn a minimum 2.0 and majors must be declared by end of first year.

Core curriculum: English, history, mathematics, biological/physical sciences, social sciences. Bachelor's: 124 hrs (30 in major).

FINANCIAL AID

Financial Aid Phone: (405) 466-3282
Financial Aid Fax: (405) 466-2986

No closing date; priority given to applications received by March 1; notifications on a rolling basis beginning about April 15. FAFSA accepted. All jobs based on need. Academic, music/drama, athletic, state/district residency, leadership, alumni affiliation and minority scholarships available.

STUDENT SERVICES

Campus student services include: academic center, career and personal counseling, employment service for undergraduates, health services, mathematics and writing labs, placement services, reduced course load program, remedial instruction, special counselor, tutoring. ROTC: Air Force, Army.

SPORTS

Varsity Sports: Baseball, basketball, football, track and field. NAIA.

WHAT MAJOR?

Bachelor's: Accounting, agricultural business and management, agricultural economics, agricultural sciences, animal sciences, biology, business administration, business education, chemistry, communications, computer sciences, economics, education, elementary education, English, environmental science, food sciences and human nutrition, geography, gerontology, health care administration, history, home economics, home economics education, hotel/motel and restaurant management, individual and family development, law enforcement and corrections, mathematics,mathematics education, music, music education, music performance, nursing, personnel management, physical education, physical sciences, physical therapy, premedicine, preveterinary, psychology, radio/television, radio/television technology, secondary education, secretarial and related programs, social sciences, social studies education, sociology, special education, textiles and clothing, urban studies, zoology.

Historical & Special Interest:

Langston University was established March 12, 1897 and is Oklahoma's only historically Black college. The University is an integral part of the Oklahoma State System for Higher Education and offers graduate programs in Teaching English as a Second Language, Bilingual/Multicultural Education, Elementary Education and Urban Education. It is both a land-grant and urban institution with centers in Oklahoma City and Tulsa. Langston has over 2,000 students from 27 states and 18 foreign countries studying on three campuses. The institution was expanded in 1978 as part of the "Urban Mission" which developed an Urban Center in both Oklahoma City and Tulsa.

The unique 1984 established, American Institute for Goat Research continues to attract national and international research scientists.

Master Key: *He who spends before he strives will surely beg before he dies.*

HBCU Third Edition
© Jireh & Associates, Inc.
Wilmington, DE

JIREH
& ASSOCIATES, INC.

LAWSON STATE COMM. COLLEGE
BIRMINGHAM, AL

SCHOOL INFO

Established in 1965. 2-year public community college, coed. Suburban campus in large city of Birmingham.

ACCREDITATON:
Southern Association of Colleges & Schools

CAMPUS ENROLLMENT:
Undergraduate: Approximately 2041 men & women. **Transfer students:** 93 men & women. **Freshman ethnic enrollment:** African American-833, Caucasian-37

WHAT DO I NEED?

Open admissions. Advanced placement option for licensed practical nurses (LPN) and nursing education. Application fee $10. No closing date; notifications on a rolling basis. Deferred and early admissions program available.

UNIQUE PROGRAMS

The following programs are available: double major, student-designed major, 2-year transfer program, 2-year degree allied health program available requiring 1 year study at University of Alabama at Birmingham.

ACADEMIC REQUIREMENTS

Minimum GPA for freshmen is 1.5 and majors must be declared on application.

Associate: 96 hours (72 in major). Core curriculum: English and mathematics.

STUDENT SERVICES

Campus student services include: career and personal counseling, employment service for undergraduates, health services, placement services, learning center, reduced course load program, remedial instruction, special counselor, tutoring verterans counselor, services for handicapped.

WHAT MAJOR?

Associate: Accounting, allied health, business administration, business and office, business data processing, business education, criminal justice studies, data processing technology, drafting, education, electrical and electronics equipment repair, electrical installation, electrodiagnostic technologies, engineering and engineering-related technologies, English, English education, food production/management/services, history, industrial equipment maintenance and repair, law enforcement and corrections technologies, legal secretary, liberal/general studies, library assistant, mathematics, mathematics education, medical assistant, medical laboratory technologies, medical records technology, medical secretary, microcomputer software, music education, nursing, occupational therapy assistant, personal services, physical education, physical therapy assistant, pre-dentistry, pre-law, pre-medicine, pre-pharmacy, pyschology, radiograph medical technology, recreation and community services technologies, respiratory therapy technology, science education, science technologies, secretarial and related programs, social sciences, sociology, teacher aide.

Historical & Special Interest:

Lawson State Community College is the first and only state-supported, two-year, predominantly Black institution in central Alabama. Lawson serves the needs of its highly industrialized community which is mostly low-income students. It has an Academic Division offers A.A., A.S. or A.A.S. and Technical Division offering certificates in 15 programs.

ADDRESS:

LAWSON STATE COMM. COLLEGE
3060 WILSON RD. S.W.
BIRMINGHAM,   AL   35221
Principal Official: Dr. Perry W. Ward

TYPES OF DEGREES AWARDED:
A, F.

ACADEMIC CALENDAR:
Quarter . Summer sessions limited.

CONTACT INFORMATION

Admissions Officer: Ms. Myra Davis, Registrar
Phone: (205) 925-2515   **Fax:** (205) 929-6316
Web Site: http://web.fie.com/web/mol/fice/001059/

DOLLARS AND SENSE

TUITION & FEES:	$1,134.00
ROOM & BOARD:	$0.00
BOOKS & SUPPLIES:	$400.00
OTHER EXPENSES:	$725.00
OUT OF STATE TUITION:	$668.00
*ANNUAL TOTAL:	$2,259.00

(*Annual Total does not include out-of-state tuition .)

FINANCIAL AID

Financial Aid Phone:
Financial Aid Fax:
No closing date for aid applications, notifications on a rolling basis beginning around August 1; must reply within 2 weeks. FAFSA accepted. Pell grants, loans, jobs available. Athletic scholarships available.

SPORTS

Varsity Sports: Basketball, track and field, volleyball. Intramural Sports: Baseball, tennis. NJCAA.

Master Key: *Information breeds confidence.*

LEMOYNE-OWEN COLLEGE

MEMPHIS,   TN

Web Site:
www.mecca.org/LOC/page/LOC.ht

SCHOOL INFO

Established in 1862. 4-year private liberal arts, coed college. Affiliated with United Church of Christ on urban campus in very large city; approximately 200 miles from Nashville.

ACCREDITATON:
Southern Association of Colleges & Schools

CAMPUS ENROLLMENT:
Undergraduate: 1200 men & women. **Graduate:** 150 men & women. **Transfer students:** 105 men & women .**Freshman ethnic enrollment :** Not available.

WHAT DO I NEED?

High school achievement record, test scores, interview, letter of recommendation. Consideration to alumni children. College preparatory program. SAT or ACT (ACT preferred) scores by July 30. Application fee $25 may be waived based on need. Closing date August 15; notifications on a rolling basis; replies with 2 weeks. Interview required. Deferred admission program available.

UNIQUE PROGRAMS

The following programs are available: cooperative education, cross-registration, double major, honors program, independent study, internships, student-designed major, study abroad, teacher preparation; liberal arts/career combination in engineering. **Special Facilities:** Art Gallery

ACADEMIC REQUIREMENTS

Freshmen must earn a minimum 2.0 and majors must be declared by end of second year.

Core curriculum: arts/fine arts, computer science, English, history, mathematics, philosophy/religion, biological/physical sciences, social sciences. Bachelor's: 130 hrs.

STUDENT SERVICES

Campus student services include: academic center, aptitude testing, career and personal counseling, employment service for undergraduates, health services, placement services, pre-admission summer program, remedial instruction, special counselor, tutoring, veterans counselor. ROTC: Air Force, Army.

WHAT MAJOR?

Bachelor's: Accounting, biochemistry, biological and physical sciences, biology, business and management, chemistry, computer and information sciences, computer programming, economics, engineering, English, health/physical education/recreation, history, humanities and social sciences, mathematics, political science and government, secondary education, social sciences, social work, sociology, visual and performing arts.

Historical & Special Interest:

LeMoyne-Owen College came into existence with the 1968 merger of LeMoyne College and Owen College. LeMoyne-Owen College however, traces its roots back to 1862 and is operated under the authority of the United Church of Christ and the Tennessee Baptist Missionary and Educational Convention.

Its fifteen-acre campus serves non-resident students only and offers a general education program for all freshmen and a cooperative education program in which all students participate. LeMoyne-Owen College is a UNCF school.

ADDRESS:

LEMOYNE-OWEN COLLEGE
807 WALKER AVENUE
MEMPHIS,   TN   38126
Principal Official: Dr. George Johnson

TYPES OF DEGREES AWARDED:
BA, BS.

ACADEMIC CALENDAR:

CONTACT INFORMATION

Admissions Officer: Jean Saulsberry
Phone: (901) 774-9090   **Fax:** (901) 942-6272
Web Site: www.mecca.org/ LOC/ page/ LOC.ht

DOLLARS AND SENSE

TUITION & FEES:	$3,300.00
ROOM & BOARD:	$1,013.00
BOOKS & SUPPLIES:	$500.00
OTHER EXPENSES:	$200.00
OUT OF STATE TUITION:	
*ANNUAL TOTAL:	$5,013.00

(*Annual Total does not include out-of-state tuition .)

FINANCIAL AID

Financial Aid Phone: (901) 942-7379
Financial Aid Fax:

No closing date; priority given to applications received by April 15; notifications on a rolling basis beginning around April 1; must reply within 10 days. FAFSA accepted. Pell grants, loans, jobs based on need.

SPORTS

Varsity Sports: Baseball, basketball, cross-country. Intramural Sports: Badminton, baseball, basketball, football, golf, gymnastics, softball, swimming, tennis, track and field, volleyball. NCAA.

Master Key: *If lonely or fearful you might be, turn your attention to Psalm 23.*

HBCU Third Edition
© Jireh & Associates, Inc.
Wilmington, DE

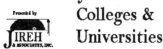
LEWIS COLLEGE OF BUSINESS

DETROIT, MI

Web Site:
Not provided.

SCHOOL INFO

Established in 1874. 2-year private coed college on urban campus in a very large city.

ACCREDITATON:
North Central Association of Colleges & Schools

CAMPUS ENROLLMENT:
Undergraduate: 322 women & men. **Transfer students:** 68 men & women. **Freshman ethnic enrollment:** African American-192, Caucasian-3

WHAT DO I NEED?

Open admissions. Interviews on or off campus available by appointment. Must be graduate of accredited high school or GED completion.

UNIQUE PROGRAMS

The following programs are available: Independent study, college-work study, Michigan Independent Adult Part-Time Program

ACADEMIC REQUIREMENTS

1st semester students must maintain a 2.0 cumulative GPA. Majors must be declared on application.

All students, including veteran students must complete all core requirements with a minimum cumulative GPA of 2.0 to be eligible to receive a degree. Minimum of 60 credit hours must be earned. Core curriculum: computer science, English, mathematics, social science. Associate's: 62 hrs.

STUDENT SERVICES

Campus student services include: personal counseling and placement services.

ADDRESS:

LEWIS COLLEGE OF BUSINESS
17370 MEYER RD.
DETROIT,   MI   48235
Principal Official: Dr. Marjorie Harris

TYPES OF DEGREES AWARDED:
A, A.A.

ACADEMIC CALENDAR:
Semester.

CONTACT INFORMATION

Admissions Officer: Frank L. Gillespie, IV,
Phone: (313) 862-6300   **Fax:** (313) 862-1027
Web Site: Not provided.

DOLLARS AND SENSE

TUITION & FEES:	$4,900.00
ROOM & BOARD:	$0.00
BOOKS & SUPPLIES:	$500.00
OTHER EXPENSES:	$408.00
OUT OF STATE TUITION:	$5,687.00
*ANNUAL TOTAL:	$5,808.00

(*Annual Total does not include out-of-state tuition.)

FINANCIAL AID

Financial Aid Phone: (313) 862-6240
Financial Aid Fax: (313) 862-1027
Each local high school and involved church receives five scholarships each to be awarded to students based on counselors/ministers recommendations. FAFSA accepted. Pell grants, loans, jobs available. The College also awards scholarships to both high school graduates and local church members.

SPORTS

Information not available.

WHAT MAJOR?

Associate:

Accounting, business administration, Computer Information Systems, Office Information Systems (Executive, Legal and Medical). Certificates in stenography and clerk typist.

Historical & Special Interest:

Lewis Business College was founded in 1928 at the beginning of the Great Depression in a store front by Dr. Violet T. Lewis, a double minority - an African American female. Dr. Lewis was possessed with the idea of providing education at the post secondary level, in office occupations, for the African-American young adults in Indianapolis, Indiana. Due to the segregation laws at that time, the private and public post secondary schools in Indiana did not accept African-American students.

In 1938, Lewis Business College received a letter from the Detroit Chamber of Commerce requesting Dr. Lewis to consider opening a business school in Detroit, Michigan. Dr. Lewis visited Detroit and found that there were no vocational schools in the city that would accept African-American students and in September 1939, Lewis Business College opened a branch school at West Warren and McGraw, in Detroit, Michigan.

The College received full accreditation from NCA in 1978 and was reaffirmed in 1982 and 1987. In September 1987, the Michigan Historical Commission erected a Michigan historical marker at the first permanent sit of the College at John R. and Ferry Streets in Detroit, Michigan. It now sits on an 11-acre campus in Northwest Detroit. Lewis is the oldest Black college in Michigan awarding Associate of Arts degrees. All students participate in its Cooperative Education Program.

Master Key: *Money is a great servant but a terrible master.*

HBCU Third Edition
© Jireh & Associates, Inc.
Wilmington, DE

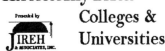
LINCOLN UNIVERSITY

JEFFERSON, MO

Web Site:
www.lincolnu.edu

SCHOOL INFO

Established in 1866. 4-year public coed teachers university on a 52-acre suburban campus in large town; 132 miles from St. Louis, 152 miles from Kansas City.

ACCREDITATON:
North Central Association of Colleges & Schools

CAMPUS ENROLLMENT:
Undergraduate: 702 men & 942 women. **Graduate:** 23 men & women. **Transfer:** 259.
Freshman ethnic enrollment: Native Am.-45, African Am.-18, Asian-17, Caucasian-2163, Hisp.-19.

WHAT DO I NEED?

Open admissions; ACT and School and College Ability test required for placement only. Application Fee $60; no closing date and priority to applications received by July 15; applicants notified on a rolling basis. Music education applicants must audition. Deferred admission program available.

UNIQUE PROGRAMS

The following programs are available: cooperative education, accelerated program, double major, concurrent enrollment/early admission program for high school students, honors program, independent study, internships.

ACADEMIC REQUIREMENTS

Freshmen must have GPA of 2.0 and major must be declared by end of second year.

Core curriculum: English, history, mathematics, biological/physical sciences, social sciences. Associate: 62 hrs. Bachelor's: 124 hrs.

STUDENT SERVICES

Campus student services include: pre-admission summer program, reduced course load program, remedial instruction, special counselors, tutoring, support services for learning disabled students. ROTC: Army.

ADDRESS:

LINCOLN UNIVERSITY
820 CHESTNUT ST.
JEFFERSON,   MO   65101
Principal Official: Dr. Donald Muellett

TYPES OF DEGREES AWARDED:
AA, AAS, B, BA, BS, MBA, MA, M.Ed.

ACADEMIC CALENDAR:
Semester. Summer sessions limited.

CONTACT INFORMATION

Admissions Officer: Jimmy Arrington
Phone: (573) 681-5599   **Fax:** (573) 681-5889
Web Site: www.lincolnu.edu

DOLLARS AND SENSE

TUITION & FEES:	$2,516.00
ROOM & BOARD:	$3,398.00
BOOKS & SUPPLIES:	$500.00
OTHER EXPENSES:	$500.00
OUT OF STATE TUITION:	$4,882.00
*ANNUAL TOTAL:	$6,914.00

(*Annual Total does not include out-of-state tuition .)

FINANCIAL AID

Financial Aid Phone: (573) 681-5003
Financial Aid Fax: (573) 681-6074

No application closing date; priority given to applications received by March 7, notifications on a rolling basis beginning about April 1; must reply within 10 days. FAFSA accepted. Academic, music/drama, art, athletic scholarships available.

SPORTS

Varsity Sports: Basketball, cross-country, golf, softball, tennis, track and field, volleyball. NCAA.

WHAT MAJOR?

Associate: Computer sciences, drafting, drafting and design technology, electronic technology, graphic and printing production, law enforcement and corrections technologies, nursing, secretarial and related programs.

Bachelors: Accounting, agricultural sciences, biology, business administration, business economics, chemistry, criminal justice studies, elementary education, English, fashion merchandising, food sciences and human nutrition, French, history, home economics, journalism, mathematics, philosophy, physics, political science and government, psychology, public administration, radio/television, secretarial and related programs, social sciences, sociology, special education.

Historical & Special Interest:

At the close of the American Civil War, the soldiers and officers of the 62nd United State Colored Infantry - stationed at Fort McIntosh, Texas, (composed principally of Missourians) decided to establish Lincoln Institute. Members of the 62nd Colored Infantry contributed $5,000 to open the school and they appealed for help to the 65th Colored Infantry, which gave $1,324.50. The school was incorporated by the organization committee which became its Board of Trustees and its doors opened to the first class in an old building in Jefferson City on September 17, 1866.

Lincoln moved to its present site in 1869 and the following year it received aid from the State for teacher training. In 1877, college-level work was added to the curriculum and the passage of the Normal School Law permitted Lincoln graduates to teach for life in Missouri without examination. The school formally became a state institution in 1879 with the deeding of the property to the State. Lincoln became a land-grant institution in 1890 and industrial agricultural courses were added to the curriculum. The high school division was accredited in 1925, the teacher-training program in 1926, and the four-year college of arts and sciences in 1934 by the North Central Association of Colleges and Secondary Schools.

Master Key: *The driver is safer when th eroads are dry;the roads are safer when the driver is dry.*

LINCOLN UNIVERSITY

LINCOLN   PA

Web Site:
www.lincoln.edu

SCHOOL INFO

Established in 1854. 4-year private liberal arts, coed college on rural campus in rural community; 45 miles from Philadelphia.

ADDRESS:

LINCOLN UNIVERSITY
LINCOLN HALL
LINCOLN UNIVERSITY,   PA   19352
Principal Official: Dr. Niara Sudarkasa

TYPES OF DEGREES AWARDED:
AA, BA, BS, M.

ACADEMIC CALENDAR:
Semester.

CONTACT INFORMATION

Admissions Officer: Dr. Robert Laney, Jr.
Phone: (610) 932-8300   **Fax:** (610) 932-1209
Web Site: www.lincoln.edu

ACCREDITATON:
Middle States Association of Colleges & Schools

CAMPUS ENROLLMENT:

Undergraduate: 1443 men & women. **Graduate:** 357 men & women. **Freshman ethnic enrollment:** Not provided.

WHAT DO I NEED?

Academic achievement record, community and school activities, essay and test scores. College preparatory program. SAT or ACT (SAT preferred); scores by August 22. Application fee $10 may be waived based on need. No closing date; notifications on a rolling basis; replies within 2 weeks. Interview recommended for provisional applicants. Deferred and early admission program available.

UNIQUE PROGRAMS

The following programs are available: accelerated program, cooperative education, double major, dual enrollment of high school students, honors program, independent study, internships, study abroad, teacher preparation, visiting/exchange student program, liberal/arts career combination in engineering.

ACADEMIC REQUIREMENTS

Freshmen must earn a minimum 2.0 and majors must be declared by end of second year.

Core curriculum: arts/fine arts, computer science, English, foreign languages, history, humanities, mathematics, biological/physical sciences, philosophy/religion, social sciences. Associate: 64 hrs. Bachelor's: 120 hrs (24 in major).

DOLLARS AND SENSE

TUITION & FEES:	$4,715.00
ROOM & BOARD:	$4,060.00
BOOKS & SUPPLIES:	$500.00
OTHER EXPENSES:	$750.00
OUT OF STATE TUITION:	$7,025.00
*ANNUAL TOTAL:	$10,025.00

(*Annual Total does not include out-of-state tuition .)

FINANCIAL AID

Financial Aid Phone: (610) 932-8300 x3566
Financial Aid Fax: (610) 932-1298

Closing date March 15; notifications on a rolling basis beginning about May 15; must reply by June 15. FAFSA accepted. Pell grants, PHEAA Grant, FSEOG; Fed Perkins loans, work-study, institutional work-aid; FFSL and PLUS loans.

Presidential, University, and alumni affiliation scholarships available.

STUDENT SERVICES

Campus student services include: academic center, career and personal counseling, employment service for undergraduates, freshman orientation, health services, placement services, preadmission summer program, reduced course load program, remedial instruction, special counselor, services for handicapped, tutoring. ROTC: Air Force, Army.

SPORTS

Varsity Sports: Baseball, basketball, bowling, cross-country,softball, soccer, swimming, tennis, track and field, volleyball, wrestling,. NCAA.

WHAT MAJOR?

Associate: Recreation and community services technologies, teacher aide.

Bachelor's: Accounting, banking and finance, biology, business administration, business economics, chemistry, communications, computer sciences, criminal justice studies, early childhood education, economics, elementary education, engineering and engineering-related technologies, English, English education, fine arts, foreign languages education, French, health education, history, human services, industrial and organizational psychology, international relations, public service, journalism, mathematics, mathematics education, music, music education, philosophy, physical education, physical sciences, physics, political science and government, pre-engineering, psychology, public affairs, recreation and community services technologies, recreation therapy, religious education, science education, secondary education, social studies education, social work, sociology, Spanish.

Historical & Special Interest:

Lincoln University was founded in 1854 as the "first insititution established anywhere in the world to provide higher education for male youth of African Descent in the Arts and Sciences." It is currently co-educational, non-sectarian, state-related liberal arts institution. Lincoln takes pride in its science programs, including LASER (Lincoln Advanced Science and Engineering Reinforcement) and MARC (Minority Access to Research Careers).

During the first 100 years of its existence, Lincoln graduates made up approximately 20 percent of the Black physicians and more than 10 percent of the Black attorneys in the U.S. At least ten alumni have been United States ambassadors or mission chiefs, heads of state and; its alum have headed 36 colleges and universities, countless prominent churches; and are federal, state and municipal judges, and mayors.

Master Key: *For the resolute and determined there is time and opportunity. Ralph Waldo Emerson*

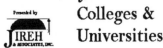

Historically Black Colleges & Universities

LIVINGSTONE COLLEGE
SALISBURY, NC

Web Site:
www.ci.salisbury.nc.us/livingstone/html

SCHOOL INFO

Established in 1879. 4-year private, coed liberal arts college. Affiliated with African Methodist Episcopal Zion Church on 75-acre urban campus in town of Salisbury; 44 miles from Charlotte, North Carolina.

ACCREDITATON:
Southern Association of Colleges & Schools

CAMPUS ENROLLMENT:
Undergraduate: 629 men & women. **Transfer students:** 26 men & women. **Freshman ethnic enrollment:** Not available

WHAT DO I NEED?
Test scores, academic record, recommendations important. SAT or ACT; scores by August 1. Application fee: $10 which may be waived based on need. Closing date August 1; notifications on a rolling basis beginning about May 15; replies within 2 weeks. Interview recommended for provisional applicants.

UNIQUE PROGRAMS
The following programs are available: double major, independent study, internships, teacher preparation, liberal arts/career combination in engineering, health sciences..

ACADEMIC REQUIREMENTS
Freshmen must earn a minimum 1.25 and majors must be declared by end of second year.

Core curriculum: English, foreign languages, history, humanities, mathematics, philosophy/religion, biological/physical sciences, social sciences. Bachelor's: 124 hrs (30 in major).

STUDENT SERVICES
Campus student services include: academic center, aptitude testing, career and personal counseling,, employment service for undergraduates, health services, placement services, reduced course load program, remedial instruction, special counselor, tutoring, veterans counselor. ROTC: Army.

ADDRESS:

LIVINGSTONE COLLEGE
701 WEST MONROE ST.
SALISBURY,   NC   28144
Principal Official: Dr. Burnett Joiner

TYPES OF DEGREES AWARDED:
BA, BS.

ACADEMIC CALENDAR:
Semester. Summer sessions limited.

CONTACT INFORMATION

Admissions Officer: Ms. Diedre Stewart
Phone: (704) 638-5502   **Fax:** (704) 638-5426
Web Site: www.ci.salisbury.nc.us/livingstone/html

DOLLARS AND SENSE

TUITION & FEES:	$11,190.00
ROOM & BOARD:	$4,150.00
BOOKS & SUPPLIES:	$954.00
OTHER EXPENSES:	$850.00
OUT OF STATE TUITION:	
*ANNUAL TOTAL:	$17,144.00

(*Annual Total does not include out-of-state tuition .)

FINANCIAL AID

Financial Aid Phone:
Financial Aid Fax:

Closing date May 15; priority given to applications received by May 1; notifications on a rolling basis beginning about June 15; must reply August 15. FAFSA accepted. Pell grants, loans, jobs available all based on need. Academic, athletic, music/drama, state/district residency scholarships available.

SPORTS

Varsity Sports: Basketball, golf, football, tennis, track and field, wrestling. NCAA.

WHAT MAJOR?
Bachelor's: Accounting, biology, business administration and management, chemistry, computer and information sciences, criminal justice studies, dramatic arts, economics, education, elementary education, English, English education, history, mathematics, mathematics education, music, music education, pharmacy, physical education, political science and government, predentistry, preelementary education, psychology, science education, social science education, social sciences, social studies education, social work, sociology, sports management.

Historical & Special Interest:

Livingstone College was founded in 1879 by the African Methodist Episcopal Zion Church and named for the missionary, philanthropist and legendary explorer, David Livingstone. Its 21 buildings add to the symmetry of the campus which is located in the historic city of Salisbury, N.C. and readily accessible to Greensboro and Charlotte.

The Hood Theological Seminary offers professional training leading to the Master of Divinity and Religious Education. The undergraduate College of ARts and Sciences offer non-sectarian academic programs leading to B.A. and B.S. degrees.

The College has a large and active athletic program, fielding teams for men's inter-collegiate competition in football, basketball, golf, tennis and wrestling. The College also offers a women's sports program offering basketball, softball and track.

Livingstone College is a UNCF school.

Master Key: *The wise man is one who know the difference between good sound reasons and reasons that sound good.*

HBCU Third Edition
© Jireh & Associates, Inc.
Wilmington, DE

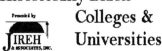

MARY HOLMES COLLEGE

WEST POINT, MS

Web Site:
www.theology.org/APCU/mh.htm

SCHOOL INFO

Established in 1892. Private, coed, 2-year junior college. Affiliated with Presbyterian Church (USA) on rural campus in large town.

ACCREDITATON:
Southern Association of Colleges & Schools

CAMPUS ENROLLMENT:
Undergraduate: 790 men & women. **Freshman ethnic enrollment: Not available.**

ADDRESS:

MARY HOLMES COLLEGE
P.O. DRAWER 1257
WEST POINT,   MS   39773
Principal Official: Dr. Elvalee Banks

TYPES OF DEGREES AWARDED:
AA, AS.

ACADEMIC CALENDAR:
Semester.

CONTACT INFORMATION

Admissions Officer: Brenda Carter
Phone: (601) 494-6820   **Fax:** (601) 494-6625
Web Site: www.theology.org/APCU/mh.htm

DOLLARS AND SENSE

TUITION & FEES:	$4,100.00
ROOM & BOARD:	$3,800.00
BOOKS & SUPPLIES:	$700.00
OTHER EXPENSES:	$500.00
OUT OF STATE TUITION:	$0.00
*ANNUAL TOTAL:	$9,100.00

(*Annual Total does not include out-of-state tuition .)

WHAT DO I NEED?

Academic record, recommendations, and extracurricular activites considered important. No Fee; no closing date and priority to applications received by July 31; applicants notified on a rolling basis. Interview and essay recommended. Deferred admission program available.

UNIQUE PROGRAMS

The following programs are available: honors program, independent study, internships, mini-semester Fall and Spring (7-wk intensive program), 2-year transfer program.

ACADEMIC REQUIREMENTS

Freshmen must maintain a minimum 2.0 and majors must be declared by end of first year.

Core curriculum: Arts/Fine arts, computer science, English, history, humanities, mathematics, biological/physical sciences, philosophy/religion, social sciences. Associate: 64 (24 in major).

FINANCIAL AID

Financial Aid Phone:
Financial Aid Fax:

No application closing date; priority given to applications received by July 1, notifications on a rolling basis beginning about July 1; must reply within 30 days. FAFSA accepted. Pell grants, loans, jobs available. Religious affiliation scholarships available.

STUDENT SERVICES

Campus student services include: academic center, aptitude testing, campus daycare, career personal counseling, freshmen orientation, health services, reduced course load program, remedial instruction, special advisor for adult students, tutoring, Upward Bound-summer enrichment program, veterans counselor, services for handicapped.

SPORTS

Varsity Sports: Baseball, basketball, soccer, softball, volleyball. NJCAA.

WHAT MAJOR?

Associate: Accounting, biological and physical sciences, biology, botany, business administration, business and management, business data processing and related programs, business education, chemical technology, chemistry, child development/care/guidance, communications, computer programming, economics, education, elementary education, engineering, English, health education, humanities and social sciences, liberal/general studies, mathematics, mathematics education, music, nursing, physical education, physics, pre-dentistry, pre-elementary education, pre-law, pre-medicine, pre-pharmacy, preveterinary, psychology, religion, secondary education, secretarial and related programs, social science education, social sciences, social studies education, special education, zoology.

Historical & Special Interest:

Mary Holmes College was founded by the Board of Freedmen of the Presbyterian Church in 1892.

It serves 90 percent Mississippian and neighboring states' students and the majority of those who graduate transfer to senior colleges and universities. Mary Holmes offers such programs as the Special Services Program and Upward Bound to its disadvantaged and first generation college students.

Master Key: *There is no medicine, except love, to cure hatred. African Proverb*

HBCU Third Edition
© Jireh & Associates, Inc.
Wilmington, DE

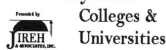
MEHARRY MEDICAL COLLEGE

NASHVILLE, TN

Web Site:
www.mmc.edu

SCHOOL INFO

Meharry Medical College was founded in 1876 as the Medical Department of Central Tennessee College of Nashville by the Freedman's Aid Society of the Methodist Episcopal Church in 1866.

ACCREDITATON:
Southern Association of Colleges & Schools/Liaison Committee of Medical Education of the AMA

CAMPUS ENROLLMENT:

ADDRESS:

MEHARRY MEDICAL COLLEGE
1005 - 18TH AVE. NORTH
NASHVILLE,   TN   37208
Principal Official: Office of the President

TYPES OF DEGREES AWARDED:
D, DDS, M, MD, MS.

ACADEMIC CALENDAR:
Semester. One freshman class per yr is admitted.

CONTACT INFORMATION

Admissions Officer: Sharon Hurt
Phone: (615) 327-6223   **Fax:** (615) 327-6228
Web Site: www.mmc.edu

WHAT DO I NEED?

Admission by selection under Committee on Admissions by division. One freshman class is admitted each year on a competitive basis: scholarship, intelligence, aptitude, character, and general fitness considered. Specific requirements of the school or division must be met. School of Medicine applicants must apply through the American Medical College Application Service and request their files to Meharry.

UNIQUE PROGRAMS

The following programs are available: Basic sciences review, combined liberal arts-medicine curriculum, early decision program, early entry program, special medical scholars program, special medical program and the International Center for Health Sciences.

ACADEMIC REQUIREMENTS

Consideration will be given to applicants who present: 1) graduation from an approved secondary school or its equiv.; 2) At least 3 full yrs of academic years of acceptable college credit at an approved college or institute of technology; 3) Satisfactory completion of 3 yrs premedical education by Sept. of admission year.

Students are eligible for the degree of Doctor of Medicine and graduation if they successfully complete the prescribed curriculum; successfully pass Part I & Part II National Board of Medical Examiners. Candidates must also be recommended by the faculty to the Board of Trustees as a person of good character and acceptable scholastic attainment.

STUDENT SERVICES

Cross-registration with Fisk, Tennessee State and Vanderbilt-Peabody, lectureships, Kresge Learning Resources Center, Meharry Learning and Enrichment Preschool, readmission, Table Clinic Day, student faculty housing, health service, Student Research Day, student organizations.

DOLLARS AND SENSE

TUITION & FEES:	$14,031.00
ROOM & BOARD:	$0.00
BOOKS & SUPPLIES:	$250.00
OTHER EXPENSES:	
OUT OF STATE TUITION:	
*ANNUAL TOTAL:	$14,281.00

(*Annual Total does not include out-of-state tuition .)

FINANCIAL AID

Financial Aid Phone:
Financial Aid Fax:
Meharry offers a variety of academic, memorial and merit scholarships. FAFSA accepted

SPORTS

None.

WHAT MAJOR?

Meharry Medical College offers **Associate of Applied Sciences, Bachelors and Doctorates** in the following areas: biomedical sciences, dentistry, health sciences, medicine, microbiology, pharmacology, physiology.

Historical & Special Interest:

The Meharry Medical College is accredited to offer academic work leading to the following degrees: Doctor of Philosophy, Doctor of Medicine, Doctor of Dental Surgery, Master of Medical Sciences, and Master of Public Health.

The School of Medicine is accredited by the Liaison Committee of Medical Educatin of the American Medical Association and the American Association of Medical Colleges, and recognized by the Examining Board in England of the Royal College of Physicians of London and by the Royal College of Surgeons of England.

The School of Dentistry is a member of the American Association of Dental School and is governed by its rules and by those of the Council on Dental Educatin of the American Dental Association. It is registered by the Dental Examining Boards of each state in the United State. The School of Dentistry is approved by the Council on Dental Education of the American Dental Association.

Master Key: *Ignore what a man desires and you ignore the very source of his power... Walter Lippmann*

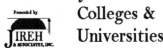
MILES COLLEGE
BIRMINGHAM, AL

Web Site:
Not provided.

SCHOOL INFO

Established in 1905. 4-year private liberal arts college, coed, affiliated with Christian Methodist Episcopal Church. Urban campus in large town; 6 miles from downtown Birmingham.

ACCREDITATON:
Southern Association of Colleges & Schools

CAMPUS ENROLLMENT:
Undergraduate: 1424 men & women. **Transfer students:** 99 men & women. **Freshman ethnic enrollment: Not available.**

WHAT DO I NEED?

Open admissions. Selective admission to education program based on 2.0 high school GPA, SAT or ACT; scores due by 7/31. Application fee $25; closing date by July 15.

UNIQUE PROGRAMS

The following programs are available: cooperative education, double major, dual enrollment of high school students, honors program, independent study, internships, visiting/exchange student program, cross-registration; liberal arts/career combination in health sciences.

ACADEMIC REQUIREMENTS

Minimum GPA for freshmen is 2.0 and majors must be declared by end of first year.

Core curriculum: arts/fine arts, computer science, English, history, humanities, mathematics, philosophy/religion, biological/physical sciences, social sciences. Bachelor's: 127 hours (in major: 72).

STUDENT SERVICES

Campus student services include: aptitude testing, career and personal counseling, employment service for undergraduates, health services, placement services, reduced course load, remedial instruction, special counselor, tutoring, reading/writing laboratories, services for handicapped.

WHAT MAJOR?

Bachelor's: Biology, business administration, chemistry, communications, education early childhood, elementary education, elementary education, English, mathematics, modern languages, music education, music performance, political science & government, social science.
Pre-Professional - Medicine and Dentistry

Historical & Special Interest:

Miles was founded in 1905 by the Colored Methodist Episcopal Church, now the Christian Methodist Episcopal Church. It is located on 45 acres in the Western section of Birmingham and home to approximately 1424 students, 80% of whom commute from within the city, and 94% ow whom receive financial aid. Miles College operates under five academic divisions: Education; Humanities; Social and Behavioral Sciences; Business and Economics and Natural Sciences and Mathematics. In addition, it offers several supportive and developmental programs. These services include three tutorial programs and a Student Support Services Program designed to attract and motivate student who may have experienced economic and/or educational deprivation. The college has never been restrictive in admissions and remains open to all qualified persons. Miles College is a UNCF school.

ADDRESS:

MILES COLLEGE
P.O. BOX 3800
BIRMINGHAM,   AL   35208
Principal Official: Dr. Albert J.H. Sloan II

TYPES OF DEGREES AWARDED:
BA, BS

ACADEMIC CALENDAR:
Semester. Summer sessions limited.

CONTACT INFORMATION

Admissions Officer: Ms. Brenda Grant-Smith
Phone: (800) 445-0708   **Fax:** (205) 929-1668
Web Site: Not provided.

DOLLARS AND SENSE

TUITION & FEES:	$4,450.00
ROOM & BOARD:	$2,750.00
BOOKS & SUPPLIES:	$400.00
OTHER EXPENSES:	$500.00
OUT OF STATE TUITION:	
*ANNUAL TOTAL:	$8,100.00

(*Annual Total does not include out-of-state tuition .)

FINANCIAL AID

Financial Aid Phone:
Financial Aid Fax:
No closing date for aid applications those received by April 15; notifications on a rolling basis beginning on or about July 15 and must reply within 2 wks. FAFSA accepted. Pell grants, loans, jobs based on need. Academic scholarships available.

SPORTS

Varsity Sports: Baseball, basketball, cross-country, football, track and field.   NCAA.

HBCU Third Edition
© Jireh & Associates, Inc.
Wilmington, DE

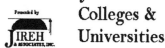
MISSISSIPPI VALLEY STATE UNIV.

ITTA BENA, MS

Web Site:
www.mvsu.edu

SCHOOL INFO

Established in 1946. Public, coed, 4-year university on rural campus in small town; 120 miles north of Jackson.

ACCREDITATON:
Southern Association of Colleges & Schools

CAMPUS ENROLLMENT:
Undergraduate: 2207 men & women. Graduate: 7 men & women. Transfer students: 155 men & women. Freshman ethnic enrollment: African American-565, Caucasian-6

WHAT DO I NEED?

Academic record, test scores, state residency important. College prep. program. SAT/ACT composite (ACT preferred). Scores by August 22. No Fee; closing date June 1st; notifications beginning about August 1. Must reply within 3 weeks. Deferred and early admission program available.

UNIQUE PROGRAMS

The following programs are available: cooperative education, honors program, internships.

ACADEMIC REQUIREMENTS

Freshmen must earn a minimum 2.0 and majors must be declared by end of second year.

Core curriculum: Fine arts/arts, English, history, humanities, mathematics, biological/physical sciences, social sciences. Bachelor's: 124 hrs.

STUDENT SERVICES

Campus student services include: academic center, freshmen orientation, career and personal counseling, health services, placement services, reduced course load program, remedial instruction, special advisor for adult students, services for handicapped, tutoring, veterans counselor. ROTC: Air Force, Army.

WHAT MAJOR?

Bachelor's: Art, biology, business administration, communication, computer sciences, criminal justice, elementary education, English, English education, environmental health, health/physical education and recreation, industrial technology, mathematics, music education, political science, social work, sociology, speech.

Historical & Special Interest:

Mississippi Valley State University was founded in 1946 and offers degree programs in the arts and sciences, business, and education. It also offers a Master's degree in Elementary Education and Environmental Health.

MVSU is home to a renowned band which has performed at the Rose Bowl, the United States Presidential Inauguration, Disney World, and the Indy 500; Mississippi's first nationally accredited art and environmental health program; and national athletic champions.

ADDRESS:

MISSISSIPPI VALLEY STATE UNIV.
P.O. BOX 61
ITTA BENA,   MS   38941
Principal Official: Dr. William W. Sutton

TYPES OF DEGREES AWARDED:
BA, BS, MS.

ACADEMIC CALENDAR:
Semester. Summer sessions.

CONTACT INFORMATION

Admissions Officer: Maxine Rush
Phone: (601) 254-3347   **Fax:** (601) 254-7900
Web Site: www.mvsu.edu

DOLLARS AND SENSE

TUITION & FEES:	$2,792.00
ROOM & BOARD:	$2,786.00
BOOKS & SUPPLIES:	$450.00
OTHER EXPENSES:	$450.00
OUT OF STATE TUITION:	$5,430.00
*ANNUAL TOTAL:	$6,478.00

(*Annual Total does not include out-of-state tuition .)

FINANCIAL AID

Financial Aid Phone: (601) 254-9041
Financial Aid Fax: (601) 254-7900

No application closing date; priority given to applications received by June 1, notifications on a rolling basis beginning about August 15; must reply within 3 weeks. FAFSA accepted. Pell Grants and state student incentive grant, loans, jobs available. Academic, music, athletic scholarships available.

SPORTS

Varsity Sports: Baseball, basketball, football, golf, tennis, track and field. SWAC/NCAA.

Master Key: *I always wanted to be somebody, but I should have been more specific. Lily Tomlin*

Historically Black Colleges & Universities

MOREHOUSE COLLEGE
ATLANTA, GA

Web Site:
www.morehouse.edu

SCHOOL INFO
Established in 1867. 4-year private college men only on urban campus in very large city; 2 miles from downtown.

ACCREDITATON:
Southern Association of Colleges & Schools

CAMPUS ENROLLMENT:
Undergraduate: 2990 men only. **Transfer students:** 0. **Freshman ethnic enrollment:** African American -647, Other-13

WHAT DO I NEED?
High school GPA, test scores, interview, extra-curricular activities, recommendations, essays important. SAT or ACT (SAT preferred). Scores by February 15. $25 application fee (which may be waived based on need). Closing date April 15; and applicants notified on rolling basis beginning on December 11. Reply required by May 1. Deferred and early admission program available. Admissions Director, Sterling Hudson, 1-800-992-0642.

UNIQUE PROGRAMS
The following programs are available: cooperative education, dual degree programs, honors program, international studies, cross-registration; liberal arts/career combination in engineering, pre-law, pre-med, student exchange, study abroad.

ACADEMIC REQUIREMENTS
Minimum GPA for freshmen 2.0. Math 3, English 4, natural sciences 1, social sciences 2 units. Major declared by end of second year.

Minimum 2.0 cumulative GPA. Core curriculum: Arts/Fine arts, English, history, humanities, foreign languages, mathematics, biological/physical sciences, philosophy/religion, and social sciences. Bachelor's: 124 semester hours (60 hrs. in major).

STUDENT SERVICES
Campus student services include: career and personal counseling, employment services for undergraduates, health services, placement services, reduced course load program, remedial instruction, tutoring, veterans counselor. ROTC: Air Force, Army, Naval.

ADDRESS:

MOREHOUSE COLLEGE
830 WESTVIEW DRIVE, S.W.
ATLANTA,   GA   30314
Principal Official: Dr. Walter E. Massey

TYPES OF DEGREES AWARDED:
BA, BS.

ACADEMIC CALENDAR:
Semesters (2). Summer programs.

CONTACT INFORMATION

Admissions Officer: Andre Patillo
Phone: (404) 681-2800   **Fax:** (404) 524-5635
Web Site: www.morehouse.edu

DOLLARS AND SENSE

TUITION & FEES:	$9,158.00
ROOM & BOARD:	$6,972.00
BOOKS & SUPPLIES:	$1,500.00
OTHER EXPENSES:	$1,000.00
OUT OF STATE TUITION:	
*ANNUAL TOTAL:	$18,630.00

(*Annual Total does not include out-of-state tuition .)

FINANCIAL AID

Financial Aid Phone:
Financial Aid Fax:
Closing date April 15. Notifications on a rolling basis beginning March 15. Reply required by May 1 or within 2 weeks of notification. FAFSA accepted; SEOG, Perkins loan, college work-study, Pell Grant, GA Student Incentive and tuition equalization grants.

SPORTS
Varsity Sports: basketball, cross-country, football, tennis, track and field. Intramural Sports: Basketball, swimming, tennis. NCAA Div. II & SIAC. (Men only)

WHAT MAJOR?

Bachelor's: Accounting, African-American studies, art, banking & finance, biological and physical sciences, biology, business administration, business economics, chemistry, communications, computer sciences, criminal justice, drama, economics, education, elementary education, engineering, English, fine arts, French, German, history, international studies, journalism, mathematics, music, philosophy, physics, political science, psychology, radio/television, religion, secondary education, sociology, Spanish, urban management, urban studies.

Historical & Special Interest:
Beginning in 1867 in the basement of Augusta's Springfield Baptist Church as the Augusta Institute, the College was founded to prepare blacks for teaching and the ministry. After moving to Atlanta in 1879, it underwent two name changes, first becoming the Atlanta Baptist Seminary and then the Atlanta Baptist College. In those days the curriculum consisted of a course of study similiar to that of a present day elementary school and an academy resembling that of a high school.

A new era dawned with the appointment of Dr. John Hope as president in 1906, the school's first black president and a Phi Beta Kappa graduate of Brown University. Dr. Hope expanded the College's curriculum to include educating leaders in all areas of American life rather than the traditional vocational and agricultural skills. Dr. Hope endorsed the name which still stands in honor of Henry Lyman Morehouse, the corresponding secretary of the American Baptist Home Mission Society. The seeds of the Atlanta University Center were planted by Hope in 1929 when a cooperative agreement was made among Atlanta University, Spelman College, and Morehouse College and later expanded to include Clark College, Morris Brown College, the Interdenominational Theological Center and the Morehouse School of Medicine. The Center allows students to use the facilities of a large university community while still attending a small liberal arts college. In 1940, Morehouse came under the leadership of Dr. Benjamin E. Mays and in 1957 received full accreditation by the Southern Association of Colleges and Schools meeting and surpassing standards established for what were then predominantly white institutions. Morehouse College is a UNCF school.

Master Key: *The quality of a person's life is in direct proportion to their commitment to excellence, regardless of their chosen field of endeaoor. Vincent T. Lombardi*

HBCU Third Edition
© Jireh & Associates, Inc.
Wilmington, DE

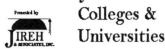
MOREHOUSE SCHOOL OF MEDICINE

ATLANTA, GA

Web Site:
www.msm.edu

SCHOOL INFO

Established in 1975. 4-year private college men only on urban campus in very large cityl; 2 miles from downtown.

ACCREDITATON:
Southern Association of Colleges & Schools

CAMPUS ENROLLMENT:
Undergraduate: 140 men approximately. **Transfer students:** 0. **Freshman ethnic enrollment:** African American -120, Other-20

WHAT DO I NEED?
High school GPA, test scores, interview, extra-curricular activities, recommendations, essays important. SAT or ACT (SAT preferred). Scores by February 15. $25 application fee (which may be waived based on need). Closing date April 15; and applicants notified on rolling basis beginning on December 11. Reply required by May 1. Deferred and early admission program available. Admissions Director, Sterling Hudson, 1-800-992-0642.

UNIQUE PROGRAMS
The following programs are available: cooperative education, dual degree programs, honors program, international studies, cross-registration; liberal arts/career combination in engineering, pre-law, pre-med, student exchange, study abroad.

ACADEMIC REQUIREMENTS
Minimum GPA for freshmen 2.0. Math 3, English 4, natural sciences 1, social sciences 2 units. Major declared by end of second year.

Minimum 2.0 cumulative GPA. Core curriculum: Arts/Fine arts, English, history, humanities, foreign languages, mathematics, biological/physical sciences, philosophy/religion, and social sciences. Bachelor's: 124 semester hours (60 hrs. in major).

STUDENT SERVICES
Campus student services include: career and personal counseling, employment services for undergraduates, health services, placement services, reduced course load program, remedial instruction, tutoring, veterans counselor. ROTC: Air Force, Army, Naval.

WHAT MAJOR?
Bachelor's: Doctor of Medicine

Historical & Special Interest:

In 1978 Morehouse College, after six years of preparation, launched the third predominantly Black medical school, the Morehouse School of Medicine. A professional degree of Doctor of Medicine is awarded upon completion of licensing and academic requirements.

The medical school has been an independent institution since 1981.

Morehouse College, renowned for producing leaders, is a place where young men grow interpersonally and intellectually. Morehouse College is a UNCF school.

ADDRESS:

MOREHOUSE SCHOOL OF MEDICINE
830 WESTVIEW DRIVE, S.W.
ATLANTA,   GA   30314
Principal Official: Dr. Walter E. Massey

TYPES OF DEGREES AWARDED:
BA, BS.

ACADEMIC CALENDAR:
Semesters (2). Summer programs.

CONTACT INFORMATION

Admissions Officer: Dr. Angela Franklin
Phone: (404) 752-1650   **Fax:** (404) 752-1512
Web Site: www.msm.edu

DOLLARS AND SENSE

TUITION & FEES:	$19,968.00
ROOM & BOARD:	$6,972.00
BOOKS & SUPPLIES:	$1,500.00
OTHER EXPENSES:	$300.00
OUT OF STATE TUITION:	
*ANNUAL TOTAL:	$28,740.00

(*Annual Total does not include out-of-state tuition .)

FINANCIAL AID

Financial Aid Phone: (800) 992-2632
Financial Aid Fax:

Closing date April 15. Notifications on a rolling basis beginning March 15. Reply required by May 1 or within 2 weeks of notification. FAFSA accepted; SEOG, Perkins loan, college work-study, Pell Grant, GA Student Incentive and tuition equalization grants.

SPORTS

Varsity Sports: basketball, cross-country, football, tennis, track and field. Intramural Sports: Basketball, swimming, tennis. NCAA Div. II & SIAC. (Men only)

HBCU Third Edition
© Jireh & Associates, Inc.
Wilmington, DE

Historically Black Colleges & Universities

MORGAN STATE UNIVERSITY
BALTIMORE, MD

Web Site:
www.morgan.edu

SCHOOL INFO

Established in 1867. 4-year public coed university of arts and sciences and business, engineering, teachers college on urban campus in a very large city; 45 miles northeast of Washington, D.C. and 100 miles south of Phildelphia.

ACCREDITATON:
Middle States Assn of Colleges & Second. Schools

CAMPUS ENROLLMENT:
Undergraduate: 5900 men & women. **Graduate:** 300 total; **Part-time:** 908. **Transfer students:** 400 men & women. **Freshman ethnic enrollment: AA:** 94%; **Asian:** 1%; **Cauc.:** 2%; **Hisp.** 1%; **Foreign:** 2%.

WHAT DO I NEED?

Test scores and official transcript. GPA 2.5/ 850 SAT or 17 ACT; GPA 2.0/900 SAT or 19 ACT. Scores due by August 1. Application fee $25 which may be waived based on need. Closing date August 1; priority to applications received by April 15; applicants notified on a rolling basis and must reply by May or within 4 weeks. Deferred and early admission program available.

UNIQUE PROGRAMS

The following programs are available: cooperative education, cross-registration, double major, dual enrollment of high school students, independent study, internships, teacher preparation, weekend college. Honors program Reqmts.: Instate - 3.0/1000 SAT & 22 ACT; Out state - 3.0/1100 SAT & 24 ACT.

ACADEMIC REQUIREMENTS

Minimum GPA of 2.0 and majors must be declared by end of second year.

Core curriculum: arts/fine arts, English, history, humanities, mathematics, philosophy/religion, biological/physical sciences, social sciences. Bachelor's: 120 hours (54 in major).

STUDENT SERVICES

Campus student services include: academic center, aptitude testing, campus daycare, career and personal counseling, employment services for undergraduates, freshman orientation, health services, placement services, reduced course load program, remedial instruction, services for handicapped, tutoring, veterans counselor. ROTC: Army. **Learning Disabled:** Supporting documentation needed, extended time for exams, exams admin. in counseling ctr., use of computer and special equipment.

WHAT MAJOR?

Bachelor's: Accounting, African studies, African-American studies, Fine Arts, Biology, Medical Technology, Pre-Dentistry, Pre-Medicine, Chemistry, Pre-Pharmacy, Computer Science, Economics, English and Language Arts, Journalism, Speech Communication, History and Geography, Mathematics, Philosophy & Religious Studies, Physics, Political Science, Psychology, Sociology, Telecommunications, Civil Engineering, Electrical Engineering, Industrial Engineering, Business Administration, Finance, Information Systems, Health, Physical Education & Recreation, Community Health, Health Administration, Environmental Health, Elementary & Secondary, Human Ecology, Social Work & Mental Health, Teacher Education and Administration.

Graduate Programs: City/Regional Planning, Economics, Educational Admin. & Supv., Elementary & Middle School Education, Engineering , English, History, International Studies, Landscape Architecture, Mathematics, Music, Science, Sociology, Teaching (MAT), and Transportation.

Historical & Special Interest:

Morgan State University is located in the Northeastern section of Baltimore City. The institution began in 1867 as the Centenary Bible institute, having been established by the Baltimore Conference of the Methodist Episcopal Church to train Black ministers.

The campus is in the process of adding a new School Science Complex and renovating the physical education instructional center. The school has an urban mandate as a public institution and offers doctorates emphasizing teaching, research and public service.

ADDRESS:

MORGAN STATE UNIVERSITY
COLD SPRING LAND & HILLEN RD.
BALTIMORE,   MD   21239
Principal Official: Dr. Earl S. Richardson

TYPES OF DEGREES AWARDED:
BA, BS, MA,MS,MBA, ME, MLA, MCRP, EdD,

ACADEMIC CALENDAR:
Semester. Summer sessions limited.

CONTACT INFORMATION

Admissions Officer: Clelsia Miller
Phone: (800) 332-6674   **Fax:** (410) 319-3684
Web Site: www.morgan.edu

DOLLARS AND SENSE

TUITION & FEES:	$3,126.00
ROOM & BOARD:	$4,918.00
BOOKS & SUPPLIES:	$1,000.00
OTHER EXPENSES:	$300.00
OUT OF STATE TUITION:	$7,288.00
*ANNUAL TOTAL:	$9,344.00

(*Annual Total does not include out-of-state tuition .)

FINANCIAL AID

Financial Aid Phone: (410) 319-3170
Financial Aid Fax: (410) 319-3852

No aid applications closing date; priority given to applications received by April 1 and notified on or about June 1; must reply within 2 weeks. FAFSA accepted. Pell grants, loans, jobs are available. **Scholarships available:** Full Scholarships plus books & laptop -In state 3.5 GPA and 1400 SAT; Partial - In state 3.2 GPA/1100 SAT/24 ACT; Out state 3.2 GPA/1200 SAT/27 ACT.

SPORTS

Varsity Sports: Basketball & football, tennis, track and field, volleyball, softbal. NCAA.

Master Key: *Personality will open many doors, but it is character that will keep them open.*

HBCU Third Edition
© Jireh & Associates, Inc.
Wilmington, DE

MORRIS BROWN COLLEGE

ATLANTA, GA

Web Site:
Not provided.

SCHOOL INFO

Established in 1881. 4-year private liberal arts coed college, affiliated with African Methodist Episcopal Church on urban campus in a very large city; 2 miles from downtown Atlanta.

ACCREDITATON:
Southern Association of Colleges & Schools

CAMPUS ENROLLMENT:
Undergraduate: 2030 men & women. **Transfer students:** 114 men & women. **Freshman ethnic enrollment:** Not available.

WHAT DO I NEED?

High school achievement record, followed by SAT (preferred) or ACT test scores and alumni/counselor recommendation strongly considered. SAT or ACT (SAT preferred). College Preparatory Program. Scores by June 30. Application fee $20 which may be waived based on need. No closing date; and applicants notified within 3 weeks of completed application. Reply required within 2 weeks of acceptance. Essay recommended. Early admission program available.

UNIQUE PROGRAMS

The following programs are available: accelerated program, cooperative education, double major, honors program, independent study, internships, cross-registration; liberal arts/career combination in engineering, study abroad.

ACADEMIC REQUIREMENTS

Minimum GPA for freshmen 2.0 and major must be declared by end of second year.

Core curriculum: Arts/fine arts, computer science, English, foreign languages, history, humanities, mathematics, biological/physical sciences, philosophy/religion, and social sciences. Bachelor's: 124 hours.

STUDENT SERVICES

Campus student services include: academic testing & assessment, academic advisement, career planning, Early Alert System, employment services for undergraduates, freshmen orientation, health services, personal counseling, placement & co-op program for graduates, remedial instruction, special counseling, special services program for socioeconomically deprived students, tutoring. ROTC: Air Force, Army, Naval.

WHAT MAJOR?

Bachelor's: Accounting, airway computer science, allied health, architecture, biology, business administration, business and management, business and office, business data processing and related programs, business economics, chemical engineering , chemistry, city/community/regional planning, civil engineering, communications, community health work, computer sciences, criminal justice studies, dramatic arts, economics, education of the emotionally handicapped, education of the physical handicapped, education of the mentally handicapped, electrical/electronics/communications engineering, elementary education, English literature, fashion design, fashion merchandising, fine arts, food sciences and human nutrition, French, geography, health education, history, hospitality administration, industrial design, industrial engineering, journalism, marketing management, mathematics, mathematics, mechanical engineering, medical illustrating, medical records technology, music, music performance, nursing, paralegal studies, philosophy, physical education, physics, political science and government, preelementary education, psychology, public relations, radio/television, recreation therapy, religion, secretarial and related programs, sociology Spanish, specific learning disabilities, speech/debate/forensics, textiles and clothing, therapeutic recreation, urban studies.

Historical & Special Interest:

Morris Brown was founded in 1881 by the African Methodist Episcopal Church "for the Christian Education of Negro Boys and Girls in Atlanta." The statement was appropriate at the time because of the limited educational opportunities for newly emancipated Negroes. On October 15, 1885, under the charter granted by the state of Georgia, Morris Brown College opened with two teachers and 107 students. The school operated until 1894 on the primary, secondary, and normal school levels. Tailoring, dressmaking, nursing education, home economics, printing, and commerce were offered, as well as the regular academic programs. The College Department was established in 1894 and graduated its first class in 1898. A Theological Department of the College was established in 1894 for the training of ministers. Six years later, its name was changed to Turner Theological Seminary in honor of the Senior Bishop of the AME Church. In 1960, the Seminary was separated from the College. Morris Brown College is a UNCF school.

ADDRESS:

MORRIS BROWN COLLEGE
643 MLK, JR. DR. N.W.
ATLANTA,   GA   30314
Principal Official: Dr. Samuel D. Jolley, Jr.

TYPES OF DEGREES AWARDED:
BA, BS.

ACADEMIC CALENDAR:
Semester .

CONTACT INFORMATION

Admissions Officer: Rev. Debora S. Grant
Phone: (404) 220-0152   **Fax:** (404) 659-4315
Web Site: Not provided.

DOLLARS AND SENSE

TUITION & FEES:	$11,120.00
ROOM & BOARD:	$2,122.00
BOOKS & SUPPLIES:	$600.00
OTHER EXPENSES:	$500.00
OUT OF STATE TUITION:	$0.00
*ANNUAL TOTAL:	$14,342.00

(*Annual Total does not include out-of-state tuition .)

FINANCIAL AID

Financial Aid Phone:
Financial Aid Fax:

Closing date June 15, priority given to applications received by April 15. Notifications on a rolling basis beginning July 1. Reply required within 15 days of notification. FAFSA accepted. Pell grants, loans, and jobs available. Academic and presidential scholarships, band awards, choir/music, athletic-in-aid, scholarships available.

SPORTS

Varsity Sports: basketball, football. Intramural Sports: Basketball, soccer, softball, volleyball, tennis. NCAA.

Master Key: *Always do your best. What you plant now you will harvest later. Og Mandino*

HBCU Third Edition
© Jireh & Associates, Inc.
Wilmington, DE

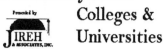
MORRIS COLLEGE
SUMTER, SC

Web Site:
www.icusc.org/morris

SCHOOL INFO

Established in 1908. 4-year private liberal arts, coed college. Affiliation with Southern Baptist Convention on urban campus in large town; 45 miles from Columbia.

ACCREDITATON:
Southern Association of Colleges & Schools

CAMPUS ENROLLMENT:
Undergraduate: 888 men & women (317/57). **Transfer students:** 70 men & women (26/44). **Freshman ethnic enrollment:** African American-911.

WHAT DO I NEED?
Open admissions; special requirements for foreign, transfer, or transient students. Graduation from an accredited high school or official GED; official high school transcript. Application fee $10 may be waived based on need. No closing date; notification a rolling basis. Replies within 10 days of notification.

UNIQUE PROGRAMS
The following programs are available: Business Admin., education, general studies, humanities, natural sciences, mathematics, social sciences, history and pre-law studies; cooperative education; honors program; adult degree; internships and teacher preparation.

ACADEMIC REQUIREMENTS
Maintain a minimum 2.0; no grade less than a 'c' in major course; class attendance mandatory, and majors must be declared by end of sophomore year.

A minimum 2.0 GPA or better. Application for graduation with a $25.00 graduation fee and exit examination. Bachelor's: 124 hrs (30 in-residence at Morris). Core curriculum: arts, English, history, humanities, mathematics, philosophy/religion, sciences, social science.

STUDENT SERVICES
Campus student services include: academic center, alumni services, aptitude testing, co-op education, counseling services, employment services, freshman orientation, health services, internships, on-campus job interviews, reduced course load program, remedial math/reading/writing, special counselor, tutoring, resume' prep. ROTC: Army.

ADDRESS:

MORRIS COLLEGE
100 W. COLLEGE ST.
SUMTER,   SC   29150
Principal Official: Dr. Luns C. Richardson

TYPES OF DEGREES AWARDED:
BA, BS, BFA, BSEd.

ACADEMIC CALENDAR:
Semester. Two summer sessions.

CONTACT INFORMATION

Admissions Officer: Queen W. Spann
Phone: (803) 775-9371   **Fax:** (803) 773-3687
Web Site: www.icusc.org/morris

DOLLARS AND SENSE

TUITION & FEES:	$5,105.00
ROOM & BOARD:	$2,691.00
BOOKS & SUPPLIES:	$850.00
OTHER EXPENSES:	$1,000.00
OUT OF STATE TUITION:	
*ANNUAL TOTAL:	$9,646.00

(*Annual Total does not include out-of-state tuition .)

FINANCIAL AID

Financial Aid Phone: (803) 775-9371 ext. 238
Financial Aid Fax: (803) 773-3687

No closing date; priority given to applications received by March 1; notifications on a rolling basis beginning about June 1; must reply by August 1. FAFSA accepted. Pell Grants, SC Tuition grants, work-study; SEOG's. Payment Option Plans: Institutional Installment Plan.

SPORTS

Varsity Sports: Baseball, basketball), softball, track and field. NAIA.

WHAT MAJOR?
Bachelor's: Biology, biology education, business administration, community health, criminal justice, early childhood education, elementary education, English, English education, health science, history, history education, liberal studies, liberal-technical studies, mathematics, mathematics education, political sciences/history, recreation administration, Christian education, Pastoral Ministry, Organizational Management, secondary education, social studies, social studies education, sociology.

Historical & Special Interest:

Under authorization granted by the Baptist Educational and Missionary Convention of South Carolina in 1906, Morris College was established in 1908 "...for the Christian and intellectual training of Negro youth." The majority of these "founding fathers" were poor and without any formal learning, but they possessed an "unfaltering faith in God and a zeal to provide for others the educational opportunities they themselves were denied."

On April 12, 1911, the College received a certificate of incorporation from the state of South Carolina. Morris College provided schooling on the elementary, high school, and college levels. The college curriculum included programs in liberal arts, in "normal" education for the certification of teachers, and a theological program. In 1915, the Bachelor of Arts degree was conferred on the first two graduates. The institution discontinued its "normal" program in 1929, its elementary school in 1930 and its high school in 1946.

During 1930-32, the school operated only as a junior college, but it resumed its full four-year program in 1933. The word "Negro" appearing in the original certificate of incorporation was eliminated on August 14, 1961, thereby opening the doors at Morris to all ethnic groups. In the seventieth year of its history, on December 13, 1978, Morris College achieved the goal of full accreditation by the Southern Association of Colleges and Schools. On January 1, 1982, it became the 42nd member of the United Negro College Fund.

Master Key: *Tell the truth the first time and you wont have to remember what it was you said.*

HBCU Third Edition
© Jireh & Associates, Inc.
Wilmington, DE

N. CAROLINA A&T STATE UNIV.

GREENSBORO, NC

Web Site:
www.ncat.edu

SCHOOL INFO

Established in 1891. 4-year public, coed liberal arts college on urban campus in small city; 91 miles from Charlotte, North Carolina.

ACCREDITATON:
Southern Association of Colleges & Schools

CAMPUS ENROLLMENT:
Undergraduate: 3020 men & 2842 women. **Graduate:** 403 men & 532 women. **Transfer students:** 137 men & 125 women. **Freshman ethnic enrollment:** Native American-25, African American-6651, Asian-80, Caucasian-657, Hisp-26.

WHAT DO I NEED?

Test scores, state residency, school achievement record and GPA important. College preparatory program. Scores by July 1. ACT or SAT (SAT preferred). Application fee: $15. Closing date June 1 and notifications on a rolling basis and replies by May 1 or within 3 weeks. Audition and portfolio recommended for music applicants art students.

UNIQUE PROGRAMS

The following programs are available: accelerated program, cooperative education, cross-registration, double major, honors program, independent study, internships, teacher preparation, weekend college.

ACADEMIC REQUIREMENTS

Freshmen must earn a minimum 1.2 and majors must be declared by end of second year.

Core curriculum: English, foreign languages, history, humanities, mathematics, biological/physical sciences, social sciences. Certificate in educational media 6-year. Bachelor's: 124 hrs (62 in major).

STUDENT SERVICES

Campus student services include: academic center, aptitude testing, career and personal counseling,, employment service for undergraduates, health services, placement services, preadmission summer program, reduced course load program, remedial instruction, special counselor, tutoring, services for handicapped, veterans counselor. ROTC: Air Force, Army.

ADDRESS:

N. CAROLINA A&T STATE UNIV.
1601 E. MARKET ST.
GREENSBORO,   NC   27411
Principal Official: Dr. Edward B. Fort

TYPES OF DEGREES AWARDED:
BA, BS, MA, MS, PhD.

ACADEMIC CALENDAR:
Semester. Summer sessions.

CONTACT INFORMATION

Admissions Officer: John Smith
Phone: (910) 334-7946   **Fax:** (910) 334-7478
Web Site: www.ncat.edu

DOLLARS AND SENSE

TUITION & FEES:	$1,561.00
ROOM & BOARD:	$3,410.00
BOOKS & SUPPLIES:	$600.00
OTHER EXPENSES:	$700.00
OUT OF STATE TUITION:	$8,715.00
*ANNUAL TOTAL:	$6,271.00

(*Annual Total does not include out-of-state tuition .)

FINANCIAL AID

Financial Aid Phone:
Financial Aid Fax:

No closing date; priority given to applications received by May 15; notifications on a rolling basis beginning about June 1; must reply within 2 weeks. FAFSA accepted. Pell grants, loans, jobs available all based on need. Academic, athletic, alumni affiliation, music/drama, leadership, minority, state/district residency scholarships available.

SPORTS

Varsity Sports: Baseball, basketball, cross-country, football, swimming, tennis, track and field, volleyball, wrestling. NCAA.

WHAT MAJOR?

Bachelor's: Accounting, agriculture business/economics/sciences, animal sciences, architectural engineering, art education, biology, business administration, business economics, business education, chemical engineering, chemistry, civil engineering, communications, computer sciences, dramatic arts, drawing, driver and safety education, electrical/electronics/communications engineering, elementary education, engineering, engineering physics, English, English education, food sciences and human nutrition, foreign languages education, forest products processing technology, French, history, home economics, home economics education, individual and family development, industrial arts education, industrial engineering, industrial technology, landscape architecture, mathematics, mathematics education, mechanical engineering, music, music education, nursing, occupational safety and health technology, painting parks and recreation management, physical education, physics, political science and government, psychology, secretarial related programs, social science education, social sciences, social work, sociology, special education, speech/debate/forensics, textiles and clothing, transportation management.

Historical & Special Interest:

North Carolina Agricultural and Technical State University was established as the Agricultural and Mechanical College for the "Colored Race" by an act of the General Assembly of North Carolina ratified March 9, 1891.

The College began operation during the school year of 1890-91, before the passage of the state law creating it. This curious circumstance arose out of the fact that the Morrill Act passed by Congress in 1890 earmarked the proportionate funds to be allocated in bi-racial school systems to the two races. The A&M College for the White Race was established by the State Legislature in 1889 and was ready to receive its share of funds provided by the Morrill Act in the Fall of 1890. Before the college could receive these funds, however, it was necessary to make provisions for "Colored" students. Accordingly, the Board of Trustees of the A&M College in Raleigh was empowered to make temporary arrangements for these students. A plan was worked out with Shaw University in Raleigh where the College operated as an annex to Shaw University during the years 1890-1893.

Master Key: *Beware of the barreness of the busy life.*

N. CAROLINA CENTRAL UNIV.

DURHAM, NC

Web Site:
Not provided.

SCHOOL INFO

Established in 1910. 4-year public, coed university on urban campus in small city; 23 miles from Raleigh, North Carolina.

ACCREDITATON:
Southern Association of Colleges & Schools

CAMPUS ENROLLMENT:
Undergraduate: 4339 men & women. **Graduate:** 3075 men & women. **Transfer students:** 303 men & women.

WHAT DO I NEED?

Test scores, academic achievement important. College preparatory program. Minimum SAT combined: 600; scores by August 1. ACT or SAT. Application fee: $15. Closing date August 1 and priority given to applications received by June 1; notifications on a rolling basis and replies by June 1 for college housing. Audition recommended for music applicants.

UNIQUE PROGRAMS

The following programs are available: Cooperative education, double major, honors program, education specialist degree, independent study, internships, teacher preparation.

ACADEMIC REQUIREMENTS

Freshmen must earn a minimum 2.0 and majors must be declared by end of first year.

Core curriculum: arts/fine arts, English, foreign languages, history, humanities, mathematics, biological/physical sciences, social sciences. Bachelor's: 124 hrs (30 in major).

STUDENT SERVICES

Campus student services include: academic support program, aptitude testing, career and personal counseling, employment service for undergraduates, freshman orientation, health services, placement services, remedial instruction, special counselor, tutoring, veterans counselor, services for handicapped. ROTC: Air Force, Army.

ADDRESS:

N. CAROLINA CENTRAL UNIV.
P.O. BOX 19717
DURHAM,   NC   27707
Principal Official: Atty. Julius L. Chambers, Chancellor

TYPES OF DEGREES AWARDED:
BA, BS, MA, MS, MBA, F.

ACADEMIC CALENDAR:
Semester. Summer sessions.

CONTACT INFORMATION

Admissions Officer: Ms. Nancy Rowland
Phone: (919) 560-6100   **Fax:** ((919) 560-5462
Web Site: Not provided.

DOLLARS AND SENSE

TUITION & FEES:	$1,789.00
ROOM & BOARD:	$3,270.00
BOOKS & SUPPLIES:	$450.00
OTHER EXPENSES:	$386.00
OUT OF STATE TUITION:	$8,943.00
*ANNUAL TOTAL:	$5,895.00

(*Annual Total does not include out-of-state tuition .)

FINANCIAL AID

Financial Aid Phone:
Financial Aid Fax:

Closing date May 1; priority given to applications received by March 1; notifications on a rolling basis beginning about May 15; must reply within 2 weeks. FAFSA accepted. Grants, loans, jobs available all based on need. Academic, athletic, art, religious affiliation, music/drama, leadership, state/district residency scholarships available.

SPORTS

Varsity Sports: Baseball, basketball, golf, soccer, softball, tennis, volleyball. NAIA.

WHAT MAJOR?

Bachelor's: Accounting, actuarial sciences, African-American studies, art education, banking and finance, biology, business administration, business management, business economics, business education, chemistry, computer sciences, dramatic arts, education, elementary education, English, English education, fine arts, food sciences, human nutrition, foreign languages education, French, geography, health education, history, home economics education, jazz, law enforcement and corrections, marketing and distribution, mathematics, mathematics education, music, music education, music performance, nursing, parks and recreation management, philosophy, physical education, physics, political science and government, preelementary education, psychology, sacred music, science education, secondary education, social science education, social sciences, social studies education, sociology, Spanish, speech/communication/theater education, textiles and clothing, visual and performing arts, visual communications.

Historical & Special Interest:

North Carolina Central University was founded in 1910 by Dr. James E. Shepard who coined the school's slogan "Truth and Service." It is one of 16 institutions of the University of North Carolina System with over 5,000 students and is the first state-supported liberal arts college for Blacks.

NCCU offers a comprehensive educational program at the undergraduate, graduate, and first professional degree levels. Its School of Graduate Studies coordinates advanced degrees in business, education, the arts and sciences, and library and information sciences.

Master Key: *Good resolutions like a screaming child should be carried out.*

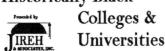
NORFOLK STATE UNIVERSITY
NORFOLK, VA

SCHOOL INFO

Established in 1935. 4-year public university of arts and sciences and nursing college on urban campus in large city in metropolitan Tidewater areas: Portsmouth, Hampton, Newport etc.

ADDRESS:

NORFOLK STATE UNIVERSITY
2401 CORPEW AVENUE
NORFOLK,   VA   23504
Principal Official: Dr. Marie V. McDemmond, President

TYPES OF DEGREES AWARDED:
AS, BA, BS, MA, MS, MBA., PhD

ACADEMIC CALENDAR:
Semester. Summer sessions extensive.

CONTACT INFORMATION

Admissions Officer: Dr. Frank Cool
Phone: (757) 683-8396   **Fax:** (757) 683-2078
Web Site: www.nsu/edu

ACCREDITATON:
Southern Association of Colleges & Schools

CAMPUS ENROLLMENT:

Undergraduate: 7000 men and women (55%). **Transfer:** 1500; **Graduate:** 1100 men and women. **Freshman ethnic enrollment: African American** 82%, **Asian** 1%, **Caucasian** 15%, **Hispanic** 1%.

DOLLARS AND SENSE

TUITION & FEES:	$3,000.00
ROOM & BOARD:	$4,566.00
BOOKS & SUPPLIES:	$425.00
OTHER EXPENSES:	$300.00
OUT OF STATE TUITION:	$6,802.00
*ANNUAL TOTAL:	$8,291.00

(*Annual Total does not include out-of-state tuition.)

WHAT DO I NEED?

High school GPA 2.0, 2 letters of recommendation required. SAT or ACT for placement and counseling only; scores by September 1. Application fee $20 may be waived based on need. No closing date; priority given to applications received by May 1; notifications on a rolling basis around February 1; must reply by May 1. Deferred and early admissions program available.

UNIQUE PROGRAMS

The following programs are available: accelerated program, cooperative education, double major, cross-registration, honors program, independent study, internships, teacher preparation, study abroad, national science institute.

FINANCIAL AID

Financial Aid Phone: (757) 683-8381
Financial Aid Fax:

No closing date; priority given to applications received by April 15; notifications on a rolling basis beginning 2-3 weeks; must reply by May 1. FAFSA and institutional form required. Pell grants, loans, jobs based on need. AMS payment plan available. Academic, Presidential, National Institute and City Norfolk and non-residential Scholarships available.

ACADEMIC REQUIREMENTS

Freshmen must earn a minimum 1.6 and majors must be declared by end of second year.

Core curriculum: English, mathematics, biological/physical sciences, social sciences. Associate: 62 hrs. Bachelor's: 120 hrs.

STUDENT SERVICES

Campus student services include: academic center, aptitude testing, campus daycare, career and personal counseling, employment services for undergraduates, health services, placement services, reduced course load, remedial instruction, special counselor, veterans counselor, services for handicapped. ROTC: Army, Navy, Marine Corps.

SPORTS

Varsity Sports: Baseball, football, wrestling, basketball, cross-country, tennis, track and field, volleyball, softbal. NCAA Division I.

WHAT MAJOR?

Associates: Construction, drafting, electronic technology, library science, nursing, secretarial and related programs, textiles and clothing.
Bachelor's: Accounting, art education, biology, business and management, business education, chemistry, computer and information sciences, drafting and design technology, economics, electrical/electronics/communications engineering, elementary education, English, English education, family/consumer resource management, fine arts, food sciences and human nutrition, foreign languages education, health care administration, health education, history, home economics, home economics education, individual and family development, industrial arts education, institutional/home management/supporting programs, journalism, labor/industrial relations, liberal/general studies, mathematics, mathematics education, medical laboratory technologies, medical records administration, music, music education, nursing, occupational safety and health technology, parks and recreation management, physical education, physics, political science and government, psychology, radio/television, reading education, secretarial and related programs, social work, sociology, special education, speech pathology/audiology.

Historical & Special Interest:

Norfolk State University is located on over 122 acres, utilizes 23 modern buildings and enrolls 8,000 plus students. It is a fully accredited, four-year, co-educational institution of nine schools offering seven Associate degree programs, 49 Bachelors degrees, 2 Doctoral Programs and 15 Masters degree programs. Classroom buildings include a technology center; a life science center with a planetarium; a new ROTC/physical educational and basketball arena complex; and a communications center with laboratories for television and 1000 watt FM radio station. Its programs are nationally accredited by American Corrective Therapy Association, the National Accrediting Agency for Clinical Laboratory Sciences, National League for Nursing, Council on Social Work Education and National Association of Schools of Music, American Medical Records Association, American Dietics Association, American Psychological Association and the Committee on Allied Health Education and Association as well as the Southern Association of Colleges and Schools.

Master Key: *Building boys is easier than mending men.*

HBCU Third Edition
© Jireh & Associates, Inc.
Wilmington, DE

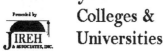

Historically Black Colleges & Universities

OAKWOOD COLLEGE
HUNTSVILLE, AL

Web Site:
www.oakwood.edu

SCHOOL INFO
Established in 1896. 4-year private liberal arts college, coed, affiliated with Seventh-day Adventists. Suburban campus in small city; 5 miles from downtown.

ACCREDITATON:
Southern Association of Colleges & Schools

CAMPUS ENROLLMENT:
Undergraduate: 1334 men & women. **Transfer students:** 67 men & women. **Freshman ethnic enrollment:** African American-297, Caucasian-1, Other-1.

WHAT DO I NEED?
Achievement record, test scores and essay recommended. Consideration given to provisional applicants. College-prepreparatory program. SAT or ACT for placement and counseling only; score report by Aug 15. Application fee $10 may be waived based on need. No closing date; notifications on a rolling basis.

UNIQUE PROGRAMS
The following programs are available: cooperative education, double major, honors program, study abroad.

ACADEMIC REQUIREMENTS
Minimum GPA for freshmen is 2.0 and majors must be declared by end of the first year.

Core curriculum: arts/fine arts, computer science, English, history, humanities, mathematics, philosophy/religion, biological/physical sciences, social sciences. Associate: 96 hours. Bachelor's: 192 hours. Hours in major: 59 and 60 respectively.

STUDENT SERVICES
Campus student services include: aptitude testing, career and personal counseling, employment service for undergraduates, health services, campus day care, learning center, placement services, reduced course load program, remedial instruction, special counselor, tutoring, special advisors, veterans counselor.

ADDRESS:

OAKWOOD COLLEGE
P.O. BOX 107
HUNTSVILLE,   AL   35896
Principal Official: Dr. Benjamin Reaves

TYPES OF DEGREES AWARDED:
AA, AS, BA, BS.

ACADEMIC CALENDAR:
Quarter. Summer sessions limited.

CONTACT INFORMATION
Admissions Officer: Ms. Tanya Bowman, Assoc.
Phone: (800) 824-5312   **Fax:** (205) 726-7154
Web Site: www.oakwood.edu

DOLLARS AND SENSE

TUITION & FEES:	$8,349.00
ROOM & BOARD:	$5,082.00
BOOKS & SUPPLIES:	$600.00
OTHER EXPENSES:	$1,845.00
OUT OF STATE TUITION:	$8,349.00
*ANNUAL TOTAL:	$15,876.00

(*Annual Total does not include out-of-state tuition .)

FINANCIAL AID
Financial Aid Phone:
Financial Aid Fax:
No closing date; priority given to applications received by April 15; notifications on a rolling basis; must reply within 15 days. FAFSA accepted. Pell grants, loans, jobs available.

SPORTS
Varsity Sports: Baseball, basketball, golf, gymnastics, soccer, softball, tennis, volleyball.

WHAT MAJOR?
Associate: Accounting, Bible studies, child development/care/guidance, communications, graphic design, illustration design, nursing, office supervision and management.

Bachelor's: Accounting, biochemistry, biology, business administration, business economics, business education, business management, chemistry, communications, computer and information sciences, computer mathematics, elementary education, English, English education, food sciences and human nutrition, history, home economics, home economics education, human development and family studies, information sciences and systems, liberal/general studies, management information systems, mathematics, mathematics education, music, music education, nursing, office supervision and management, pre-elementary education, psychology, religion, religious education, science education, secondary education, social science education, social sciences, social work, theological studies.

Historical & Special Interest:

Oakwood College, founded in 1896, is a four-year Christian institution that is owned and operated by the General Conference of Seventh-Day Adventists. It sits on an 1,185-acre beautifully landscaped campus. Academic programs are available in Natural Sciences and Mathematics, Behavioral and Social Sciences, Humanities, Religion and Theology, and Applied Sciences and Education.

Oakwood College endeavors to "Challenge and motivate its students for service to humanity and to God...". Its current president, Dr. Benjamin F. Reaves, is a 1955 graduate of Oakwood College. Oakwood College is a UNCF school.

Master Key: *If there is a way to do it better... find it. Thomas A. Edison*

HBCU Third Edition
© Jireh & Associates, Inc.
Wilmington, DE

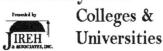
PAINE COLLEGE
AUGUSTA, GA

Web Site:
www.paine.edu

SCHOOL INFO

Established in 1882. 4-year private liberal arts coed college, affiliated with Christian Methodist Episcopal Church on urban campus in a large town; 74 miles from Columbia, South Carolina.

ACCREDITATON:
Southern Association of Colleges & Schools

CAMPUS ENROLLMENT:
Undergraduate: 686 men & women. **Transfer students:** 26 men & women. **Freshman ethnic enrollment:** African American-225

WHAT DO I NEED?

High school academic record, recommendations and test scores considered. Scores by July 15. $10 application fee. Closing date June 15; and applicants notified on rolling basis. Interview recommended; for music education audition required. Essay required. Early admission program available.

UNIQUE PROGRAMS

The following programs are available: cooperative education, honors program, independent study, internships, cross-registration; teacher preparation, study abroad.

ACADEMIC REQUIREMENTS

Minimum GPA 1.7. A core of at least 34 hours is required for each major. Major must be declared by the end of second year.

Core curriculum: Arts/fine arts, computer science, English, foriegn languages, history, mathematics, biological/physical sciences, philosophy/religion, and social sciences. Bachelor's: 124 hours (48 in major).

STUDENT SERVICES

Campus student services include: aptitude testing, career and personal counseling, employment services for undergraduates, freshmen orientation, health services, placement service for graduates, preadmission summer program, reduced course load program, remedial instruction, services for handicapped, tutoring, veterans counselor. ROTC: Army.

WHAT MAJOR?

Bachelor's: Biology, business administration, chemistry, communications, early childhood education, English, history, mass communications, mathematics, middle grades education, music education, philosophy, psychology, religion, sociology.

Historical & Special Interest:

After the Civil War, the Black members of the Methodist Episcopal Church, formed the Colored (now Christian) Methodist Episcopal Church. Realizing the need for an institution of learning designed to train ministers and teachers, Bishop Lucius H. Holsey and other leaders of the C.M.E. requested assistance of the mother church in the organization and support of the school.

In 1882, each church appointed three of its members to a committee which established Paine Institute, named in honor of Bishop Robert Paine. Six months after incorporation, classes began in rented quarters on Broad Street in Augusta, GA. The present site was acquired in 1886. In those days, the campus looked more pastoral than collegiate with barns, chickens, mules, and cultivated fields, in addition to its classrooms, library and residences.

In 1903, Paine Institute was re-chartered as Paine College. However, there were no public schools for Blacks at that time, and Paine continued to provide secondary education for its students as well as college work. It was not until 1945, when the first public high school for Blacks was opened in Augusta, that Paine discontinued preparatory programs.

Almost since its beginning, Paine's faculty has been interracial. Dr. John Wesley Gilbert, Paines' first student and first graduate, furthered his education at Brown University and Athens, Greece and returned in 1888 to become Paine's first Black faculty member.

ADDRESS:

PAINE COLLEGE
1235 - 15TH ST.
AUGUSTA,   GA   30910
Principal Official: Dr. Shirley A. R. Lewis

TYPES OF DEGREES AWARDED:
BA, BS.

ACADEMIC CALENDAR:
Semester. Summer sessions.

CONTACT INFORMATION

Admissions Officer: Ellen King
Phone: (800) 476-7703   **Fax:** (706) 821-8293
Web Site: www.paine.edu

DOLLARS AND SENSE

TUITION & FEES:	$7,220.00
ROOM & BOARD:	$3,520.00
BOOKS & SUPPLIES:	$400.00
OTHER EXPENSES:	$800.00
OUT OF STATE TUITION:	
*ANNUAL TOTAL:	$11,940.00

(*Annual Total does not include out-of-state tuition .)

FINANCIAL AID

Financial Aid Phone:
Financial Aid Fax:

No closing date; priority given to applications received by May 15. Notifications on a rolling basis beginning June 1. Reply required within 2 weeks of notification. FAFSA acceptedd. Pell grants, loans, and jobs available and based on need. Music and drama scholarships available.

SPORTS

Varsity Sports: baseball, basketball, cross-country, softball, track and field, volleyball. NCAA.

Master Key: *Silence cannot be misquoted. Murdock*

HBCU Third Edition
© Jireh & Associates, Inc.
Wilmington, DE

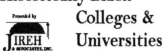
PAUL QUINN COLLEGE

DALLAS, TX

Web Site:
Not provided.

SCHOOL INFO

Established in 1872. 4-year private liberal arts coed college with African Methodist Episcopal Church on 130-acre urban campus in Dallas, in the former home of Bishop College.

ACCREDITATON:
Southern Association of Colleges & Schools

CAMPUS ENROLLMENT:
*Undergraduate: 750 total; 250 men and 500 women. **Freshman ethnic enrollment:** A.A. - 83%; Asian - 2%; Hisp. - 15%.

WHAT DO I NEED?

2.0 GPA required. SAT or ACT (required); deadline for Fall by July 1; deadline for Spring by November 15th. Application fee - $15. Notifications on a rolling basis. EDP-F. Deferred admission program available.

UNIQUE PROGRAMS

The following programs are available: cooperative education, double major, honors program, internships, cooperative program with Texas State Technical Institute for Bachelor of Applied Science in 24 fields.

ACADEMIC REQUIREMENTS

T. Assessment Skills Proficiency (TASP) required and must be passed by close of Sophomore year. Freshmen must earn a minimum 2.0 and majors must be declared by end of second year.

GRE test required prior to graduation. Core curriculum: arts/fine arts, computer science, English, history, mathematics, philosophy/religion, biological/physical sciences, social sciences. Bachelor's: 128 hrs (36 in major).

STUDENT SERVICES

Campus student services include: aptitude testing, career and personal counseling, employment service for undergraduates, freshmen orientation, health services, reduced course load program, remedial instruction, special counselor, tutoring. ROTC: Air Force.

WHAT MAJOR?

Bachelor's: Accounting, biology, business administration and management, business and office, communications, computer and information sciences, computer technology, criminal justice studies, drafting and design technology, elementary education, English, history, laser elctro-optic technology, mathematics, medical laboratory, music, occupational safety and health technology, religion, secondary education, social education, social work, sociology.

Historical & Special Interest:

Paul Quinn College was begun by a group of African Methodist Circuit Riders in a one room building in Austin, Texas in 1872. They saw a need for a trade school to teach newly freed slaves skills in carpentry, blacksmithing, saddlery and tanning. The school was named after Bishop William Paul Quinn and chartered in May 1881 by the state of Texas and was moved to Waco, Texas. It is the oldest liberal arts college established by Negroes, west of the Mississippi River.

At Paul Quinn twenty bachelor degrees in ten areas are offered. A cooperative relationship with Baylor University and the Texas State Technical Institute allows the college to offer nearly 30 other degree opportunities.

The archives for the African Methodist Episcopal Church national and state of Texas memorabalia is housed in the Johnson Library-Learning Resource Center. Paul Quinn College is a UNCF school.

ADDRESS:

PAUL QUINN COLLEGE
3837 SIMPSON STEWART ROAD
DALLAS,   TX   75241
Principal Official: Dr. Lee E. Monroe

TYPES OF DEGREES AWARDED:
BA, BS.

ACADEMIC CALENDAR:
Semester. Summer sessions limited.

CONTACT INFORMATION

Admissions Officer: Ralph Spencer
Phone: (214) 302-3520   **Fax:** (214) 302-3613
Web Site: Not provided.

DOLLARS AND SENSE

TUITION & FEES:	$4,590.00
ROOM & BOARD:	$3,525.00
BOOKS & SUPPLIES:	$700.00
OTHER EXPENSES:	$0.00
OUT OF STATE TUITION:	
*ANNUAL TOTAL:	$8,815.00

(*Annual Total does not include out-of-state tuition .)

FINANCIAL AID

Financial Aid Phone: (214) 302-3530
Financial Aid Fax: (214) 302-3013

Fall closing date June 1; notifications on a rolling basis; student must reply by July 1 or if notified after the 15, within 2 weeks. FAFSA accepted. Pell grants, loans based on need. Four Academic Merit scholarships; 7 Activity Scholarships available.

SPORTS

Varsity Sports: Baseball, basketball, softball, track and field, and volleybal. NAIA.

Master Key: *A diamond cannot be polished without friction, nor can man be perfected without trials. Anonymous*

HBCU Third Edition
© Jireh & Associates, Inc.
Wilmington, DE

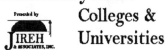
PHILANDER SMITH COLLEGE

LITTLE ROCK, AR

Web Site:
www.philander.edu

SCHOOL INFO

Established in1877. A 4-year private liberal arts college, coed, affiliated with United Methodist Church on urban campus in small city in downtown area.

ADDRESS:

PHILANDER SMITH COLLEGE
812 WEST 13TH ST.
LITTLE ROCK,   AR   72202
Principal Official: Dr. Myer L. Titus

TYPES OF DEGREES AWARDED:
BA, BS.

ACADEMIC CALENDAR:
Semester. Summer sessions limited.

CONTACT INFORMATION

Admissions Officer: Ms. Beverly Richardson
Phone: (501) 375-9845   **Fax:** (501) 370-5225
Web Site: www.philander.edu

ACCREDITATON:
North Central Association of Colleges & Schools

CAMPUS ENROLLMENT:
*Undergraduate: 657 Total men and women. Part-time: 194. **Freshman ethnic enrollment: Not available.**

WHAT DO I NEED?
Open admissions. Application fee $10 may be waived based on need. No closing date; notifications on a rolling basis.

UNIQUE PROGRAMS
The following programs are available: Internships, Teacher Certificate, and Double Major.

ACADEMIC REQUIREMENTS

Minimum GPA of 2.0 for freshmen and major must be declared on enrollment.

Core curriculum: English, foreign languages, humanities, mathematics, philosophy/religion, biological/physical science, social science. Bachelor's: minimum 124 hrs.

STUDENT SERVICES
Campus student services include: aptitude testing, employment services for undergraduates, personal and career counseling, special counseling, tutoring, veterans counselor.

DOLLARS AND SENSE

TUITION & FEES:	$3,538.00
ROOM & BOARD:	$2,746.00
BOOKS & SUPPLIES:	$1,075.00
OTHER EXPENSES:	$350.00
OUT OF STATE TUITION:	$3,538.00
*ANNUAL TOTAL:	$7,709.00

(*Annual Total does not include out-of-state tuition .)

FINANCIAL AID

Financial Aid Phone: (501) 370-5350
Financial Aid Fax: (501) 370-5357

No closing date; priority given to applications received by May 1; notifications on a rolling basis; must reply within 2 weeks. FAFSA accepted. Pell grants, SEOG, loans, work-study and Arkansas Student Assistance Grants available. Payment Option Plans available.

SPORTS

Varsity sports: Basketball.

WHAT MAJOR?

Bachelor's: Biology, business administration, elementary education, English, psychology, physical education, political science, sociology, special education, political science, computer science, organizational management.

Historical & Special Interest:

Philander-Smith is the result of one of the early attempts to make education available to freed men west of the Mississippi River by the United Methodist Church. It has a rich Christian heritage that emphasizes service in its faculty, students, and educational philosophy. The General Board of Higher Education and Campus Ministry of the United Methodist Church has historically financed the College Program. It is located in the historic Little Rock area on approximately 20 acres.

Philander-Smith College is a UNCF school.

Notable Alumni:

Dr. Joycelyn Elders, Sherman Tate, Rev. Dr. Cecil Wayne Cone, Dr. Eddie Reed, Dr. Collins A. Mbanugo.

Master Key: *The greatest mistake a man can make is to be afraid of making one. Elbert Hubbard*

HBCU Third Edition
© Jireh & Associates, Inc.
Wilmington, DE

PRAIRIE VIEW A&M COLLEGE

PRAIRIE VIEW, TX

Web Site:
www.pvamu.edu

SCHOOL INFO

Established in 1876. 4-year public coed college of arts and sciences, agriculture, engineering, nursing and teachers in rural campus in Prairie View; 40 miles northwest of Houston.

ACCREDITATON:
Southern Association of Colleges & Schools

CAMPUS ENROLLMENT:
*Undergraduate: Full-time: 2317 men and 2412 women. Part-time: 188 men and 244 women. **Graduate:** Full-time: 52 men and 74 women. Part-time: 185 men and 340 women.

WHAT DO I NEED?

Rank top half of high school senior class, GPA 2.0, and SAT combined 700 or ACT composite 15. SAT or ACT; scores before second semester. No application fee. No closing date; notifications on a rolling basis. Essay required for Honors College. Deferred and early admission program available.

UNIQUE PROGRAMS

The following programs are available: cooperative education, double major, dual enrollment of high school students, education specialist degree, honors program, independent study, internships, teacher preparation; combined bachelor's/graduate program in business administration.

ACADEMIC REQUIREMENTS

Freshmen must earn a minimum 2.0 and majors must be declared by end of second year.

Core curriculum: English, history, mathematics, biological/physical sciences, social sciences. Honors college (applied science) participation in symposia/seminars. Bachelor's: 120 hrs.

STUDENT SERVICES

Campus student services include: academic center, aptitude testing, career and personal counseling, freshman orientation, health services, campus daycare, placement services, reduced course load program, special counselor, services for handicapped, tutoring. ROTC: Army, Naval.

ADDRESS:

PRAIRIE VIEW A&M COLLEGE
P.O. BOX 3089
PRAIRIE VIEW,   TX   77446
Principal Official: Dr. Charles Hines

TYPES OF DEGREES AWARDED:
BA, BA, BFA, MA, MS, MBA.

ACADEMIC CALENDAR:
Semester. Summer sessions.

CONTACT INFORMATION

Admissions Officer: Deborah Dungey
Phone: (409) 857-2618   **Fax:** (409) 857-2699
Web Site: www.pvamu.edu

DOLLARS AND SENSE

TUITION & FEES:	$1,816.00
ROOM & BOARD:	$3,764.00
BOOKS & SUPPLIES:	$513.00
OTHER EXPENSES:	$1,302.00
OUT OF STATE TUITION:	$6,952.00
*ANNUAL TOTAL:	$7,395.00

(*Annual Total does not include out-of-state tuition .)

FINANCIAL AID

Financial Aid Phone:
Financial Aid Fax:
No closing date; priority given to applications received by April 16; notifications on a rolling basis beginning around June 1; must reply within 2 weeks. FAFSA accepted. Pell grants, loans based on need. Academic, music/drama, minority scholarships available.

SPORTS

Varsity Sports: Baseball, basketball, cross-country, football, golf, tennis, track and field. NAIA.

WHAT MAJOR?

Bachelor's: Accounting, agricultural economics/engineering/sciences, agronomy, animal sciences, architecture, banking and finance, biology, business economics, business education, chemical engineering, chemistry, civil engineering, communications, computer and information sciences, computer technology, computer-aided drafting and design, drafting and design technology, dramatic arts, electrical technology/communications engineering, elementary education, English, fashion design, food sciences and human nutrition, geography, health education, history, individual and family development, industrial arts education, industrial design, indusrial education, industrial engineering, industrial technology, journalism, law enforcement and corrections, management science, marketing management, mathematics, mechanical design technology, mechanical engineering, music, music performance, nursing, office administration, physical education, physics, political science and government, psychology, radio/television, secondary education, social work, sociology, Spanish, speech correction, speech/debate/forensics, trade and industrial education.

Historical & Special Interest:
Prairie View A&M University, a land-grant institution, is the second oldest institution of higher education in the state of Texas. Its beginnings were in the Texas Constitution of 1876, which, in separate articles, established an "agricultural and mechanical college" and pledged that "separate schools shall be provided for the white and colored children, and impartial provisions shall be made for both."

As a consequence of these constitutional provisions, the Fifteenth Legislature, on August 14, 1876, established the Agricultural and Mechanical College of Texas for Colored Youths and placed responsibility for its management with the Board of Directors of the Agricultural and Mechanical College at Bryan. The A&M College Board of Directors authorized the teaching of 13 subjects on the elementary and secondary levels with E.H. Anderson as principal in 1879. His brother, L.C. Anderson became principal in 1885, served for 12 years, and was the founder of the politically active Colored Teachers Association of Texas. In 1889, the Twenty-Sixth Legislature changed the name of the school to Prairie View State Normal and Industrial College reflecting the expanded curriculum. The first three degrees were granted in 1903. The name Prairie View Normal and Industrial College was changed by the forty-Ninth Legislature in 1945 to Prairie View University.

Master Key: *Failure is only the opportunity to more intelligently begin again. Henry Ford*

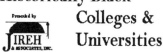

ROXBURY COMMUNITY COLLEGE
ROXBURY MA

Web Site:
Not provided.

SCHOOL INFO
Established in 1972. 2-year public coed community college on urban campus in a very large city.

ACCREDITATON:
New England Association of Colleges & Schools, NLNAC, MBNR.

CAMPUS ENROLLMENT:
Undergraduate: 1400 men & women. **Freshman ethnic enrollment:** Native American-1%, African American-63%, Asian-3%, Caucasian-6%, Hispanic-17.5%, Other-1.

WHAT DO I NEED?
Admissions open. Interviews and/or recommendations for specialized programs. High school diploma, GED or equivalent. Proof of citizenship or immigration status, proof of state residency. Application fee $10 in-state; $35 out-of-state.

UNIQUE PROGRAMS
The following programs are available: independent study, interships, cross-registration and 2-year transfer program. Joint admissions with Massachusetts 4-year colleges and universities. Tuition advantage (33% discount) at public institutions upon transfer if 'B' or better grade maintained at RCC.

ACADEMIC REQUIREMENTS
Minimum GPA of 1.79; majors must be declared on enrollment.

Core curriculum: arts/fine arts, computer science, English, foreign languages, history, humanities, mathematics, philosophy/religion, biological/physical sciences, social sciences. Associate: 60 hours.

STUDENT SERVICES
Campus student services include: Library, health services, disabilities counselor, student activities office, learning center, remedial instruction, tutoring.

ADDRESS:

ROXBURY COMMUNITY COLLEGE
1234 COLUMBUS AVENUE
ROXBURY CROSSING,   MA   02120
Principal Official: Dr. Grace Carolyn Brown

TYPES OF DEGREES AWARDED:
AA, AS and Certificates.

ACADEMIC CALENDAR:
Semester. Summer sessions limited.

CONTACT INFORMATION

Admissions Officer: Dr. Rudolph Jones
Phone: (617) 541-5310   **Fax:** (617) 427-5316
Web Site: Not provided.

DOLLARS AND SENSE

TUITION & FEES:	$2,662.00
ROOM & BOARD:	$0.00
BOOKS & SUPPLIES:	$600.00
OTHER EXPENSES:	$265.00
OUT OF STATE TUITION:	$6,550.00
*ANNUAL TOTAL:	$3,527.00

(*Annual Total does not include out-of-state tuition .)

FINANCIAL AID

Financial Aid Phone: (617) 541-5322
Financial Aid Fax: (617) 541-5390

Closing date for applications August 1; applicants notified on a rolling basis. FAFSA accepted. Pell grants, state scholarships, SEOG, loans, jobs available.

SPORTS
Varsity Sports: Basketball. Intramural Sports: Basketball, gymnastics, tennis. NJCAA.

WHAT MAJOR?
Associate: Accounting, aeronautical technology, business administration, business management, computer sciences, biology, drafting, pre-engineering and engineering-related technologies, environmental management, legal secretary, liberal arts, marketing and distribution, mechanical design technology, medical laboratory technologies, medical secretary, pre-nursing, nursing, physical sciences, precision metal work, secretarial and related programs, social science, early childhood, office technology, micro-computer, computer info systems, theatre visual arts, music, arts & humanities, retail management, criminal justice, hospitality.

Certificates: Allied health, paralegal, bookkeeping, computers, Computer-Assisted Drafting, Office Technology.

Master Key: *He who masters his time masters his life. Murdock*

HBCU Third Edition
© Jireh & Associates, Inc.
Wilmington, DE

75

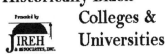
RUST COLLEGE
HOLLY SPRINGS, MS

Web Site:
Not provided.

SCHOOL INFO
Established in 1866. Private, coed, 4-year liberal arts college. United Methodist affiliation on rural campus in small town; 45 miles southeast of Memphis, TN.

ADDRESS:

RUST COLLEGE
150 RUST AVENUE
HOLLY SPRINGS,   MS   38635
Principal Official: Dr. David L. Beckley

TYPES OF DEGREES AWARDED:
AS, BA, BS.

ACADEMIC CALENDAR:
Semester. Summer sessions limited.

CONTACT INFORMATION

Admissions Officer: JoAnn Scott
Phone: (601) 252-8000   **Fax:** (601) 252-6107
Web Site: Not provided.

ACCREDITATON:
Southern Association of Colleges & Schools

CAMPUS ENROLLMENT:
Undergraduate: 287 men & 442 women. **Transfer students:** 15 men & 19 women;
Part-time: 61 men & 147 women. **Freshman ethnic enrollment:** African American-871, Caucasian-19; Foreign-47

WHAT DO I NEED?
Academic record, test scores, recommendations important. College preparatory program. SAT or ACT (ACT preferred) scores by August 15. Application Fee $10 which may be waived with need; no closing date and priority to applications received by August 1; notifications on a rolling basis beginning about May 1; replies within 2 weeks. Early admission program available.

UNIQUE PROGRAMS
The following programs are available: cooperative education/internships, double major, honors program, independent study, internships, study abroad, teacher preparation, health sciences, liberal arts/career combination in engineering.

ACADEMIC REQUIREMENTS
Freshmen must earn a minimum 2.0 and majors must be declared by end of second year.

Core curriculum: Computer science, English, foreign languages, history, humanities, mathematics, biological/physical sciences, philosophy/religion, social sciences. Associate: 66 hrs. Bachelor's: 124 (36 in major).

STUDENT SERVICES
Campus student services include: academic center, basic skills laboratories, career and personal counseling, health services, campus daycare, placement services, reduced course load program, remedial instruction, special counselor, tutoring. ROTC: Army.

DOLLARS AND SENSE

TUITION & FEES:	$7,300.00
ROOM & BOARD:	$0.00
BOOKS & SUPPLIES:	$220.00
OTHER EXPENSES:	$135.00
OUT OF STATE TUITION:	$0.00
*ANNUAL TOTAL:	$7,655.00

(*Annual Total does not include out-of-state tuition .)

FINANCIAL AID

Financial Aid Phone: (601) 252-8000 x4061
Financial Aid Fax: (601) 252-8895 ext 4915

Application closing date August 1; notifications on a rolling basis beginning about July 10; must reply within 2 weeks. Grants, loans, work programs available. FAFSA accepted. Academic, alumni affiliation, music/drama, minority, religious affiliation, special scholarships available. **Payment Plan Options:** Deferred Payment Plan (monthly installments).

SPORTS

Varsity Sports: Baseball, Volleyball, basketball, cross-country, tennis, track and field. NCAA.

WHAT MAJOR?
Associate: Business and office, secretarial and related programs.

Bachelors: Business administration (Accounting, Computer Science, Economics, Management, Marketing, Office Administration), Elementary education, Early Childhood Education, Health-Physical Education and Recreation, Secondary Education (Business, English, Music, Science Mathematics, Social Science), English/Liberal ARts, English/Journalism, Mass Communication/Print Journalism, Music, Music Media, Biology, Chemistry, Computer Science, Mathematics, Physics, Political Science and Legal Studies, Sociology, Social Work, (Engineering and Nursing and Biology - dual degree program with other institutions) Medical Technology - Cooperative program with other institutions).

Historical & Special Interest:
Rust College was established in 1866 by the Freedman's Aid Society of the Methodist Episcopal Church. Its founders were missionaries from the North who opened a school in Asbury Methodist Episcopal Church, accepting adults of all ages, as well as children, for instruction in elementary subjects. A year later, the first building on the present campus was erected.

In 1870, the school was chartered as Shaw University, honoring the Reverend S.O. Shaw, who made a gift of $10,000 to the new institution. In 1892, the name was changed to Rust University as a tribute to Richland S. Rust, Secretary of the Freedman's Aid Society and to avoid confusion with another Shaw University. The name was again changed to Rust College. High school and college courses were added to the curriculum and in 1878 two students were graduated from the college department. As public school for Negroes became more widespread, the need for private schools decreased and in 1930 the grade school was discontinued. The high school continued to function in 1953. A significant change in the administration of the institution took place in 1920 when Dr. M. S. Davage became president, the first Negro to hold that position. Among approximately 20,000 students of Rust, many completed only their elementary or secondary education. However, more than 5,000 have graduated from the college department. Rust College is a UNCF school.

Master Key: *No man fails who does his best... Orison Swett Marden*

HBCU Third Edition
© Jireh & Associates, Inc.
Wilmington, DE

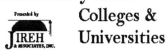
SAINT AUGUSTINE'S COLLEGE

RALEIGH, NC

Web Site:
www.staugustinescollege.com

SCHOOL INFO

Established in 1867. 4-year private, liberal arts coed college with Episcopal Church affiliation on urban campus in small city; 170 miles from Charlotte, North Carolina.

ACCREDITATON:
Southern Association of Colleges & Schools

CAMPUS ENROLLMENT:
Undergraduate: 1918 men & women. **Transfer students:** 73 men & women. **Freshman ethnic enrollment:** African American-696, Caucasian-6

WHAT DO I NEED?

Test scores, academic record, recommendations considered important. College preparatory program. Minimum SAT score report by August 1. ACT or SAT (SAT preferred). Application fee: $25. Closing date August 1; notifications on a rolling basis.

UNIQUE PROGRAMS

The following programs are available: accelerated program, honors program, independent study, internships, study abroad, teacher preparation, cross-registration; liberal arts/career combination in engineering.

ACADEMIC REQUIREMENTS

Freshmen must earn a minimum 2.0 and majors must be declared by end of second year.

Core curriculum: Computer Science, English, foreign languages, history, mathematics, biological/physical sciences, philosophy/religion, social sciences. Bachelor's: 126 hrs (36 in major). The college offers high quality programs to prepare students for a profession, graduate school and a career.

STUDENT SERVICES

Campus student services include: career and personal counseling, employment service for undergraduates, freshman orientation, health services, placement services, remedial instruction, tutoring, veterans counselor. ROTC: Air Force, Army.

ADDRESS:

SAINT AUGUSTINE'S COLLEGE
1315 OAKWOOD AVENUE
RALEIGH,   NC   27610-2298
Principal Official: Dr. Bernard W. Franklin

TYPES OF DEGREES AWARDED:
BA, BS.

ACADEMIC CALENDAR:
Semester.

CONTACT INFORMATION

Admissions Officer: Keith Powell
Phone: (919) 516-4012   **Fax:** (919) 516-5801
Web Site: www.staugustinescollege.com

DOLLARS AND SENSE

TUITION & FEES:	$5,769.00
ROOM & BOARD:	$2,146.00
BOOKS & SUPPLIES:	$0.00
OTHER EXPENSES:	$0.00
OUT OF STATE TUITION:	$5,769.00
*ANNUAL TOTAL:	$7,915.00

(*Annual Total does not include out-of-state tuition .)

FINANCIAL AID

Financial Aid Phone: (919) 516-4131
Financial Aid Fax: (919)516-5805
Closing date April 15; notifications on a rolling basis; must reply within 4 weeks. FAFSA accepted. Pell grants, loans, jobs available all based on need. Academic, music/drama, leadership, state/district residency scholarships available.

SPORTS

Varsity Sports: Baseball, basketball, bowling, cross-country, fencing, golf, softball, tennis, track and field, volleyball.

WHAT MAJOR?

Bachelor's: 36 Majors and areas of concentration. Accounting, aerospace and African-American studies, art studies, biological and agricultural engineering, biology, biology education, business education, business administration, chemical engineering, chemistry, civil engineering, clinical laboratory science, communication, computer sciences, criminal justice, elementary education, English, English education, exceptional children's education, history, human performance (physical education [non-teaching]), industrial engineering, industrial mathematics, international business, materials engineering, mathematics, mathematics education, mechanical engineering, modern foreign languages (French & Spanish), music business, music education, music performance, physical education, political science, pre-medical sciences, psychology, social studies education, sociology, theatre/dance/film.

Historical & Special Interest:

St. Augustine's College was founded in 1867 and has close ties with the Protestant Episcopal Church. Its past president of twenty-four years, Dr. Prezell R. Robinson is a 1946 graduate of Saint Augustine's College. Its current president is Dr. Bernard W. Franklin. St. Augustine is a private, accredited, four-year, co-educational liberal arts institution. St. Augustine's College is strong in business and administration, the natural sciences and mathematics, communications and teacher education.

St. Augustine's College is a UNCF school.

Master Key: *A new year is not really new if we live the same old life.*

HBCU Third Edition
© Jireh & Associates, Inc.
Wilmington, DE

SAINT PAUL'S COLLEGE
LAWRENCEVILLE, VA

Web Site:
www.stpaul.html

SCHOOL INFO

Established in 1888. 4-year private liberal arts coed college on rural campus setting in small town; 80 miles from Richmond.

ADDRESS:

SAINT PAUL'S COLLEGE
406 WINSOR AVENUE
LAWRENCEVILLE,   VA   23868
Principal Official: Dr. Thomas Law

TYPES OF DEGREES AWARDED:
BA, BS.

ACADEMIC CALENDAR:
Semester. Summer sessions limited.

CONTACT INFORMATION

Admissions Officer: Mary Ransom
Phone: (804) 848-3984   **Fax:** (804) 848-0403
Web Site: www.stpaul.html

ACCREDITATON:
Southern Association of Colleges & Schools

CAMPUS ENROLLMENT:
Undergraduate: 701 men & women. **Transfer students:** 69 men & women. **Freshman ethnic enrollment:** African American-192, Caucasian-4.

DOLLARS AND SENSE

TUITION & FEES:	$10,800.00
ROOM & BOARD:	$4,040.00
BOOKS & SUPPLIES:	$486.00
OTHER EXPENSES:	$950.00
OUT OF STATE TUITION:	
*ANNUAL TOTAL:	$16,276.00

(*Annual Total does not include out-of-state tuition .)

WHAT DO I NEED?
Academic record, extracurricular activities, school recommendations considered, college preparatory program. ACT/SAT(SAT preferred) for placement and counselling only; scores by August 1. Application fee $15. Closing date August 1; notifications on a rolling basis around November 1; must reply by May 1 or within 2 weeks if after May 1.

UNIQUE PROGRAMS
The following programs are available: accelerated program, cooperative education, honors program, internships, teacher preparation; liberal arts/career combination in health sciences.

FINANCIAL AID

Financial Aid Phone:
Financial Aid Fax:
 No closing date; priority given to applications received by June 1; notifications on a rolling basis beginning around March 1; must reply by May 1 or within 2 weeks if after May 1. FAFSA accepted. Pell grants, loans, jobs based on need. Academic, state/district residency scholarships available.

ACADEMIC REQUIREMENTS
Freshmen must earn a minimum 1.4 and majors must be declared by end of second year.

Core curriculum: arts/fine arts, computer science, English, history, humanities, mathematics, biological/physical sciences, philosophy/religion, social sciences. Bachelor's: 120 hrs (30 in major).

STUDENT SERVICES
Campus student services include: academic center, career and personal counseling, employment services for undergraduates, freshman orientation, health services, placement services, preadmission summer program, reduced course load program, remedial instruction, special counselor, tutoring, services for handicapped. ROTC: Army.

SPORTS
Varsity Sports: Baseball, basketball, football, golf, softball, tennis, track and field, volleyball. NCAA.

WHAT MAJOR?
Bachelor's: Accounting, biology, business management, business education, education, elementary education, marketing and distribution, marketing management, mathematics, mathematics education,office supervision and management, physical sciences, political science and government, science education, social sciences, social studies education, sociology.

Historical & Special Interest:

Founded as Saint Paul's Normal and Industrial School in 1888, Saint Paul's College has a long tradition of academic excellence. The name of the institution was changed to Saint Paul's Polytechnic Institute in 1941, and authority was granted to offer a four-year degree program. In 1957, the name was changed to Saint Paul's College.

Saint Paul's College, a private, Episcopalian church-related, coeducational institution with a Christian heritage, has created an environment in which the attributes of integrity, objectivity, resourcefulness, scholarship, and responsible citizenship are emphasized. Its beautifully landscaped 75-acre campus is situated among the rolling lowlands of southern Virginia, approximately 1 1/2 hours from Richmond, VA and 2 hours from Raleigh.

The College is accredited by and holds membership in the Southern Assocation of Colleges and Schools. It is approved by the Virginia State Board of Education and is a member of the Central Intercollegiate Athletic Association and the National Collegiate Athletic Association.

Master Key: *Seek not to be better than your neighbor, but better than yourself.*

HBCU Third Edition
© Jireh & Associates, Inc.
Wilmington, DE

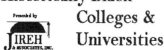
SAVANNAH STATE COLLEGE
SAVANNAH, GA

SCHOOL INFO

Established in 1890. 4-year public arts and sciences and business coed college on urban campus in a small city adjacent to city limits and a part of the University System of Georgia.

ACCREDITATON:
Southern Association of Colleges & Schools

CAMPUS ENROLLMENT:
Undergraduate: 2872 men & women. **Transfer students:** 100 men & women. **Freshman ethnic enrollment:** African American-654, Asian-3, Caucasian-15, Hispanic-4, Other-10

WHAT DO I NEED?
Academic record and GPA considered. SAT/ACT accepted. Students lacking requirements admitted on provisional basis. Scores due by September 1. Application fee $10 which may be waived based on applicant need. Closing date September 1; and applicants notified on rolling basis on or about March 1. Deferred and early admission program available.

UNIQUE PROGRAMS
The following programs are available: cooperative education, double major, dual enrollment of high school students, honors program, independent study, internships, cross-registration; liberal arts/career combination in engineering.

ACADEMIC REQUIREMENTS

Minimum GPA for freshmen 2.0 and major must be declared by end of second year.

Core curriculum: English, history, humanities, mathematics, biological/physical sciences, and social sciences. Credits required for Associate: 110 hours (53 in major). Bachelor's: 195 hours.(100 in major).

STUDENT SERVICES
Campus student services include: aptitude testing, career and personal counseling, employment services for undergraduates, health services, learning center, placement services, remedial instruction, special counselor, tutoring, veterans counselor. ROTC: Army, Naval.

ADDRESS:

SAVANNAH STATE COLLEGE
STATE COLLEGE BRANCH
SAVANNAH,   GA   31404
Principal Official: Dr. John T. Wolfe, Jr.

TYPES OF DEGREES AWARDED:
AS, BA, BS, MA, MBA.

ACADEMIC CALENDAR:
Quarter. Summer sessions.

CONTACT INFORMATION

Admissions Officer: Dr. Roy A. Jackson
Phone: (912) 356-2181   **Fax:** (912) 356-2256
Web Site: www.peachnet.edu/borweb/inst/info

DOLLARS AND SENSE

TUITION & FEES:	$1,815.00
ROOM & BOARD:	$3,310.00
BOOKS & SUPPLIES:	$775.00
OTHER EXPENSES:	$650.00
OUT OF STATE TUITION:	$6,009.00
*ANNUAL TOTAL:	$6,550.00

(*Annual Total does not include out-of-state tuition .)

FINANCIAL AID

Financial Aid Phone:
Financial Aid Fax:
Closing date August 1. Notifications on a rolling basis beginning July 1. FAFSA accepted. Pell grants, loans, and jobs available and based on need. Academic, athletic, music and drama scholarships available.

SPORTS

Varsity Sports: Baseball and football, basketball, cross-country, tennis, track and field, volleyball. NCAA.

WHAT MAJOR?

Associate: Civil technology, computer technology, drafting and design technology, electronic technology, engineering and engineering-related technologies, mechanical design technology.

Bachelor's: Accounting, biology, business administration, business management, chemical manufacturing technology, chemistry, civil technology, communications, computer sciences, criminal justice studies, electronic technology, English, environmental science, history, information sciences and systems, journalism, management information systems, marine biology, marketing and distribution, marketing management, mathematics, mechanical design technology, medical laboratory technologies, music, parks and recreation management, physics, political science and government, radio/television, social work, sociology, urban studies.

Historical & Special Interest:

By Act of the General Assembly, the State of Georgia "...established in connection with the State University, and forming one of the departments thereof, a school for the education and training of Negro students." on November 26, 1890.

The Commission on the School for Negro Students was designated as the Board of Trustees for the School, with perpetual succession subject to the general Board of trustees of the University of Georgia. The Chancellor of the University of Georgia was given general supervision of the school. A preliminary session of the school was held between June 1 and August 1, 1891, at the Baxter Street School building in Athens, Georgia. Richard R. Wright the first principal, and three other instructors comprised the faculty. In the following year the school was moved to its present site, which is approximately five miles southeast of the Courthouse of Savannah, Georgia. The school was given the name "The Georgia State Industrial College for Colored Youths." Major Wright served as President for thirty years with the first women students admitted as boarders in 1921.

Master Key: *A fool is thirsty in the midst of water. African Proverb*

HBCU Third Edition
© Jireh & Associates, Inc.
Wilmington, DE

79

Historically Black
Colleges &
Universities

JIREH
& ASSOCIATES, INC.
Presented by

SELMA UNIVERSITY
SELMA, AL
Web Site:
Not provided.

SCHOOL INFO
Established in 1878. 4-year private university, coed, affiliated with Alabama Baptist Convention. Urban campus in large town; 50 miles west of Montgomery.

ACCREDITATON:
None

CAMPUS ENROLLMENT:
Undergraduate: 107 men & women. **Transfer:** 50 men & women. **PT:** 20. **Graduate:** 15.
Freshman ethnic enrollment: Not available.

WHAT DO I NEED?
Open admissions. Required tests: SAT or ACT (ACT preferred) for placement and counseling only. Application fee is $10; closing date-September 12; notifications on a rolling basis beginning around August 1st.

UNIQUE PROGRAMS
The following programs are available: students with deficiencies from high school or low test scores must take remedial courses. Reduced course load, remedial instruction, special counselor, tutoring.

ACADEMIC REQUIREMENTS
Minimum GPA for freshmen is 2.0.

Core curriculum: arts, English, history, humanities, mathematics, philosophy religion, biological/physical sciences, social sciences. Associate: 66 hours. Bachelor's: 126 hours.

STUDENT SERVICES
Campus student services include: aptitude testing, career and personal counseling.

ADDRESS:

SELMA UNIVERSITY
1501 LAPSLEY ST.
SELMA,   AL   36701
Principal Official: Dr. Willie L. Muse

TYPES OF DEGREES AWARDED:
AA, AS, BA, BS.

ACADEMIC CALENDAR:
Semester. Summer sessions limited.

CONTACT INFORMATION

Admissions Officer: Estella Davis-Baynes, Ira
Phone: (334) 872-2533   **Fax:** (334) 872-7746
Web Site: Not provided.

DOLLARS AND SENSE

TUITION & FEES:	$3,500.00
ROOM & BOARD:	$4,538.00
BOOKS & SUPPLIES:	$250.00
OTHER EXPENSES:	$220.00
OUT OF STATE TUITION:	$3,500.00
*ANNUAL TOTAL:	$8,508.00

(*Annual Total does not include out-of-state tuition .)

FINANCIAL AID

Financial Aid Phone:
Financial Aid Fax: (334) 872-7746
No closing date for aid applications.FAFSA accepted. Priority given to applications received by September 15; notifications on a rolling basis beginning around August 23 and must reply within 2 weeks. Pell grants, jobs available.

SPORTS
Varsity Sports: Baseball, basketball, volleyball. NJCAA.

WHAT MAJOR?
Associate: Accounting, Bible studies, biochemistry, biology, botany, business administration, business management, business and office, business data processing and related programs, business economics, communications, computer sciences, computer programming, data processing, health sciences, liberal/general studies, marketing management, mathematics, microcomputer software, political science, nursing, pre-medicine, psychology, secretarial and related programs, sociology, word processing.

Bachelor's: Business Administration, management information science, religion, theological studies.

Historical & Special Interest:
The early history of Selma University dates back to 1873, when Dr. W.H. McAlpine of the Alabama Colored Baptist State Convention originated a plan to establish a school in the Selma area to further the educational and spiritual aspirations of the Baptist constituency in the Black Belt region. His resolution for the creation of the so-called Alabama Baptist Normal and Theological School passed unanimously in the Convention at Tuscaloosa, and plans were undertaken to determine a central location for the institution. On January 1, 1878, the school opened at the Saint Philip Street Baptist Church, now First Baptist Church of Selma. In 1881, the institution was incorporated by an act of the state legislature and underwent several name changes in succeeding years. The name "Selma University" was first adopted, then changed to Alabama Baptist Colored University."

In 1889, the American Baptist Home Mission Society adopted the University and, for more than half a century, contributed substantially to its support. Support for the new school was also provided by the newly organized Women's Baptist State Convention which became a leading exponent in the advancement of education and the construction of two girls dormitories on the campus. On May 14, 1908, the present name of the University was adopted through an amendment of the institutions's charter. By 1948, Cleveland Hall was constructed out of salvaged materials from two dismantled, historically significant buildings in Selma, the Vickers Home (Alabama's first mansion) and the Old Arcade Hotel and serves as a bridge to the histories of the University and the city of Selma.

Master Key: *Your future begins with what you have in your hands today. Murdock*

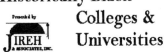
SHAW UNIVERSITY
RALEIGH, NC

Web Site:
Not provided.

SCHOOL INFO

Established in 1865. 4-year private, liberal arts coed college with North Carolina Baptist Convention on urban campus in the city of Raleigh, the capital of the state.

ADDRESS:

SHAW UNIVERSITY
118 EAST SOUTH STREET
RALEIGH, NC 27601
Principal Official: Dr. Talbert O. Shaw

TYPES OF DEGREES AWARDED:
AA, BA, BS.

ACADEMIC CALENDAR:
Semester. Summer sessions.

ACCREDITATON:
Southern Association of Colleges & Schools, National Council for Accred. of Teacher Ed

CAMPUS ENROLLMENT:
Undergraduate: 2105 men & women. **Part-Time:** 222; **Transfer students:** 360 women & men . **Freshman ethnic enrollment:** Native American-4, African American-2236, Asian-2, Caucasian-70, Hispanic-11 & Other-4.

WHAT DO I NEED?
SAT or ACT test scores, min. HS GPS 2.0, GED considered. College preparatory program. Minimum SAT scores by August 1. ACT or SAT. Application fee: $10. Closing date July 30 (priority); notifications on a rolling basis and replies by registration deadline.

UNIQUE PROGRAMS
The following programs are available: Accelerated Prgm, independent study, distance learning double majors, cross-registration, ESL, mentoring Prgm, ROTC, Child Devel. Assoc. Prgm (CDA), Environmental Protection Agency Prgm (EPA), Lyceum Prgms, Veterans Affairs Bennefits Prgm and 2-year transfer program and Early Admissions.

ACADEMIC REQUIREMENTS
In general, students whose grade point aveages indicate they stand a probable chance of meeting the University's graduation standards are considered to be making at least minimal academic progress.

AA degree candidates must satisfactorily complete a min. of 60 sem. hrs. BA/BS degree candidates must satisfactorily complete a min. of 120 semester hours 120 hrs. All candidates must satisfy University core and major requirements, meet a min. cum. GPA of 2.0, complete at least 30 semester hours at Shaw, and successfully complete all required exams, projects and assignments.

STUDENT SERVICES
Campus student services include: Housing, Academic Tutoring, Career Development, Counseling Center, Learning Resource Center, Security, Chapel, employment service for undergraduates, Health Services Center, Pan Hellenic Council, choir, music ensembles, Shaw Players drama group.
ROTC: Army

CONTACT INFORMATION

Admissions Officer: Keith Smith
Phone: (800) 214-6683 **Fax:** (919) 546-8271
Web Site: Not provided.

DOLLARS AND SENSE

TUITION & FEES:	$6,494.00
ROOM & BOARD:	$4,174.00
BOOKS & SUPPLIES:	$750.00
OTHER EXPENSES:	$1,132.00
OUT OF STATE TUITION:	$0.00
*ANNUAL TOTAL:	$12,550.00

(*Annual Total does not include out-of-state tuition .)

FINANCIAL AID

Financial Aid Phone: (800) 475-6190
Financial Aid Fax: (919) 546-8356

No closing date, priority given to applications received by June 15; notifications on a rolling basis beginning about July 1; must reply within 10 days. FAFSA accepted. All jobs based on need. Pymt. Option: AMS (9 mo. pymt plan); University (30 day pymt plan). Federal Perkins Loan, Federal Stafford, National Direct Student Loan, PLUS, Federal Pell, FSEOG, State Guaranteed Loans, NCSCSF, NCSIG, NCLTG, FWS, UWA. Scholarships available: Vary

SPORTS

Intercollegiate Men: Basketball, baseball, track/cross country, tennis, softball, volleyball.

Various intramural sports.

WHAT MAJOR?

Associate: Business Management and Criminal Justice.

Bachelor's: Adapted Physical Education and Kinesiotherapy, Recreation, speech pathology and audiology, accounting, business mgmt., public administration, criminal justice, education, English, international relations, mass communications, mathematics computer science, computer info systems, liberal studies, gerontology, biology, chemistry, environmental science, physics, religion and philosophy, sociology, psychology, music, theatre arts.

Historical & Special Interest:
Shaw University was founded in 1865 as a private Baptist Church affiliated liberal arts school. The University offers specialized degrees in Engineering and Computer Studies, International Relations, Pre-Therapy, Radio/Television/Film, and Speech Pathology & Audiology.

The CAPE program (Center for Alternative Programs of Education) allows students an opportunity to pursue an academic degree through independent study, flexible scheduling, and prior experience credit.

Shaw University's Division of International Studies offers a major in International Relations, with emphasis on Africa, the Caribbean and the Middle East. Shaw University is a UNCF school.

Notable Graduates:
Benjamin A. Quarles, educator; Willie E. Gary, Attny & Chair of Shaw Univ. Board of Trustees; James E. Cheek, former Shaw Univ. and Howard Univ. President; Shirley A. Caesar, Gospel Singer & Evangelist; James "Bonecrusher" Smith, professional boxer .

Master Key: *The freedom to fail is vital if you're going to succeed. Most successful men fail time and time again...*
Michael Korda

HBCU Third Edition
© Jireh & Associates, Inc.
Wilmington, DE

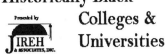

SHORTER COLLEGE

NORTH LITTLE   AR

Web Site:
www.shorter.edu

SCHOOL INFO

Established in 1886. A 2-year private junior, liberal arts college, coed, affiliated with African Methodist Episcopal Church on urban campus in small city; 1.5 miles from Little Rock.

ACCREDITATON:
North Central Association of Colleges & Schools

CAMPUS ENROLLMENT:
Full-time: 46 women and 20 men; part-time: 14 women and 10 men .

WHAT DO I NEED?

Open admissions. Student's desire for a good education and willingness to apply themselves in a higher education setting is important. Fall applications $25 fee; closing date August 31; priority to applications received to May 12; notifications on a rolling basis. Entrance exams required. Interviews recommended. Deferred and early admission program available.

UNIQUE PROGRAMS

The following programs are available: double major, external degree, internships, weekend college, independent study, 2-year transfer program, cross-registration.

ACADEMIC REQUIREMENTS

Minimum GPA for freshmen is 1.5 and major must be declared by end of first year.

Core curriculum: arts/fine arts, computer science, English, history, humanities biological/physical sciences, social sciences. Associate: 64 hours (48 in major).

STUDENT SERVICES

Campus student services include: adult education program, aptitude testing, career and personal counseling, employment services for undergraduates, freshmen orientation, pre-admission summer program, reduced course load, remedial instruction, special counselor, services for handicapped, tutoring, veterans counselor.

WHAT MAJOR?

Associate: Accounting, allied health, business management, business and office, computer sciences, education, elementary education, health sciences, humanities and social sciences, liberal/general studies, medical secretary, practical nursing, secretarial and related programs, social sciences.

Historical & Special Interest:

Shorter College, founded in 1886, is a two-year liberal arts, co-ed college with African Methodist Episcopal Church affiliation. Founded in 1886, it serves a uinque role in developmental education among institutes of higher learning in the state. Shorter College offers the A.A. and the A.S. Degree programs. Part of its stated mission is to provide a Christian education to economically and/or educationally disadvantaged individuals.

ADDRESS:

SHORTER COLLEGE
604 LOCUST STREET
NORTH LITTLE ROCK,   AR   72114
Principal Official: Dr. Irma Hunter-Brown

TYPES OF DEGREES AWARDED:
AA, AS.

ACADEMIC CALENDAR:
Semester.

CONTACT INFORMATION

Admissions Officer: Ms. Delores Voliber
Phone: (501) 374-6305   **Fax:** (501) 374-9333
Web Site: www.shorter.edu

DOLLARS AND SENSE

TUITION & FEES:	$3,267.00
ROOM & BOARD:	$2,200.00
BOOKS & SUPPLIES:	$850.00
OTHER EXPENSES:	$200.00
OUT OF STATE TUITION:	$5,687.00
*ANNUAL TOTAL:	$6,517.00

(*Annual Total does not include out-of-state tuition .)

FINANCIAL AID

Financial Aid Phone:
Financial Aid Fax:
 No closing date; priority given to applications received by May 1. FAFSA accepted. Pell grants, loans, jobs available.

SPORTS

Varsity Sports: Basketball. Intramural Sports: Basketball. NCAA.

Master Key: *Nevery spend more time one a critic than you would on a friend. Murdock*

HBCU Third Edition
© Jireh & Associates, Inc.
Wilmington, DE

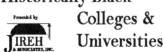

SOJOURNER-DOUGLASS COLLEGE
BALTIMORE, MD

Web Site:
www.host.sdc.edu

SCHOOL INFO
Established in 1980. 4-year private liberal arts coed college on urban campus in a very large city.

ADDRESS:

SOJOURNER-DOUGLASS COLLEGE
500 NORTH CAROLINE ST.
BALTIMORE,   MD   21205
Principal Official: Dr. Charles W. Simmons

TYPES OF DEGREES AWARDED:
BA.

ACADEMIC CALENDAR:
Trimester.

CONTACT INFORMATION

Admissions Officer: Diana Samuels
Phone: (410) 276-0306   **Fax:** (410) 675-1810
Web Site: www.host.sdc.edu

ACCREDITATON:
Middle States Association of Colleges & Schools

CAMPUS ENROLLMENT:
Undergraduate: 262 men & women. **Transfer students:** 21 men & women. **Freshman ethnic enrollment: Not available.**

WHAT DO I NEED?
Interview, autobiographical sketch, resume, and community activities important.

DOLLARS AND SENSE

TUITION & FEES:	$6,420.00
ROOM & BOARD:	$0.00
BOOKS & SUPPLIES:	$600.00
OTHER EXPENSES:	$600.00
OUT OF STATE TUITION:	$0.00
*ANNUAL TOTAL:	$7,620.00

(*Annual Total does not include out-of-state tuition .)

UNIQUE PROGRAMS
The following programs are available: accelerated program, cooperative education, honors program, independent study, internships, public administration, social work.

ACADEMIC REQUIREMENTS
Minimum GPA of 2.0.

Core curriculum: English, history, humanities, social sciences.

FINANCIAL AID

Financial Aid Phone: (410)276-0306 ext 258
Financial Aid Fax: (410) 675-1810
No applications closing date; notified on a rolling basis. FAFSA accepted. Pell grants, loans, jobs are available.

STUDENT SERVICES
Campus student services include: academic center, career and personal counseling, campus daycare, tutoring.

SPORTS
None.

WHAT MAJOR?
Bachelor's: Accounting, business economics, business management, counseling psychology, criminal justice studies, elementary education, health care administration, public administration, social work.

Historical & Special Interest:

Sojourner-Douglas College was founded in 1972 as the Homestead Montebello Center of Antioch University and on July 1, 1980 began operating as a predominantly Black, independent institution.

Sojourner-Douglas College is located in the heart of Baltimore, Maryland and offers full-time, adult evening degree programs in the Applied Social Sciences, Human and Social Resources and Human Growth and Development.

The College was founded by its current President, Charles W. Simmons, a native of Baltimore earning his doctorate in Administration of Higher Education at the Union Graduate School.

Master Key: *Hearing without doing is like chewing without swallowing.*

HBCU Third Edition
© Jireh & Associates, Inc.
Wilmington, DE

SOUTH CAROLINA STATE

N.E.   SC

Web Site:
www.scsu.edu

SCHOOL INFO

Established in 1896. 4-year public liberal arts, coed college. Affiliation with Southern Baptist Convention on urban campus in large town; 45 miles from Columbia.

ACCREDITATON:
Southern Association of Colleges & Schools

CAMPUS ENROLLMENT:
Undergraduate: 4626 men and women. **Graduate:** 334 men and women. **Transfer students:** 191 men & women. **Freshman ethnic enrollment:** African American-697, Caucasian-3.

WHAT DO I NEED?
High school achievement record, GPA, SAT test scores important. College preparatory program SAT or ACT (SAT preferred); scores by July 31. Application fee $10; $15 for out-of-state. Closing date July 31; notifications on a rolling basis; replies within 2 weeks. Portfolio required for art education applicants; audition required for music education applicants. Deferred admission program available.

UNIQUE PROGRAMS
The following programs are available: cooperative education, cross-registration, dual enrollment of high school students, education specialist degree, honors program, internships, teacher preparation; liberal arts/career combination in health sciences.

ACADEMIC REQUIREMENTS
Freshmen must earn a minimum 1.4 and majors must be declared by the end of first year.

Core curriculum: English, computer science, humanities, mathematics, biological/physical sciences, social sciences. Bachelor's: 120 hrs (72 in major).

STUDENT SERVICES
Campus student services include: academic center, career and personal counseling, freshman orientation, health services, placement services, remedial instruction, special advisor for adult students, services for handicapped, tutoring, veterans counselor. ROTC: Air Force, Army.

ADDRESS:

SOUTH CAROLINA STATE UNIVERSITY
300 COLLEGE ST.
N.E. ORANGEBURG,   SC   29117
Principal Official: Dr. Leroy Davis

TYPES OF DEGREES AWARDED:
BA, BS, M, PhD, EdD.

ACADEMIC CALENDAR:
Semester. Summer sessions limited.

CONTACT INFORMATION

Admissions Officer: Dorothy Brown
Phone: (800) 260-5956   **Fax:** (803) 536-8990
Web Site: www.scsu.edu

DOLLARS AND SENSE

TUITION & FEES:	$3,195.00
ROOM & BOARD:	$5,442.00
BOOKS & SUPPLIES:	$400.00
OTHER EXPENSES:	$400.00
OUT OF STATE TUITION:	$4,727.00
*ANNUAL TOTAL:	$9,437.00

(*Annual Total does not include out-of-state tuition .)

FINANCIAL AID

Financial Aid Phone: (803)536-7067
Financial Aid Fax: (803)536-8420

No closing date; priority given to applications received by June 1; notifications on a rolling basis beginning about July 1. FAFSA accepted. Pell grants, loans, jobs based on need.

SPORTS

Varsity Sports: Baseball, basketball, cross-country, football, golf, tennis, track and field, volleyball. NCAA.

WHAT MAJOR?

Bachelor's: Accounting, agriculture business, art education, biology, business administration and management, business economics, business education, chemistry, child development/care/guidance, civil technology, computer and information sciences, criminal justice studies, dramatic arts, electrical technology, elementary education, English, English education, food sciences and human nutrition, foreign languages educatin, industrial technology, marketing and distribution, mathematics, mathematics education, mechanical design technology, music education, music merchandising, nursing, office supervision and management, physical education, physics, political science and government, pre-law, psychology, secondary education, social sciences, social studies education, social work, sociology, Spanish, special education, speech pathology/audiology, speech/communication/theater education.

Historical & Special Interest:

South Carolina State College was founded in 1896 and is a public land-grant institution. The College is the only higher education insitution in the state that offers the graduate and undergraduate degrees in Speech Pathology and Audiology additionally, the Doctor of Education degree in Education Administration.

South Carolina State College now has over 4,000 students and offers 53 degrees in Arts and Sciences, Business, Education, Engineering Technologies, Graduate Studies and Continuing Education and Home Economics.

Master Key: *There is no achievement without goals. Robert J. McKain*

HBCU Third Edition
© Jireh & Associates, Inc.
Wilmington, DE

SOUTHERN UNIV. at BATON

BATON ROUGE, LA

Web Site:
www.subr.edu

SCHOOL INFO
Established in 1880. 4-year public coed university on urban campus in a small city; 90 miles from New Orleans.

ACCREDITATON:
Southern Association of Colleges & Schools

CAMPUS ENROLLMENT:
*Undergraduate: Full-time: 3812 women and 2873 men. Part-time: 444 women and 305 men. Graduate: Full-time: 237 women and 334 men; Part-time: 415 women and 144 men. Freshman ethnic enrollment: Not available.

WHAT DO I NEED?
Open admissions. SAT or ACT (ACT preferred) for placement and counseling; score report by August 1. Fall-term application fee $5. Closing date July 2; applicants notified on a rolling basis and early admission program available.

UNIQUE PROGRAMS
The following programs are available: cooperative education, cross-registration, double major, dual enrollment of high school students, educations specialist degree, honors program, independent study, internships, teacher preparation; liberal arts/career combination in engineering.

ACADEMIC REQUIREMENTS
Minimum GPA for freshmen 1.51 by end of first semester and major must be declared by end of first year.

Core curriculum: art/fine arts, computer science, English, foreign languages, history, humanities, mathematics, philosophy/religion, biological/physical sciences, social sciences. Associate: 66 hours. Bachelor's: 124 hours. Hours in major: 28 and 40.

STUDENT SERVICES
Campus student services include: aptitude testing, campus daycare, career and personal counseling, employment services for undergraduates, freshmen orientation, health services, learning center, placement services, preadmission summer program, reduced course load, remedial instruction, special counselor, services for handicapped, tutoring, veterans counselor. ROTC: Army, Naval.

ADDRESS:

SOUTHERN UNIV. at BATON ROUGE
J.S. CLARK ADMIN. BLDG./SOUTHERN
BATON ROUGE,   LA   70813
Principal Official: Dr. Leon Tawer

TYPES OF DEGREES AWARDED:
AA, AS, BA, BS, MA, MS, F.

ACADEMIC CALENDAR:
Semester. Summer sessions.

CONTACT INFORMATION

Admissions Officer: Wayne Brumfield
Phone: (504) 771-2430   **Fax:** (504) 771-2500
Web Site: www.subr.edu

DOLLARS AND SENSE

TUITION & FEES:	$2,454.00
ROOM & BOARD:	$5,168.00
BOOKS & SUPPLIES:	$500.00
OTHER EXPENSES:	$386.00
OUT OF STATE TUITION:	$5,894.00
*ANNUAL TOTAL:	$8,508.00

(*Annual Total does not include out-of-state tuition .)

FINANCIAL AID

Financial Aid Phone: (504)771-2790
Financial Aid Fax:

No closing date, priority given to applications received by March15. Notifications on a rolling basis. FAFSA accepted. Pell grants, loans, and jobs available and based on need. Academic, athletic, scholarships available.

SPORTS
Varsity Sports: basketball, baseball, football, tennis, track and field, volleyball. NCAA.

WHAT MAJOR?
Associate: Air conditioning/heating/refrigeration technology, electronic technology, engineering and engineering-related technologies, law enforcement and corrections.

Bachelor's: Accounting, agricultural business/economics/education, air conditioning/heating/refrigeration technology, animal sciences, art education, biology, business management, business education, business economics, cardiopulmonary therapy, chemistry, civil engineering, computer sciences,counseling psychology, cytotechnology, dramatic arts, education of the deaf and hearing impaired, education of the mentally handicapped, electrical/electonics/communications engineering, electronic technology, elementary education, English, English education, fine arts, food sciences and human nutrition, foreign languages education, French, health education, history, home economics education, individual and family development, industrial arts education, journalism, junior high education, library science, marketing management, mathematics, mathematics education, mechanical engineering, medical laboratory technology, music, music education, nursing, occupational therapy, parks and recreation management, philosophy, physical education, physical sciences, physical therapy, physics, plant sciences, political science and government, psychology, radio/television technology, rehabilitation counseling/services, science education, secondary education, social studies education, social work, sociology, soil sciences, Spanish, special education, speech correction, speech pathology/audiology, speech communcation/theater education, textiles and clothing, visual and performing arts.

Historical & Special Interest:
Southern University at Baton Rouge is situated on 884 acres which includes an Agricultural Experiment Farm for teaching and research. Southern's accomplishments are reflected in Energy and Environmental Studies, Hazardous Materials Management, NASA Industrial and Space Applications, and its women and minorities-focused Behavioral Studies.   Dr. Delores Spikes is chancellor and a summa cum laude graduate of Southern University and A&M College in Baton Rouge as well as President of the entire Southern University System.

Master Key: *People with goals succeed because they know where they are going. Earl Nightingale*

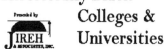

Historically Black Colleges & Universities

SOUTHERN UNIV. AT SHREVEPORT

SHREVEPORT, LA

Web Site:
www.suno.edu

SCHOOL INFO

Established in 1964. 2-year public coed community college on suburban campus in a small city.

ACCREDITATON:
Southern Association of Colleges & Schools

CAMPUS ENROLLMENT:
*Undergraduate: 187 men and 485 women full-time. 76 men and 291 women part-time.
Freshman ethnic enrollment: Not available.

WHAT DO I NEED?
Open admission. ACT scores for placement and counseling; scores by August 3. Fall-term applications no fee. No closing date; applicants notified on a rolling basis. Early admission program available.

UNIQUE PROGRAMS
The following programs are available: cross-registration and internships.

ACADEMIC REQUIREMENTS
Minimum GPA of 1.5 and major must be declared by end of first year.

Core curriculum: English, mathematics, social sciences. Associate: 62 hours.

STUDENT SERVICES
Campus student services include: health services, personal counseling, placement services for graduates, remedial instruction, special counselor, tutoring, veterans counselor.

ADDRESS:

SOUTHERN UNIV. AT SHREVEPORT
3050 MARTIN LUTHER KING DR.
SHREVEPORT,   LA   71107
Principal Official: Dr. Gullum- Interim Chancellor

TYPES OF DEGREES AWARDED:
AA, AS, AAS.

ACADEMIC CALENDAR:
Semester. Summer sessions limited.

CONTACT INFORMATION

Admissions Officer: Ms. Artie Reed
Phone: (800) 458-1472   **Fax:** (318) 674-3313
Web Site: www.suno.edu

DOLLARS AND SENSE

TUITION & FEES:	$1,200.00
ROOM & BOARD:	
BOOKS & SUPPLIES:	$300.00
OTHER EXPENSES:	$10.00
OUT OF STATE TUITION:	$1,165.00
*ANNUAL TOTAL:	$1,510.00

(*Annual Total does not include out-of-state tuition .)

FINANCIAL AID

Financial Aid Phone: (318)674-3494
Financial Aid Fax: (318)674-3313

No application closing date; applicants notified on a rolling basis beginning on or about July 15; must reply within 2 weeks. FAFSA accepted. Pell grants, loans, jobs are available. Academic, leadership, alumni affiliation, minority scholarships available.

SPORTS

None.

WHAT MAJOR?
Associate: Accounting, banking and finance, biology, business administration, chemistry, computer sciences, electronic technology, hotel/motel and restaurant management, legal assistant/paralegal, marketing and distribution, mathematics, medical assistant, medical laboratory technologies, medical records technology, mental health/human services, preelementary education, respiratory therapy technology, science technologies, secretarial and related programs, small business management and ownership, social sciences, surgical technology, teacher aide, word processing.

Historical & Special Interest:

The Southern University, Shreveport-Bossier City Campus sits on a 101 acre campus and was founded in 1964 as a two-year, co-ed, commuter community college. It is an integral part of and completes the triad Southern University system.

The College enrolls an average of 1,000 students, both full and part-time, each semester. It has a multi-national and multi-ethnic faculty with broad educational and training experience and expertise.

Master Key: *Patience is the weapon that forces deception to reveal itself.*

HBCU Third Edition
© Jireh & Associates, Inc.
Wilmington, DE

Historically Black Colleges & Universities

Presented by
JIREH & ASSOCIATES, INC.

SOUTHERN UNIV. NEW ORLEANS

NEW ORLEANS, LA

Web Site:
www.suno4.htm

SCHOOL INFO

Established in 1959. 4-year public coed university on urban campus in a small city; 90 miles from New Orleans.

ACCREDITATON:

Southern Association of Colleges & Schools

CAMPUS ENROLLMENT:

*Undergraduate: 3500 men and women **Graduate:** 200 men and women. **Freshman ethnic enrollment: Not available.**

WHAT DO I NEED?

Open admission. Selective admissions to allied health and various technical programs. Recommended high school GPA 2.5. ACT for placement and counseling; scores by August 10. Fall-term applications fee $5. No closing date; applicants notified on a rolling basis. Deferred and early admission program available.

UNIQUE PROGRAMS

The following programs are available: cooperative education, cross-registration, internships.

ACADEMIC REQUIREMENTS

No minimum GPA; students records revealing academic difficulty are reviewed individually.

ADDRESS:

SOUTHERN UNIV. NEW ORLEANS
6400 PRESS DRIVE
NEW ORLEANS,   LA   70126
Principal Official: Dr. Robert Gex, Chancellor

TYPES OF DEGREES AWARDED:

AA, AS, BA, BS, M.

ACADEMIC CALENDAR:

Semester. Summer sessions limited.

CONTACT INFORMATION

Admissions Officer: Dr. Laura Hardester
Phone: (504) 286-5314   **Fax:** (504) 286-5320
Web Site: www.suno4.htm

DOLLARS AND SENSE

TUITION & FEES:	$2,011.00
ROOM & BOARD:	$0.00
BOOKS & SUPPLIES:	$400.00
OTHER EXPENSES:	$568.00
OUT OF STATE TUITION:	$4,142.00
*ANNUAL TOTAL:	$2,979.00

(*Annual Total does not include out-of-state tuition .)

FINANCIAL AID

Financial Aid Phone: (506) 286-5000
Financial Aid Fax: (506) 286-5131

Aid applications closing date May 1; applicants notified on or about May 15; must reply within 1 week. FAFSA accepted. Pell grants, loans, jobs are available.

STUDENT SERVICES

Campus student services include: health services, personal counseling, placement services for graduates. ROTC: Air Force, Army.

SPORTS

None.

WHAT MAJOR?

Associate: Business data programming, real estate, secretarial and related programs.

Bachelor's: Accounting, biology, business administration, business economics, business management, chemistry, economics, elementary education, English, French, history, mathematics, medical laboratory, physics, political science and government, psychology, secondary education, secretarial and related programs, social sciences, social work, sociology, Spanish, visual and performing arts.

Historical & Special Interest:

Southern University at New Orleans (SUNO) began operating in September of 1959 as an urban institution. With one of the largest evening and weekend colleges among its peer institutions, SUNO is fully accredited by the Southern Association of Colleges and Schools and its School of Social Work graduate and undergraduate programs are accredited by the Council of Social Work Education.

Master Key: *Money is an instrument that can buty everything but happiness, and pay your fare to everywhere but heaven.*

HBCU Third Edition
© Jireh & Associates, Inc.
Wilmington, DE

SOUTHWESTERN CHRISTIAN
TERRELL, TX
Web Site:
Not provided.

SCHOOL INFO
Established in 1949. 4-year private, Bible, liberal arts coed college with Church of Christ affiliation on rural campus in large town; 30 miles east of Dallas.

ACCREDITATON:
Southern Association of Colleges & Schools

CAMPUS ENROLLMENT:
*Undergraduate: Full-time: 131 men and 96 women. Part-time: 7 men and 6 women.
Freshman ethnic enrollment: Not available.

WHAT DO I NEED?
Academic record, recommendations, and extracurricular activites considered important. No closing date and priority to applications received by July 31; applicants notified on a rolling basis. Interview and essay recommended.

UNIQUE PROGRAMS
The following programs are available: 2-year transfer program, independent study, internships.

ACADEMIC REQUIREMENTS
Freshmen must earn a minimum 2.0 and majors must be declared by end of second year.

Core curriculum: computer science, English, history, humanities, mathematics, philosophy/religion, biological/physical sciences. Associates: 62 hrs. Bachelor's: 124 hrs.

STUDENT SERVICES
Campus student services include: academic center, career and personal counseling, freshman orientation, reduced course load program, remedial instruction, special counselor.

WHAT MAJOR?
Associates: Accounting, Bible studies, business data entry equipment operation, business data programming, computer and information sciences, education, elementary education, engineering, liberal/general studies, mathematics, science technologies, secondary education, secretarial and related programs. **Bachelor's:** Religious education, theological studies.

Historical & Special Interest:

Southwestern Christian College was founded in 1949 for the purpose of offering a Christian education to Black youths. The school is a liberal arts, co-educational institution fully accredited by the Southern Asociation of Colleges and Schools. The student body comes from throughout the United States and several countries.

Southwestern is a junior college from which most students transfer to senior colleges and universities upon graduation. The College offers the Associate of Arts and Associate of Science degrees as well as a program in Secretarial Science.

ADDRESS:

SOUTHWESTERN CHRISTIAN COLLEGE
200 BOWSER CIRCLE
TERRELL,   TX   75160
Principal Official: Dr. Jack Evans Sr.

TYPES OF DEGREES AWARDED:
AS, BA, BS.

ACADEMIC CALENDAR:
Semester.

CONTACT INFORMATION

Admissions Officer: Thomas Fitzgerald
Phone: (972) 524-3341   **Fax:** (972) 563-7133
Web Site: Not provided.

DOLLARS AND SENSE

TUITION & FEES:	$3,028.00
ROOM & BOARD:	$2,008.00
BOOKS & SUPPLIES:	$300.00
OTHER EXPENSES:	$400.00
OUT OF STATE TUITION:	$0.00
*ANNUAL TOTAL:	$5,736.00

(*Annual Total does not include out-of-state tuition .)

FINANCIAL AID

Financial Aid Phone:
Financial Aid Fax:

Closing date July 15; notifications on a rolling basis beginning around July 15; must reply by August 23. FAFSA accepted. Pell grants, loans based on need. Academic, athletic, music/drama scholarships available.

SPORTS
Varsity Sports: Basketball, track and field. NJCAA.

HBCU Third Edition
© Jireh & Associates, Inc.
Wilmington, DE

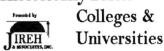

Historically Black Colleges & Universities

SPELMAN COLLEGE
ATLANTA, GA

SCHOOL INFO
Established in 1881. 4-year private liberal arts women's college on a 32-acre urban campus 2 miles southwest of downtown Atlanta. It is the oldest HBCU in the country for women.

ACCREDITATON:
Southern Association of Colleges & Schools

CAMPUS ENROLLMENT:
Undergraduate: 2026 women only. **Transfer students:** 37 women only. **Freshman ethnic enrollment:** African American-538, Other-10

WHAT DO I NEED?
Academic record, test scores, leadership, activities considered important. Two recommendations and essay are required. Completed application and all supporting documents due by February 1. Application fee $35 which may be waived based on applicant need. Closing date February 1; and applicants notified on or about March 1 and must reply by May 1. Early admission program available.

UNIQUE PROGRAMS
The following programs are available: double major, dual enrollment of high school students, honors program, independent study, internships, study abroad, teacher preparation, visiting/exchange student program, cross-registration; dual degree in engineering; program in medicine.

ACADEMIC REQUIREMENTS
Minimum GPA for freshmen 1.5 and major must be declared by end of first year.

Core curriculum: arts/fine arts, computer science, English, foreign languages, history, humanities, mathematics, philosophy/religion, biological/physical sciences, social sciences. Bachelor's: 120 hours.

STUDENT SERVICES
Campus student services include: aptitude testing, campus daycare, career and personal counseling, employment services for undergraduates, freshman orientation, health services, learning center, placement services,special counselor, tutoring special advisor for adult students, services for handicapped. ROTC: Air Force, Army, Naval.

WHAT MAJOR?
Bachelor's: Art history and appreciation, biochemistry, biology, chemistry, child development/care/guidance, computer sciences, dramatic arts, economics, engineering, English, French, German, health education, health sciences, history, mathematics, music, natural science, philosophy, physics, political science and government, psychology, religion, sociology, Spanish.

Historical & Special Interest:

Spelman College was founded in 1881 by Sophia B. Packard and Harriet E. Giles and is the nation's oldest undergraduate liberal arts college for Black women and a part of the Atlanta University Center. In 1991, Spelman received the Point of Light Award from President Bush because of its emphasis on the importance of community service. According to Spelman, its freshman classes have had the highest SAT averages of entering students at any historically Black college or university and was included in U.S. News & World Report as one of the nation's best colleges and universities.

Spelman College is a UNCF school.

ADDRESS:

SPELMAN COLLEGE
350 SPELMAN LANE
ATLANTA,   GA   30314
Principal Official: Dr. Johnetta B. Cole

TYPES OF DEGREES AWARDED:
BA, BS.

ACADEMIC CALENDAR:
Semester. One of the six sharing members of

CONTACT INFORMATION

Admissions Officer: Victoria Valle
Phone: (404) 681-3643   **Fax:** (404) 215-7788
Web Site: www.spelman.edu

DOLLARS AND SENSE

TUITION & FEES:	$9,200.00
ROOM & BOARD:	$7,200.00
BOOKS & SUPPLIES:	$1,950.00
OTHER EXPENSES:	$700.00
OUT OF STATE TUITION:	$8,150.00
*ANNUAL TOTAL:	$19,050.00

(*Annual Total does not include out-of-state tuition .)

FINANCIAL AID

Financial Aid Phone: (800) 982-2411
Financial Aid Fax: (404) 223-7523

Closing date April 1. Notifications on a rolling basis beginning June 1. Reply within 2 weeks. FAFSA accepted. Pell grants, loans, and jobs available and based on need. Academic, music/drama, state/district residency, leadership, religious affiliations scholarships available.

SPORTS
Varsity Sports: basketball, tennis, track and field, volleyball. NCAA.

Master Key: *All people fall, the great one get back up.*

HBCU Third Edition
© Jireh & Associates, Inc.
Wilmington, DE

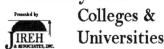
STILLMAN COLLEGE

TUSCALOOSA, AL

Web Site:
www.stillman.edu

SCHOOL INFO

Established in 1876. 4-year private liberal arts college, coed, affiliated with Presbyterian Church (USA). Suburban campus in small city; 60 miles west of Birmingham.

ACCREDITATON:
Southern Association of Colleges & Schools

CAMPUS ENROLLMENT:
Undergraduate: 888 men & women. **Transfer students:** 48 men & women. **Freshman ethnic enrollment :** African American-248

WHAT DO I NEED?

Selection criteria based on school achievement record. College preparatory program. SAT or ACT (ACT preferred) required for placement. Application fee $10 may be waived based on need. Closing date August 1; priority given to applications received by May 1; notifications on a rolling basis. Early admission program available.

UNIQUE PROGRAMS

The following programs are available: cooperative education, double major, honors program, independent study, internships, teacher preparation, health sciences.

ACADEMIC REQUIREMENTS

Minimum GPA for freshmen is 1.6 and majors must be declared by end of second year.

Core curriculum: computer science, English, history, humanities, mathematics, philosophy / religion, biological / physical sciences, social sciences. Bachelor's: 124 hours (30 in major).

STUDENT SERVICES

Campus student services include: career and personal counseling, employment service for undergraduates, freshman orientation, health services, learning center, placement services, reduced course load program, remedial instruction, special counselor, tutoring, veterans counselor. ROTC: Air Force, Army.

WHAT MAJOR?

Bachelor's: Biology, business management, chemistry, computer sciences, elementary education, English, history, international studies, mathematics, music, parks and recreation management, physics, religion, sociology, Spanish, telecommunications.

ADDRESS:

STILLMAN COLLEGE
P.O. BOX DRAWER 1430
TUSCALOOSA,　　AL　　35403
Principal Official: Dr. Cordell Wynn

TYPES OF DEGREES AWARDED:
BA, BS

ACADEMIC CALENDAR:
Semester. Summer sessions limited.

CONTACT INFORMATION

Admissions Officer: Mason Bonner
Phone: (205) 349-4240 **Fax:** (205) 366-8996
Web Site: www.stillman.edu

DOLLARS AND SENSE

TUITION & FEES:	$5,200.00
ROOM & BOARD:	$3,751.00
BOOKS & SUPPLIES:	$500.00
OTHER EXPENSES:	$300.00
OUT OF STATE TUITION:	
*ANNUAL TOTAL:	$9,751.00

(*Annual Total does not include out-of-state tuition .)

FINANCIAL AID

Financial Aid Phone:
Financial Aid Fax:

No closing date; priority given to applications received by June 15; notifications on a rolling basis; must reply within 2 weeks. FAFSA accepted. Pell grants, jobs scholarships available. Academic, music/drama, state/district residency, leadership, religious affiliation scholarships available.

SPORTS

Varsity Sports: Baseball, basketball, cross-country, tennis. NCAA.

Historical & Special Interest:

Stillman's history dates back to 1874 when a group of Presbyterians from Tuscaloosa, Alabama, headed by the Rev. Charles Allen Stillman, presented an overture to the General Assembly of the Presbyterian Church in the United States that the Church establish a training school for Negro ministers. The General Assembly authorized the opening of an institute in Tuscaloosa in the Fall of 1876 and appropriated funds for the school's operation.

Following years yielded a need for academic as well as theological training and its academic programs were enlarged. The school was renamed Stillman Institute in honor of its founder who died in 1895 and was moved in 1898 to its present location in the western section of Tuscaloosa. In 1899 the General Assembly approved the opening of the school to all women as well as men who wished to enter.

In the next five decades, the school acquired its present campus tract of over 100 acres, organized a junior and senior high school and established a junior college program which was accredited in 1937. In addition, between 1930 and 1946, it operated a hospital and nurses training school.

Master Key: *When you follow in the path of your father, you learn to walk like him. African Proverb*

HBCU Third Edition
© Jireh & Associates, Inc.
Wilmington, DE

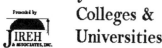
TALLADEGA COLLEGE
TALLADEGA, AL

Web Site:
Not provided.

SCHOOL INFO

Established in 1867. 4-year private liberal arts college, coed on rural campus in large town; 55 miles east of Birmingham.

ADDRESS:

TALLADEGA COLLEGE
624 WEST BATTLE ST.
TALLADEGA,   AL   35160
Principal Official: Dr. Joseph B. Johnson

TYPES OF DEGREES AWARDED:
BA

ACADEMIC CALENDAR:
Semester - Fall (August-Dec.); Spring (Jan. -

ACCREDITATON:
Southern Association of Colleges & Schools

CAMPUS ENROLLMENT:

Undergraduate Full-Time: 627 men & 396 women. **Part-Time:** 23 Males, 17-Females.
Ethnic Enrollment: African American-641, Caucasian-4, Hisp. -1.

WHAT DO I NEED?

Graduation from accredited high school with min. 22 units and official transcripts. Medical record from TC must be completed by apllicant and physician. Must supply ACT or SAT scores. report by March 1. College preparatory program. Application fee $10 must accompany application. Students encouraged to apply no later than end of 1st semester of sr. year; notifications on a rolling basis. Juniors may apply at end of junior year.

UNIQUE PROGRAMS

The following programs are available: Cooperative education with Envir. Prot. Agncy; dual-degree in Engr. with Auburn Univ.; Free Enterprise, Bloomberg Financial, Ron McNair Pgm, Min. Access to Research Careers (MARC); College Career Oppor. in Research Ed. and Trng (COR).

ACADEMIC REQUIREMENTS

Cum. GPA of 2.0 required for graduation at TC unless hardship. After one semester, student must have at least 1.5 GPA.

Evidence through exam of knowledge in the social and natural sciences; English, humanities, mathematics, biological, physical sciences, & social sciences. Staff must view quality of work sufficient to pursue work in a field of concentration.

STUDENT SERVICES

Campus student services include: new student orientation, career and personal counseling, employment service for undergraduates, health services, student government, learning center, placement services, reduced course load program, VA, honor societies, tutoring. No services for LD students. ROTC: Army.

WHAT MAJOR?

Bachelor's: Secondary Education (English, History, Music, Mathematics, Chemistry, Biology), Psychology, Social Work, Sociology, English, History, Music Education (N-12), Music Performance; Business Administration (Emphasis: Accounting, Economics, and management), Finance and Banking, Marketing, Public Administration, Biology, Chemistry, Computer Science, Mathematics, Physics.

Historical & Special Interest:

Talladega College was founded in 1867 by Freedmen and later assisted the American Missionary Association. It was charted as a college by the state of Alabama in 1869. Talladega is nationally known as a center of intellectualism, culture and learning. It has been cited in statistical studies for its particularly high percentage of graduates who earn science doctorates, degrees in medicine and other challenging disciplines i.e., for each 1,000 Talladega graduates, 8.2 acquired doctorate degrees in science. This was the best performance among graduates of Black colleges and the 18th best performance of all American colleges and universities in this category.

Talladega College is a UNCF school.

CONTACT INFORMATION

Admissions Officer: Dr. Edward L. Hall
Phone: (800) 633-2440   **Fax:** (205) 362-2268
Web Site: Not provided.

DOLLARS AND SENSE

TUITION & FEES:	$5,949.00
ROOM & BOARD:	$3,224.00
BOOKS & SUPPLIES:	$1,000.00
OTHER EXPENSES:	$800.00
OUT OF STATE TUITION:	
*ANNUAL TOTAL:	$10,973.00

(*Annual Total does not include out-of-state tuition .)

FINANCIAL AID

Financial Aid Phone: (800) 633-2440
Financial Aid Fax: (205) 761-6440

Notifications on a rolling basis beginning around February 15; must reply upon receipt of acceptance. FAFSA accepted. Federal Loans, Pell grants, jobs, academic and athletic scholarships available including special Presidential Academic Scholarships and Grants.

SPORTS

Varsity Sports: Baseball, basketball cross-country, golf, Volleyball. NAIA.

Master Key: *The amunition selected by your enemy is a clue to his fear of you. Murdock*

HBCU Third Edition
© Jireh & Associates, Inc.
Wilmington, DE

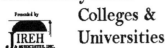
TENNESSEE STATE UNIVERSITY

NASHVILLE, TN

Web Site:
www.tustate.edu

SCHOOL INFO
Established in 1912. 4-year public coed college on urban campus in very large city.

ADDRESS:

TENNESSEE STATE UNIVERSITY
3500 JOHN MERRITT BOULEVARD
NASHVILLE,   TN   37203
Principal Official: Dr. James A. Hefner

TYPES OF DEGREES AWARDED:
AA, AS, BA, BS, MA, MS, MBA, PhD, EdD.

ACADEMIC CALENDAR:
Semester. Summer sessions limited.

CONTACT INFORMATION

Admissions Officer: Dean John Cade
Phone: (615) 963-5131   **Fax:** (615) 963-5108
Web Site: www.tustate.edu

ACCREDITATON:
Southern Association of Colleges & Schools

CAMPUS ENROLLMENT:
Undergraduate: 6605 men & women. **Graduate:** 1008 men & women. **Transfer students:** 536 men & women. **Freshman ethnic enrollment:** Native American-2, African American-669, Asian-2, Caucasian-69, Hispanic-1.

WHAT DO I NEED?
Academic record and test scores important. College preparatory program. SAT or ACT scores by August 1. Application fee $5. Closing date August 1; notified on a rolling basis. Interview required for allied health and nursing applicants. Deferred and early admission program available.

UNIQUE PROGRAMS
The following programs are available: cooperative education, cross-registration, 2-year transfer program, double major, honors program, independent study, weekend college; combination bachelor's/graduate program in business administration.

DOLLARS AND SENSE

TUITION & FEES:	$1,866.00
ROOM & BOARD:	$2,720.00
BOOKS & SUPPLIES:	$400.00
OTHER EXPENSES:	$450.00
OUT OF STATE TUITION:	$3,782.00
*ANNUAL TOTAL:	$5,436.00

(*Annual Total does not include out-of-state tuition .)

ACADEMIC REQUIREMENTS
Freshmen must earn a minimum 1.6 and majors must be declared by end of first year.

Core curriculum: computer science, English, history, humanities, mathematics, biological/physical sciences, social sciences. Credit required for an Associate: 76 hrs. Bachelor's: 132.

FINANCIAL AID

Financial Aid Phone:
Financial Aid Fax:
No closing date; priority given to applications received by April 1; notifications on a rolling basis beginning around July 15; must reply within 2 weeks. FAFSA accepted. Pell grants, loans, jobs based on need. Academic, music/drama, athletic, state/district residency, leadership, alumni affiliation, minority scholarships available.

STUDENT SERVICES
Campus student services include: academic center, aptitude testing, career and personal counseling, employment service for undergraduates, health services, placement services, remedial instruction, special counselor, tutoring, veterans counselor. ROTC: Air Force.

SPORTS
Varsity Sports: Baseball, basketball, football, racquetball, swimming, tennis, track and field.
Intramural Sports: Basketball, golf, tennis.

WHAT MAJOR?
Associate: Accounting, dental hygiene, fire control and safety technology, liberal/general studies, medical records technology, nursing, practical nursing, public affairs, secretarial and related programs.

Bachelor's: Accounting, aerospace science (Air Force), aerospace/aeronautical/astronautical engineering, agricultural sciences, animal sciences, architectural engineering, architecture, art history and appreciation, biochemistry, biological and physical sciences, biology, business administration and management, business and management, business economics, chemistry, civil engineering, communications, computer and information sciences, computer programming, criminal justice studies, dental hygiene, dramatic arts, education, engineering, engineering and other related disciplines, elementary education, English, food sciences and human nutrition, French, health care administration, history, human nutrition, health/physical education/recreation, history, home economics, humanities and social sciences, individual and family development, journalism, law enforcement and corrections, liberal/general studies, mathematics, mechanical laboratory, medical records administration, music, nursing, physical sciences, physics, political science and government, preelementary education, psychology, secondary education, secretarial and related programs, social sciences, social work, sociology, soil sciences, Spanish, special education, speech pathology/audiology, textiles and clothing.

Historical & Special Interest:
By virtue of a 1909 Act of the General Assembly, the Agricultural and Industrial State Normal School was created, along with two other normal schools in the State, and began serving Negro students on June 19, 1912. The first degrees were granted in June, 1924. In 1927 the word "Normal" was dropped from the name of the College.

The present-day Tennessee State University exists as a result of the merger on July 1, 1979, of the former Tennessee State University and the University of Tennessee at Nashville. Tiger-beles won the first national Women's Amateur Athletic Union (AAU) Track & Field Championship in 1955 and through 1968 won 25 of 40 American Women's Track & Field Olympic medals.

Master Key: *The world has the habit of making room for the man whose words and actions show that he knows where he is going. Napoleon Hill*

HBCU Third Edition
© Jireh & Associates, Inc.
Wilmington, DE

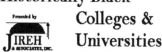
TEXAS COLLEGE

TYLER, TX

Web Site:
Not provided.

SCHOOL INFO

Established in 1894. 4-year private, liberal arts coed college with Christian Methodist Episcopal affiliation on urban campus in small city; 90 miles west of Shreveport, Louisana.

ADDRESS:

TEXAS COLLEGE
2404 NORTH GRAND AVENUE
TYLER,   TX   75702
Principal Official: Dr. Haywood L. Strickland

TYPES OF DEGREES AWARDED:
AA, BA, BS.

ACADEMIC CALENDAR:
Semester. Summer sessions limited.

CONTACT INFORMATION

Admissions Officer: Dr. T Meek Dean of
Phone: (903) 593-8311   **Fax:** (903) 593-0588
Web Site: Not provided.

ACCREDITATON:
Southern Association of Colleges & Schools

CAMPUS ENROLLMENT:

Undergraduate: Full-time: 161 men and132 women. **Transfer:** 19 men. **Part-time:** 1 men and 5 women. **Freshman ethnic enrollment:** African American-290; Asian -0; Caucasian -1; Hisp.-2.

WHAT DO I NEED?

Open admissions. Application fee $10 which may be waived based on need. Closing date August 15; notifications on a rolling basis. Music applicants auditions required. Deferred and early admission program available.

UNIQUE PROGRAMS

The following program is available: Double major. Computer literacy program fro public school students. Comprehensive services for students requiring remediation in the basic skills: Reading, Writing & Arithmetic.

ACADEMIC REQUIREMENTS

Freshmen must earn a minimum 1.5 and majors must be declared by end of second year.

Core curriculum: arts/fine arts, computer science, English, foreign languages, history, humanities, mathematics, philosophy/religion, biological/physical sciences, social sciences. Bachelor's: 124 hrs (24 in major).

STUDENT SERVICES

Campus student services include: academic center, reduced course load program, remedial instruction, tutoring.

DOLLARS AND SENSE

TUITION & FEES:	$5,220.00
ROOM & BOARD:	$2,830.00
BOOKS & SUPPLIES:	$400.00
OTHER EXPENSES:	$925.00
OUT OF STATE TUITION:	
*ANNUAL TOTAL:	$9,375.00

(*Annual Total does not include out-of-state tuition .)

FINANCIAL AID

Financial Aid Phone: (903) 593-8311
Financial Aid Fax: (903) 593-0588
Closing date May 31; notifications beginning around June 15. FAFSA accepted. Pell grants, loans, jobs based on need. Academic, athletic, music/drama scholarships available and awarded to students based on the contributions and requirements given to the institution by donors.

SPORTS

Varsity Sports: Baseball, basketball, volleyball , track and field. NAIA.

WHAT MAJOR?

Bachelor's: Arts, biology, business administration, computer and information sciences, early childhood education (A.A.), English, Elementary education, history, mathematics, music, physical education, political science, social work, sociology.

Historical & Special Interest:

Texas College was founded in 1894 and affiliated with the Christian Methodist Episcopal Church and is fully accredited by the Commission on Colleges and the Southern Association of Colleges and Schools. Over the years, the College has maintaind strong programs in teacher education and liberal arts.

More recently, Texas College has developed rapidly growing programs in business and the social sciences. In addition to offering the Bachelor of Arts and Bachelor of Science degrees, the College also offers courses required for career options in Pre-law, Pre-medicine, and Pre-dentistry.

The Texas Higher Education Coordinating Board has granted a certificate of authority to Texas College to award associate and bachelor degrees in fourteen fields. Texas College is a UNCF school.

Master Key: *Prefer a loss to a dishonest gain; the one brings pain at the moment, the other for all time. Chilon*

HBCU Third Edition
© Jireh & Associates, Inc.
Wilmington, DE

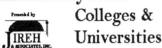
TEXAS SOUTHERN UNVERSITY

HOUSTON, TX

Web Site:
www.tsu.edu

SCHOOL INFO

Established in 1947. 4-year public coed college on urban campus in very large city; 10 miles from downtown Houston.

ACCREDITATON:
Southern Association of Colleges & Secondary Schools

CAMPUS ENROLLMENT:
Undergraduate: 4917 men and women (Full-time). **Graduate:** 1012 men and women.
Ethnic Enrollment: Native American-270, African American-5055, Asian-153, Caucasian-55, Hispanic-122.

WHAT DO I NEED?

Open admissions. Selective admissions to some programs. SAT or ACT for placement and counseling only. Application fee-$25. Notifications on a rolling basis.

UNIQUE PROGRAMS

The following programs are available: ROTC-cross-enrollment with Univ. of Houston's Dept. of Military Science; cooperative education, cross-registration, double major, honors program, internships, teacher preparation; combined bachelor's/graduate program in business administration.

ACADEMIC REQUIREMENTS

Freshmen must earn a minimum 1.5 for the first 30 semester hrs; 1.75 for 31-60 hrs; and 2.0 for over 61; and majors must be declared by end of second year.

Core curriculum: English, mathematics, biological/physical sciences, social sciences.

STUDENT SERVICES

Campus student services include: The TSU Student Support Services Program is a federally funded academic assistance program designed to meet the needs of students matriculating through a post-secondary institution who may require tutorial or remedial instruction to help ensure their academic success.

ADDRESS:

TEXAS SOUTHERN UNVERSITY
3000 CLEBURNE AVENUE
HOUSTON,   TX   77004
Principal Official: Mr. James M. Douglas

TYPES OF DEGREES AWARDED:
BA, BBS, BS, MA, MS, MPA, MBA, EdD, PhD.

ACADEMIC CALENDAR:
Semester. Summer sessions.

CONTACT INFORMATION

Admissions Officer: Joyce Waddell
Phone: (713) 313-7011   **Fax:** (713) 313-7471
Web Site: www.tsu.edu

DOLLARS AND SENSE

TUITION & FEES:	$2,006.00
ROOM & BOARD:	$4,000.00
BOOKS & SUPPLIES:	$800.00
OTHER EXPENSES:	$800.00
OUT OF STATE TUITION:	$6,600.00
*ANNUAL TOTAL:	$7,606.00

(*Annual Total does not include out-of-state tuition .)

FINANCIAL AID

Financial Aid Phone: (713) 313-4383
Financial Aid Fax:
No closing date May 1; notifications on a rolling basis beginning around June 1. FAFSA accepted. Pell grants, SEOG, FSEOG, loans, work-study based on need; Univ. Scholastic Assistance Grant; Texas Public Educational State Student Incentive Grant. Payment Option plans available.

SPORTS

Varsity Sports: Baseball, basketball, cross-country, track and field, volleyball. NAIA, NCAA.

WHAT MAJOR?

Bachelor's: Accounting, banking and finance, biology, business management, business economics, chemistry, communications, community services, computer sciences, criminal justice studies, economics, elementary education, English, French, health & Kinesiology, history, home economics, human environment and housing, individual and family development, journalism, mathematics, music, pharmacy, psychology, public administration, radio/television, radio/television technology, secondary education, sociology, Spanish, special education, speech correction, speech/debate/forensics, textiles and clothing, interdisciplinary studies.

Historical & Special Interest:

Texas Southern's history began in 1927 when Houston Colored Junior College for Negroes was transferred to the State of Texas following the passage of a bill creating Texas State University for Negroes. It was established as a state university in 1947 and is fully accredited. The University profices a variety of undergraduate, graduate, and professional degree programs. With a student enrollment of more than 10,000, TSU offers courses of study in Science and Technology, Humanities and Communications, Law, Education and Behavioral Sciences, Management and Pharmacy, and Health Sciences. The name was changed in 1951 to Texas Southern University and it is located on a beautifully pine-studded campus in the heart of Houston.

TSU is establishing the prototype for the Peace Corps Internship Foreign Studies Program.

Notable Alumni:
Joseph Fuller, Jr., NASA Deputy Director; Barbara Jordan, former member of US House of Reps.; George Leland, US House of Reps. , Hubert Laws, jazz artist.

Master Key: *The milk of human kindness never curdles and should not be bottled up.*

HBCU Third Edition
© Jireh & Associates, Inc.
Wilmington, DE

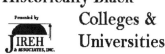
TOUGALOO COLLEGE
TOUGALOO, MS

Web Site:
www.tougaloo.edu

SCHOOL INFO

Established in 1869. Private, coed, 4-year liberal arts college. United Christian Mission Society and United Church of Christ. affiliation on suburban campus in rural community at city limits of state capital, Jackson.

ACCREDITATON:
Southern Association of Colleges & Schools

CAMPUS ENROLLMENT:
Undergraduate: 308 men & 674 women. **Transfer students:** 21 men & 39 women. Part-time: 15 men & 51 female. **Freshman ethnic enrollment:** African American-979; Asian -1; Caucasian -1; Hisp.-1.

WHAT DO I NEED?

Academic record and recommendations important. College preparatory program. SAT or ACT for admissions, placement and counseling only; scores by August 24. No fee; no closing date and notifications on a rolling basis; replies within 2 weeks. Early admission program available. Audition and portfolio required for music and art applicants, respectively.

UNIQUE PROGRAMS

The following programs are available: accelerated program, cooperative education, double major, honors program, independent study, internships, study abroad, student-designed major, teacher preparation, visiting/exchange student program, Washington semester, cross-registration, liberal arts/career combination in engineering.

ACADEMIC REQUIREMENTS

Freshmen must earn a minimum 2.0 and majors must be declared by end of second year.

Core curriculum: computer science, English, foreign languages, history, humanities, mathematics, biological/physical sciences, social sciences. Total credits for Associate: 64. Bachelor's: 124.

STUDENT SERVICES

Campus student services include: career and personal counseling, freshmen orientation, health services, placement services, reduced course load program, remedial instruction, special counselor, tutoring, veterans counselor, services for handicapped. ROTC: Army.

WHAT MAJOR?

Associate: Preelementary education, teacher aide.

Bachelor's: Accounting, African-American studies, biology, business economics, chemistry, computer programming, economics, elementary education, English, history, management science, mathematics, music, physics, political science and government, psychology, secondary education, sociology, visual and performing arts.

Historical & Special Interest:

Tougaloo College is 4-year, liberal arts, private, co-educational and church-related institution. Founded in 1869 by the American Missioary Society, the school now enrolls an average of 1,000 students. The history of the school is firmly rooted in academic excellence and this has been widely acclaimed by national publication, including the "Chronicle of Higher Education." Although the school accepts studentw with various backgrounds and preparations, fully half of Tougaloo's graduates go on to attend graduate school.

Tougaloo College is a UNCF school.

ADDRESS:

TOUGALOO COLLEGE
ADMINISTRATIVE OFFICES
TOUGALOO,   MS   39174
Principal Official: Joe A. Lee

TYPES OF DEGREES AWARDED:
AA, BA.

ACADEMIC CALENDAR:
Semester.

CONTACT INFORMATION

Admissions Officer: Carolyn Evans
Phone: (601) 977-7770   **Fax:** (601) 977-6185
Web Site: www.tougaloo.edu

DOLLARS AND SENSE

TUITION & FEES:	$6,272.00
ROOM & BOARD:	$3,446.00
BOOKS & SUPPLIES:	$500.00
OTHER EXPENSES:	$920.00
OUT OF STATE TUITION:	
*ANNUAL TOTAL:	$11,138.00

(*Annual Total does not include out-of-state tuition .)

FINANCIAL AID

Financial Aid Phone: (888) 424-2566
Financial Aid Fax: (601) 977-7739

No application closing date but priority given to applications received by April 15; notifications on a rolling basis beginning about May 1; must reply within 2 weeks. FAFSA accepted. Pell grants, loans, jobs available. Academic, music/drama, athletic, scholarships available.

SPORTS

Varsity Sports: Softball, Golf, Basketball, cross-country, track and field. NAIA.

HBCU Third Edition
© Jireh & Associates, Inc.
Wilmington, DE

TRENHOLM STATE TECH. COLLEGE

MONTGOMERY,   AL

Web Site:
Not provided.

SCHOOL INFO

Established in 1966. Public 2-year technical coed college on urban campus is small city.

ADDRESS:

TRENHOLM STATE TECH. COLLEGE
1225 AIR BASE BOULEVARD
MONTGOMERY,   AL   36108
Principal Official: Dr. Leroy Bell, Jr. (Interim)

TYPES OF DEGREES AWARDED:
AA.

ACADEMIC CALENDAR:
Quarter.

ACCREDITATON:
Southern Association of Colleges & Schools

CONTACT INFORMATION

Admissions Officer: Ms. Carolyn Silverman
Phone: (334) 832-9000   **Fax:** (334) 832-9777
Web Site: Not provided.

CAMPUS ENROLLMENT:
Undergraduate: 962 men & women. **Transfer students:** 45 men & women. **Freshman ethnic enrollment: Not available.**

WHAT DO I NEED?

Open admission. Applicants must take entrance text (ASSET examination). Min. scores on ACT: English 20 and 19.2 Math. SAT scores: 526 Math min. and 480 Verbal. No application fee. No closing date; notifications on a rolling basis beginning around July 31. Interview required for dental asst. applicants only. Closing dates for LPN only.

DOLLARS AND SENSE

TUITION & FEES:	$3,267.00
ROOM & BOARD:	$2,299.00
BOOKS & SUPPLIES:	$575.00
OTHER EXPENSES:	$850.00
OUT OF STATE TUITION:	$5,687.00
*ANNUAL TOTAL:	$6,991.00

(*Annual Total does not include out-of-state tuition .)

UNIQUE PROGRAMS

The following programs are available: cooperative education, internships, weekend college, Tech Prep, NASA, Talent Search, Student Support Services.

ACADEMIC REQUIREMENTS

Minimum 2.0 GPA for freshmen and majors must be declared on application.

Credits required for an Associate: 96 hours.

FINANCIAL AID

Financial Aid Phone: (334) 832-9000
Financial Aid Fax: (334) 832-9777

No closing date; priority given to applications received by August 31; notifications on a rolling basis. FAFSA accepted. Pell grants, FSEOG, FCWS, ASAP, Veteran Affairs Benefits, and institutional scholarships available. Scholarships available: Academic and Leadership. No other Payment Options available.

STUDENT SERVICES

Campus student services include: aptitude testing, career and personal counseling, campus daycare, learning center, remedial instruction, special counselors, special advisor for adult students, services for handicapped, tutoring, veterans counselor.

SPORTS

None.

WHAT MAJOR?

Associate: Accounting, Culinary Arts, Stenography, Medical Records, Medical Records Technology, Medical Assisting, Dental Lab Technology, Dental Assisting, EMT, Horticulture.

Historical & Special Interest:

Trenholm is a public, two-year college named after Dr. H. Council Trenholm, the former president of neighboring Alabama State University. It is the only school in Alabama that offers the Emergency Medical Technology Program, which provides training ranging from basic to advanced paramedic levels. Under a reciprocal agreement with the Community College and the U.S. Air Force, active duty and Reserve/National Guards personnel may take occupational courses at Trenholm.

Master Key: *Every season has a product. Murdock*

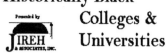

Historically Black Colleges & Universities

TUSKEGEE UNIVERSITY

TUSKEGEE, AL

Web Site:
www.tusk.edu

SCHOOL INFO
Established in 1881. 4-year private university, coed on rural campus in large town; 40 miles from Montgomery, 45 miles from Columbus, Georgia.

ACCREDITATON:
Southern Association of Colleges & Schools

CAMPUS ENROLLMENT:
Undergraduate: 3023 men & women **Graduate:** 172 men & women. **Transfer students:** 90 men & women. **Freshman ethnic enrollment:** African American-92%, Asian-1%, Puerto Rican-3, Caucasian-2%, Hispanic-1%, Native American-4%.

WHAT DO I NEED?
Academic record, essay and test scores important. ACT required for engineering and nursing applicants. College Preparatory Program. SAT or ACT/SAT preferred; score report by June 15. Closing date for admissions applications March 31st and fee $25.

UNIQUE PROGRAMS
The following programs are available: cooperative education, double major, honors program, independent study, internships, teacher preparation, engineering program with 2-year colleges; liberal arts/career combination in engineering. Trio Programs: Student Support Svcs, Talent Search, and Upward Bound identify and assist low income, first-generation students.

ACADEMIC REQUIREMENTS
Minimum GPA of 2.0 for freshmen and major must be declared by end of first year.

Core curriculum: English, computer science, history, mathematics, biological/physical sciences, social science. Bachelor's: 124 hours (33 in major).

STUDENT SERVICES
Campus student services include: aptitude testing, counseling center, residence life development, student life and development, campus daycare, freshman orientation, health services, learning center, personal and veteran counseling, placement services, reduced course program, remedial instruction, special counseling, tutoring, and services for learning disabled. ROTC: Army.

ADDRESS:

TUSKEGEE UNIVERSITY
317 KRESKE CENTER
TUSKEGEE,   AL   36088
Principal Official: Dr. Benjamin F. Payton

TYPES OF DEGREES AWARDED:
BA, BS, MS, Med, DVM, BArch.

ACADEMIC CALENDAR:
Semester. Summer sessions limited.

CONTACT INFORMATION

Admissions Officer: Elva Bradley
Phone: (334) 727-8500   **Fax:** (334) 724-4402
Web Site: www.tusk.edu

DOLLARS AND SENSE

TUITION & FEES:	$9,060.00
ROOM & BOARD:	$4,710.00
BOOKS & SUPPLIES:	$600.00
OTHER EXPENSES:	$600.00
OUT OF STATE TUITION:	
*ANNUAL TOTAL:	$14,970.00

(*Annual Total does not include out-of-state tuition .)

FINANCIAL AID

Financial Aid Phone: (800) 416-2831
Financial Aid Fax: (334) 724-4227

Closing date for aid applications March 31, priority given to applications received by March 15; notifications on a rolling basis beginning May 15. Student must reply within 2 weeks. FAFSA accepted. All grants, loans, jobs based on need. Academic, music/drama, athletic scholarships available.

SPORTS
Varsity Sports: Baseball, basketball, football, tennis, track and field, volleyball. NCAA.

WHAT MAJOR?
Bachelor's: Accounting, aerospace engineering, aeronautical engineering, astronautical engineering, agricultural business, agricultural education, ag. sciences, animal sciences, architecture, banking and finance, biology, business administration, business management, chemical engineering, chemistry, computer and information sciences, construction, construction management, dietetics, economics, education of the mentally handicapped, electrical/electronics/communications, engineering, elementary education, English, English education, food sciences, food sciences and human nutrition, history, home economics, home economics education, industrial arts education, management science, marketing management, mathematics, mathematics education, mechanical engineering, medical laboratory, nursing, nutritional sciences, occupational therapy, physical education, physics, political science and government, poultry, pre-elementary education, psychology, science education, secondary education, social science education, social work, sociology, soil sciences, technical education, textiles and clothing.

Historical & Special Interest:
Tuskegee University was founded in 1881 by Booker T. Washington and is one of the most famous universities in the United States. Its most famous professor and agricultural chemist was George Washington Carver, creator of more than 300 uses of the peanut and sweet potato. The man who revolutionized the south's farming methods, Carver is also known for his discovery of synthetics. It was, in addition, the training groung during World War II for America's first Black fighter pilots in the 99th Pursuit Squadron-- the original "Tuskegee Airmen." The average student enrollment is 3,300 with students from 40 states and 54 foreign countries. Its secondary colleges include: the College of Arts and Sciences; School of Agriculture and Home Economics; School of Business, Education, Engineering and Architecture. Tuskegee University is a UNCF school.

NOTABLE ALUMNI:
Tom Joyner-Radio Announcer; Lionel Richie, singer; Keenan Ivory Wayans, actor/producer; Daniel "Chappie" James, 1st Black 4-Star General in U.S. Armed Forces; William Dawson -Outstanding Composer/Conductor; Ralph Ellison-Author & Recipient of National Medal of Arts.

Master Key: *You will never be promoted until you become over-qualified for your present position. Murdock*

HBCU Third Edition
© Jireh & Associates, Inc.
Wilmington, DE

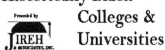
UNIV. OF ARKANSAS PINE BLUFF

PINE BLUFF, AR

Web Site:
www.uapb.edu

SCHOOL INFO

Established in 1873. 4-year public coed university on urban campus in small city; 42 miles south of Little Rock.

ADDRESS:

UNIV. OF ARKANSAS PINE BLUFF
P.O. BOX 4038
PINE BLUFF, AR 71601
Principal Official: Dr. Lawrence Davis, Chancellor

ACCREDITATON:
North Central Association of Colleges & Schools & 6 others.

CAMPUS ENROLLMENT:
*Undergraduate: men & women. **Graduate:** men & women. **Transfer students:** men & women. **Freshman ethnic enrollment:** African American-, Asian-5, Caucasian-76, Hispanic-2

WHAT DO I NEED?

Open admissions. ACT or SAT placement and counseling only; score report by August 20. No application fee; no closing date; notifications on rolling basis; must reply within 3 weeks. Deferred and early admission program available.

UNIQUE PROGRAMS

The following programs are available: Cooperative education, double major, honors program, internships, teacher preparation, 2-year transfer program.

ACADEMIC REQUIREMENTS

Minimum GPA for freshmen of 2.0 and a ACT composite score of 19 are the general requirements for unconditional admissions. A major must be declared by end of second year.

Core curriculum: English, foreign languages, history, mathematics, biological/physical sciences. Graduate study available in the area of Education. Associate: 62 hours. Bachelor's: 124 hours.

STUDENT SERVICES

Campus student services include: aptitude testing, career and personal counseling, employment services for undergraduates, health services, learning center, placement services for graduates, reduced course load program, remedial instruction, special counselor, tutoring, services for handicapped. ROTC: Army

TYPES OF DEGREES AWARDED:
AA, AS, AAS, BA, BS, MS.

ACADEMIC CALENDAR:
Semester. Summer sessions limited.

CONTACT INFORMATION

Admissions Officer: Ms. Kwurly Floyd
Phone: (501) 543-8000 **Fax:** (501) 543-8014
Web Site: www.uapb.edu

DOLLARS AND SENSE

TUITION & FEES:	$1,946.00
ROOM & BOARD:	$3,630.00
BOOKS & SUPPLIES:	$508.00
OTHER EXPENSES:	$400.00
OUT OF STATE TUITION:	$4,501.00
*ANNUAL TOTAL:	$6,484.00

(*Annual Total does not include out-of-state tuition .)

FINANCIAL AID

Financial Aid Phone:
Financial Aid Fax:

No closing date; applicants notified on a rolling basis beginning around June 1; must reply within 6 weeks. FAFSA accepted. Pell grants, loans, jobs, scholarships available. The college offers a total of $50,000 in scholarships per academic year for non-traditional minorities.

SPORTS

Varsity Sports: Basketball, football, track and field, cross-country. NAIA.

WHAT MAJOR?

Associate: Criminal justice technology, industrial technology, law enforcement and corrections technologies.

Bachelor's: Accounting, agricultural economics, agricultural education, agronomy, animal science, art, automotive technology management, biology, biology/dentistry/medicine/pharmacy, business adminstration/management, business education, business finance/marketing, chemistry, child development, community recreation, computer sciences, criminal justice, economics, economic education, early childhood education, elementary education, English, English education, fashion design/merchandising, fisheries biology, gerontology, health & physical education/elementary/secondary, history, hospitality food service mgmt/dietetics/restaurant, industrial technology/construction mgmt/electronics/manufacturing, journalism, mathematics, mathematics education, music, music education, nursing, physics, political science, preengineering, psychology, science education, social science education, sociology, special education, speech & drama/communication/theatre arts, trade and industrial education.

Historical & Special Interest:

University of Arkansas at Pine Bluff is located in a blend of oak and pine trees which comprise 318 acres of land and 41 major buildings and agricultural and aquaculture research farms. Tabbed as "Arkansas' fastest growing university" in recent years, the 83-acre main campus includes five new buildings recently constructed including a new student housing complex. Since 1986 four others have been remodeled including the student union and the women's housing complex.

Two art galleries which house the "Persistence of the Spirit" exhibit on Arkansas black history; a 430-seat theater hall, and a 650-seat fine arts concert hall also used for events by the public.

Master Key: *A life without a cause is a life without effect. Barbella*

HBCU Third Edition
© Jireh & Associates, Inc.
Wilmington, DE

Historically Black Colleges & Universities

Presented by JIREH & ASSOCIATES, INC.

UNIV. OF MARYLAND E. S.

PRINCESS ANNE, MD

Web Site:
www.umes.umd.edu

SCHOOL INFO

Established in 1886. 4-year public coed university. Fifteen minutes from Salisbury; 45 minutes from Ocean City and two-and-one-half hours from Baltimore and Washington, DC.

ACCREDITATON:
Middle States Assoc. of Colleges & Sec. Schools

CAMPUS ENROLLMENT:
Undergraduate: 2682 total men and women. **Graduate:** 228 men and women. **Transfer students:** 138. **Freshman ethnic enrollment:** African American-2178, Asian-17, Caucasian-472, Hispanic-2.

WHAT DO I NEED?

Test scores and high school achievement important. 820 SAT or 18 ACT. Official copy of high school or GED test results as appropriate. Scores due by June 30 for placement, admissions and counseling only. Application fee $25 which may be waived based on need. Closing date June 30; notifications on a rolling basis; replies within 2 weeks. Deferred and early admission program available.

UNIQUE PROGRAMS

The following programs are available: accelerated program, cooperative education, cross-registration, double major, dual enrollment of high school students, honors program, independent study, internships, teacher preparation, weekend college; liberal arts/career combination in engineering.

ACADEMIC REQUIREMENTS

Minimum GPA of 1.65 for freshmen and major must be declared by end of second year.

Core curriculum: English, computer science, history, humanities, mathematics, biological/physical sciences, social sciences. Total credits for Bachelor's: 120 hours (60 in major).

STUDENT SERVICES

Campus student services include: academic center, aptitude testing, career and personal counseling, employment services for undergraduates, freshman orientation, health services, placement services, reduced course load program, remedial instruction, services for handicapped, tutoring, veterans counselor. ROTC: Army.

ADDRESS:

UNIV. OF MARYLAND E. S.
BACKBONE RD./EASTERN SHORE
PRINCESS ANNE,   MD   21853-1299
Principal Official: Dr. Delores R. Spikes

TYPES OF DEGREES AWARDED:
BA, BS, M Ed, MA Physical Ther., MS, PhD.

ACADEMIC CALENDAR:
Semester. Summer sessions limited.

CONTACT INFORMATION

Admissions Officer: Dr. Rochell Peoples
Phone: (410) 651-6410   **Fax:** (410) 651-7922
Web Site: www.umes.umd.edu

DOLLARS AND SENSE

TUITION & FEES:	$3,455.00
ROOM & BOARD:	$4,970.00
BOOKS & SUPPLIES:	$500.00
OTHER EXPENSES:	$1,500.00
OUT OF STATE TUITION:	$9,196.00
*ANNUAL TOTAL:	$10,425.00

(*Annual Total does not include out-of-state tuition .)

FINANCIAL AID

Financial Aid Phone: (410) 651-6172
Financial Aid Fax:

Applications closing date May 1st; notified on or about May 15; must reply within 1 week. FAFSA accepted. Federal Pell grants, Federal Supplemental Ed. Opp. Grant, loans, and work-study are available. Academic, athletic, music/drama, state/district residency, leadership, minority and merit scholarships available.

SPORTS

Varsity Sports: Baseball, basketball, cross-country, golf, soccer, softball, tennis, track and field, volleyball. NCAA.

WHAT MAJOR?

Bachelor's: Airway Science: Aircraft Systems Management, Airway Electronic Systems; Agriculture: Agribusiness, Agricultural Education, General Agriculture; Business, Economics and Accounting: Accounting, Business Administration, Business Education; Computer Science and Mathematics: Computer Science, Mathematics; Criminal Justice; English and Modern Languages: English, Telecommunications; Engineering Technology: Electrical/Electronic, Mechanical Technology; Fine Arts: Art Education, Music Education; Human Ecology: Dietetics, Family & Consumer Sciences, Early Childhood Education, Interior Design, Food and Nutrition, Fashion Merchandising; Hotel and Restaurant Management; Natural and Physical Sciences: Biology, Chemistry, Environmental Science, Marine Biology; Physical Education and Rehabilitation Services: Physical Education, Rehabilitation Services; Pre-Professional Programs: Dental Hygiene, Pharmacy, Nursing, Radiologic Technology, Engineering, Physical Therapy, Dentistry and Medicine, Law; Social Sciences: Sociology, Social Science Education and Sociology/Social Work; Special Education; Technology and Construction Management: Construction Management, Technology Education. *Teacher Education Programs are available for Elementary and Secondary School Certification.

Historical & Special Interest:

A full partner in the University of Maryland System since 1970, the University of Maryland, Eastern Shore offers a variety of programs in such areas as physical therapy, engineering technology, computer science, hotel and restaurant management, and human ecology.

Member of the 1890 Land Grant Institution network on 620 acres of panoramic countryside with 30 major buildings, including instructional facilities, residence halls, radio station, and research farm. UMES is authorized to award advanced degrees in the fields of guidance and counseling, special education, agriculture and extension education, and marine-estuarine-environmental science.

Master Key: *If you can't have the best of everything, make the best of everything you have.*

HBCU Third Edition
© Jireh & Associates, Inc.
Wilmington, DE

Historically Black Colleges & Universities

JIREH & ASSOCIATES, INC.

UNIV. OF THE VIRGIN ISLANDS

ST.THOMAS, USV

Web Site:
www.uvi.edu

SCHOOL INFO

The University of the Virgin Islands is comprised of two campuses: St. Thomas and St. Croix.

ACCREDITATON:
CIHE Middle States / Assoc. of Colleges & Schools.

CAMPUS ENROLLMENT:
Undergraduate: 2989 men & women. **Graduate:** 256 men & women. **Freshman ethnic enrollment:** Native Am.: 3, African Am.: 2143, Asian: 27, Caucasian: 121, Hispanic: 98.

WHAT DO I NEED?

High school diploma or equivalent. SAT or ACT required. Closing date: April 30. Rolling basis. Student reply date: July 15. Application fee $20 ($10 late fee).

UNIQUE PROGRAMS

The following programs are available: Business administration, education, humanities, nursing, science & mathematics, social sciences.

ACADEMIC REQUIREMENTS

A minimum GPA is required for freshmen 1.70. School achievement record very important; test scores - important. Basic requirement for admission to all academic programs is four years of high school english. Majors must be declared at enrollment.

Successful completion of English Proficiency and Computer Literacy Examination. Core curriculum: humanities, mathematics, natural sciences, social sciences, and physical education. Associate: 62 (32 in major) credits. Bachelor degree: 120 (66 in major) credits.

STUDENT SERVICES

Realization of Academic Potential (REAP) Program, Drug & Alcohol Education Prevention Program, advising, orientation, health services, placement and counseling, housing on St. Thomas campus, Early Admission Program, National Student Exchange.

ADDRESS:

UNIV. OF THE VIRGIN ISLANDS
2 JOHN BREWER'S BAY
ST.THOMAS,   USVI 00802-0990
Principal Official: Dr. Orville Lean

TYPES OF DEGREES AWARDED:
AA, AS, BA, BS, MAE, MBA, MPA.

ACADEMIC CALENDAR:
Semester. Summer sessions.

CONTACT INFORMATION

Admissions Officer: Judith Edwin
Phone: (809) 776-9200   **Fax:** (809) 693-1155
Web Site: www.uvi.edu

DOLLARS AND SENSE

TUITION & FEES:	$2,346.00
ROOM & BOARD:	$5,126.00
BOOKS & SUPPLIES:	$700.00
OTHER EXPENSES:	$650.00
OUT OF STATE TUITION:	$6,660.00
*ANNUAL TOTAL:	$8,822.00

(*Annual Total does not include out-of-state tuition .)

FINANCIAL AID

Financial Aid Phone: (809) 693-1090
Financial Aid Fax:
Pell grants, loans, scholarships, work-study jobs available. FAFSA accepted.

SPORTS

Varsity: Volleyball and soccer. Intramural: volleyball, basketball, track & field.

WHAT MAJOR?

Associate: Accounting, business management, data processing, hotel & restaurant management (offered on a part-time basis), nursing, office machines, physics, police science & administration.

Bachelor's: Accounting, business administration, elementary education, vocational education, English, humanities, music education, Spanish, biology chemistry, chemistry with physics, marine biology, mathematics, Caribbean studies, psychology, social sciences, social work and nursing.

Historical & Special Interest:

The University of the Virgin Islands was founded in 1962 by the Legislature of the Virgin Islands. With a total student enrollment of 2,600, it is a public, co-educational, land-grant institution. The University has two campuses: St. Thomas, the main campus, and St. Croix. It offers the Master of Arts, Bachelor of Arts, Bachelor of Science, and the Associate degrees.

The University of the Virgin Islands holds active membership in the Middle States Association of Colleges and Schools and is accredited by the Commission on Institutions of Higher Education of the Middle States Association.

Master Key: *The starting point of all acheivement is desire. Weak desires bring weak results. Napoleon Hill*

HBCU Third Edition
© Jireh & Associates, Inc.
Wilmington, DE

Historically Black
Colleges &
Universities

JIREH
& ASSOCIATES, INC.
Presented by

UNIVERSITY OF D. C.
WASHINGTON, DC

Web Site:
www.udc.edu

SCHOOL INFO

Established in 1975. 4-year public coed university on urban campus in very large city.

ADDRESS:

UNIVERSITY OF D. C.
4200 CONNECTICUT AVE. N.W.
WASHINGTON,   DC   20008
Principal Official: Dr. Tilden J. LeMelle

ACCREDITATON:
Middle States Association of Colleges & Schools

CAMPUS ENROLLMENT:
Undergraduate full-time: women 2216, 1605 men. **Part-time:** women 4257 and 3083 men.
Graduate full-time: women 140 and 101 men; part-time: 271 women and 196 men.

WHAT DO I NEED?

Selective admissions to nursing, art, and music programs. Fall applications $10 fee. Closing date August 1; priority to applications received by July 1. Notification on rolling basis. Interview, audition, or portfolio recommended for nursing, music and art applicants. It is an open admissions institution whose only requirement for entrance is a high school diploma or a GED certificate.

UNIQUE PROGRAMS

The following programs are available: cooperative education, cross-registration, dual enrollment of high school students, honors program, independent study, internships, weekend college, 2-year transfer program.

ACADEMIC REQUIREMENTS

Minimum GPA for freshmen 2.0 and majors must be declared by end of first year.

Core curriculum: English, foreign languages, history, mathematics, philosophy/religion, biological/physical sciences, social sciences. Associate: 65 hours. Bachelor's: 120 hours. Hours in major: 53 and 90 respectively.

STUDENT SERVICES

Campus student services include: career and personal counseling, employment service for undergraduates, health services, learning center, preadmission summer program, placement services, remedial instruction,services for handicapped, tutoring, veterans counselor. ROTC: Air Force, Army, Naval.

TYPES OF DEGREES AWARDED:
AA, AS, BA, BS, MA, MS, MBA.

ACADEMIC CALENDAR:
Semester. Summer sessions limited.

CONTACT INFORMATION

Admissions Officer: Michael O'Leary
Phone: (202) 274-5000 **Fax:** (202) 994-0325
Web Site: www.udc.edu

DOLLARS AND SENSE

TUITION & FEES:	$1,392.00
ROOM & BOARD:	$0.00
BOOKS & SUPPLIES:	$400.00
OTHER EXPENSES:	$1,300.00
OUT OF STATE TUITION:	$4,964.00
*ANNUAL TOTAL:	$3,092.00

(*Annual Total does not include out-of-state tuition .)

FINANCIAL AID

Financial Aid Phone:
Financial Aid Fax:
No closing date; priority given to applications received by April 15; notifications on a rolling basis beginning around June 1; must reply by July 1 or within 10 days. FAFSA accepted. Pell grants, loans, jobs based on need. Academic, athletic scholarships available.

SPORTS

Varsity Sports: Baseball, basketball, football, soccer, tennis, track and field, volleyball. NCAA.

WHAT MAJOR?

Associate: Accounting, aeronautical technology, air pollution control technology, aircraft mechanics, architectural technologies, banking and finance, business administration and management, business and office, business computer/console peripheral equipment operation, business data processing and related programs, child development/care/guidance, civil technology, computer technology, criminal justice technology, criminology, electronic technology, engineering and related technologies, fashion merchandising, fire control and safety technology, food production/management services, mortuary science, graphic and printing production, graphic arts technology, history, law enforcement and corrections technologies, legal paralegal, marine biology, marketing and distribution, mechanical design technology, medical laboratory technologies,music, nursing, philosophy, physical sciences, public affairs, radiograph medical technology, respiratory therapy technology, secretarial and related programs.
Bachelor's: Accounting, animal sciences, anthropology, art education, banking and finance, biology, business management, chemistry, city planning, civil engineering, clothing and textiles management, communications, computer and information sciences, construction, construction management, criminal justice studies, dramatic arts, economics, electrical/electronics and communications engineering, elementary education, English, environmental science, film arts, fire control and safety technology, food sciences, food sciences and human nutrition, French, geography, German, health education, history home economics/education, information sciences and systems, journalism, library science, mathematics, mechanical engineering, music, music education, nursing, ornamental horticulture, philosophy, physical education, physics, political science and government, psychology, public administration, radio/television, reading education, secondary education, secretarial and related programs, social foundations, social work, sociology, Spanish, special education, speech correction, speech pathology/audiology, studio art, textiles and clothing, urban studies.

Historical & Special Interest:
The roots of the University of District of Columbia began in 1851 when Myrtilla Miner opened a school to prepare "colored girls to teach." The University of D.C. was created in 1976 from the consolidation of three existing public institutions of post-secondary education: D.C. Teachers College; Federal City College and Washignton Technical Institute. UDC was opened in 1977 as the nation's only metropolitan, land-grant institution of higher education.

Master Key: *To speak kindly does not hurt the tongue.*

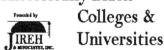
VIRGINIA STATE UNIVERSITY

PETERSBURG, VA

Web Site:
www.vsu.edu

SCHOOL INFO

Established in 1882. 4-year public coed university on suburban campus setting in large town; 25 miles from Richmond.

ACCREDITATON:
Southern Association of Colleges & Schools

CAMPUS ENROLLMENT:
*Undergraduate: Full-time: 1220 men and 1675 women. Part-time:140 men and 170 women. **Graduate:** Full-time: 25 men and 40 women. Part-time: 135 men and 440 women. **Freshman ethnic enrollment:** Not available.

WHAT DO I NEED?

Academic record, school recommendation required, essay recommended. SAT or ACT (SAT preferred); report by May 1. Application fee $10. Closing date May 1; notifications on a rolling basis around November 1; must reply by May 1 or within 2 weeks if after May 1. Music applicants require audition.

UNIQUE PROGRAMS

The following programs are available: cooperative education, double major, dual enrollment of high school students, honors program, internships, study abroad, teacher preparation.

ACADEMIC REQUIREMENTS

Freshmen must earn a minimum 1.5 and majors must be declared by end of first year.

Core curriculum: arts/fine arts, computer science, English, history, humanities, mathematics, biological/physical sciences, social sciences. Bachelor's: 120 hrs (42 in major).

STUDENT SERVICES

Campus student services include: career and personal counseling, employment services for undergraduates, freshman orientation, health services, placement service for graduates, reduced course load program, remedial instruction, special counselor, services for handicapped, tutoring, veterans counselor. ROTC: Army.

WHAT MAJOR?

Bachelor's: Accounting, agricultural business, agricultural economics, agricultural sciences, animal sciences, art education, biology, business management, business economics, business education, business home economics, chemistry, computer and information sciences, elementary education, engineering and engineering-related technologies, English, English education, environmental sciences, foreign languages (multiple emphasis), foreign languages education, geology, history, home economics, home economics education, hotel/motel and restaurant management, international relations, international studies, mathematics, music, physical education, physics, political science and government, psychology, public administration, social work, sociology, soil sciences, special education, statistics, trade and industrial education, visual and performing arts.

Historical & Special Interest:

Virginia State University was founded March 6, 1882 when the legislature of Virginia passed a bill introduced by Alfred W. Harris, a black attorney in Petersburg and representative in the General Assembly for Dinwiddie County, to charter the Virginia Normal and Collegiate Institute.

The University is situated on a 201-acre campus and a 416-acre farm where Randolph Farm-teaching, research, and cooperative extension laboratories are located.

The University is one of the two land-grant universities in the Commonwealth of Virginia overlooking the Appomattox River and borders on the cities of Petersburg and Colonial Heights.

ADDRESS:

VIRGINIA STATE UNIVERSITY
P.O. BOX 18
PETERSBURG, VA 23803
Principal Official: Dr. Eddie N. Moore, Jr.

TYPES OF DEGREES AWARDED:
BA, BS, MA, MS.

ACADEMIC CALENDAR:
Semester. Summer sessions.

CONTACT INFORMATION

Admissions Officer: Lisa Winn
Phone: (804) 524-5906 **Fax:** (804) 524-5055
Web Site: www.vsu.edu

DOLLARS AND SENSE

TUITION & FEES:	$1,950.00
ROOM & BOARD:	$4,845.00
BOOKS & SUPPLIES:	$450.00
OTHER EXPENSES:	$475.00
OUT OF STATE TUITION:	$2,980.00
*ANNUAL TOTAL:	$7,720.00

(*Annual Total does not include out-of-state tuition.)

FINANCIAL AID

Financial Aid Phone:
Financial Aid Fax:

No closing date; priority given to applications received by March 31; notifications on a rolling basis beginning around April 1; must reply by May 1 or within 2 weeks if after May 1. FAFSA accepted. Pell grants, loans, jobs based on need. Academic, state/district residency, alumni affiliation, minority scholarships available.

SPORTS

Varsity Sports: Baseball, basketball, cross-country, football, golf, softball, tennis, track and field, wrestling. NCAA.

Master Key: *Swallowing your pride occasionally, will never give you indigestion.*

HBCU Third Edition
© Jireh & Associates, Inc.
Wilmington, DE

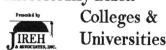
VIRGINIA UNION UNIVERSITY

RICHMOND, VA

Web Site:
Not provided.

SCHOOL INFO

Established in 1865. 4-year private coed university affiliated with American Baptist Churches in the USA on urban campus setting in the city of Richmond; 90 miles from Norfolk.

ACCREDITATON:
Southern Association of Colleges & Schools

CAMPUS ENROLLMENT:
*Undergraduate: Total: 1209 men and women.   Graduate: 134 men and women.
Freshman ethnic enrollment: Not available.

WHAT DO I NEED?

Academic record, SAT or ACT scores and 2.0 GPA, college preparatory program. ACT or SAT (SAT preferred); scores by June 1. Academically provisional applicants may be conditionally accepted with interview. Application fee $10 may be waived based on need. No closing date; notifications on a rolling basis; replies within 2 weeks if after May 1. Music applicants auditions required.

UNIQUE PROGRAMS

The following programs are available: cooperative education, honors program, independent study, internships; liberal arts/career combination in engineering.

ACADEMIC REQUIREMENTS

Freshmen must earn a minimum 1.8 and majors must be declared by end of second year.

Core curriculum: English, history, humanities, mathematics, biological/physical sciences, philosophy/religion, social sciences. Bachelor's: 124 hrs (36 in major).

STUDENT SERVICES

Campus student services include: aptitude testing, career and personal counseling, employment services for undergraduates, health services, placement services, reduced course load program, remedial instruction, tutoring. ROTC: Army.

ADDRESS:

VIRGINIA UNION UNIVERSITY
1500 NORTH LOMBARDY ST.
RICHMOND,   VA   23220
Principal Official: Dr. S. Dallas Simmons

TYPES OF DEGREES AWARDED:
BA, BS, M. Div., Doctor of Ministry.

ACADEMIC CALENDAR:
Semester. Summer sessions limited.

CONTACT INFORMATION

Admissions Officer: Gil Powell
Phone: (804) 257-5600   **Fax:** (804) 524-5055
Web Site: Not provided.

DOLLARS AND SENSE

TUITION & FEES:	$8,579.00
ROOM & BOARD:	$3,780.00
BOOKS & SUPPLIES:	$250.00
OTHER EXPENSES:	$400.00
OUT OF STATE TUITION:	
*ANNUAL TOTAL:	$13,009.00

(*Annual Total does not include out-of-state tuition .)

FINANCIAL AID

Financial Aid Phone:
Financial Aid Fax:
Closing date August 1; priority given to applications received by July 1; notifications on a rolling basis beginning around June 1; must reply within 2 weeks. FAFSA accepted. Pell grants, loans, jobs based on need.

SPORTS

Varsity Sports: Basketball, football, golf, tennis, track and field. NCAA.

WHAT MAJOR?

Bachelor's: Accounting, biology, business administration and management, chemistry, elementary education, English, French, history, journalism, mathematics, music, philosophy, political science and government, psychology, special education.

Historical & Special Interest:

Virginia Union University was founded in 1865 to provide educational opportunities to newly emancipated blacks in Virginia. It is the result of a 1899 merger of two institutions (Wayland Seminary and Richmond Theological Institute) which had been established by the American Baptist Home Mission Society. Later, Hartshorn Memorial College of Richmond and Storer College of Harpers Ferry, WV, merged with Virginia Union as it became a "union" of educational institutions.

From its earliest years, Virginia Union has exhibited strength as a Christian institution offering students of every race and economic group the opportunity to acquire the knowledge and skills to be successful in life. The focus of the University has been on rigorous, intellectual discipline, with emphasis on religious convictions and commitment.

The Lynchburg College/VUU Exchange Partnership provides both universities with unique opportunities to interact, share resources and obtain cultural diversity on their campuses (Lynchburg is predominantly white). Its nationally recognized Kenan Project is administered by the Center for Teacher Effectiveness at VUU and is designed to prepare high school students for college entry and successful completion of degree requirements. It is a cooperative program between the University and Richmond Public Schools and funded by the William Kenan Charitable Trust. There is a dual-degree program with Howard University, University of Michigan, and University of Iowa.

Virginia Union University is a UNCF school.

Master Key: *Money talks and often says "Good-bye".*

HBCU Third Edition
© Jireh & Associates, Inc.
Wilmington, DE

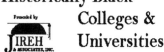
VOORHEES COLLEGE

DENMARK, SC

Web Site:
www.icusc.org/voorhees

SCHOOL INFO

Established in 1897. 4-year private liberal arts, coed college. Affiliation with Episcopal Church on rural campus in small town; 50 miles from Columbia.

ACCREDITATON:
Southern Association of Colleges & Schools

CAMPUS ENROLLMENT:
*Undergraduate: 578 men and women.

ADDRESS:

VOORHEES COLLEGE
1411 VOORHEES ROAD
DENMARK,   SC   29042
Principal Official: Dr. Leonard E. Dawson

TYPES OF DEGREES AWARDED:
BA & BS.

ACADEMIC CALENDAR:
Semester. Summer sessions.

CONTACT INFORMATION

Admissions Officer: Cedric W. Baker
Phone: (803) 793-3351   **Fax:** (803) 793-3068
Web Site: www.icusc.org/voorhees

WHAT DO I NEED?

Open admissions. SAT or ACT for placement and counseling only; test scores by August 22. Application fee $10 may be waived based on need. No closing date; notifications on a rolling basis.

UNIQUE PROGRAMS

The following programs are available: Academic Achievement Center, honors program, independent study and internships.

DOLLARS AND SENSE

TUITION & FEES:	$8,034.00
ROOM & BOARD:	$2,866.00
BOOKS & SUPPLIES:	$300.00
OTHER EXPENSES:	$500.00
OUT OF STATE TUITION:	$8,034.00
*ANNUAL TOTAL:	$11,700.00

(*Annual Total does not include out-of-state tuition.)

ACADEMIC REQUIREMENTS

The academic program is administered through four divisions: Business, Humanities, Education, Fine Arts, Natural Sciences, Mathematics, Computer Science and Social Science.

Core curriculum: computer science, English, history, mathematics, philosophy/religion, biological/physical sciences, social sciences. Associate: 78 hrs. Bachelor's: 122 hrs (72 in major).

FINANCIAL AID

Financial Aid Phone: (803) 793-3351 x7313
Financial Aid Fax:

Closing date July 30; priority given to applications received by May 1; notifications on a rolling basis beginning about June 15. FAFSA accepted. Federal Pell grants, Supplemental tuition grants, loans, and work-study jobs based on need. Institutional Academic scholarships and UNCF scholarships available.

STUDENT SERVICES

Campus student services include: academic center, aptitude testing, career and personal counseling, health services, placement services, reduced course load program, remedial instruction, special advisors, tutoring. ROTC: Army.

SPORTS

Varsity Sports: Baseball, basketball, cross-country, softball, track and field. NAIA.

WHAT MAJOR?

Bachelor's: Accounting, biology, business and administration and management, chemistry, computer and information sciences, criminal justice, early childhood education, elementary education, English, health & recreation, mathematics, mathematics education, physical education, political science, and sociology.

Historical & Special Interest:

Voorhees College was founded in 1897 by Elizabeth Evelyn Wright and is affiliated with the Episcopal Church. It was the first predominantly Black institution in South Carolina to achieve full accreditation by the Southern Association of Colleges and Schools. It offers four academic divisions: Business and Economics, Education/Humanities, Natural Sciences and Mathematics, and Social Sciences.

The school is situated on 350 acres in a park-like setting and more importantly students learn in a 'family' environment where they are treated as individuals.

Voorhees College is a UNCF school.

Master Key: *It is better to deserve honors and not have them than to have them and not deserve them. Mark Twain*

HBCU Third Edition
© Jireh & Associates, Inc.
Wilmington, DE

WEST VIRGINIA STATE COLLEGE

INSTITUTE, WV

Web Site:
wvsc.wvnet.edu

SCHOOL INFO

Established in 1891. 4-year public coed liberal arts college on suburban campus setting in small town; 8 miles from Charleston.

ACCREDITATON:
North Central Association of Colleges & Schools

CAMPUS ENROLLMENT:
*Undergraduate: Full-time: 1230 men and 1330 women. Part-time: 794 men and 1298 women. Freshman ethnic enrollment: Not available.

WHAT DO I NEED?

Academic record, test scores, college preparatory program. Minimum ACT comp. 14. ACT or SAT (ACT preferred); scores by August 27. No application fee and no closing date; notifications on a rolling basis. Nuclear medicine technology , regents of bacholor of arts, and borderline applicants- interview recommended. Deferred and early admissions program available.

UNIQUE PROGRAMS

The following programs are available: cross-registration, cooperative education, dual enrollment of high school students, external degree, internships, teacher preparation, transfer program (2-yr).

ACADEMIC REQUIREMENTS

Freshmen must earn a minimum 2.0 and majors must be declared by end of second year.

Core curriculum: arts/fine arts, humanities, mathematics, biological/physical sciences, social sciences. Associate: 60. Bachelor's: 121 (34 in major).

STUDENT SERVICES

Campus student services include: academic center, aptitude testing, career and personal counseling, employment services for undergraduates, freshman orientation, health services, placement services, reduced course load program, remedial instruction, special counselor, skills enhancement program for ROTC students, tutoring, services for handicapped, veterans counselor. ROTC: Army.

ADDRESS:

WEST VIRGINIA STATE COLLEGE
P.O. BOX 1000
INSTITUTE,   WV   25112
Principal Official: Dr. Hazo W. Carter

TYPES OF DEGREES AWARDED:
AA, AS, AAS, BA, BS.

ACADEMIC CALENDAR:
Semester. Summer sessions limited.

CONTACT INFORMATION

Admissions Officer: Robin Green, Assoc. Dir.
Phone: (304) 766-3221   **Fax:** (304) 766-5182
Web Site: wvsc.wvnet.edu

DOLLARS AND SENSE

TUITION & FEES:	$2,050.00
ROOM & BOARD:	$3,450.00
BOOKS & SUPPLIES:	$420.00
OTHER EXPENSES:	$920.00
OUT OF STATE TUITION:	$4,866.00
*ANNUAL TOTAL:	$6,840.00

(*Annual Total does not include out-of-state tuition .)

FINANCIAL AID

Financial Aid Phone:
Financial Aid Fax:

Closing date August 10; priority given to applications received by March 1; notifications on a rolling basis; must reply within 2 weeks. FAFSA accepted. Pell grants, loans, jobs based on need. Academic, athletic, art, music/drama, state/district residency, leadership, religious affiliation, minority scholarships available.

SPORTS

Varsity Sports: Baseball, basketball, cross-country, football, softball, tennis, track and field. NAIA.

WHAT MAJOR?

Associates: Accounting, architectural drafting technology, banking and finance, chemical technology, communications, community behavioral health technology, computer sciences, computer programming, computer-aided drafting and design technology, criminal justice, electronics engineering technology, gerontology, hospitality managment, management, medical assisting, merchandising, nuclear medicine technology, office administration, postal service managment, radiologic technology.
Bachelor's: Accounting, art, biology, business administration, chemistry, communications, criminal justice, economics, education, secondary education, elementary education, English, English education, foreign languages, health, physical education and recreation, history, mathematics, military science, music education, philosophy, physics, political science, psychology, social work, sociology, special education, technical and business writing.
Historical & Special Interest:
West Virginia State College had its orgins with federal legislation known as the Second Morrill Act passed by the U.S. Congress in 1890. The Act provided that no land grant institution of higher education could enjoy the benefits of federal funds provided by the Act unless adequate provision were made for the education of black youth as well as white youth.

To assure federal funds for West Virginia University, the W. Virginia Legislature enacted legislation to create a new land grant institution in Kanawha County for black students. The new institution was known as West Virginia Colored Institute. During the first year, the main purpose of the Institute was to teach agriculture, horticulture, mechanical arts and domestic science. Teacher training was added the second year and has remained an important emphasis throughout the school's history. In 1915 the name was changed to West Virginia Collegiate Institute and changed again in 1929 to W. Virginia State College. The institution was first accredited by the North Central Association of Coleges and Schools in 1927 and has remained continously accredited since that date. Within the next few years, the enrollment increased dramatically and West Virginia State College was transformed to a racially integrated institution. It gained nationwide recognition as a "living laboratory of human relations."

Master Key: *Honesty is the first chapter in the book of wisdom.*

HBCU Third Edition
© Jireh & Associates, Inc.
Wilmington, DE

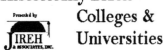
WILBERFORCE UNIVERSITY

WILBERFORCE, OH

Web Site:
www.wilberforce.edu

SCHOOL INFO

Established in 1856. 4-year private liberal arts, coed college on rural campus located on 120 acres. Affiliated with the African Methodist Episcopal Church.

ADDRESS:

WILBERFORCE UNIVERSITY
1055 NORTH BICKETT ROAD
WILBERFORCE, OH 45384
Principal Official: Dr. John L. Henderson

TYPES OF DEGREES AWARDED:
BA, BS.

ACADEMIC CALENDAR:
Semester. Summer sessions.

ACCREDITATON:
North Central Association of Colleges & Schools

CONTACT INFORMATION

Admissions Officer: Kenneth Christmon
Phone: (973) 376-2911 **Fax:** (937) 376-4751
Web Site: www.wilberforce.edu

CAMPUS ENROLLMENT:
Undergraduate: 800 men & women. **Transfer students:** 47 men & women. **Freshman ethnic enrollment:** African American-195.

WHAT DO I NEED?
Achievement record, interview, and test scores. SAT or ACT (ACT preferred); scores by July 1. Application fee: $10 may be waived based on need. Closing date June 1; notifications on a rolling basis and must reply within 3 weeks. Interview recommended. Deferred and early admissions programs.

DOLLARS AND SENSE

TUITION & FEES:	$7,510.00
ROOM & BOARD:	$4,260.00
BOOKS & SUPPLIES:	$550.00
OTHER EXPENSES:	$970.00
OUT OF STATE TUITION:	
*ANNUAL TOTAL:	$13,290.00

(*Annual Total does not include out-of-state tuition .)

UNIQUE PROGRAMS
The following programs are available: cooperative education, cross-registration, honors program, independent study, internships, study abroad; liberal arts/career combination in engineering, health sciences.

FINANCIAL AID

Financial Aid Phone:
Financial Aid Fax:

Closing date June 1; priority given to applications received by April 30; notifications on a rolling basis beginning about March 15; must reply within 2 weeks. FAFSA accepted. All jobs based on need. Academic, leadership, religious and alumni affiliation, scholarships available.

ACADEMIC REQUIREMENTS
Freshmen must earn a minimum 1.5 and majors must be declared by end of second year.

Core curriculum: arts/fine arts, computer science, English, humanities, history, mathematics, philosophy/religion, biological/physical sciences, social sciences. Bachelor's: 126 hrs (45 in major).

STUDENT SERVICES
Campus student services include: career and personal counseling, employment service for undergraduates, freshmen orientation, health services, placement services, remedial instruction, special counselor, tutoring, veterans counselor.
ROTC: Air Force, Army.

SPORTS
Varsity Sports: Basketball, track and field.
Intramural Sports: Baseball, basketball, softball, table tennis, tennis, volleyball.

WHAT MAJOR?

Bachelor's: Accounting, banking and finance, biological and physical sciences, biology, business administration, business economics, chemical engineering, chemistry, civil engineering, comparative literature, computer sciences, economics, electrical/electronics/communications engineering, English, fine arts, health care administration, information sciences and systems, journalism, liberal/general studies, marketing and distribution, mathematics, mechanical engineering, music, political science and government, psychology, sociology.

Historical & Special Interest:

Wilberforce University was founded in 1856 and is the oldest, private, African-American liberal arts college in the nation. It is affiliated with the African Methodist Episcopal Church and serves a predominantly Black and international population. The University's mission is to develop the total person and prepare him for today's complex job market. With a student body of approximately 850, Wilberforce University can provide each individual student with a high degree of personalized attention. The school offers dual-degree programs including a joint degree in law with St. John's University.

Wilberforce University is a UNCF school.

Master Key: *Time lost never returns—lost time is never found.*

HBCU Third Edition
© Jireh & Associates, Inc.
Wilmington, DE

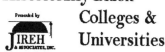

WILEY COLLEGE
MARSHALL, TX

Web Site:
www.wiley.edu

SCHOOL INFO
Established in 1873. 4-year private, liberal arts coed college with United Methodist Church affiliation on 63-acre urban campus near downown Marshall; 38 miles west of Shreveport, Louisana and 145 miles east of Dallas, Texas.

ACCREDITATON:
Southern Association of Colleges & Schools

CAMPUS ENROLLMENT:
*Undergraduate: Full-time: 602 men and women. Part-time:20 men and women.

ADDRESS:

WILEY COLLEGE
711 WILEY AVENUE
MARSHALL,   TX   75670
Principal Official: Dr. Lamore J. Carter

TYPES OF DEGREES AWARDED:
AA, BA, BS.

ACADEMIC CALENDAR:
Semester. Summer sessions extensive.

CONTACT INFORMATION

Admissions Officer: Frederick Pryor
Phone: (903) 927-3300   **Fax:** (903) 938-8100
Web Site: www.wiley.edu

DOLLARS AND SENSE

TUITION & FEES:	$3,960.00
ROOM & BOARD:	$3,138.00
BOOKS & SUPPLIES:	$200.00
OTHER EXPENSES:	$900.00
OUT OF STATE TUITION:	$4,860.00
*ANNUAL TOTAL:	$8,198.00

(*Annual Total does not include out-of-state tuition .)

WHAT DO I NEED?
Open admissions. SAT or ACT for placement; score report by August 20. No application fee. Closing date March 1 or within 2 weeks if after March 1; notifications on a rolling basis. Music applicants must audition. Deferred and early admission program available.

UNIQUE PROGRAMS
The following programs are available: honors program and internships.

ACADEMIC REQUIREMENTS
Freshmen must earn a minimum 2.0 and majors must be declared on enrollment.

Core curriculum: computer science, English, history, humanities, mathematics, philosophy/religion, biological/physical sciences, social sciences. Associates: 65 hrs. Bachelor's: 124 hrs. Hours in major: 50 and 30 respectively.

FINANCIAL AID

Financial Aid Phone:
Financial Aid Fax:
Closing date September 1; priority given to applications received by June 1; notifications on a rolling basis beginning around June 15. FAFSA accepted. Pell grants, loans, jobs based on need. Academic, athletic, music/drama, state/district residency, leadership, religious affiliation scholarships available.

STUDENT SERVICES
Campus student services include: academic center, aptitude testing, career and personal counseling, employment services for undergraduates, freshman orientation, placement services, reduced course load program, remedial instruction, special counselor, veterans counselor, services for handicapped.

SPORTS
Varsity Sports: Baseball, basketball, softball , track and field, volleyball. NAIA.

WHAT MAJOR?
Associates: Business data processing and related programs, computer programming, secretarial and related programs.

Bachelor's: Biology, business management, business and office, business education, chemistry, communications, computer and information sciences, elementary education, English, English education, history, hotel/motel and restaurant management, liberal/general studies, mathematics, mathematics education, music, music education, music performance, philosophy physical education, physics, religion, secondary education, social science education, social sciences, sociology, special education.

Historical & Special Interest:

Wiley College is a four-year, co-educational institution founded in 1837 in Marshall, Texas by the Methodist Episcopal Church. It has the distinction of being the oldest accredited Black college west of the Mississippi and serves not only student from the United States but those from other countries as well.

The College awards the Associate of Arts, Bachelor of Arts, Bachelor of Science and Bachelor of Business Administration degrees in fifteen academic areas. The College is committed to providing a balanced education with a wide range of social cultural and religious activities to include: national organizations such as Beta Kappa Chi, Alpha Phi Omega, and Gamma Sigma Sigma plus, departmental and city clubs.

Wiley College is a UNCF school.

Master Key: *Oh, what a tangled web we weave when first we practice to deceive.*

HBCU Third Edition
© Jireh & Associates, Inc.
Wilmington, DE

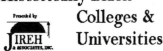
WINSTON-SALEM STATE UNIV.

WINSTON-SALEM, NC

Web Site:
www.wssu.edu

SCHOOL INFO

Established in 1892. 4-year public, coed university on an 85-acre tract urban campus in small city; 28 miles from Greensboro, North Carolina.

ACCREDITATON:
Southern Association of Colleges & Schools and numerous other agencies.

CAMPUS ENROLLMENT:
*Undergraduate: 2576 men and women.

ADDRESS:

WINSTON-SALEM STATE UNIV.
601 MARTIN LUTHER KING DR.
WINSTON-SALEM, NC 27110
Principal Official: Dr. Alvin J. Schexnider

TYPES OF DEGREES AWARDED:
BA, BS.

ACADEMIC CALENDAR:
Semester. Summer sessions.

CONTACT INFORMATION

Admissions Officer: Dr.Alvin Schexnider
Phone: (910) 750-2000 **Fax:** (910) 750-2079
Web Site: www.wssu.edu

WHAT DO I NEED?

SAT test scores, academic record, health, character, abilities important. College preparatory program. Individual consideration is given to candidates graduating from non-accredited high schools and GED certified applicants. Application fee: $15. No closing date; notifications on a rolling basis; must reply within 3 weeks. Interview recommended; audition required for music applicants.

UNIQUE PROGRAMS

The following programs are available: continuing education, cooperative education, double major, honors program, independent study, internships, language/speech laboratory, Health Careers Opportunity Program.

ACADEMIC REQUIREMENTS

Freshmen must earn a minimum 1.5 and majors must be declared by end of second year.

Core curriculum: English, history, mathematics, biological/physical sciences, philosophy/religion, social sciences. Bachelor's: 127 hrs. minimum.

DOLLARS AND SENSE

TUITION & FEES:	$1,552.00
ROOM & BOARD:	$3,300.00
BOOKS & SUPPLIES:	$500.00
OTHER EXPENSES:	$200.00
OUT OF STATE TUITION:	$7,868.00
*ANNUAL TOTAL:	$5,552.00

(*Annual Total does not include out-of-state tuition .)

FINANCIAL AID

Financial Aid Phone: (910) 750-3280
Financial Aid Fax:

Priority given to applications received by May 15; notifications on a rolling basis beginning about May 25; must reply within 2 weeks. FAFSA accepted. All grants and jobs based on need. Academic, music/drama, art, athletic, alumni affiliation, minority and special Chancellor's and Incentive scholarships available.

STUDENT SERVICES

Campus student services include: career and personal counseling, employment service for undergraduates, freshmen orientation, health services, placement services, PLATO learning center, Project Upward Bound, reduced course load program, special counselor, services for handicapped, special advisor for LD students, supplemental education program, testing center, tutoring, veterans counselor.

SPORTS

Varsity Sports: Basketball, cross-country, football, golf, softball, tennis, track and field, volleyball, wrestling. Central Intercollegiate Athletic Association and NCAA

WHAT MAJOR?

Bachelor's: Accounting, applied science, art, biology, business administration, chemistry, commercial music, computer science, early childhood education,economics, elementary/intermediate/middle grades education, English, history, mass communications, mathematics, medical technology, music education, nursing, physical education, political science, psychology, recreation therapy, sociology, Spanish, special education, sports management, urban affairs.

Historical & Special Interest:

Winston-Salem University was founded as the Slater Industrial Academy on September1892. It began in a one-room frame structure with 25 pupils and one teacher. In 1895, the school was recognized by the state of North Carolina, and in 1897 it was chartered by the state as the Slater Industrial and State Normal School.

The school's leadership in training teachers merited it a new charter, extending its curriculum above high school; changed its name to Winston-Salem Teachers College making it the first Negro institution in the nation to grant degrees for teaching in the elementary grades.

In 1963 the General Assembly authorized the changing of the name from Winston-Salem Teachers College to Winston-Salem State College following curriculum expansion and in 1969, a statute designating Winston-Salem University received legislative approval.

Master Key: *There is no right way to do something wrong.*

HBCU Third Edition
© Jireh & Associates, Inc.
Wilmington, DE

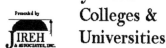
XAVIER UNIVERSITY OF LOUISANA

NEW ORLEANS,   LA

Web Site:
www.xula.edu

SCHOOL INFO

Established in 1915. 4-year private coed university affiliated with Roman Catholic Church on urban campus in a very large city; 1 mile from downtown.

ACCREDITATON:
Southern Association of Colleges & Schools

CAMPUS ENROLLMENT:
*Undergraduate: 850 men and 1973 women. **Transfer Students**: 80 men and 189 women.
Ethnic Enrollment: AA- 3133, NAm- 79, Asian - 76, Cauc.- 196, Hisp.- 20.

WHAT DO I NEED?

Academic record, GED test scores, test results, and recommendation from counselor. Application fee $25; closing date July 15; notifications on a rolling basis; replies within 3 weeks. Deferred admission program available. Audition and portfolio recommended for music and art applicants, respectively.

UNIQUE PROGRAMS

The following programs are available: cooperative education, cross-registration, double major, dual enrollment of high school students, honors program, independent study, internships, teacher preparation; liberal arts/career combination in engineering; combined bachelor's/graduate program in business administration.

ACADEMIC REQUIREMENTS

Minimum GPA of 2.0 and major must be declared by end of second year.

Core curriculum: African American Culture/history, fine arts, English, foreign languages, history, mathematics, philosophy/religion, biological/physical sciences, social sciences. Bachelor's: 128 hours.

STUDENT SERVICES

Campus student services include: career and personal counseling, employment services for undergraduates, health services, learning center, placement services, preadmission summer program, reduced course load program, remedial instruction, special counselor, services for handicapped, tutoring. ROTC: Air Force, Army, Naval.

WHAT MAJOR?

Associate: Radio/television.

ADDRESS:

XAVIER UNIVERSITY OF LOUISANA
7325 PALMETTO ST.
NEW ORLEANS,   LA   71025
Principal Official: Dr. Norman C. Francis

TYPES OF DEGREES AWARDED:
BA, BS, M, MA, MS, Pharm. D., F, .

ACADEMIC CALENDAR:
Semester. Summer sessions limited.

CONTACT INFORMATION

Admissions Officer: Winston Brown
Phone: (504) 486-7411   **Fax:** (504) 482-1508
Web Site: www.xula.edu

DOLLARS AND SENSE

TUITION & FEES:	$8,840.00
ROOM & BOARD:	$5,200.00
BOOKS & SUPPLIES:	$960.00
OTHER EXPENSES:	$500.00
OUT OF STATE TUITION:	
*ANNUAL TOTAL:	$15,500.00

(*Annual Total does not include out-of-state tuition .)

FINANCIAL AID

Financial Aid Phone: (504) 483-3517
Financial Aid Fax: (504) 482-6258

Applications closing date March 1st priority given to those applications received by July 21; applicants notified on a rolling basis by April 1; must reply by May 1. FAFSA accepted. Pell grants, loans, work study are available. Academic, art, athletic, and religious affiliation scholarships available. Payment Option Plan: PEARL (Pay Early and Return Late)

SPORTS

Varsity Sports: Basketball. Intramural Sports: Badminton, basketball, softball, swimming, table tennis, tennis, and cross country track and field, volleyball. NCAA.

Bachelor's: Accounting, art education, biochemistry, biology, business administration, business economics, chemistry, computer and information sciences, elementary education, English, English education, environmental chemistry, fine arts, French, history, information sciences and systems, journalism, mathematics, mathematics education, microbiology, music, music education, music performance, pharmacy, philosophy, physical education, physics, political science and government, pre-dentistry, pre-elementary education, pre-law, pre-medicine, psychology, science education, sociology, Spanish, special education, speech correction, speech pathology/audiology, statistics.

Historical & Special Interest:

Xavier University was founded in 1915 by Katherine Drexel and the Sisters of the Blessed Sacrament, a Catholic religious community she established to serve American minorities. Mother M. Katharine Drexel came to New Orleans at the request of the local Catholic archbishop because of the limited higher educational opportunities for black youth, denied admission to area colleges and universities.

Xavier opened with a college preparatory school in 1915, then added a normal school in 1917 to help provide sorely needed teachers. In 1925, a College of Arts and Sciences was established and, in 1927, a College of Pharmacy. The colleges and the preparatory school, all showing rapid growth were confined in the University's original quarters on Magazine Street.

In 1929 Katharine Drexel sought land near Washington and Carrollton Avenue for a campus for Xavier University. The present site was selected, and in 1932 the college division moved to the new campus, occupying the Gothic administrative/academic building complex that has become a landmark to New Orleans. Xavier University is a UNCF school.

Master Key: *When you get in the present of God your best ideas will surface. Murdock*

HBCU Third Edition
© Jireh & Associates, Inc.
Wilmington, DE

CONTACTS
WEBSITES & MORE

Jireh & Assoc., Inc.

The Best College Planning Web-sites

COLLEGE RESOURCES   www.collegeresources.com
Visit our web-site and find admissions information for HBCUs,
direct links to HBCUs with web-sites, workshops, and a preview of the
Bestselling Handbook of Historically Black Colleges & Universities..

College Planning Network   www.collegeplan.org
Information on college selection, admission, financial aid and
scholarships. Plus direct links to the other college planning sites.

FASTWEB   www.fastweb.com
Financial aid search through the WEB. As many as 500 scholarship
awards are added daily. Establish your own personal mailbox with
awards matching your profile.

College View Online Database   www.collegeview.com
Search for the university that's right for you using College View's online
database of over 3,500 two and four-year schools.

College Board Online   www.collegeboard.com
Educational and informative resources from the College Board, includes
Fund Finder - scholarship database to look for private scholarships.

Fin-Aid   www.finaid.com
The Financial Aid Information Page provides a wide variety of resources to
help students and parents understand college financial aid, sponsored by the
National Association of Student Financial Aid Administrators (NASFAA).

HIGHER EDUCATION INFORMATION CENTER   WWW.HEIC.ORG
Provides academic, financial aid and career information and counseling,
originating from Boston and serving New England. A nonprofit
organization with extensive college planning services.

MOLIS-Minority Online Information Svc.   //web.fie.com/web/mol
A service of the Federal Information Exchange. It provides information
about HBCU institutions, scholarships, and fellowships for minorities.

NACME, INC.   WWW.NACME.ORG
The nation's largest privately funded source for scholarships for
minority engineering students.

Mapping Your Future   www.mapping-your-future.org
Provides information to make higher education and career
dreams a reality i.e., career planning, selecting a school, paying
for educational opportunities and much more.

Jireh & Associates, Inc.
Wilmington, DE

GLOSSARY OF TERMS

GLOSSARY OF TERMS

The following are definitions of commonly used terms varying from campus to campus. More detailed information may be found in the college catalog of the individual school.

Accelerated Programs.
A program of study completed in less time than is usually required, usually by attending classes in summer or by taking extra courses during the regular academic terms. An example of acceleration is completion of a bachelor's degree program in two or three years.

Accreditation.
Official recognition given to a college which has met certain acceptable standards in its education programs, services, and facilities. That recognition is given by an accrediting organization or agency. *Regional accreditation* applies to a college as a whole as opposed to any particular programs or courses of study. *Specialized accreditation* of specific types of schools, such as Bible colleges or trade and technical schools, may also be determined by a national organization. Accreditation by regional accrediting associations and by national accrediting organizations is included in this *Handbook* descriptions of colleges. Information about the accreditation of specialized programs within a college may be found in *Accredited Institutions of Post secondary Education* published for the Council on Post secondary Accreditation by the American Council on Education.

Achievement Tests (ACH).
Tests developed by the College Board in specific secondary school subjects and given at test centers in the United States and other countries on specified dates throughout the year. These tests are used by colleges in helping with decisions about admissions, course placement and exemption of enrolled freshmen.

Advanced Placement.
The admission or assignment of a freshman to an advanced course in a certain subject on the basis of evidence that the student has already completed the college's freshman equivalent in that subject.

Advanced Placement (AP) Program.
High schools implement college courses and administer the Advanced Placement Examinations to interested students, who are then eligible for advanced placement, college credit, or both, on the basis of satisfactory grades. This service is provided by the College Board. It provides high schools with course descriptions in college subjects and AP examinations in those subjects.

American College Testing Program Assessment (ACT).
The American College Testing Program's test battery, given at test centers in the United States and other countries on specific dates throughout the year. Tests in English, mathematics, reading, and science reasoning are given. The average of students' scores on these four tests is called the ACT composite score.

Associate Degree.
Upon completion of a two-year full-time program of study or its part-time equivalent, this degree is conferred by a college or university. After students complete a program of study similar to the first two years of a four-year college curriculum, the associate of arts (AA) or associate of science (AS) degrees are granted. Usually, students can transfer to four-year colleges to complete bachelor's degrees after earning either of these degrees. The associate in applied science (AAS) however, is awarded by many colleges upon completion of technological or vocational program of study.

Bachelor's, or Baccalaureate Degree.
This degree is conferred after the satisfactory completion of a four- or five-year, full-time program of study, or its part-time equivalent, at a college or university. The most common baccalaureates are the bachelor of arts (BA) and bachelor of science (BS) degrees.

Calendar.
An institution may divide its year into shorter periods and the most common calendars are those based on the semester, trimester, quarter, and 4-1-4.

Jireh & Associates, Inc.
Wilmington, DE

College-Level Examination Program (CLEP).

Students and adults are provided the opportunity to demonstrate college-level achievement by taking a program of examinations in undergraduate college courses. Credit is awarded based on these examinations to entering freshmen and adults completing their education. Business, industry, government, and professional groups also use them to satisfy educational requirements for advancement, licensing, and admission to training programs.

College-Preparatory Subjects.

A term used to describe subjects from the fields of English, history and social studies, foreign languages, mathematics, science, and the arts required for admission to or recommended as preparation for college.

College Scholarship Service (CSS).

A service of the College Board that measures a family's financial strength and analyzes its ability to contribute to college costs. CSS provides the Financial Aid Form (FAF) with which students may apply for some nonfederal aid programs.

Combined Bachelor's/Graduate Degree.

Students accepted for this type of study at both the undergraduate and graduate levels can be completed in less time than two individual programs.

Cooperative Education.

This college program allows a student to alternate between periods of full-time study and full-time employment in a related field. Students are paid for their work. To complete a bachelor's degree under the cooperative plan, five years are usually required. However, graduates have the advantage of about a year's practical work experience in addition to their studies. This sort of program should not be confused with the federally sponsored College Work-Study Program.

Cross-Registration.

The practice of permitting students enrolled at one college or university to enroll in courses at another institution without formally applying for admission to the second institution. This is usually done through reciprocal agreements.

Deferred Admission.

Students are permitted to postpone enrollment for one year after acceptance to the college.

Degrees. See list at end of Glossary

Double major.

When a student completes the requirements of two majors concurrently.

Dual Enrollment.

High school seniors are allowed to enroll in certain courses while completing their senior year. These students are not, however, considered full-time college students.

Early Admission.

Students of exceptional ability who have not completed high school (usually who have completed their junior year) are admitted. These students are enrolled as full-time college students.

Early Decision.

Students who are sure of the college they want to attend and are likely to be accepted by that college. The student initiates the early decision application and is then notified of the college's decision earlier than usual-generally by December 15th of the senior year.

Early Decision Plan (EDP-F, EDP-S).

A common schedule for early decision applicants. Two plans exist: under the first-choice plan (EDP-F), the student must withdraw applications from all other colleges as soon as he or she is notified of acceptance by the first-choice college. Under the single-choice plan (EDP-S), the student may not apply to any colleges other than his or her first choice unless rejected by that institution. If a college follows either type of plan, applications (including financial aid applications) must be received by a specified date no later than November 15, and the college agrees to notify the applicant by a specified date no later than December 15.

External Degree Program.

A program of study whereby a student earns credit toward a degree through independent study, college courses, proficiency examinations, and personal experience. External degree colleges generally have no campus or classroom facilities.

Jireh & Associates, Inc.
Wilmington, DE

Federal Pell Grant Program.

A financial aid program that is sponsored and administered by the federal government and provides grants to undergraduate students based soley on need. Congress sets the dollar range annually and it currently cannot exceed $2,700 per year.

Federal Perkins Loan Program.

This program was formerly called the National Direct Student Loan Program (NDSL). This federally funded program is administered by colleges and provides low-interest loans of up to $3,000 per year during undergraduate study not to exceed $15,000 for the total undergraduate program. The total loans available to an individual (undergraduate and graduate) is $30,000 combined cumulative.

Federal Stafford Loan.

This federally funded program allows students to borrow money for educational expenses directly from banks and other lending institutions (sometimes the colleges themselves). The amounts that may be borrowed are limited by the students year in school. The total amount for an undergraduate is $23,000 and graduate students may borrow to an aggregate amount including undergraduate borrowing to $65,000.

Federal Supplemental Educational Opportunity Grant Program (FSEOG).

This federally funded program is administered by colleges and provides grants of up to $1,000 a year for undergraduate students based on need.

Federal Work-Study Program.

This is a program which is awarded by the college and allows students to work and attend college. It is an integral part of the financial aid package to pay for college, if available. The average work-study award is $1,000 per year and cannot be awarded to students who are ineligible to receive it. Students are required to work no more than ten hours per week.

Financial Aid Form (FAF).

See Free Application for Federal Student Aid.

4-4-1. One type of the semester calendar system, it consists of two terms of about 16 weeks each followed by a one-month term used for intensive short courses, independent study, off-campus work, or other types of instruction.

4-1-4. Another type of the semester calendar system, the 4-1-4 calendar consists of two terms of about 16 weeks each, with a one-month term between them used for intensive short courses, independent study, off-campus work, or other types of instruction.

Free Application for Federal Student Aid (FAFSA).

To apply for the federal financial aid programs, students must complete the need analysis form distributed by the federal government for use by students applying for federal campus-based aid. Some private colleges may require the FAF, and to apply for state financial aid programs, or the FAFSA may be the only form required. Students should check with the state agency to learn if any other application forms need to be submitted i.e., PHEAA Aid Information Request (PAIR) of the Pennsylvania Higher Education Assistance Agency (Pennsylvania applicants only).

General Educational Development (GED).

A series of five tests that adults who did not complete high school may take through their state education system to qualify for a high school equivalency certificate. These tests are also administered at centers outside the United States and to members of the armed services through the United States Armed Forces Institute. The tests cover correctness and effectiveness of expression, interpretation of reading materials in the social studies, interpretation of reading materials in the natural sciences, interpretation of literary materials, and general mathematics ability. Many colleges accept satisfactory GED test results in lieu of high school graduation.

Grade-Point Average or Ratio (GPA).

The evaluation system used to determine the overall scholastic performance of a student. It is calculated by taking the number of grade points a student has earned for each completed course and dividing the sum of all grade points by the total hours of course work completed. If you do not know your grade points for a course, multiply the number of hours for a course by the grade received from the course. (A=4, B=3, C=2, D=1 and E or F=0 are the most commonly used numerical values for grades.)

Honors Program.

Any special program for high or potentially high achieving students that offers the opportunity for educational enrichment, independent study, acceleration, or some combination of these.

Jireh & Associates, Inc.
Wilmington, DE

Independent Study.

A program that allows students to study independently instead of attending scheduled classes and completing group assignments. Typically, students plan programs of study in consultation with a faculty adviser or committee, to whom they may report periodically and submit a final project or report for evaluation.

Interdisciplinary.

Refers to programs or courses that use some combination of the knowledge from a number of academic disciplines, such as biology and physical sciences or of engineering and business.

Internships.

Are programs that provide short-term, supervised work experiences, usually related to a student's major field and allows them to earn academic credit. The work can be full- or part-time, on or off campus, paid or unpaid. Student teaching and apprenticeships are examples.

Liberal Arts and Career Combination.

A program in which a student may complete two or three years of study in the liberal arts field followed by two or three years of professional/technical study (i.e., engineering or forestry) Upon completion, the student is awarded the bachelor of arts and bachelor of science degrees. Often referred to as 2 +3 or 3 +2 programs.

Need Analysis Form.

To apply for the federal financial aid programs, students must complete the need analysis form distributed by the federal government for use by students applying for federal campus-based aid. These forms are used to determine the estimated amount of money a family is able to contribute to a student's college expenses. Some private colleges may require the FAF, and to apply for state financial aid programs, or the FAFSA may be the only form required. Students should check with the state agency to learn if any other application forms need to be submitted i.e., PHEAA Aid Information Request (PAIR) of the Pennsylvania Higher Education Assistance Agency (Pennsylvania applicants only).

Open admissions.

The policy of admitting high school graduates and other adults into college generally without regard to conventional academic qualifications, such as high school subjects, high school grades, and admissions test scores. Virtually all applicants with high school diplomas or their equivalent are accepted.

Prueba de Aptitude Academica (PAA).

This is a Spanish-language college aptitude test similar to the SAT which was also developed by the College Board. It is required by many colleges in Puerto Rico.

Preliminary Scholastic Aptitude Test/National Merit Scholarship Qualifying Test (PSAT/NMSQT).

This is a shorter version of the Scholastic Aptitude Test and is administered by high schools each year in October. The PSAT/NMSQT serves as the qualifying test for scholarships awarded by the National Merit Scholarship Corporation and the National Hispanic Scholar Awards Program.

Quarter.

Approximately 11 weeks of an academic calendar. Four quarters make up an academic year, but at many colleges using the quarter system, students attend three quarters each year and make normal progress.

Reserve Officers' Training Corps (ROTC).

Programs conducted in cooperation with the United States Air Force, Army, and Navy in many colleges. Detailed information about these program can be found at the local recruiting office or at participating colleges.

Residency Requirements.

Residency requirements may refer to the minimum amount of time a student is required to have lived in a state in order to be eligible for in-state tuition at a public (state-controlled) college or university. Or it can pertain to the minimum number of required terms that a student must spend on that particular campus (as opposed to independent study or transfer credits from other colleges) to be eligible for graduation.

Rolling Admissions.

A procedure whereby each student's application is considered as soon as all the required credentials have been received (i.e., test scores, school records, etc.).

Jireh & Associates, Inc.
Wilmington, DE

S.A.T.

An acronym which means Scholastic Achievement Test. Developed by the College Board and measures developed verbal and mathematical reasoning abilities. This test is required by many colleges and financial aid grantors. The new SATI: Reasoning Test took the place of the SAT and the SAT II: Subject Tests replaced the Achievement Tests (ACT) in March of 1994.

Semester.

This is approximately a 17 week period that makes up half of the academic year of many college campuses.

Study Abroad.

A program which allows a student to study in another country to complete some part of a their college program for a semester or a summer. A college may operate a campus or have a cooperative agreement with an institution in another country.

Teacher Preparation.

This a teacher certification program which prepares students to meet the requirements as teachers in elementary or secondary schools.

Terminal Program.

These programs are deisgned to prepare students for immediate employment and can usually be completed in less than four years beyond high school. These types of programs are frequently available in junior, vocational-tech, or community colleges.

Transfer Program.

This is primarily for students who plan to continue their studies in a four-year college or university and will transfer from a two-year college (or a four-year college that offers associates).

Transfer Student.

Any student who has attended another college for any period from a single term up to three years depending on the receiving school. The student may receive full or partial credit for the courses successfully completed before the transfer.

Trimester.

A 15-week period of an academic calendar which contains three trimesters. Normal progression is made by attending two trimesters and can be accelerated by attending all three in one or more years.

United Nations Semester.

This is a program which allows students to take courses at a college in the New York City metropolitan area while participating in an internship program at the United Nations.

Upper Division.

The junior and senior level of study. Some colleges only offer upper-division study where the student must have already completed the lower division at another institution.

Visiting/Exchange Student Program.

This is a program where a student is allowed to study for a semester or more at another college without extending the amount of time required for a degree.

Washington Semester.

This is a program which allows students to take courses at a college in the Washington D.C. metropolitan area while participating in an internship program at a government agency or department in Washington.

Weekend College.

This type of program allows a student to complete a course of study by attending classes only on the weekend.

Work-Study.

This is a program which allows students to work and attend college. It is an integral part of the financial aid package to pay for college, if available. A cooperative education program is an arrangement that is a part of the academic program and is sometimes referred to as work-study (now referred to as Federal Work-Study).

Types of Degrees listed on next page.

Jireh & Associates, Inc.
Wilmington, DE

Types of Degrees:

These are some of the types of degrees awarded at colleges and universities. It is not an exhaustive list.

A	Associate Degree (General Studies)
A.A.	Associate of Arts
AAS	Associate of Applied Science
B.A.	Bachelor of Arts
B.Arch	Bachelor of Architecture
B.B.A.	Bachelor of Business Administration
B.F.A.	Bachelor of Fine Arts
B. Music	Bachelor of Music
B. Music Ed.	Bachelor of Music Education
B.S.	Bachelor of Science
B.S. in Chem. Eng.	Bachelor of Science in Chemical Engineering
B.S. in Civil Eng.	Bachelor of Science in Civil Engineering
B.S.E.E.	Bachelor of Science in Electrical Engineering
B.S. in Sys.&Comp. Sci.	Bachelor of Science in Systems and Computer Science
B.S.M.E.	Bachelor of Science in Mechanical Engineering
B.S. in CLS	Bachelor of Science in Clinical Lab Science
B.S.N.	Bachelor of Science in Nursing
B.S.N.S.	Bachelor of Science in Nutritional Sciences
B.S.O.T.	Bachelor of Science in Occupational Therapy
B.S.P.T.	Bachelor of Science in Physical Therapy
B.S. in P.A.	Bachelor of Science in Physician Assistant
B.S. in R.T.T.	Bachelor of Science in Radiation Therapy Technology
M.A.	Master of Arts
M.A.P.A.	Master of Arts in Public Administration
M.A.T.	Master of Arts in Teaching
M.A.R.S.	Master of Religious Studies
M.B.A.	Master of Business Administration
M.C.J.	Master of Comparative Jurisprudence
M.Ed.	Master of Education
M.Eng.	Master of Engineering (Civil, Electrical & Mechanical)
M.F.A.	Master of Fine Arts
M.Mus.	Master of Music
M.Mus.Ed.	Master of Music Education
M.P.A.	Master of Public Administration
M.S.	Master of Science
M.S. Chem Eng.	Master of Science in Chemical Engineering
M.S.N.	Master of Science in Nursing
M.C.S.	Master of Computer Science
M.S.W.	Master of Social Work
M.S. in P.T.	Master of Science in Physical Therapy
Ed.D.	Doctor of Education
D. of Min.	Doctor of Ministry
Ph.D.	Doctor of Philosophy
D.D.S	Doctor of Dental Surgery
J.D.	Juris Doctor
M.D.	Doctor of Medicine
Pharm.D.	Doctor of Pharmacy
M.Div.	Master of Divinity

6

ADMISSIONS APPLICATIONS

Claflin College
Cuyahoga Community College
Elizabeth City State University
Florida A & M University
Florida Memorial College
Hampton University
Jackson State University
Kentucky State University
Knoxville College
Lane College
Morehouse College
North Carolina A & T State University
Roxbury Community College
Saint Augustine's College
South Carolina State University
Southern University at Baton Rouge
Southern University at New Orleans

Claflin College   Office of Admissions   400 College Avenue N.E.   Orangeburg, South Carolina 29115

Application for admission

Date you wish to enter   ☐ Fall 19____   ☐ Spring 19____   ☐ Summer 19____
Please print in INK.

1. Name _____
               last   first   middle

2. Social Security No. _____   Age _____   Gender _____

3. Home Address (permanent mailing address)

   _____
      number and street   city   state   zip   telephone

4. Religious Affiliation (denomination) _____

5. Date of Birth _____
                  month/day/year

6. Do you plan to attend: ☐ full time   ☐ part time

7. What is your intended field of study? _____

8. Family History

   Father: ☐ living ☐ deceased   Mother: ☐ living ☐ deceased

   Name _____   Name _____

   Occupation/Title _____   Occupation/Title _____

   Employer _____   Employer _____

   Business Address _____   Business Address _____

   _____   _____

   Business Telephone No. _____   Business Telephone No. _____

   If your parents are divorced or separated, with whom do you live? ☐ Father ☐ Mother
   If you live with a guardian, list his or her name and address.

   _____

9. School Data *List all schools and colleges you have attended, in chronological order, beginning with the present school. Additional information can be continued on reverse side in Section 16.*

Dates of Attendance	Name and Location of School	Diploma, Degree or Type of Discharge
from/to		
from/to		
from/to		

10. College Entrance Examinations (SAT/ACT)

	Verbal	Math	Total	Date Taken		Composite Score	Date Taken
SAT					ACT		
SAT							

Jireh & Associates, Inc.
Wilmington, De

11. If you are a freshman applicant, list any courses you have taken or are taking at a college.

Course	College/University	Grade Received	Dates Attended
_____	_____	_____	_____
_____	_____	_____	_____
_____	_____	_____	_____

12. Are you interested in applying to the Claflin Honors College? ☐ Yes ☐ No

13. Do you plan to live on campus? ☐ Yes ☐ No

14. Please answer the following questions:
    a. Have you ever been convicted of a criminal offense? ☐ Yes ☐ No
    b. Have you ever been placed on probation, suspended or expelled from any
       educational institution? ☐ Yes ☐ No
    c. Has there been any gap in your educational experience longer than a summer? ☐ Yes ☐ No
    d. Do you have any physical or emotional handicaps? ☐ Yes ☐ No
    If the answer to any of the above questions is yes, please explain on a separate sheet.

15. If you are not a U.S. citizen, state the type of visa you hold. _____

    If English is not your primary language, please specify that which is. _____

16. Please state in your handwriting your reasons for applying to Claflin College and your future plans.

The undersigned agrees that the information furnished on this application is complete and correct, and that any deliberate omission or falsification of information may result in denial of admission or dismissal.

Signature of Applicant _____ Date _____

Parents' or Guardians' Signature (if applicant is a dependent)

Father/Guardian _____ Date _____

Mother/Guardian _____ Date _____

Claflin College's policy on nondiscrimination on the basis of race, color, religion, national origin, sex, handicap, and age is in conformity with applicable federal laws and regulations.

Cuyahoga Community College

APPLICATION FOR ADMISSION or READMISSION

PRINT CLEARLY in ink

01 02 03

Social Security Number:
(or previously assigned Student Number)

Entry Term (ex: Fall, 1998): _____

Legal Name: _____
Last   First   Middle   Former

Mailing Address: _____
Street

City   State   ZIP Code   County

Home Phone: (　)   **Work Phone:** (　)

Business Address:

Sex: ☐ Female ☐ Male   **Date of Birth** (month/day/year) :   **Country of Birth:** (if not U.S.)

Ethnicity:
☐ (1) American Indian or Alaska Native
☐ (2) Black (Non-Hispanic)
☐ (3) Asian, Pacific Islander, or Indian Subcontinent
☐ (4) Hispanic / Spanish Culture
☐ (5) White (Non-Hispanic)
☐ (7) Other (please specify):

Citizenship: (Non-citizen applicants must show proof of legal presence.)
☐ (Y): U.S. Citizen
☐ Non-Citizen   Visa type: _____ Issue date: _____ Expiration date: _____ Country of Citizenship: _____
☐ Permanent Resident   Alien reg # _____ Issue date: _____ Expiration date: _____

Student Type:
☐ (D G N) First time enrolling for credit classes (Includes auditing a credit class).
☐ (R) Returning CCC student.   Last attendance date: _____
☐ (X) Transfer (From another college or university).
☐ (T) Transient (This term only, with permission of home college or university).
☐ (A) Only non-credit classes. (Does not include auditing a credit course.)
☐ (E) Postsecondary Enrollment Options Program
☐ (S) Program 60 (Ohio resident 60 years or older, not for credit)

NON-CREDIT STUDENTS:

Complete this block, then skip to the signature block on the next page.

Campus I plan to attend: ☐ East ☐ Metro ☐ West ☐ Off-campus ☐ Telecourse/Distance Learning ☐ UTC

Home Address (NOT a P.O. box; *if same as Mailing Address, write "SAME"*):

Street

City   State   ZIP Code   County

	RESIDENCY INFORMATION	RES

RESIDENCY

Have you lived at your current address for at least 12 months?   ☐ Yes   ☐ No

ONLY IF "NO", this RESIDENCY INFORMATION must be completed by legal residents of the U.S. and will be used to determine your residency status. If additional information is needed to determine your status, you will be required to present evidence. The burden of proof to clearly demonstrate residency lies with the student.

List all addresses where you have lived for the past 12 months:

Street	City	State	County	From	To

Are you employed in Cuyahoga county?   ☐ Full time   ☐ Part time   ☐ Not employed

Firm Name: _____   Phone Number: _____ ext _____

If you are a dependent, is your spouse / parent / legal guardian employed in Cuyahoga county?   ☐ Yes ☐ No

rev 5/97

Jireh & Associates, Inc
Wilmington, De

Selective Service (To be completed by all males):   Selective Service Number: _____

NOTICE: Under section 3345.32 of the Revised Code of the State of Ohio, if you are a male age **18** through **26**, you are required to complete this information. Failure to do so will result in tuition penalty charges. If you have not registered, you must indicate below the reason you are not required to register.

I certify that I am not required to be registered with Selective Service, and I qualify for exemption for the following reason:

☐ I am with the armed forces of the United States **excluding** training in a reserve or national guard unit.
☐ I have not reached my 18th birthday.
☐ I am 27 years of age or older.
☐ I am a permanent resident of the Trust Territory of the Pacific Islands or the Northern Mariana Islands and I am not a citizen of the United States.
☐ I am a nonimmigrant alien lawfully in the United States in accordance with Section 101(A)(15) of the "Immigration and Nationality Act" U.S.C. 1161, as amended.

Planned course of study: Select the code that best fits your area of interest from the Major Code list.

List the 4-digit code: ☐☐☐☐

FOR OFFICE USE ONLY   Deg ☐☐☐   Col ☐☐
Dept ☐☐☐   Mjr ☐☐☐

Highest Previous Education Level: ☐ (00) no high school diploma or GED   ☐ (01) high school graduate

☐ (02) GED   ☐ (03) certificate   ☐ (04) 2-year degree   ☐ (05) 4-year degree
☐ (06) master's degree   ☐ (07) post-graduate work   ☐ (08) doctoral degree   ☐ (09) some college

Educational Goal at CCC:

☐ (01) To obtain an associate degree for the job market
☐ (02) To obtain an associate degree then transfer to a four-year college or university
☐ (03) To obtain a certificate
☐ (04) To transfer to a four-year college or university before completing a degree or certificate
☐ (05) To train for a new career by taking only selected courses
☐ (06) To upgrade skills for current job by taking only selected courses
☐ (07) To obtain knowledge for personal interest
☐ (08) To obtain GED
☐ (09) To prepare for college courses
☐ (10) To complete a single course

FOR OFFICE USE ONLY

I will enroll as a: ☐ **Full** Time Student (at least 12 credits each term)   ☐ **Part** Time Student (less than 12 credits each term)

Did either of your parents earn a 4-year (Bachelor's) Degree?   ☐ Yes ☐ No   FOR OFFICE USE ONLY

High School you currently attend or last attended: *If you plan to apply for federal financial aid, follow the "Full-Time Admission" instructions.*

Name: _____   City & State/Country: _____

GRADUATION DATE (Month/Year): _____   If you did not graduate, did you receive a GED? ☐ Yes ☐ No   Date: _____

Colleges or Universities you have attended or are currently attending (list most recent first):   *For transcript mailing procedure, see "Full-Time Admission" instructions.*

Institution	City & State or Country	Dates Attended (from/to)	Degree(s) earned	FOR OFFICE USE ONLY

Confidentiality: The College may disclose Directory Information (i.e. student name, address, telephone number, date and place of birth, major field of study, participation in officially recognized activities and sports, weight and height of members of athletic teams, dates of attendance, degrees awarded and received, and most recent previous school attended) to publicize student involvement in College-related activities without prior written consent from you.

Do you want this information to be kept confidential?   ☐ Yes   ☐ No

➤ By signing and dating this application, I certify that the information I have provided hereon is complete and correct in every respect.
➤ I understand that falsifying any part of this application may result in cancellation of admission.
➤ I agree to abide by the policies, rules, and regulations of Cuyahoga Community College.
➤ I will bear full responsibility for any consequences resulting from my failure to promptly report a new address or change in name.
This application and all supporting documents become the property of Cuyahoga Community College and will not be returned to you, forwarded to another institution, or duplicated for any purpose.

Legal Signature: _____   **Date:** _____

rev 5/97

Elizabeth City State University

Application for Admission

Office of Admissions
Elizabeth City State University
Campus Box 901
Elizabeth City, North Carolina 27909
1-800-347-3278 or (919) 335-3305

Please include $15 application fee

PERSONAL INFORMATION

Social Security number
☐☐☐-☐☐-☐☐☐☐

Semester you
will enroll: ☐ Fall ☐ Spring ☐ Summer _____
Year

Last name | First | Middle | Previous name(s) if any

Street address | City | State and zip code

( )
Home phone | Date of birth (Month / Day / Year) | ☐ Female ☐ Male | ☐ Married ☐ Unmarried

Ethnicity: ☐ African American ☐ Asian ☐ Native American ☐ Caucasian ☐ Hispanic ☐ Other

RESIDENCY INFORMATION

U.S. citizen: ☐ Yes ☐ No | On active duty military: ☐ Yes ☐ No

Are you claimed as a dependent by a parent or guardian? ☐ Yes ☐ No | Is the parent or guardian employed full-time in North Carolina? ☐ Yes ☐ No

State of residency* | If North Carolina resident, **list county** | What year did residency begin?

If previously a non-resident, and applying for state residency for tuition purposes, you must complete a Residence-Tuition Status Application

PARENT/GUARDIAN INFORMATION

(Person to contact in case of emergency)

Name | Relationship to applicant

Address

City and State | Zip

( ) | ( )
Home phone | Work phone

Occupation

ACADEMIC INFORMATION

Entrance Status (check one): ☐ Beginning Freshman ☐ Transfer* ☐ Attended ECSU ☐ Special ☐ Transient
☐ Teacher certification candidate (college graduates)

High school attended | City | State | Graduation date

Did you receive a General Education Development Certificate (GED)? ☐ Yes ☐ No Date _____

Intended major | Minor(s)

(Continued on reverse)
Jireh & Associates, Inc
Wilmington, De

College/university attended	City	State	Dates of attendance	Degree earned

College/university attended	City	State	Dates of attendance	Degree earned

College/university attended	City	State	Dates of attendance	Degree earned

*TRANSFER STUDENTS

Please answer the following questions: Are you eligible to return to your previous institution? ❏ Yes ❏ No

If you answered No, please indicate if this action is for academic, conduct, or other reasons? _____

(If additional space is needed please attach a separate sheet)

APPLICANT CERTIFICATION

Have you been convicted of a criminal offense other than a minor traffic violation? ❏ Yes ❏ No

Are there such criminal charges pending against you at this time? ❏ Yes ❏ No

(If you answered Yes to any of the questions above, please explain the circumstances on a separate sheet)

The information submitted above is complete and accurate to the best of my knowledge. I understand that misrepresentation of facts on this application will be cause for refusal of admission, cancellation of admission, or dismissal from the university. The university also reserves the right to revoke any degree or diploma that may have been awarded in reliance on information contained in the application for admission if it subsequently transpires that this information was a fraudulent misrepresentation of fact. By signing this application, I agree to abide by the policies and regulations of the University. I understand this application will not be processed until I have signed on the line below.

Signature _____ Date _____

If under 18, signature _____ Date _____
of Parent or Legal Guardian

UNDERGRADUATE MAJORS AND CONCENTRATIONS

DEPARTMENT OF ART
Art (Studio)
Art (Education, K-12)
DEPARTMENT OF BIOLOGY
Biology
Biology (Concentration in Cellular Biology)
Biology (Concentration in Ecology)
DEPARTMENT OF BUSINESS AND ECONOMICS
Accounting
Business Administration
Business Education
Business Administration
  (Concentration in Marketing)
Business Administration
  (Concentration in Economics & Finance)
MINOR- *Business Administration*
DIVISION OF EDUCATION
Elementary Education, K-6
Special Education, K-12
Psychology
MINOR- *Middle Grades Education*
       Secondary Education
DEPARTMENT OF GEOSCIENCE
Geology
MINOR- *Geology*
       Environmental Science
       GIS/Remote Sensing

DEPARTMENT OF LANGUAGE, LITERATURE, & COMMUNICATION
English
English (Concentration in Drama)
English (Concentration in News Media)
English (Concentration in Pre-Professional Speech Pathology)
MINOR- *English*
       Modern Languages
       Speech and Drama

DEPARTMENT OF MATHEMATICS AND COMPUTER SCIENCE
Mathematics
Applied Mathematics
Computer and Information Science
  (Concentration in Science)
Computer and Information Science
  (Concentration in Business Administration)
MINOR- *Mathematics*
       Computer Science and
         Information Science
       Statistics
       Applied Mathematics
       Airway Science
DEPARTMENT OF MUSIC
Music (Concentration in Applied Music)
Music (Concentration in Theory of Composition)

Music (Concentration in Music Business Administration)
Music Industry Studies (Concentration in Music Engineering and Technology)
MINOR- *Music*
DEPARTMENT OF PHYSICAL SCIENCES
Chemistry
Physics
MINOR- *Chemistry*
       Physics
DEPARTMENT OF SOCIAL SCIENCES
Criminal Justice
History
Political Science
Sociology
Sociology/Social Work
MINOR- *American History*
       Criminal Justice
       Black Studies
       Juvenile Justice
       Correctional Sociology
       Political Science
DEPARTMENT OF TECHNOLOGY
Technological Education
Industrial Technology

FLORIDA A & M UNIVERSITY

Complete each item. Incomplete forms will not be processed. Type or print in black ink.

1. ____/____/____
U.S. Social Security Number

Last Name _____ Jr., III, etc. ____

First Name _____

Middle Name _____

2. For which term, in which year, do you seek admission?
August, 19____   January, 19____   May, 19____   June, 19____

3. This application is for enrollment as:
☐ First time in college **Freshman**
☐ Undergraduate **Transfer**
☐ **Second** Bachelors Degree
☐ Former Degree student **returning** (no application fee required)
☐ **One-term** enrollment only for transfer credit (Transient).
☐ Other:_____

4. If your transcripts, test scores, etc. might arrive under any name(s) other than those listed above, enter here:_____

5. Nation of Citizenship:
_____

6. ☐ Male
☐ Female

7. Date of birth: ____/____/____
Mo.   Day   Yr.

9. Ethnic Origin, check one:
(Requested in compliance with Title VI of the Civil Rights Act of 1964).
☐ White (not of Hispanic origin)
☐ Black (not of Hispanic origin)
☐ Hispanic
☐ Asian or Pacific Islander
☐ American Indian or Native Alaskan

10. If your native language is other than English, how many years have you spoken or studied English?

_____

12. If you would like the appropriate campus organization notified, enter your religious preference:

_____

8. Print your permanent address. All correspondence will be mailed to this address.

_____
Street Address   Apt No.

_____
City   County (or Province)   State/Nation

_____
Zip Code   (___) Telephone Number   (___) Daytime Telephone Number

(___)_____
Fax Number   Email Address (if available)

11. In case of an emergency, indicate the person you request the university to contact:

_____
Last Name   First Name   M.I.

_____
Name and Street Address   Apt No.

_____
City   State/Nation   Zip Code

(___)_____ (___)_____
Telephone Number   Daytime Telephone Number

Relationship: ☐ Mother
☐ Father   ☐ Legal Guardian
☐ Other:_____

13. In which academic division do you wish to enroll?   What is your planned major?

(e.g., the College or School within the university)_____   _____

14. High School Graduation Date: ____/____
Month   Year

High School Code:_____
(Ask your counselor for the 6-digit CEEB Number)

(___)_____
High School Area Code and Telephone Number

High School Name (Official transcript must be provided)
_____

City _____ State/Nation _____

If High School was completed by GED, enter year: 19____
(Official copy of test scores and official partial high school transcript required.)

15. An official transcript from each post-secondary school you have attended must be provided.
You must list in chronological order every post-secondary institution (including dual enrollment) you have attended or will attend prior to entering this university. (You must include schools even if you did not complete a term.) Include this university if you attended previously. For multi-campus institutions, indicate the specific campus. **Failure to list all institutions could result in your application being denied.** *Use a separate sheet if necessary.*

Enter dates of attendance (including present enrollment) and degrees earned or expected before attending this university. Include Associate Degrees, certificates or diplomas.

Enter credit earned or expected from each institution attended

School Please do not abbreviate.	City, State or Nation	Dates of Attendance From Mo	From Yr	To Mo	To Yr	Degree/Date Earned/Expected Type	Mo	Yr	Credit Hours Earned/Expected Number	Unit Sem/Qtr.

16. For Non-US Citizens Only:
What VISA do you presently hold? ☐ F1 ☐ F2 ☐ J1 ☐ J2 ☐ None ☐ Other:_____ I-94 Expiration Date: ___/___
What VISA are you applying for? ☐ F1 ☐ F2 ☐ J1 ☐ J2 ☐ None ☐ Other:_____   Mo   Yr
Which institution issued your last I-20?_____ Did you attend? ☐ Yes ☐ No
If a permanent immigrant, enter the alien registration number shown on your I-551 form:_____
You must provide a photocopy of your Alien Registration card, front and back.

Jireh & Associates, Inc
Wilmington, De

17. Important: Complete the resume of your activities since leaving high school. List chronologically how you have spent or plan to spend your time prior to entering this university (employment, military service, etc.). Use a separate sheet if necessary.

Activity	City, State or Nation	From Mo	Yr	To Mo	Yr

18. If you have taken or plan to take any of the tests below, enter the month and year. Official records of all test scores must be provided.

Test	1st Time	2nd Time Mo	Yr	3rd Time Mo	Yr	Mo	Yr
ACT							
SAT							
TOEFL							
CLAST							

19. Additional information you wish to be considered for review of your application should be provided below or on a separate sheet and enclosed with your application, e.g., offices held, prizes won honors achieved; participation in school clubs or activities such as drama, debate, music, athletics, student government, etc.; extracurricular activities or community service. You are encouraged to submit a statement regarding your selection of this university to pursue your educational objectives_____
_____
_____

20. Present High School/College Enrollment

a. If you are currently enrolled in a high school, college or university, list all high school and college level courses which you are now taking or expect to complete before entering this university. Use separate sheet if necessary.

b. If you are not currently enrolled and do not expect to complete any courses, check here. ☐

Courses for Which You Are Now Enrolled
Name of Institution: _____

Courses You Expect to Complete Before Entering
Name of Institution: _____

Title of Course	Course No.	Date Course Will End Mo	Yr	Credit Hrs. (Sem/Qtr)	Title of Course	Course No.	Date Course Will End Mo	Yr	Credit Hrs. (Sem/Qtr)

21. If your answer to any of the following is yes, you must submit a full statement of relevant facts on a separate sheet attached to this form. You may be required to furnish the university with copies of all official documentation explaining the final disposition of the proceedings.

a. ☐ Yes ☐ No. Have you ever been charged with or subject to disciplinary action for scholastic or any other type of misconduct at any educational institution?

b. ☐ Yes ☐ No. Have you ever been charged with a violation of the law which resulted in probation, community service, a jail sentence, or the revocation or suspension of your driver's license (including traffic violations which resulted in a fine of $200 or more)?

If your records have been expunged pursuant to applicable law, you are not required to answer yes to these questions. If you are unsure whether you should answer yes to 21a or 21b, we strongly suggest that you answer yes and fully disclose all incidents. By doing so, you can avoid any risk of disciplinary action or revocation of an offer of admission.

22. OPTIONAL INFORMATION:

a. Are you a Veteran?
☐ Yes   ☐ No

b. Check whether any of the following attended college:
☐ Yes ☐ No Mother   ☐ Yes ☐ No Father
☐ Yes ☐ No Sister(s)   ☐ Yes ☐ No Brother(s)
☐ Yes ☐ No Grandmother(s)   ☐ Yes ☐ No Grandfather(s)

c. Name(s) of your immediate family who have attended this university:
Name: Relationship:
_____
_____
_____

d. If you wish to request special admission consideration based on a disability, check here. ☐ **(See page 1 for comments).**

Important. You must read and sign the following section in order to complete your application to this university.

I understand that this application is for admission to the university designated on page 1 and is valid only for the term indicated in item 2 on page 2. I also understand and agree that I will be bound by the university's regulations concerning application deadline dates and admission requirements. I further agree to the release of any transcript, student record, and test scores to this institution (including any SAT-I, SAT-II, and ACT score reports that this institution may request from the College Board or ACT).

I certify that the information given in this application is complete and accurate, and I understand that to make false or fraudulent statements within this application or residence statement may result in disciplinary action, denial of admission and invalidation of credits or degrees earned. If admitted, I hereby agree to abide by the policies of the Board of Regents and the rules and regulations of the university. Should any of the information I have given change prior to my entry to the university, I shall immediately notify the Office of Admissions.

I understand that the $20 check or money order I submit with this application is a nonrefundable fee.

_____   _____   _____
Applicant's Original Signature (in ink)   U.S. Social Security Number   Date

admission forms / part 1

admission application

Return All Items to:
Admissions Office
Florida Memorial College
15800 NW 42nd Avenue
Miami, Florida 33054
305.626.3751
800.822.1362
www.fmc.edu

Applicant Information

TERM/YEAR OF ENTRANCE	LOCATION

NAME (LAST, FIRST, MIDDLE)	SOCIAL SECURITY NUMBER

STREET ADDRESS	CITY	STATE	ZIP

HOME PHONE	APPLICATION STATUS ☐ First Time ☐ Transfer ☐ Re-admit ☐ Other

GENDER	AGE	BIRTHDATE (MONTH/DAY/YEAR)	MARITAL STATUS	ETHNIC ORIGIN

NATION OF BIRTH	NATION OF CITIZENSHIP (IF DIFFERENT THAN BIRTH)

Scholastic Information

HIGH SCHOOL ATTENDED	CITY	STATE	COUNTY

HIGH SCHOOL PHONE	DATE OF GRADUATION (MONTH/DAY/YEAR)	ESTIMATED GRADE POINT AVERAGE	HIGH SCHOOL EQUIVELANCY (GED)

INTENDED MAJOR	S.A.T. VERBAL	S.A.T. QUANTITATIVE	A.C.T. MATH	A.C.T. ENGLISH	A.C.T. READING

Other Information

Do you plan to live on campus? ☐ Yes ☐ No   Do you plan to apply for Financial Aid? ☐ Yes ☐ No

IN CASE OF AN EMERGENCY, CONTACT:	RELATIONSHIP TO APPLICANT	PHONE ( )

STREET ADDRESS	CITY	STATE	ZIP

Transfer Students Only (If you've attended more than two schools, list additional information on reverse side.)

COLLEGE/UNIVERSITY	ADDRESS	CITY/STATE	YEAR(S) OF ATTENDANCE

Have you ever been placed on Academic or Social Probation? ☐ Yes ☐ No   If yes, explain briefly:

Have you ever missed a signifigant number of days from school or had your academic efficiency impaired because of physical, mental or other reasons? ☐ Yes ☐ No   If yes, explain briefly:

Have you ever been convicted or found guilty of violating any federal, state or local law/ordinance other than a traffic violation? ☐ Yes ☐ No   If yes, explain briefly:

REFERRED TO FLORIDA MEMORIAL COLLEGE BY	ADDRESS	PHONE

I certify that the information I have provided is accurate.	SIGNATURE	DATE

FMC
FLORIDA
MEMORIAL
COLLEGE

admission forms/part 2

official transcript release form

Return All Items to:
Admissions Office
Florida Memorial College
15800 NW 42nd Avenue
Miami, Florida 33054
305.626.3751
800.822.1362
www.fmc.edu

prospective student:

Please complete the required information below and forward to your High School or College. If you need additional Transcript Release forms, photocopy this one.

REQUEST IS HEREBY MADE FOR THE RELEASE OF MY OFFICIAL TRANSCRIPT AND TEST SCORES IN ORDER TO COMPLETE THE ADMISSION PROCESS AT **FLORIDA MEMORIAL COLLEGE.**

School Information

HIGH SCHOOL/COLLEGE NAME

STREET ADDRESS   CITY   STATE   ZIP

Student Information

APPLICANT NAME (LAST, FIRST, MIDDLE)   SOCIAL SECURITY NUMBER

PERMANENT ADDRESS   CITY   STATE   ZIP

BIRTHDATE (MONTH/DAY/YEAR)   DATE OF LAST ATTENDANCE   STUDENT'S SIGNATURE

HAMPTON UNIVERSITY
UNDERGRADUATE APPLICATION

PLEASE TYPE OR PRINT IN BLACK INK. USE CODES ON INSIDE COVER TO COMPLETE THE APPLICATION.

I am applying to:

❑ School of Liberal Arts and Education

❑ School of Pure and Applied Science
❑ School of Business

❑ Undecided

COLLEGE OF HEALTH
❑ School of Nursing
❑ Dept. of Communication Disorders

The application must be returned with the non-refundable application fee of $25.00.
NO PERSONAL CHECKS WILL BE ACCEPTED.

PERSONAL DATA

Legal Name _____ SS# _____
  Last   First   Middle (Complete) Jr., etc.

Former Last Name(s) if any:_____

Are you applying as a first year ❑   or transfer student ❑ ?   for term beginning_____ 19____

Permanent home address: _____
  Street Address

_____
  City or Town   County   State (1)   Zip   Citizenship (2)

If different from above, please give your mailing address for all admission correspondence:

_____
  Number and Street   Apt. #   City or Town   County   State   Zip

Telephone at mailing address: _____ _____   Permanent Home Telephone: _____ _____
  Area Code Number   Area Code Number

Birthdate: _____   Gender: ❑ Male ❑ Female   Ethnicity:* (SEE BACK PAGE) _____
                                                                                      (3)

Religion: _____   State of Legal Residence:_____   Veteran Status _____
            (4)   (1)   (5)

Intended major:_____   Are you requesting on-campus housing? ❑ Yes ❑ No
                                   (9)

Will you be a candidate for financial aid?   ❑ Yes ❑ No .

Name and address of closest living relative: _____
                                            Last Name   First Name

_____ Relationship:_____

HIGH SCHOOLS ATTENDED	NAME OF HIGH SCHOOL	CEEB CODE	CITY AND STATE	DATES ATTENDED FROM - TO	DATE GRADUATED
MOST RECENT FIRST					
HAVE TRANSCRIPTS SENT					
COLLEGES ATTENDED MOST RECENT FIRST	NAME OF COLLEGE	CEEB CODE	CITY AND STATE	DATES ATTENDED FROM - TO	DATE GRADUATED
FAILURE TO DECLARE ATTENDANCE AT ANOTHER INSTITUTION WILL RESULT IN DENIAL OF CREDIT FOR SUCH WORK OR IMMEDIATE DISMISSAL.					

Jireh & Associates, Inc
Wilmington, De

TEST INFORMATION. Hampton University cannot guarantee consideration of any applicant whose file does not include the scores from the required Scholastic Aptitude Test (SAT) or the American College Test (ACT). **Please list test plans below, specifying month, day and year of the test date. All scores must be reported officially from the testing agency.**

	American College Test (ACT)	Scholastic Aptitude Test (SAT)	Achievement Tests (ACH)	Achievement Test Subjects		
Dates taken or	_____	_____	_____	(EN/ES) _____	(M1/M2) _____	(3rd) _____
to be taken	_____	_____	_____	(EN/ES) _____	(M1/M2) _____	(3rd) _____

FAMILY. Note: For purpose of this application reference to mother and father also means stepmother and stepfather, if appropriate.

Mother or Guardian's full name: _____ Living? _____

Home address if different from yours: _____

Occupation: _____
(Describe briefly)   (Name of business or organization)

Name of college attended (if any): _____ Degree: _____ Year: _____

Name of professional or graduate school (if any): _____ Degree: _____ Year: _____

Father or Guardian's full name: _____ Living? _____

Home address if different from yours: _____

Occupation: _____
(Describe briefly)   (Name of business or organization)

Name of college attended (if any): _____ Degree: _____ Year: _____

Name of professional or graduate school (if any): _____ Degree: _____ Year: _____

Has any other member of your family ever attended Hampton University? If yes, please give name and dates of attendance.

_____

_____

_____

_____

Please give names and ages of your brothers or sisters. If they have attended college, give the names of the institutions attended, degrees, and approximate date.

_____

_____

_____

_____

ACADEMIC HONORS

Briefly describe any scholastic distinctions or honors you have won since the 9th grade: Include such accomplishments as Valedictorian, Honor Society, Governor's School appointment, etc.

_____

_____

_____

_____

EXTRACURRICULAR AND PERSONAL ACTIVITIES AND HONORS

Please list your principle extracurricular, community, and family activities and hobbies in the order of their interest to you. Include specific events and/or major accomplishments such as musical instrument played, varsity letters earned, etc.

_____

_____

_____

_____

_____

_____

_____

_____

Have you ever been convicted of any crime?   ❏ Yes   ❏ No
If yes, give date(s) and nature of offense(s).

_____

Have you ever been dismissed from any school or college?   ❏ Yes   ❏ No
If yes, give reason(s), date(s), time(s).

_____

Have you ever been previously enrolled at Hampton University?   ❏ Yes   ❏ No
If yes, please indicate dates of attendance and reason(s) for leaving.

_____

How did you first learn about Hampton University?
Check one:
__ family member   __ alumni*   __ visit to my high school   __ magazine or newspaper
__ mail correspondence __ college tour   __ college fair   title_____
__ other _____

*Please provide name and include a letter of recommendation.

PERSONAL STATEMENT

This essay section is an opportunity for you to help us become acquainted with you in a way separate from objective data. Please write an essay on the topic listed below. Your essay may be between 150-300 words.

Respond to the question: How can I prepare educationally for the 21st century?

_____   _____   _____
Signature of Applicant   Date   Signature of Parent or Guardian

OFFICE OF ADMISSIONS AND FINANCIAL AID

JACKSON STATE UNIVERSITY

1400 John R. Lynch Street

P. O. Box 17330

Jackson, MS 39217-0133

TELEPHONE:

(601) 968-2227 *(Locally)* or 1-800-848-6817 *(In or Out-of-State)*

UNDERGRADUATE APPLICATION FOR ADMISSIONS

INSTRUCTIONS: PLEASE PRINT CLEARLY. The following information will become part of your permanent record. All blanks MUST be filled in. The admission record is not complete until all required credentials are received.

SEE CODES ON THE BACK OF THIS SHEET

1. [ ] Social Security Number 2. [ ] Last Name [ ] First Name [ ] MI

3. [ ] Permanent Address / Street No. & Name [ ] City, State or County [ ] Zip Code [ ] Telephone Number (Including Area Code)

4. [ ] County Code 5. [ ] State Code 6. [ ] Race Code 7. [ ] Sex Code 8. [ ] Marital Status Code 9. [ ] Religious Code 10. [ ] Res. Alien Citizen 11. [ ] Date of Birth (Include Mon. / Day / Year)

12. [ ] Enrollment Semester 13. [ ] Classification Code 14. [ ] Readmit? 15. [ ] Transfer? 16. [ ] Enroll Intent 17. [ ] Full/Part Time 18. [ ] Type Classes 19. [ ] Major Code 20. [ ] Highest Ed.

21. [ ] GI Bill 22. [ ] Financial Aid 23. [ ] Housing 24. [ ] Date of Application 25. [ ] Disabled? (Optional) 26. [ ] U Office Use ONLY

INSTRUCTIONS

No.	Description
1.	Social Security Number (Example: 123-45-7890)
2.	Student Name (Last, First, MI)
3.	Permanent Address (street, city, state, zip code & phone no.)
4.	Resident county code (see codes on back of this sheet)
5.	Resident state code (see codes on back of this sheet)
6.	Race code (use following codes):

    1 - African American   4 - Spanish American

    2 - American Indian   5 - Caucasian

    3 - Asian/Oriental   6 - Other (Specify) _____

7. Sex Code: M or F

8. Marital Status Code: (1 single or 2 married)

9. Religion Code (use following codes):

    01 - Baptist   13 - Catholic

    09 - Methodist   15 - Other

    12 - Presbyterian   16 - No Preference

10. U. S. Citizen? (Y-yes or N-no)

11. Date of Birth (Example: 08-17-96)
    mo. day yr.

12. Semester and year you expect to enroll: (Example: 9/97)

    1 - Spring   6 - Summer Session   9 - Fall

13. Classification Code (use following)

    0 - Special admit (21 years or older)

    1 - Freshman   2 - Sophomore   3 - Junior   4 - Senior

14. Have you ever attended school at JSU? (Y - yes, N - no)

15. Will you transfer credits to JSU? (Y - yes, N - no)

No.	Description
16.	Indicate your enrollment intent.

    1 - To earn credits to transfer elsewhere

    3 - To upgrade skills

    4 - To earn Bachelor's Degree

    7 - To earn Certificate/Work

    9 - To earn ROTC Crossover Credit

17. Expect to enroll as:

    1 - Full-time student (12 or more credit hours)

    2 - Part-time student (less than 12 credit hours)

    3 - Summer (Full-time 6 or more credit hours)

    4 - Summer (Part-time less than 6 credit hours)

18. Type classes expected to enroll in primarily:

    1 - Day classes   2 - Evening classes   3 - Weekend classes

19. Major (see codes on back of this sheet)

20. Highest education at present time (see codes on back of this sheet)

21. Will you receive Veteran benefits? (Y - Yes, N - no)

22. Financial aid plans:

    1 - Have applied for financial aid

    2 - Will not apply for financial aid

    3 - Will apply for financial aid

23. Housing Plans:

    1 - Have applied for campus housing

    2 - Will not apply for campus housing

    3 - Will apply for campus housing

24. Date of application (Example: 02-15-97)
    mo. day yr.

25. Do you have any physical disabilities? (Y - yes, N - no)

SUPPLEMENTARY INFORMATION

A. Give your current address (if different from your permanent address).

_____ _____ _____ _____

Rural Route, P. O. Box, Street No. & Name   City / State   Zip Code   Telephone No. (Including Area Code)

B. ACADEMIC PREPARATION: List high school and all colleges and universities attended (including JSU). An official transcript from each of the institutions MUST be submitted before action can be taken on your application.

Name of Institution	Address: City and State	Dates of Attendance	Degree Awarded	Field of Study

C. Number of years lived in Mississippi: Applicant _____ Parents (Guardian) or Spouse _____

D. Names under which your transcript(s) is/are listed, if different from above _____

5

E. Request ACT Waiver: * Yes * No (NOTE: Applies to applicants 21 years of age and over).

F. Country of Origin _____

I certify that the information contained in this application is true and correct. I understand that misrepresentation or omission of information will be cause for dismissal and loss of credit. Furthermore, I give permission for a copy of my academic transcript(s) to be released according to the policies of the Institution.

_____
Signature of Applicant

APPLICATION: THE FOLLOWING CODES LISTED ARE TO BE USED IN COMPLETING THE ADMISSIONS APPLICATION

STATE CODES

01 Alabama	12 Indiana	23 Missouri	34 Oklahoma	45 Washington
02 Arizona	13 Iowa	24 Montana	35 Oregon	46 West Virginia
03 Arkansas	14 Kansas	25 Nebraska	36 Pennsylvania	47 Wisconsin
04 California	15 Kentucky	26 Nevada	37 Rhode Island	48 Wyoming
05 Colorado	16 Louisiana	27 New Hampshire	38 South Carolina	49 Alaska
06 Connecticut	17 Maine	28 New Jersey	39 South Dakota	50 Hawaii
07 Delaware	18 Maryland	29 New Mexico	40 Tennessee	51 District of Columbia
08 Florida	19 Massachusetts	30 New York	41 Texas	52 Puerto Rico
09 Georgia	20 Michigan	31 North Carolina	42 Utah	99 Out-of-Country
10 Idaho	21 Minnesota	32 North Dakota	43 Vermont	(Foreign Students)
11 Illinois	22 Mississippi	33 Ohio	44 Virginia	

COUNTY CODES FOR MISSISSIPPI ONLY

01 Adams	13 Clay	25 Hinds	37 Lamar	49 Montgomery	61 Rankin	73 Union
02 Alcorn	14 Coahoma	26 Holmes	38 Lauderdale	50 Neshoba	62 Scott	74 Walthall
03 Amite	15 Copiah	27 Humphreys	39 Lawrence	51 Newton	63 Sharkey	75 Warren
04 Attala	16 Covington	28 Issaquena	40 Leake	52 Noxubee	64 Simpson	76 Washington
05 Benton	17 Arizona	29 Itawamba	41 Lee	53 Oktibbeha	65 Smith	77 Wayne
06 Bolivar	18 Forrest	30 Jackson	42 Leflore	54 Panola	66 Stone	78 Webster
07 Calhoun	19 Franklin	31 Jasper	43 Lincoln	55 Pearl River	67 Sunflower	79 Wilkinson
08 Carroll	20 George	32 Jefferson	44 Lowndes	56 Perry	68 Tallahatchie	80 Winston
09 Chickasaw	21 Green	33 Jefferson Davis	45 Madison	57 Pike	69 Tate	81 Yalobusha
10 Choctaw	22 Grenada	34 Jones	46 Marion	58 Pontotoc	70 Tippah	82 Yazoo
11 Claiborne	23 Hancock	35 Kemper	47 Marshall	59 Prentiss	71 Tishomingo	99 Out-of-State
12 Clark	24 Harrison	36 Lafayette	48 Monroe	60 Quitman	72 Tunica	

HIGHEST EDUCATION

1. Have not graduated from high school
2. Have passed GED
3. High school graduate
4. Have completed 1 year of college
5. Have completed 2 years of college
6. Have graduated from junior college
7. Have completed 3 years of college

MAJORS OFFERED AT JACKSON STATE UNIVERSITY: USE CODES ONLY TO COMPLETE ITEM 19

CODES	MAJORS	CODES	MAJORS	CODES	MAJORS
ACCT	ACCOUNTING	FNGB	FINANCE	MUED	MUSIC EDUCATION
ART	ART	PE	HEALTH, PHYSICAL ED. AND		Instrumental
BIOL	BIOLOGY		RECREATION		Vocal
	Biology Education		Therapeutic Recreation		Keyboard
	Pre-Nursing		Health		Jazz
	Pre-Dental		Physical Education	MUS	MUSIC-PIANO PERFORMANCE
	Pre-Medicine	HCA	HEALTH CARE ADMINISTRATION	OFAD	OFFICE ADMINISTRATION
	Pre-Optometry	HIST	HISTORY	PHYS	PHYSICS
	Pre-Pharmacy		American History		Atmospheric Physics
	Pre-Physical Therapy		European History		Theoretical Physics
	Pre-Dental Hygiene		African American History		Applied Physics
	Pre-Veterinary Medicine	IT	INDUSTRIAL TECHNOLOGY		Computational Physics
	Pre-Physician Associate		Computer Technology		Chemical Physics
	Pre-Health Records Adm.		Construction Management Technology		General Physics
	Marine Science		Drafting and Design Technology	PS	POLITICAL SCIENCE
	Environmental Science		Electronics Technology		Pre-Law
BSAD	BUSINESS ADMINISTRATION		Industrial Management Technology		International Studies
BSED	BUSINESS EDUCATION		Manufacturing Technology		American Politics
CHEM	CHEMISTRY		Hazardous Materials Management	PSY	PSYCHOLOGY
	Chemical Education		Airway Science	SS	SOCIAL SCIENCE EDUCATION
	Pre-Chemical Engineering		Electronic Engineering Technology		Ethnic Studies
	American Chemical Society	MGNT	MANAGEMENT	SW	SOCIAL WORK
	Certification	MKTG	MARKETING	SOC	SOCIOLOGY
CCFE	CHILD CARE FAMILY ED.	MC	MASS COMMUNICATIONS	SPED	SPECIAL EDUCATION
CSC	COMPUTER SCIENCE		Broadcast Journalism	SPCH	SPEECH
	Information Systems		Broadcast Production		Speech Communication Studies
	Mathematics-Oriented		News Editorial		Dramatic Art
CJCS	CRIMINAL JUSTICE		Advertising		Communicative Disorders
	Corrections		News Editorial/Public Relations		Speech Education
	Law Enforcement	MATH	MATHEMATICS	TCED	TECHNOLOGY EDUCATION
	Juvenile Justice		Pre-Engineering	UA	URBAN STUDIES
ECON	ECONOMICS	MTED	MATHEMATICS EDUCATION	UND	UNDECIDED
ELED	ELEMENTARY EDUCATION	MET	METEOROLOGY		
ENGL	ENGLISH				
FLG	FOREIGN LANGUAGES				

6

KENTUCKY STATE UNIVERSITY
Application for Admission
PLEASE PRINT

U.S. Social Security Number _____

Name _____
         LAST   FIRST   MI   MAIDEN

Home Address_____
                              STREET

_____
        CITY   STATE   ZIP   COUNTY

_____
     PROVINCE   COUNTRY   (AREA CODE) PHONE

Current Mailing Address_____
                                       STREET

_____
        CITY   STATE   ZIP   COUNTY

_____
        COUNTRY   PROVINCE

_____
     (COUNTRY OF BIRTH)   (AREA CODE) PHONE

Citizenship ____ U.S.   ____ Other _____
                        SPECIFY COUNTRY, TYPE OF VISA, DATE VISA EXPIRES

         Resident Alien Number _____

Type of Visa _____ Date Visa Expires _____

Emergency Contact Person _____
                                        NAME

_____
        RELATIONSHIP   (AREA CODE) PHONE

_____
                      STREET

_____
        CITY   STATE   ZIP

RESIDENCY (*You must complete all four questions.*)

a. Have you lived in Kentucky for the last 12 consecutive months?   Yes   No
   If no, please list city, state, and dates of residence._____

   _____

b. Have you received financial support from an individual out-of-state during the last
   12 months?   ___Yes   ___ No
c. Does either parent (or legal guardian) live in Kentucky? ___ Yes ___ No

High School_____
                                   NAME

_____
        CITY   STATE

_____
        ZIP   (AREA CODE) PHONE

Graduated _____
                    MONTH/YEAR

___I have taken   ___I will take

___I have taken   ___I will take

___I have taken   ___I will take

Program of study. If unsure, write "undecided." _____. A list of majors can be found on page 2 of this booklet.

Please complete the following items:
Have you ever applied to KSU.?   Yes   No
If yes, specify year and term_____
I am applying as: ___ Full-time   ___ Part-time

____ **degree-seeking** -interested in a KSU degree
____ **non-degree student** (currently not interested
        in a degree from KSU)
____ **visiting student** (will transfer back to original
        institution
____ **non-degree to degree seeking**
____ **international student** (non-citizen of the US)

____ **First-time Freshman** - no college experience
____ **Freshman Transfer** - less than 24 credit hours
____ **Transfer** - 24 or more credit hours
____ **Veteran** - military affiliation
Applying for:
___ Fall ___Spring ___Summer   19_____
Date of Birth _____/_____/_____
Ethnic Group (for reporting purposes only)
___ Black   ___ White   ___ American Indian
___ Hispanic   ___Asian or Pacific Islander
___ Resident Alien   ___ Other
Gender (for reporting purposes only)
___ Male   ___ Female
Special Programs
___(CER) Teacher Certification
___(KSP) Kentucky State Police Academy
___ (VIS)Visiting Student
___(EAD) Early Admission
___(SRC) Senior Citizen

For Office Use Only

AC ____/____/____ ____ ____
AC ____/____/____ ____ ____
AC ____/____/____ ____ ____
DE ____/____/____ ____ ____
DE ____/____/____ ____ ____
AP ____/____/____ ____ ____

Received ____/____/____ ____
Entered ____/____/____ ____
Paid ____/____/____ ____
Check_____ Money Order_____

Will Graduate_____
                        MONTH/YEAR

___the ACT ___the SAT ___the TOEFL on_____
                                                MONTH/YEAR

___the ACT ___the SAT ___the TOEFL on_____
                                                MONTH/YEAR

___the ACT ___the SAT ___the TOEFL on_____
                                                MONTH/YEAR

Received GED _____
                        MONTH/YEAR

over

Jireh & Associates, Inc.
Wilmington, De

All Students. List, in order, beginning with your high school (if you are still in high school) or college (if you are currently in college), all other universities/institutions of higher learning which you have attended. Official grade reports or mark sheets must be received directly from each institution attended. Place name of school, date of attendance (month/year) on Line A. Write the complete address on Line B. On Line C, write the phone number, including area code, and degree received (if any).

1 a._____

   b_____

   c. _____

2 a._____

   b_____

   c. _____

3 a._____

   b_____

   c. _____

4 a._____

   b_____

   c. _____

(For Visiting Students Only) Please be advised that if you are a visiting student, a Letter of Good Standing from the institution which you plan to transfer the KSU course back to must accompany this application.

(For Non-Degree Applicants Only) I understand that if I am classified as a Non-Degree student, I am not eligible for university, state or federal financial aid. If, at some time, I wish to pursue a degree at Kentucky State University, it will be necessary for me to submit, in writing, my desire to seek a degree at Kentucky State University. I understand that it will be necessary for me to supply all documentation for admission in effect at the time. Finally, I understand that if I become a degree-seeking student at a future time, credits earned as a non-degree student will be evaluated and *may* be applied toward my degree based on the degree requirements in effect at the time of my admission as a degree-seeking student.

(For All Applicants) I affirm that all information supplied to this application is true and complete. I understand that withholding information or supplying false information and/or documentation will make me ineligible for admission and/or make my enrollment subject to cancellation. With this in mind, I certify that the above statements are correct and complete.

Signature_____   Date_____

It is the policy of Kentucky State University not to discriminate against any individual in its educational program, activities or employment on the basis of race, color, national origin, sex, disability, veteran status, age, religion or marital status.

March 1998

KNOXVILLE COLLEGE
Application for Admission

For Office Use Only
ID# _____
Appl rec'd _____
Appl Fee Paid _____
Status _____
Adm. Type _____

Type or print using a ball point pen.

1. Social Security Number _____ - _____ - _____

2. Name _____, _____, _____,   3. Sex ___ M ___F
               Last   First   M.I.

4. Home Address _____

       City _____ State _____ Zip Code _____

5. Telephone Number (_____) _____ - _____ Alternate Number (_____) _____ - _____

6. Ethnic Origin: ___ African-American (B) ___ Caucasian (W) ___ Hispanic (H) ___ Non-resident alien (N)
     (Optional)
               ___ Asian/Pacific Islands (A) ___ Native American (I) ___ Other (U)

7. Religion *(optional)* _____ 8. Marital Status ___ M ___ S

9. Date of Birth _____ Place of Birth _____ State _____

10. U.S. Citizen ___ Yes ___ NO   If not, country of citizenship _____

11. Name of Parent or Guardian

      _____, _____, _____,   Relationship to you _____
               Last   First   M.I.

      Address _____ Telephone Number (_____) _____ - _____

12. In case of emergency, contact: Name _____

      Address _____ Telephone Number (_____) _____ - _____

13. Describe any disabilities of which we should be aware *(Optional)* _____
_____

FOREIGN STUDENTS ONLY

14. If not a U.S. Citizen, indicate TOEFL score _____ Date TOEFL Taken _____

15. ESL Program? _____ Yes _____ No   Where? _____ When? _____

16. VISA? _____ Yes _____ No   Type of VISA _____ Requested VISA? _____ Yes _____ No

      Alien Number _____ Date and City of Issue _____ _____

EDUCATIONAL HISTORY

17. All high schools/colleges/and/or universities attended.

Name	City and State	Dates Attended	Diploma/Degree/GED Date

18. Total SAT score _____ ACT composite score _____

19. High school rank _____ / _____ High school class size _____ High school /College GPA _____

20. Have you previously attended Knoxville College? _____ Yes, When? _____ No _____

Jireh & Associates, In
Wilmington, De

21. Have you been suspended or been on probation for _____ poor scholarship or _____ Disciplinary reasons?

22. Have you ever been convicted of a criminal offense? _____ Yes _____ No   If so, explain below

_____

_____

23. Check if you have a relative who attended the Knoxville campus _____ .

Name _____ Relationship _____ Years attended _____

24. Semester and year you plan to enroll _____ Fall 19 ___, _____ Spring 19 ___, _____ Summer 19 ___

25. Entrance status: _____ Entering freshman   _____ Special (non-degree) student

      _____ Readmit student   _____ Transfer student   _____ Transient student

26. You plan to live in _____ a campus residence hall or _____ Commute

---

27. **Select your intended major course of study at Knoxville College by indicating the alphabetic code found in item 7 of the instructions: Major _____**

---

28. Indicate the sports, clubs, or other interests you participated in high school or at another college by using the four digit numeric codes for those activities listed in item 8 of the application instructions.

_____   _____   _____   _____   _____

29. Indicate which of the following influenced you to apply to Knoxville College:

_____ Admissions Counselor   _____ Current Knoxville College Student   _____ Campus visit
_____ Guidance Counselor   _____ Knoxville College Alumnus   _____ Letter from Admissions
_____ Parents   _____ College Literature   _____ Telephone call from College
_____ Friend   _____ Minister   _____ Internet

30. References are required, so indicate the names, addresses, and titles of at least three persons who can write in support of your application. Persons may include the Principal, Counselors, Teachers, or a Minister, or any other person in a responsible position who knows you.

Name	Address
Name	Address
Name	Address
Name	Address

AGREEMENT WITH KNOXVILLE COLLEGE

All applications and academic records are reviewed for completeness prior to enrollment. The College reserves the right to cancel any acceptance or adjust the type of acceptance as determined to be appropriate. All applicants agree to the terms stated and attests the following:

Every statement herein is correct to the best of my knowledge. I realize that misrepresentation of any statement may result in denial of admission or subsequent dismissal and forfeiture of all fees to Knoxville College. I understand that I am responsible for presenting all materials to the Director of Admissions, Knoxville College, Knoxville, Tennessee 37921.

If accepted, I agree to abide by the rules and regulations of Knoxville College.

_____   _____
Signature of Applicant   Date

Knoxville College does not discriminate on the basis of sex, religion, national origin, age, of status in its admissions procedures and educational programs.

MOREHOUSE COLLEGE

830 Westview Drive, S.W.
Atlanta, Georgia 30314

APPLICATION FOR ADMISSION

Please attach a recent photo

1. Social Security Number ☐☐☐ – ☐☐ – ☐☐☐☐
   (This will be your student identification number at Morehouse. Please check for accuracy.)

2. Name _____
   Last   First   Middle

   Address _____

   _____
   City   State   Zip Code   County

   ☐☐☐ – ☐☐☐ – ☐☐☐☐
   Area Code   Telephone Number

4. Are you a U.S. citizen? ☐ Yes ☐ No   If not, state country of citizenship and type of visa you hold.

   _____

Non-U.S. Citizens Only   Primary Language: _____ Language of Education _____

Test of English as a Foreign Language (TOEFL)? ☐ Yes ☐ No   When? _____

Have you ever enrolled in an ESL (English as a Second Language) program? ☐ Yes ☐ No   Where? _____

Type of Visa: _____ ☐ Requested?   Permanent Resident Alien? ☐ Yes ☐ No   If yes, Alien Number _____
           ☐ Currently held   *(If yes, attach copy of I-551 or I-151.)*   Date Issued: _____

5. Sex _____   6. Racial or Ethnic Origin   ☐ Black   ☐ Hispanic   ☐ White   ☐ Other

7. Religious Denomination (optional) _____   8. Marital Status _____

9. Date of Birth ☐☐ – ☐☐ – ☐☐   10. Place of Birth _____   11. Height _____ Weight _____

13. Describe any disability of which we should be aware.

    _____

    _____

14. Name of Parent or Guardian
    (Person to receive all bills, grades, etc.) _____
                              Last   First   Middle Initial

15. Street Address _____

    _____
    City   State   Zip Code   County

    ☐☐☐ – ☐☐☐ – ☐☐☐☐   (H)
    Area Code   Telephone Number

    ☐☐☐ – ☐☐☐ – ☐☐☐☐   (W)
    Area Code   Telephone Number

16. Planned Entrance Date   ☐ Fall, 19 _____   ☐ Spring, 19 _____

17. Entrance Category   ☐ Regular Entering Freshman   ☐ Early Admission Freshman   ☐ Special Student
              ☐ Transfer Student from Another College   ☐ Transient Student from Another College

Jireh & Associates, Inc
Wilmington, De

18. Do you plan to live in a campus residence hall? ☐ Yes ☐ No

19. Intended major at Morehouse.

☐ Accounting	☐ English	☐ Philosophy
☐ Actuarial Science	☐ French	☐ Physics
☐ Art	☐ German	☐ Physics/Engineering
☐ Banking and Finance	☐ Health & Physical Education	☐ Political Science
☐ Biology	☐ History	☐ Psychology
☐ Business Management	☐ Insurance	☐ Religion
☐ Chemistry	☐ Interdisciplinary Science	☐ Social Welfare
☐ Chemistry/Engineering	☐ Interdisciplinary Science/Engineering	☐ Sociology
☐ Computer Science	☐ International Studies	☐ Spanish
☐ Computer Science/Engineering	☐ Marketing	☐ Urban Studies
☐ Drama	☐ Mathematics	☐ Undecided
☐ Economics	☐ Mathematics/Engineering	
☐ Education	☐ Music	

NOTE: Pre-medicine and pre-dentistry students normally major in biology or chemistry. Pre-law students normally major in political science or English. Engineering is a 3-2 program with the bachelor's degree in a science or mathematics awarded by Morehouse and a bachelor's degree in an area of engineering awarded by the Georgia Institute of Technology after five years of study.

20. High School _____
       Name   City   State   Zip Code

       _____
            Address   Phone

    High School College Board code number _____(May be obtained from high school counselor)

    Control of High School   ☐ Public   ☐ Parochial   ☐ Private

21. List in chronological order, all high schools and colleges you have attended. Failure to provide **complete and accurate** information may result in your dismissal from Morehouse College or the withholding of transfer credit.

High School(s)	City and State	Dates Attended
_____	_____	_____
_____	_____	_____
_____	_____	_____
College(s)		
_____	_____	_____
_____	_____	_____
_____	_____	_____

22. Do you wish to apply for financial aid at Morehouse? ☐ Yes ☐ No If yes, file FAF.

23. In the spaces below, please list your extracurricular activities, hobbies, and special interests. Indicate any leadership positions held and/or honors won.

_____

_____

24. Are you interested in participating in ROTC? ☐ Yes ☐ No

    If so, please specify the branch   ☐ Army   ☐ Navy   ☐ Air Force (Georgia Tech)

25. Are you a legal resident of Georgia? ☐ Yes ☐ No   If not, of what state are you a legal resident? _____

26. Have you taken the College Board's Scholastic Aptitude Test (SAT)? ☐ Yes ☐ No

    Have you taken the American College Test (ACT)? ☐ Yes ☐ No

    If not, when do you plan to take one of these exams?   ☐ SAT   Exam Date:_____

    ☐ ACT   Exam Date:_____

27. Have you previously applied to or been enrolled at Morehouse? ☐ Yes ☐ No

    If so, what semester(s) and year(s)? _____

28. Have you ever been expelled or suspended from any school or college for disciplinary reasons? ☐ Yes ☐ No

    Have you ever been arrested for, or convicted of, any criminal offense other than a traffic violation? ☐ Yes ☐ No

    Have you ever been suspended because of academic deficiencies from an educational institution or from a particular program of study? ☐ Yes ☐ No

    If you answered "Yes" to any of the above, please explain in the remarks section on the next page.

29. Father's name _____
               Last   *First*   *Middle*

    Is he living? ☐ Yes ☐ No   His occupation _____

    Highest education completed _____ Morehouse alumnus? ☐ Yes ☐ No

                                           If yes, in class of _____

30. Mother's name _____
               Last   *First*   *Middle*

    Is she living? ☐ Yes ☐ No   Her occupation _____

    Highest education completed _____

31. Essay

Write a brief essay that provides a description of yourself and the reasons why you seek admission to Morehouse College.

_____

_____

_____

_____

_____

_____

_____

_____

_____

_____

_____

_____

_____

_____

_____

_____

_____

_____

I certify that the above statements are true. If accepted, I agree to abide by the rules and regulations of Morehouse College.

Date _____   _____
                                                        Signature of Applicant

The Application Fee is $35.00. Payments must be made with certified checks or money orders. Personal checks will not be accepted. First-time freshmen also should submit an official high school transcript and SAT or ACT scores. Transfer students are required to have a 2.50 or better cumulative college grade-point average. A minimum of 26 semester hours (39 quarter hours) of college credit earned must be presented for admission. A maximum of 60 semester hours (90 quarter hours) may be transferred to Morehouse College. An interview may be a part of the admissions procedure. You will be contacted by the college if an interview is necessary.

APPLICATION FOR ADMISSION

Lane College
Office of Admissions
545 Lane Avenue
Jackson, Tennessee 38301
(901) 426-7532   (800) 960-7533

Please print. Return completed application to the address above.

            Last   First   Middle

Name: _____

                                     Date of Birth

Social Security Number: _____   _____ ; _____ / _____

Permanent Address: _____ City: _____

         State: _____ County: _____ Zip: _____

Telephone Number: (   ) _____(H)   (   ) _____(W)

U.S. Resident: Yes (   )   No (   )

Tennessee Resident: Yes (   )   No (   )   Sex: Male (   )   Female (   )

Veteran: Yes (   )   No (   )

African-American (   )   White (   )   American Indian (   )   Hispanic (   )   Other _____

Religious Affiliation: _____ Home Church: _____

         Semester applying for: Fall 19 _____   Spring 19 _____   Summer 19 _____

Intended Major: _____   Special Interest(s): _____

Have you previously attended Lane College? Yes (   )   No (   )   If yes, when? 19 _____ - 19 _____

Do you plan to live: On-Campus (   )   Off-Campus (   )

Application status: Freshman (   )   Transfer (   )   Special (   )   Transient (   )

* Any student expecting to receive Financial Aid must complete the Free Federal Application for Student Aid!
Have you applied for Financial Aid? Yes (   )   No (   )

Have you taken the ACT? Yes (   )   No (   )   If yes, when? _____

Have you taken the SAT? Yes (   )   No (   )   If yes, when? _____

List all schools which you have previously attended. You must provide addresses and dates of attendance and any degree earned from each.

         Name   Address   Degree   Date Attended

High
School: _____

Community
College: _____

College/
University: _____

                                          *CONTINUED ON BACK...

Jireh & Associates, Inc
Wilmington, De

Father: _____   Mother: _____

Address: _____   _____

_____   _____

Employer: _____   _____

Occupation: _____   _____

College Attended: _____   _____

Please list any family members who have attended Lane College:

Name   Relationship   Dates of Attendance

_____

_____

_____

I hereby certify that the information furnished on this application is complete and accurate. I fully understand that any deliberate omission or falsification of information may result in denial of admission to or dismissal from Lane College. If accepted at Lane College, I do hereby agree to abide by all rules and regulations set forth by Lane College.

_____   ____ _____
            Date   Applicant's Signature

LANE COLLEGE

545 Lane Avenue
Jackson, Tennessee 38301
(901) 426-7532   (800) 960-7533

NORTH CAROLINA AGRICULTURAL AND TECHNICAL STATE UNIVERSITY
Greensboro, NC 27411

APPLICATION FOR UNDERGRADUATE ADMISSION

Please answer all questions, making entries legible with a typewriter or black pen.

OFFICE USE 002	HAVE YOU PREVIOUSLY APPLIED TO A & T?	☐ Yes_____ (YEAR) ☐ No	HAVE YOU EVER ENROLLED IN CLASSES AT A&T?	☐ Yes_____ (YEAR) ☐ No

206 003 DATE OF APPLICATION:

SOCIAL SECURITY NUMBER

I am voluntarily providing on this form my social security number with the understanding that it will be used only as a personal identifier for the internal record keeping and data processing operations of this institution.

COMPLETE LEGAL NAME | Last | First | Middle Initial | Family/Maiden

CURRENT ADDRESS | Number and Street | Apt. No. | City/Town

State or Country | Zip Code | Area Code and Home Phone | Area Code and Bus. Phone

Permanent Address or Parent(s) Address | Number and Street | Apt. No. | City/Town

State or Country | Zip Code | Area Code and Home Phone | Area Code and Bus. Phone

007 Date of Birth | Mo. | Day | Year | Place of birth (City/State) | COUNTY OF RESIDENCE

SEX ☐ Male ☐ Female

ETHNIC GROUP/RACE *(Used for reporting purposes only. Check one.)*
- ☐ American Indian or Alaskan Native
- ☐ Black (non-hispanic origin)
- ☐ Asian or Pacific Islander
- ☐ Hispanic
- ☐ Caucasian
- ☐ Other

ARE YOU A CITIZEN OF THE UNITED STATES? ☐ Yes ☐ No
If no, Permanent Resident Alien #_____ or VISA Type_____
Native Country

MILITARY STATUS, VETERAN BENEFITS *(Check only one.)*
- ☐ Veteran Receiving Benefits
- ☐ Veteran Not Receiving Benefits
- ☐ Veteran's Dependent with Benefits
- ☐ Active Duty with Benefits
- ☐ Active Duty without Benefits
- ☐ Not Applicable _____

Next of Kin Mr. / Ms. / Mr. & Mrs.

Nearest relative's full name

Relationship: father ☐ mother ☐ guardian ☐ spouse ☐ other ☐

Street address/P.O. Box | City | State | Zip | ( ) Area code/phone

206

ADMISSION TYPE: ☐ Regular Admission   ☐ Special   ☐ Other (Specify)

ADMISSION STATUS:
- ☐ New Freshman
- ☐ Transfer
- ☐ Continuing Education
- ☐ Second Baccalaureate Degree
- ☐ Full Time
- ☐ Part Time
- ☐ Day
- ☐ Evening

TERM OF ENTRY: ☐ Fall ☐ Spring 19_____

INTENDED MAJOR: First Choice_____ Second Choice_____

209

OFFICE USE CODE | HIGH SCHOOL FROM WHICH YOU WILL (OR HAVE) GRADUATE(D) | OFFICE USE RECORD RECEIVED

NAME OF SCHOOL | CITY & STATE | MONTH/YEAR OF GRADUATION | DATES OF ATTENDANCE

In accordance with the University Regulations, **you must attach an application fee of $25.00.** This fee is not refundable. The University does not accept fee waivers. Please make check payable to NC A&T State University. Please consider your cancelled check as your receipt. If you do not receive a confirmation within 10 days that we have received your application, contact the Admissions Office at (910) 334-7946 or 1-800-443-8964 Toll Free for North Carolina.

SOCIAL SEC # _____ TERM: ( ) FALL ( ) SP YEAR: 19_____

NAME _____
Last   First   Middle

ADDRESS _____

CITY & STATE _____

ZIP CODE

Jireh & Associates, Inc
Wilmington, De

Have you attended any post-secondary schools since graduation from
High School? _____Yes _____No; If yes, complete the section below.

211	OFFICE USE CODE		LIST ALL POST-SECONDARY SCHOOLS AND COLLEGES ATTENDED, INCLUDING SUMMER SESSIONS, CORRESPONDENCE, AND EXTENSION WORK. ATTACH A SECOND SHEET IF NECESSARY.				OFFICE USE RECORD RECEIVED
			College/University	Location	Month/Year	Number of Hours	Degree	

COURSES IN PROGRESS: Transfer applicants, list courses in which you are currently enrolled, or will enroll, prior to transfer. *Response required!*

000	If you did not attend any post-secondary schools since graduation from high school or if your educational attendance has been interrupted for any reason, please list the types of activities in which you have been engaged (i.e., military, work, etc.). _____

ARE YOU ELIGIBLE TO RETURN TO THE COLLEGE LAST ATTENDED? Yes_____ No_____ If no, Give reason below.

WHY DID YOU DECIDE TO TRANSFER? _____

206	DO YOU WISH INFORMATION ON: *(Check all that apply)*	□ Financial Aid □ On Campus Housing □ Services for Disabled Students □ Army ROTC □ Air Force ROTC
000	PLEASE INDICATE ANY OTHER COLLEGES/UNIVERSITIES TO WHICH YOU HAVE APPLIED, OR INTEND TO APPLY.

000	HOW DID YOU FIRST LEARN OF A&T STATE UNIVERSITY?

DID ONE OR BOTH PARENT(S) GRADUATE FROM A FOUR YEAR COLLEGE OR UNIVERSITY? □ YES □ NO

ARE YOUR PARENTS GRADUATES OF A&T? □ Yes □ No If yes, please list

Mother's Name _____ Father's Name _____

208	HONORS AND AWARDS *(Check each that applies)*	□ Class Officer □ Who's Who	□ Governor's School □ NMSQT Finalist or Semifinalist	□ National Honor Society □ Girls' or Boys' State

ATHLETICS *(List)* _____ Religious Preference (Optional) _____

OTHER SPECIAL TALENTS *(List)* _____

007	Residence Information

I certify that I am a bona fide resident of _____ in _____ and
County State

have been a resident from_____ until_____
inclusive dates

Signature _____ Date _____

If you are a dependent student please complete the following

Father's occupation _____ Employer _____

Mother's occupation _____ Employer _____

Signature (Parent/Guardian Signature if applicant is under 18) Date

By signing this application, I agree to abide by the policies and regulations of North Carolina A&T State University and to the best of my knowledge, the information I have given is true. I understand that any misrepresentation of facts on this application will be cause for refusal of admission, cancellation of admission, or suspension from the university.

Signature _____ Date _____

150,000 copies of this public document were printed at a cost of $4093.50, $.0273 per copy.

RCC Application for Admission

Personal Information

Last (family) name   First name   Middle initial

Maiden name   Date of Birth   Social Security #

Mailing Address

Street

City   State   Zip code   Country

Telephone number   Facsimile number

Permanent Address

Street

City   State   Zip Code   Country

Telephone number   E-mail address

Citizenship

Country of Birth

Are you a U.S. citizen? ☐ Yes ☐ No (If yes, go to the next section)

Alien registration number

Institution that issued last I-20

Will you need a temporary student visa (I-20) to attend RCC? ☐ Yes ☐ No

Current Visa status (check one) ☐ F1 ☐ F2 ☐ B1 ☐ B2 ☐ Other

If in U.S., expiration date of 1-94

Educational Background

Name of high school or place of GED   Date of Graduation

Street   City   State   Zip Code

Colleges/Universities Attended

Street   City   State   Zip Code

Expected date of graduation from RCC

Sex:

☐ Male ☐ Female

How did you hear about RCC?

☐ TV
☐ Subway Advertising
☐ Friend
☐ Newspaper
☐ Radio
☐ College fair
☐ Community Agency
☐ RCC Student/Alumni
☐ Leaflet/Flyer
☐ RCC Staff/Faculty
☐ High School Visit
☐ Other

Type of Application (check all that apply)

Applying As:

☐ New Student
☐ Readmitting
☐ Transfer
☐ Joint Admission
☐ Dual Enrollment
☐ 100 Careers

Applying for:

☐ September 19
☐ January 19

☐ Day
☐ Evening

☐ Full Time
☐ Part Time

Veteran: ☐ Yes ☐ No

Campus Location Preference:

☐ Columbus Avenue
☐ BBS Campus

Limited English proficiency: ☐ Yes ☐ No

Will you be studying English as a second language?: ☐ Yes ☐ No

I hereby certify that all information stated in this application is complete and accurate, and I understand that falsification or omission of information may result in disqualification or dismissal. I understand that this application for admission will not be complete until all documents are submitted to the Office of Admissions.

Applicants Signature   Date

Jireh & Associates, In
Wilmington, De

Academic Degree Programs

Please check the box in front of the program of interest to you (be sure to check only one major).

Associate of Arts Degrees (Liberal Arts)

- ☐ GL   General Concentration
- ☐ AH   Arts and Humanities
- ☐ MU   Musical Arts
- ☐ TA   Theater
- ☐ VA   Visual Arts
- ☐ RS   Biological Science
- ☐ BA   Business Administration
- ☐ EN   English
- ☐ EP   Environmental Management and Pollution Prevention
- ☐ MA   Mathematics
- ☐ PS   Physical Science
- ☐ PE   Pre-Engineering
- ☐ PN   Pre-Nursing
- ☐ SS   Social Science

Associate of Science Degrees

- ☐ AN   Accounting
- ☐ BM   Business Management
- ☐ IS   Computer Information Systems
- ☐ EE   Early Childhood
- ☐ MI   Microcomputer Applications
- ☐ NR   Nursing (1,2)

    Office Technology:
- ☐ ES   Executive Secretary
- ☐ LS   Legal Secretary
- ☐ MS   Medical Secretary
- ☐ RM   Retail Management
- ☐ WP   Word Processing

Certificate Degrees

- ☐ HC   Allied Health
- ☐ BC   Bookkeeping
- ☐ CC   Computer Information Systems-Microcomputer Applications
- ☐ SC   Computer Information Systems-Spreadsheet Applications
- ☐ EC   Engineering and Architectural Design and CAD (1)
- ☐ DC   CAD Mechanical Drafting (1)
- ☐ TC   Office technology-Training
- ☐ WC   Office Technology-Word Processing

Note: (1) Day only (2) Upon completion of Nursing Program prerequisites

Demographic Information

Roxbury Community College does not discriminate on the basis of sex, race, national and ethnic origin, or handicapped status. The following optional information is requested for affirmative action purposes only.

Ethnic Origin: ☐ African ☐ African American ☐ Asian/Pacific Islander ☐ English Caribbean ☐ French ☐ Caribbean ☐ Hispanic ☐ Middle Eastern ☐ Native American ☐ White American ☐ Cape Verdean ☐ Other

Saint Augustine's College

1315 Oakwood Avenue
Raleigh, NC 27610-2298
(Fully-Accredited Four-Year Liberal Arts College)
("A New Era of Excellence")

CHARACTERISTICS:

- Church affiliated, co-educational, liberal learning with strong focus on teacher preparation and professional studies including: Computer Information Systems, Biology, Pre-Med, Accounting, Music, Journalism, Industrial Hygiene, Medical Technology, Political Science, Pre-Law, Psychology, Biblical Studies, etc.

- 36-degree granting programs including internships, service learning experiences and study abroad opportunities.

- Honors Program rewards gifted students with unique challenging opportunities as well as an Academic Achievers Program with its unparalleled ways to upgrade academic standing through tutoring and counseling.

- Intercollegiate and intramural athletics.

- Values steeped in the appreciation of cultural diversity, family orientation, religious emphasis, social, economic and political awareness.

- As the state's capital, Raleigh encompasses theaters, restaurants, sports arenas and other recreational activities. Only 1-2 hours away from Atlantic Ocean beaches and the majestic Blue Ridge Mountains.

FOR CHALLENGE & EXCITEMENT COME TO SAINT AUGUSTINE'S COLLEGE!

I would like to know more about Saint Augustine's College!
(Please *Copy* and Mail to Address Below)

Name_____ SS# _____ Sex _____ Major _____

Mailing Address_____
        (Street or Route/Box Number)   (City)   (State)   (Zip Code)

Home Telephone _(___)___-_____ High School _____
                                                   (Name)   (City)   (State)

Graduation Date _____ High School Class: ☐Freshman ☐Sophomore ☐Junior ☐ Senior ☐Transfer

Scores: SAT_____ GPA_____ Class Rank_____

Please Send: ☐ Information   ☐ Application for Admission   ☐ Application Financial Aid

        <u>MAIL TO:</u>   *Saint Augustine's College*
                        Office of Enrollment Management
                1315 Oakwood Avenue, Raleigh, NC 27610-2298
                Telephone: (919) 516-4016/Fax: (919) 516-5801

Jireh & Associates, Inc.
Wilmington, De

SOUTH CAROLINA STATE UNIVERSITY

UNDERGRADUATE

ADMISSIONS APPLICATION

PLEASE PRINT IN INK OR TYPE

Applying For: AUGUST, 19_____   JANUARY, 19_____   SUMMER, 19_____

GENERAL INSTRUCTIONS:

- Complete and return this application along with a non-refundable application fee of $25.00. A cashier's check, money order or personal check will be accepted. **Please do not send cash through the mail.**

- Application Deadlines: July 31 for the fall semester.   November 30 for the spring semester. May 1 for the **summer** session.

- Forward completed application and all requested documents to: **Office of Admissions & Recruitment, South Carolina State University, 300 College Street, NE Orangeburg, South Carolina 29117-0001.**

FRESHMAN: After completing the first two pages, please give this form to your counselor who will furnish your high school transcript, including courses currently enrolled in, GPA, rank-in-class and SAT I or ACT score.

TRANSFER: If you have earned fewer than 30 semester hours of college credit, submit an official copy of your high school transcript, GPA, rank-in-class and SAT I or ACT score. Submit a complete, official transcript from each college/university attended.

TRANSIENT: A signed approval form from the currently enrolled college/university must be submitted.

SPECIAL or NATIONAL EXCHANGE PROGRAM: Submit official copy of high school or college transcript.

ADMISSION STATUS: Freshman ____   Transfer ____   Transient ____   Special ____

Social Security No._____   Date of Birth_____

Month   Date   Year

Name _____

Last   First   Middle/Maiden

Mailing Address _____
Street, P.O. Box, Etc.

_____

City   State   Zip Code

County_____   Telephone Number (_____)_____

Legal resident of South Carolina? Yes____ No____ If no, list resident state _____

Country of Citizenship _____   Language Spoken in Home_____

Religious Preference _____   Sex ____Male   Marital Status ___Single
                                                              ____Female   ___Married

Race or Ethnic Group   African American/Black ___   Caucasian ___   American Indian/Alaskan Native __
Asian or Pacific Islander ___   Hispanic ___   Other (specify)

Jireh & Associates, Inc
Wilmington, De

_____

Father   Address

_____

Mother   Address

Did either parent attend South Carolina State University?   Father: Yes____   No____
Mother: Yes____   No____   If mother attended, give maiden name _____

Education of parents (Highest degree or grade completed):   Mother_____   Father_____

College Entrance Examination: SAT ___ ACT ___   Date taken or will be taken _____ 19_____

Provide information for each high school or college attended, begin with current high school or college.

Name of High School or College	City and State	Dates Attended		Type of Degree/Diploma
		From	To	

United States Veteran?   Yes ____   No ____

Have you ever been convicted of a felony?   Yes ____   No ____   (If yes, attach an explanation)

Do you plan to enroll at another college/university prior to entering South Carolina State University?
Yes ____ No ____ If yes, when and where _____

List Activities: Community, church, athletics, dramatics, publications, music, art, important offices
                held. List prizes, awards, and honors received.

_____

_____

_____

_____

_____

_____

_____

_____

_____

SOUTHERN UNIVERSITY and A.M. COLLEGE
BATON ROUGE, LOUISIANA 70813-9901
APPLICATION FOR UNDERGRADUATE ADMISSION

Deadlines to apply for Admissions and submit supporting documents.

July 1 . . . . Fall Semester
November 1 . . Spring Semester
April 1 . . . . . Summer Semester

FOR OFFICE USE ONLY				
MO	CC	DATE RECEIVED	APPROVED BY	INPUT

DIRECTIONS: Read carefully before completing application.

1. Please enclose fee with application: $5.00 – U.S. Citizen, Permanent Resident, and Refugee with Evidence of Status; $10.00 – Non U.S. Citizen. (Application fee should be submitted as a Money Order. No cash, drafts or personal checks accepted.)

2. Attach your recent photograph.

3. Submit all required documents or credentials to complete application (see section on admission requirements).

4. Mail application to: Office of Admissions, P.O. Box 9901, Southern University, Baton Rouge. LA 70813-9901.

Note: Application will be returned if all items applicable to you are not completed. For information on **out-of-state exemptions** contact the Office of Admissions (504) 771-2430. Exemption deadlines: October 1– Spring, April 1 – Summer, July 1 – Fall. Exemption of the non-resident fee will not be granted after the deadline and/or during any registration period.

If you are a student who has special needs, please contact Disabilities Services (504) 771-3950.

ADMISSION STATUS (Check One)

☐ New Freshman   ☐ New Transfer   ☐ Readmit   ☐ Special   ☐ Summer Only   ☐ Exchange

Planned Entry Date to University   Semester _____ Year _____

Indicate Special Disabilities _____ Do you have special needs? Yes ____ No ____ What are your needs?

SOCIAL SECURITY NUMBER	APPLICANT'S FULL NAME (Last. First. Middle)	

PERMANENT MAILING ADDRESS	PERMANENT CITY. STATE/COUNTRY	ZIP CODE

LOCAL STREET ADDRESS (No P.O. Box Accepted)	LOCAL CITY. STATE/COUNTRY	ZIP CODE

HOME TELEPHONE NUMBER   DATE OF BIRTH   PLACE OF BIRTH   SEX

AREA CODE   NUMBER   MONTH   DAY   YEAR   COUNTRY   MALE ☐   FEMALE ☐

RELIGIOUS PREFERENCE

U.S. MILITARY STATUS

Date of Active Duty

Month	Day	Year

(Indicate Religious Preference)

☐ Veteran
☐ Non-Veteran

CITIZENSHIP

U.S. Citizen ☐
U. S. Resident Alien ☐
Non-Citizen ☐
Citizen of what country?

ETHNIC CATEGORY (Required for Federal Reports by Civil Rights Act 1964) Check One

☐ Asian American   ☐ Black American   ☐ Hispanic   ☐ Native American   ☐ White American
☐ Other _____   Give name of country.

PARENT OR GUARDIAN'S FULL NAME (Must Be Legal Guardian)   DID PARENT GRADUATE FROM SOUTHERN UNIVERSITY?

Yes ☐   No ☐   If yes, give year

_____ NAME AT LEFT   Parent ☐   Guardian ☐

Jireh & Associates, Inc
Wilmington, De

Name of High School _____

High School Address _____ City/State _____ Date of High School Graduation _____

Parish _____

List below all colleges and universities attended, including Southern University in Baton Rouge.

Institution	Location	Dates Attended	Date Graduated
_____	_____	_____	_____
_____	_____	_____	_____
_____	_____	_____	_____
_____	_____	_____	_____

Currently enrolled? ☐ Yes ☐ No If yes, give name of Institution _____

Previous major at Southern University _____

Has applicant participated in the LSU/SU COOP Program? ☐ Yes ☐ No

List your choice of major _____

List the source of your financial support _____

Have you ever been on probation or sentenced to jail/prison as a result of a felony conviction or guilty plea?

I understand that any falsification of any information may result in my not being accepted or in my being dismissed from Southern University.

Signature _____ Date _____
      Applicant

Signature _____ Date _____
      Parent or guardian (if applicant is under 18 years of age)

What will be your major subject during your enrollment at Southern University?
Beginning Freshman must also choose a major when applying.

UNDERGRADUATE DEGREES OFFERED
(Please Check One)

COLLEGE OF AGRICULTURAL, FAMILY AND CONSUMER SCIENCES

☐ Bachelor of Science in Agriculture Sciences
☐ Bachelor of Science in Agriculture Economics
☐ Bachelor of Science in Family and Consumer Sciences
☐ Bachelor of Science in Urban Forestry

COLLEGE OF ARTS AND HUMANITIES

☐ Associate of Arts in Jazz with emphasis in Louisiana music
☐ Bachelor of Arts in English
☐ Bachelor of Arts in Fine Arts
☐ Bachelor of Arts in French
☐ Bachelor of Arts in History
☐ Bachelor of Arts in Mass Communications
☐ Bachelor of Music
☐ Bachelor of Arts in Spanish
☐ Bachelor of Arts in Speech Communications
☐ Bachelor of Arts in Theatre

COLLEGE OF BUSINESS

☐ Bachelor of Science in Accounting
☐ Bachelor of Science in Business Economics
☐ Bachelor of Science in Business Management
☐ Bachelor of Science in Marketing

COLLEGE OF EDUCATION

☐ Bachelor of Arts in Elementary Education
☐ Bachelor of Arts in Special Education
☐ Bachelor of Music Education
☐ Bachelor of Science in Secondary Education
☐ Bachelor of Science in Therapeutic Recreation and Leisure Studies

COLLEGE OF ENGINEERING

☐ Associate of Applied Science in Electronics Engineering Technology
☐ Bachelor of Science in Civil Engineering
☐ Bachelor of Science in Electrical Engineering
☐ Bachelor of Science in Electronics Engineering Technology
☐ Bachelor of Science in Mechanical Engineering

COLLEGE OF SCIENCES

☐ Associate of Science in Law Enforcement
☐ Bachelor of Science in Biology
☐ Bachelor of Science in Chemistry
☐ Bachelor of Science in Computer Science – Scientific Option
☐ Bachelor of Science in Computer Science – Business Option
☐ Bachelor of Science in Mathematics

☐ Bachelor of Science in Physics

COLLEGE OF SCIENCES (Cont.)

☐ Bachelor of Science in Psychology
☐ Bachelor of Science in Rehabilitation Services
☐ Bachelor of Science in Social Work
☐ Bachelor of Science in Sociology
☐ Bachelor of Science in Speech Pathology and Audiology

SCHOOL OF ARCHITECTURE

☐ Bachelor of Architecture

SCHOOL OF NURSING

☐ Bachelor of Science in Nursing

SCHOOL OF PUBLIC POLICY

☐ Bachelor of Arts in Political Science

PART II
PERSONAL DATA SECTION
Southern University
at New Orleans

DIRECTIONS: Please read carefully before completing this section:

NOTE: Application will be returned if all items applicable to you are not completed.
1. Type or print in ink all information.
2. Place only one letter or number in one space.
3. The application form must be submitted one month prior to the semester the applicant plans to enroll.

PLEASE CHECK ONE:
☐ REGULAR DAY
☐ EVENING DIVISION
☐ WEEKEND COLLEGE

CARD 1

SOCIAL SECURITY NO.
1 9

APPLICANTS FULL NAME (LAST NAME, FIRST, MIDDLE INITIAL)
10 31

HOME STREET ADDRESS OR MAILING ADDRESS
32 51

HOME CITY AND STATE
52 72

HOME ZIP CODE
75 79   1   80

CARD 2

HOME TELEPHONE
AREA CODE | EXCHANGE | NUMBER
10 19

DATE OF BIRTH
MONTH | DAY | YEAR
20 25

PLACE OF BIRTH

SEX
1. ☐ M
2. ☐ F
27

RELIGIOUS PREFERENCE (CHECK ONE)
1. ☐ BAPTIST   3. ☐ METHODIST   5. ☐ JEWISH
2. ☐ CATHOLIC   4. ☐ PRESBYTERIAN   6. ☐ OTHER
28

MILITARY STATUS
1. ☐ VETERAN
2. ☐ NON-VET.
29

DATE ACTIVE DUTY
FROM:
TO:

ETHNIC ORIGIN (CHECK ONE)
1. ☐ NON-CITIZEN   3. ☐ WHITE (CAUCASIAN) AMERICAN   5. ☐ SPANISH AMERICAN   7. ☐ OTHER
2. ☐ BLACK (NEGRO) AMERICAN   4. ☐ AMERICAN INDIAN   6. ☐ ORIENTAL AMERICAN
30

HIGH SCHOOL YOU GRADUATED FROM
PARISH:
SCHOOL NAME: DATE
CITY NAME:

ADMISSIONS ONLY
PARISH | HI-SCH
31 35

HAVE YOU ENROLLED AT SUNO BEFORE?
☐ YES   ORIGINAL ENTRY DATE
☐ NO   PLANNED DATE OF ENTRY

ENTRY DATE
MONTH | YEAR
36 39

PARENT OR GUARDIAN'S FULL NAME
45 65

NAME ENTERED AT LEFT IS:
☐ PARENT   ☐ GUARDIAN

DID PARENT OR GUARDIAN GRADUATE
FROM A LOUISIANA COLLEGE?
[ ] YES   ☐ NO

IF YES, GIVE NAME OF AND ADDRESS BELOW:
COLLEGE:
ADDRESS:

2
80

DO NOT WRITE BELOW THIS LINE—A D M I S S I O N ' S   U S E   O N L Y

CARD 4

COL | DEPT | CL | MAJOR | MINOR | HRS ATTEMPTED | HRS EARNED | QUALITY POINTS | CUM AVG | TRANSFER HRS

SEM AVG | MID SEM AVG | LSE | ADM | STAT | C MOD | EXT | EXM | GRAD | HET | ROTC | DEL | REGISTRATION FEE | ADVISOR SOC SEC NO
40   50   54   57   58   59   60   61   62   63   64   65   66   71   80   4

Jireh & Associates, Inc
Wilmington, De

PART V. EDUCATIONAL DATA

1. List below all colleges including SUNO you have attended. Failure to acknowledge attendance at a college or university may result in dismissal from the University.

Name of College	City & State	Dates (Month & Year)	Degree Earned
Last one attended _____	_____	From _____ Thru _____	_____
Others _____	_____	From _____ Thru _____	_____
Others _____	_____	From _____ Thru _____	_____
Others _____	_____	From _____ Thru _____	_____
Others _____	_____	From _____ Thru _____	_____
Others _____	_____	From _____ Thru _____	_____
Others _____	_____	From _____ Thru _____	_____

2. Are you attending school now? ☐ Yes ☐ No   Institution: _____
   If "Yes", when do you intend to complete this enrollment? _____

3. You are required to have all official transcripts mailed directly to this office. Have you made these necessary arrangements?
   Yes _____ (NOTE: Transcripts are not accepted from students.)

4. Have you been suspended or dismissed from any college or university for scholastic or disciplinary reasons? ☐ Yes ☐ No
   If "Yes", give name of institution, date and reason for this action: _____

PART VI. STATEMENT OF SELECTIVE SERVICE REGISTRATION STATUS

WARNING: If you are required to register for the federal draft under the Military Selective Service Act, Louisiana law requires that you must register for such draft before you enroll in any post-secondary school which receives any state or federal funds. Southern University at New Orleans is a state-supported school. If you purposely give false or misleading information, you will be denied enrollment at Southern University at New Orleans, or, if enrolled, will be immediately suspended. You may also be subject to any applicable Louisiana law.

☐ I certify that I am registered with Selective Service.
☐ I certify that I am not required to be registered with Selective Service, because:
    ☐ (1) I am female
    ☐ (2) I am in the armed services on active duty (Note: Does not apply to members of the Reserves and National Guard who are not on active duty)
    ☐ (3) I have not reached my 18th birthday
    ☐ (4) I was born before 1960
    ☐ I am a permanent resident of the Federated States of Micronesia, the Marshall Islands or the Republic of Palau

I CERTIFY THAT THE ANSWERS I HAVE GIVEN TO EACH AND ALL OF THE FOREGOING QUESTIONS ARE TRUE TO THE BEST OF MY KNOWLEDGE. I KNOW THAT FALSIFICATION OF ANY INFORMATION ON THIS FORM WILL SUBJECT ME TO DISMISSAL FROM THE UNIVERSITY. I FURTHER CERTIFY THAT I HAVE READ AND UNDERSTAND THE INSTRUCTIONS FOR THE COMPLETION OF THIS APPLICATION.

_____
DATE

_____
SIGNATURE OF APPLICANT (SIGN IN INK)

Application Fee
$5.00

International Fee
$15.00

Return your application to:

THE OFFICE OF ADMISSIONS
SOUTHERN UNIVERSITY AT NEW ORLEANS
6400 PRESS DRIVE
NEW ORLEANS, LOUISIANA 70126